GARDENING
BASICS

GARDENING BASICS

How to design, plant and maintain your garden

Reader's Digest

PUBLISHED BY THE READER'S DIGEST ASSOCIATION LIMITED
LONDON • NEW YORK • SYDNEY • CAPE TOWN • MONTREAL

A READER'S DIGEST BOOK

Published by The Reader's Digest Association Limited
11 Westferry Circus
Canary Wharf
London E14 4HE

ISBN 0 276 42371 2

A CIP data record for this book is available from the
British Library

A Berry Book, conceived, edited and designed by
Susan Berry for Collins & Brown Limited, London House,
Great Eastern Wharf, Parkgate Road, London SW11 4NQ

Gardening Consultant: Joanna Chisholm
Editors: Alison Freegard, Jacqueline Jackson, Amanda Lebentz,
Hilary Mandleburg and Ginny Surtees
Editorial Assistant: Lisa Pendreigh

Senior Designer: Kevin Williams
Designers: Dave Crook, Claudine Meissner and Allan Mole
Design Consultant: Tim Foster
Art Director: Roger Bristow

Special photography: Howard Rice and George Taylor
Illustrations: Ian Sidaway
Garden designs: Tim Newbury
Planting plans: Yvonne Innes

Reproduction by Hong Kong Graphic and Printing Ltd
Printed by Midas, Hong Kong

Contents

Designing the Garden 20

How to use this book

The aim of this book is to help people with relatively little gardening knowledge make informed choices about how to plan and maintain their gardens. It is designed with the fact in mind that it is much easier to cope with small amounts of relevant information than with large quantities of advice and instruction from which you have to extract what is really useful. *Gardening Basics* provides all the basic information a new or inexperienced gardener will need. It discusses how plants grow and what you can do to ensure optimum conditions. It gives insights into garden style and introduces you to some of the wide range of style possibilities. Finally, it talks about the origin of the garden plants we have come to know and love, how they are classified, and where to obtain the plants you require. *Gardening Basics* is divided into four, easy-to-manage principle sections, with a useful appendix at the end of the book.

Designing the Garden

This section of the book offers you the basic information you need to make a considered choice when it comes to planning and designing your garden, whether it be the whole garden or a part of it.

Any garden requires a structure and this is usually provided by inanimate material – walls, fences, paving, and so on – but sometimes by living material in the form of hedges and screening plants.

Designing the Garden shows you how to construct a garden plan and decide on this structure. In addition, it explains how to go about designing a single area of planting, such as a perennial border or bed, or, on a smaller scale, a hanging basket or wall pot.

Photographs illustrate a variety of garden designs

Versions of the plan are adapted for different shapes of garden

Plans provide inspiration plus practical information on transforming the garden

Plants for the Garden

This section provides the reference you need to furnish your garden with plants, whether it be the largest tree or the smallest annual. It features an illustrated A-Z directory of carefully selected plants in each of the different categories – *Trees, Shrubs, Climbers and Wall Shrubs, Perennials, Bulbs, Annuals and Biennials*. Each entry gives a description of the plant, often with an accompanying colour photograph, its hardiness, eventual height and its individual cultivation needs.

Clear page headings indicate categories of plant, such as Trees and Shrubs, plus particular groups within categories

Specially commissioned portraits of plants

Plants are listed alphabetically by Latin name within their grouping

Additional named plants are included to extend the chooser's guide

Full cultivation details are given for each entry

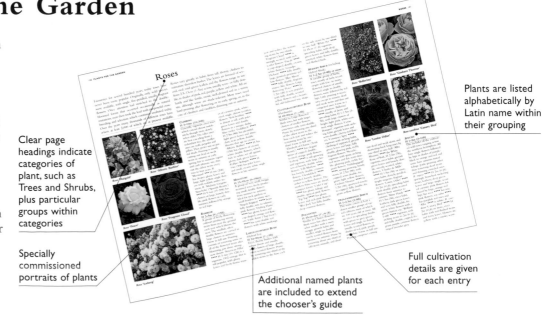

Vegetables, Fruit and Herbs

Each plant has a clear photograph for identification

Detailed text gives all the basic cultivation information, including sowing, planting, propagation and harvesting advice

Practical, easy-to-follow tips and photographs

Boxed information on points of special interest

This section provides essential information on planning and maintaining the edible garden. It has three separate sections within it: one on vegetable growing, with detailed plant by plant cultivation information, one on fruit with similar detailed cultivation information for the different types of fruit, and finally a short section on both culinary and medicinal herbs, again with helpful cultivation details.

Care and Maintenance

This section includes all the information you require to keep your garden in good order throughout the year. It advises on the principal tools you will need and explains how to cultivate the soil, how to feed, water and nurture your plants and how to propagate them. It also provides useful information on creating compost in order to feed plants successfully, and on the most common pests and diseases and how to deal with them effectively.

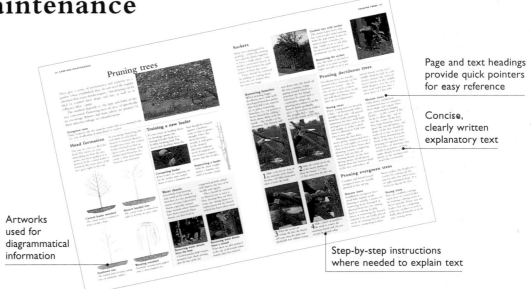

Page and text headings provide quick pointers for easy reference

Concise, clearly written explanatory text

Artworks used for diagrammatical information

Step-by-step instructions where needed to explain text

Appendix

This final section includes two calendars for the garden, listing the basic tasks each season for both an ornamental and edible garden. In addition, plants lists are included for a variety of different planting purposes, cross-referring to the *Plants for the Garden* section. There is a special section on pests and diseases that commonly attack edible crops and a fully comprehensive index, with cross references to common and Latin names for plants.

Calendar of work divided into four major seasons

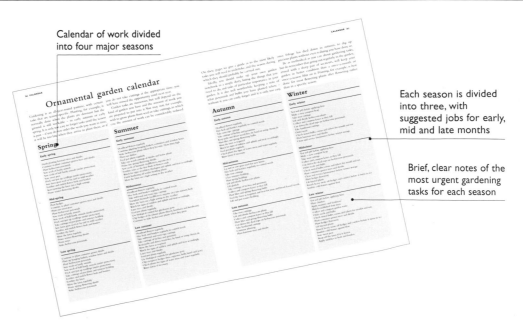

Each season is divided into three, with suggested jobs for early, mid and late months

Brief, clear notes of the most urgent gardening tasks for each season

First steps in gardening

Many people, confronted with a garden for the first time in their lives, feel intimidated by their lack of knowledge and the seemingly vast amount they think they will have to know if they are to succeed in managing their garden, let alone trying to make any improvements to it. In fact, gardening need not be difficult, especially nowadays when, for instance, nurseries supply a huge range of container-grown plants that may, to begin with, require nothing more than a planting hole to be dug for them.

As you gain confidence, you will quickly find your gardening horizons widening and your taste in plants becoming more esoteric. You will start to look for different forms of the same plant so that, instead of simply growing, for example, the honeysuckle commonly available in your local garden centre, you will want three different types, each painstakingly sought out at specialist nurseries.

As you visit other gardens, your understanding of and taste in plants will improve, and you will see how other, more experienced gardeners have confronted precisely the same problems that you have faced. You will begin to take cuttings from friends' plants, and collect the seed of favourite perennials. And, like the seed, your gardening knowledge will eventually grow, flower, and bear fruit!

How plants grow

The essential principle to grasp is that the plants in your garden have the same needs as those growing in the wild. The only difference is that you have chosen to put your garden plants there (except for those that mysteriously seed themselves) and so you are, to a greater or lesser degree, in control of their fate and fortune.

Plants need air, light, water and nutrients to flourish, but they vary in their needs. Some, for instance, require evenly moist conditions at all times for healthy growth, while others can survive long periods of drought. The amount of light needed varies greatly too. Many plants, grasses especially, will soon look sick if grown in shade, whereas others are able to survive in such situations because they are better adapted to make use of limited light. Many gardeners find shade the hardest of all conditions to deal with. However, although the choice of plants is more limited, there are attractive foliage plants, in particular, that thrive in low light levels – although you will not be able to create the colourful exuberance of a traditional perennial border.

Since plants vary so much in how much air, light, water and nutrients they need, it is not surprising to find the character of wild vegetation varies from place to place. As gardeners, we should learn from this. For example, moist, fertile soils are inhabited by fast-growing, lush grasses, perennials and shrubs, so it is sensible to concentrate on plants like these if your garden has similar conditions.

At the other extreme, cold windswept land, with poor, acidic soil, is covered in a mat of heathers, wiry, dwarf shrubs and clump-forming grasses, along with birch trees and conifers. Gardeners in such areas should concentrate on growing similar plants: the results will be both beautiful and trouble-free.

Mediterranean garden
Olive and cherry trees and grey-leaved sun-loving plants such as lavender and santolina flourish in a hot climate.

Garden in the shade
Woodland plants – ferns, irises and primulas – are specially adapted to make the most of the low light levels of dappled shade.

Special needs

In the wild, plants will thrive if they have the correct conditions, and will fail if not. However, in the garden you want all your plants to do well. By planting your garden with the plants you want rather than with those that would grow there naturally if given the chance, you have started to interfere with natural selection and natural habitats.

You may also have crammed plants in, clipped them, trained them and forced them into growth. The price to be paid for all this is that you have to put in some work to keep your plants healthy and strong. If you do not, no matter how brilliantly you have planned your garden and how well you have chosen your plants, it will not flourish. So, the first rule of successful gardening should be to select plants to suit the prevailing conditions. Those who try to go against the conditions they have, such as by adding quantities of peat and chemicals to grow rhododendrons on soil where they would not naturally grow, are making work for themselves as well as spending a lot of money and contributing to environmental damage in the process.

Self-seeded aquilegias
A few aquilegias planted in a spot where conditions are favourable will quickly multiply to make a splendid show.

Sources of information

Gardening reference books give information on the widest possible range of plants and conditions, but for information on plants that might be suitable for your garden, visit local gardens that are open to the public. Here you can see plants *in situ*, and can judge which thrive and which do less well. You may even have the opportunity to talk to the owners and discuss the particular gardening problems they have faced. Gardening clubs are yet another good source of information on what does well in your area. Here you also have the chance to meet other local gardeners, exchange experiences, seeds and cuttings, and perhaps hear specialist speakers. Finally, reputable nurseries usually have knowledgeable staff who will be able to answer many of your questions.

A well-stocked nursery
Nurseries often have the specialist staff you need to advise you on what plants to grow and how to cultivate them.

Plant health

When grown in conditions that suit them, plants generally stay healthy. The single most important lesson in gardening is to allow the conditions to dictate the choice of plants. Even so, you should watch for problems and take quick action against them.

Insects and other creatures such as slugs and snails attack plants, as do fungal or bacterial diseases. All these are less of a problem in gardens with a wide range of plants, for not only do the problems not spread so fast, but they are less noticeable. Bear in mind that chemical treatments are often time consuming, and ineffective unless rigorously applied. They can also cause environmental damage. Other problems may be the result of poor growing conditions. These include wilting and premature leaf-drop caused by drought, to leaf-yellowing and spotting due to a variety of chemical imbalances in soil.

A varied border
In a border with a wide variety of different plants, there is less chance of disease and pests spreading quickly.

Creating a style

When planning a garden, deciding on the style you like most and one that will suit the adjoining house or flat is one of the most difficult tasks. By far the greatest number of gardens are in fairly small urban plots in which the house's architecture is an inescapable feature. In these situations especially, any garden that is not designed with the architecture of the house in mind will look strangely unsatisfactory.

If choosing a single style for your garden is difficult, you do have the option of using more than one. You could consider having a formal garden near the house, with a much wilder area at the back, perhaps partially screened by a hedge. This adds a sense of mystery and surprise and is a trick that can be used even in quite a small garden.

You also need to consider the purposes the garden will have to fulfil. If you have small children, they will need plenty of space to play and you might want to include structures such as a sandpit or play house. This does not mean that the garden need be reduced to a featureless football pitch: children like a garden that inspires the playing of imaginative games – places to hide and little paths wending their way around bushes.

Grown-up entertainment creates rather different needs. If you like barbecues and parties, or simply to eat *al fresco* as often as possible, you will need plenty of flat space. 'Hard landscaping' – paved areas, decking, built-in seating and so on – is therefore particularly important to the sociable gardener.

When thinking about your garden style, remember the possibility of including a water feature. This can bring a feeling of tranquillity, relaxation and coolness even to the smallest plot. It also allows you interesting variations in your planting as plants that enjoy damp conditions look strikingly different from those that thrive on dry soil.

And finally, do not forget the part that colour and scent can play in your choice of garden style. Colour arouses strong feelings: vibrant colours and clear contrasts are loved by many, but are seen as garish and vulgar by others, so be sure you know which you prefer. Or you could choose scent as your garden theme. A garden filled with roses, lavender, herbs, jasmine and tobacco plants is marvellous on long summer evenings, when the fragrance of the flowers can be enjoyed as night falls and it wafts through open windows.

A town garden
Cobblestones, a granite table and a formal style of planting (above) help make this garden an organic part of the surrounding architecture.

A walled cottage garden
Plants jostle for attention in an apparently haphazard planting (left) that perfectly suits a country-style setting.

A plantsman's garden
A passion for collecting certain plants – here herbs (right) – provides the theme for an exuberant, flower-filled garden.

Choosing a style

Your choice of style will, to some extent, be governed by the size of your garden. Normally, people choose their home first and get the garden that comes with it. Only a very keen gardener, or perhaps a professional, is likely to choose a house because of its garden. So, you have to make the most of what you have, whether it be a large, rambling country garden with an orchard, or a tiny, handkerchief-sized urban plot.

Generally, a large garden lends itself best to an informal style, while a small garden suits a more formal look, if only because the architecture of the house is so much more prominent. Some of the garden styles shown on the following pages would suit small gardens, some large, some either. Whichever style you choose, make sure you really like it, and that it suits your needs. For example, if you have the spare time and enjoy cooking, an edible garden or potager is worth considering. If you have a busy lifestyle, but want a good-looking garden in which to relax, opt for a low maintenance approach with easy-care shrubs and hard surfaces rather than grass.

Formal and informal

A garden is a place where art and nature work together. In formal gardens, the element of human control is uppermost, with plants used in the way that artists use paint, or sculptors stone or metal. Informal gardens are more naturalistic and take greater account of the growth habits of their plants.

Most of us think of a formal garden as one that is angular and geometrical, with an abundance of clipped shrubs in straight lines and stone statuary. But as well as this classical type of formal garden, there are also more modern versions, where blocks of single plant species are juxtaposed to create dramatic effects of colour and form. Clear separation of the hard and soft elements conveys a sense of clarity and order. Informal gardens can take many forms. Flowing 'organic' shapes are commonly used for beds, terraces, lawns and water features, along with planting that mixes and blends plant varieties, the plants being encouraged to develop their natural shapes. Maintenance is minimal, as little clipping to shape is done, while the mixed, dense planting reduces opportunities for weeds.

Some of the great gardens are those that combine the formal and informal, where a clear framework of clipped shrubs and hedges encloses burgeoning, flower-filled planting. Even a naturalistic style of planting, one inspired by wildflower meadows, can look effective when accompanied by very formal shaped trees. In larger gardens you can create a formal area close to the house, with a progressively more relaxed style the further you move away from it, culminating in a wild-flower meadow, perhaps, at the end of a formal lawn.

Classical yet modern

This small garden breaks some rules but is still unmistakeably in the classical tradition.

Flowing informality

A large, informal garden merges seamlessly into the lush green countryside beyond.

Low maintenance

People who want to spend time enjoying their garden rather than gardening need a low maintenance garden, often with plenty of hard surfaces for tables, chairs and barbecue equipment. Paving has always been the traditional material for this, but decking is becoming increasingly popular, especially since it is easier to build out over a slope. Other low maintenance surfaces include pebbles and gravel, but bear in mind that standing furniture on these is not very satisfactory.

Since hard surfaces can look rather bare, containers are often used as well. They can be moved around and replanted as and when necessary, and so are highly flexible. Other planting should consist of species that require little attention.

Water looks particularly effective next to hard surfaces, and adds yet another dimension. A water feature is also much appreciated in hot summer weather. With so much choice, there is no need for a low maintenance garden to be dull.

Oriental influence
Bold foliage shapes, along with the clever use of pebbles, rock, gravel and water combine to make a trouble-free garden.

Edible potager

This type of garden is not nearly as difficult or time-consuming as you might suppose and can be very rewarding. Beans, lettuces, tomatoes, raspberries and strawberries can all be grown even in a small plot or, in the case of tomatoes, strawberries and lettuces, in nothing more than a simple container.

Traditionally, the growing of fruit and vegetables meant a utilitarian garden, often located in a separate area away from the main ornamental garden. But modern thinking is introducing us to the possibility of ornamental vegetable gardening, or of integrating vegetables with flowering plants. Those separate, uninspired kitchen gardens are definitely a thing of the past.

Usefulness and beauty
A modern potager with ornamental cabbages, herbs and fruit proves that practical need not mean utilitarian.

Nature garden

With much countryside used for crops and building developments, gardens are more important than ever to wild flora and fauna. We should all do our best to encourage wildlife in our gardens, but you can devote your garden to it entirely, for instance, growing locally native wild flowers and shrubs rather than imported exotics.

The most effective nature gardens are in rural areas where the existing vegetation can be managed so that it is difficult to tell where the garden ends and the countryside begins. However, even a town garden can be home to an extraordinarily wide range of birds, animals and insects. Simply by installing the tiniest pond, you will soon attract frogs and aquatic insects.

Nature runs riot
A wild-flower meadow studded with colour at the height of summer provides food for insects as well as a feast for the eyes.

Year-round garden

A garden that looks good all year round is the dream of many, but is not always easy to achieve, especially in the smaller garden. Good planning and a knowledge of a wide variety of plants are both essential.

Starting with bulbs and shrubs that begin to flower in late winter, it is possible to have some interest all year, ending with a flourish of perennials in the autumn, and perhaps some exciting leaf and berry colour. Winter days can be enlivened with evergreen foliage and the coloured stems of willows and dogwoods. In the smaller garden there is little space to pack in a lot of plants, so it is important to concentrate on those that flower for a long time and that have attractive foliage, remembering that leaves always have a longer season than flowers.

In a small garden, you may also like to include bedding plants – temporary plants that add colour and can be removed when they have finished flowering, to be replaced with others.

A green oasis
The use of strongly architectural plants and decorative ornaments make this a garden to be enjoyed all year round.

Large and small gardens

Large gardens offer the keen gardener exciting possibilities, yet to the not so keen, they can seem daunting and burdensome. Small gardens offer the scope to develop an intimate style, yet can feel terribly cramped to the ambitious. In a large garden, maintenance is often the major issue, so a relaxed approach to the planting is often necessary to help keep it manageable. The double perennial borders of grand country houses are too much work for the average household: a naturalistic approach to planting is more appropriate for modern lifestyles. Because of the maintenance problem, far too many large gardens are nothing more than barren swathes of grass with a few scattered shrubs. But rather than trying to keep a large lawn neat, why not leave some of it as meadow grass,

Unobstructed view
A wall of pleached lime trees divides a large garden into two separate 'rooms'.

to be cut only once or twice a year? Alternatively, you could devote more of the garden to shrubs and trees. You have the opportunity to grow fine specimen trees or to sculpt the landscape with shrubs, using them to separate one area of the garden from another.

In many ways, small gardens are more difficult to plan as any mistakes are clearly visible. Maintaining or redesigning a small garden to remove mistakes is much easier though. The limited space means that the garden has to be multi-purpose, with a variety of needs satisfied by the same area. The most successful small gardens are densely planted, making use of all the available space. There will be climbers on the vertical surfaces, flowers spilling out of pots and containers positioned on walls and other hard surfaces, and carefully planned planting that provides a succession of colour and interest for as long as possible.

A floral abundance
Perennials supplemented by annuals spill from every nook and cranny in a tiny town garden.

Cottage garden

The cottage-garden style is a modern interpretation of the traditional country plot, where vegetables, fruit and herbs were grown alongside decorative flowers. The appearance is one of romantic confusion: there appears to be no obvious overall plan. In reality it can be quite a task to create such an apparently artless look.

One reason why cottage gardens have become so popular is that they offer the opportunity to grow everything we want in one space: it is perfectly acceptable to alternate flowers with rows of vegetables, or to stick some raspberry canes in between the roses. It is also a good style to adopt if you do not want to have a lawn: the plants are grown in wide borders and are reached by means of narrow paths.

Old rose varieties, scented flowers, wild flowers, herbs (culinary and medicinal) and simple natural-looking flowers are all essential to the cottage garden. Any modern hybrids or exotic plants will detract from the effect.

The artless look

Plants completely obscure the garden path in this traditional-style cottage garden. The planting appears quite random but in fact a lot of thought has gone into the positioning of the different heights of plants and the planning of the blocks of colour.

Romantic garden

For many people, romance is an important part of a garden's appeal. It is, of course, like beauty, in the eye of the beholder, but for most of us a romantic garden is one with an abundance of colour and scent, and a sense of seclusion from the world. Intimacy can be created by fences and hedges separating parts of the garden, while climbers can be grown up fences and walls to soften hard surfaces.

Soft textures and pastel colour combinations are another vital feature of such a garden, as are billowing flower shapes and graceful foliage plants. Finally, places to sit and enjoy the view are essential. Surround them with lush planting, preferably scented. A simple seat in a corner can be enough to create the effect or, if you want something more elaborate, install a summer-house or rose-covered bower in a good viewing spot.

Romantic appeal

A winding path leads past luxuriant planting to more secluded spots beyond.

Where garden plants come from

The range of plants commonly grown in gardens includes species from all over the world, with certain concentrations from particular places. Most of the late-summer and autumn-flowering perennials for example, come from eastern North America which has a spectacular and rich flora of such species. China and Tibet are the source of many of the best shrubby plants found in our gardens – camellias and rhododendrons for example – while the Mediterranean basin is the origin of a number of favourite sun-loving shrubs such as rock roses (*Cistus*), lavenders and many herbs.

The nineteenth and early twentieth centuries saw many intrepid botanists devoting their lives to seeking out new plants in areas practically unknown to Europeans: David Douglas in North America, Frank Kingdon Ward, and Ernest Wilson in the China-Tibet border region being three of the most notable. Funded by wealthy landowners trying to outdo each other in creating spectacular gardens, the story of the plant-hunters is one of heroism, endurance and romance. While many of their introductions are still with us as unchanged natural species, breeders have since developed many new creations. Nearly all the camellias now sold, and most of the rhododendrons, are the result of many years' work to produce plants with desirable characteristics for the garden – compact habit, colourful flowers freely produced, and resistance to disease and environmental stress.

European native
Crocus dalmaticus *is a late-winter and early-spring flowerer that is native to central and southern Europe but is now grown in gardens all across the northern hemisphere.*

A plant from the Orient
Camellias, which are now bred prolifically in many countries of the world, originated from the cool mountain slopes of China and Tibet.

Classification

All naturally occurring plant species have an internationally used two-part scientific name written in italics, for example, *Rhododendron ponticum*. The first part of the name is the genus, which can include anything from one to several hundred species: the second part is the specific epithet. There are hundreds of rhododendrons, but only those with mauve flowers and certain other characteristics can be called *Rhododendron ponticum*.

Plant genera (the plural of genus) are grouped together into families. The *Ericaceae* or heather family includes not only ericas (heathers), but also rhododendrons and vacciniums (blueberries and similar shrubs). *Rosa* species are part of the *Rosaceae* family which also includes *Malus* (apple) and *Prunus* (cherries and plums). It can be useful for the gardener to have an awareness of these families as plants in them often share the same characteristics. Nearly all members of the heather family, for example, grow best on acid soils, whereas most members of the rose family do best on fertile, deep soils.

If there is a third element in a plant's name, written with inverted commas, for instance *Rhododendron ponticum* 'Variegatum', then this means that the plant is a cultivar, or variety that has been selected as a good garden plant. If a plant is a cultivated hybrid species – the result of crossing two species or two other hybrids in the genus – then its specific name is preceded by a multiplication sign.

Species
The simple, but attractive, leaves of a species pelargonium, Pelargonium tomentosum.

Cultivar
Pelargonium *'Lady Plymouth' is grown primarily for its scented, silver-edged leaves.*

CLASSIFICATION DIAGRAM

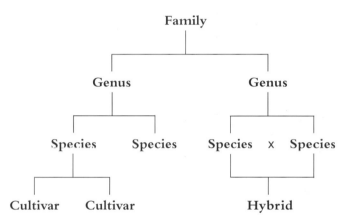

Hybrid
The abundant, large flowers of a hybrid pelargonium, bred precisely for its flower power.

Plant-breeding

Modern plant-breeding can produce plants with characteristics that are desirable for farmers or gardeners. Farmers want crops with higher yields and resistance to disease or to chemicals used for pest control. Gardeners also want plants that are disease-resistant, and may require more decorative features too, such as a compact habit, special coloration, or double instead of single flowers.

Roses, for example, are very highly bred plants, resulting from several centuries of selection and constant crossings between varieties. Characteristics have been developed which are entirely unnatural to roses but which appeal to gardeners, such as double flowers or unusual colours – bright orange is one. Nearly all hybrids and many cultivars cannot be propagated by seed as the seed will produce progeny with a wide variety of characteristics. Often none of these will resemble the parent, but many will look like the original wild plant. That is why plants which self-seed in the garden appear to change over the years. Polyanthus primroses, for example, seem to change to yellow, but this colour change is really the result of new seedling plants that have reverted to the coloration of the original wild primrose.

For many hybrids, the only means of propagation is by cuttings or division which maintains the characteristics of the parent plant, or by very careful pollination of the flowers under controlled conditions. Highly bred plants, as opposed to naturally occurring species, can give gardeners problems unless the breeding has been done to improve on naturally occurring characteristics. There is now a move to use species plants, and to pick plants that enjoy local conditions instead.

A simple rose
Rosa glauca *is a vigorous species rose with single flowers.*

Highly bred rose
Breeding has produced the double flowers of Rosa *'Louise Odier'.*

Selecting plants

It is important that you learn a little about the planted material with which you intend to furnish your garden. You do not need a great deal of specialized knowledge to start with, but plants, like people, differ in their characteristics and attributes, and if you are going to create a successful garden, you need to understand the basic differences. On the previous pages, it was explained where plants originate from, and how subsequently we have bred them to suit our purposes, and how we have grouped them according to their different characteristics. At the most basic level, plants can be distinguished by general category (see below), which governs their overall form. The biggest and most durable are trees, then come shrubs and climbers with woody stems, smaller perennial plants which re-grow every year (the foliage of many dying in winter, to re-grow the following spring), bulbs (which lie dormant for part of the year) and annuals and biennials, which grow, flower and die in one year (annuals) and over two years (biennials). You need a mixture of these in your garden, and you can buy the plants from nurseries or garden centres, or you can grow your own.

Plant categories

Trees and shrubs are together known as woody plants, trees being distinguished by having a single stem or trunk, whereas shrubs form multiple stems from the base. Their growth rate, relative to herbaceous plants, is slow, which makes them a more long-term proposition for the gardener. However, their size and permanence make them an essential part of the garden framework. Fruit bearing trees can also be an important feature of the garden. Included in the category of shrub are small, low-growing twiggy plants like heathers, lavender, sage and rock roses (*Cistus*) which usually have their origins in harsh and stressful environments. They are usually faster to establish in the garden than larger shrubs, and their attractive ground-hugging habit makes them an important feature in many gardens.

Plants that do not form woody growth are known as 'herbaceous' plants.

Herbaceous perennials go through an annual cycle of growth, producing a whole new set of stems and leaves above ground every year, and in the main, dying back completely during the winter. Bulbs and tuberous plants are specialised perennials which die back to a compact storage organ during their dormant season.

Annuals are plants that germinate from seed to grow, flower and produce more seed all in the space of a year. They are useful for the gardener as they are quick to establish and very colourful. Often counted as annuals are perennials from tropical climates which are discarded after they have flowered as they would not survive a winter outside in more temperate conditions.

Biennials are plants that are grown from seed one year, and then flower and die the next. The majority of vegetables are annuals although some, such as the root vegetables carrots and parsnips, are strictly speaking biennials but are harvested before they flower.

Tree
Carpinus betulus *'Fastigiata'* is an award-winning cultivar of the common hornbeam. Its shape becomes more open with age.

Shrub
The rounded white flowerheads of the deciduous shrub Hydrangea arborescens *'Annabelle' appear in summer.*

Perennial
With its tall spikes of pink and purple and its glossy foliage, the perennial Acanthus spinosus *makes a bold statement.*

Bulbs
Each bulb of Tulipa tarda *produces several star-shaped yellow-tinged cream flowers in early to mid-spring.*

Where to buy

Garden centres stock a good range of basic plants, but they ignore many equally good, but less common ones. However, like supermarkets, their staff sometimes know little and care less about what they are selling. As an alternative, there is much to be said for visiting specialist nurseries to buy plants, particularly as your enthusiasm for and knowledge of gardening increases. Specialist nurseries have the advantage of growing many of the less usual plants and their owners are often very knowledgeable, enthusiastic and helpful. Look

out for specialist nurseries at plant and garden fairs and shows. They often exhibit there, giving you the chance to see a wider range of plants than you would otherwise, as well as the opportunity to buy from a number of far-flung sources.

Mail order is another, traditional way of buying plants, and is still a very good one, especially if you live far from good nurseries or garden centres.

Many specialist nurseries offer mail-order services of a high standard. In fact, if you want fruit trees and bushes it is often best to buy them by mail order, as this is an extremely specialized business, done well by only a few firms.

Flower shows
Flower shows provide the opportunity to see plants grown by specialists from all over the country. With plants often 'forced' into growth for these occasions, you may also see flowers at a time when they would not usually be in season.

Raising plants

Growing from seed is one of the most rewarding and least expensive ways of raising plants. You can grow annuals and most biennials from seed as well as many perennials, most of which will flower in the second year after sowing. It is even possible to raise trees and shrubs from seed, although they may take many years to reach maturity.

Division and taking cuttings are other ways of obtaining plants. These produce quicker results and are also inexpensive.

Growing from seed
Many popular garden plants can be raised from seed, some without any specialized equipment.

Division
Some perennials are easily divided simply by separating the roots using two hand forks.

Cuttings
Plants have different requirements as to when during their growing cycle cuttings can be taken.

Choosing a healthy plant

When you buy a plant from a garden centre or nursery, you are buying the product of many years', sometimes many generations' work. Most garden centres have a quick turnover, so there is usually little risk of buying an old, pot-bound plant. However, you should check by looking underneath the pot. If it is a woody plant and has a mass of roots coming out of the bottom, do not buy it as its roots have not had enough room to grow and may have been damaged for life. Perennials that look unhappy having been in a pot for the whole summer are less of a problem: they will quickly recover once

they are planted out in the garden. Also look carefully to check the plant has a good shape, without any long, leafless or dead stems. If it is in leaf, the leaves should be sturdy and a good colour. If it is a flowering plant, check that it has plenty of buds: a plant in full flower will be attractive now, but may be past its best within a week or two. Try to avoid buying a large plant for an instant look, it is better to buy a young one: it will be more vigorous and so will establish more readily.

A container-grown plant
Any plant you buy should be in good shape. Avoid any with broken stems, discoloured leaves or roots growing out of the base of the pot.

Well-branched open shape

Healthy new shoots

Leaves in good condition

Healthy root system

DESIGNING THE GARDEN

With a little know-how, it is possible to transform the most neglected or untidy plot into a garden that is as beautiful as it is practical. Designing a garden is about making the best of the space that you have. It involves organizing the various features and elements you wish to include in a cohesive, appealing way. But most important, it is about turning your garden into what you really want it to be. With designs for every shape and size of plot, it is easier than ever to become your own landscape gardener. You will find all the help you need to draw up your own plan and see it through to completion, including simple, step-by-step guides to adding features such as brick surfaces and paving, building steps and timber decks, and pagodas or fencing. With suggestions on what to plant and where, how to deal with problem areas, how best to disguise eyesores, lay lawns, make ponds and more, this chapter gives you the basic information to create a good-looking yet practical garden.

The need for design

To be successful, a garden has to both look good and be practical, too. The best way to realize these two aims is to start off with a design.

For every beautiful garden that has evolved without careful planning, there are many more that, despite considerable investments of time, effort and money, fail to work because they are either impractical or unattractive. This is because an unplanned garden is rather like a small house which is extended bit by bit, as and when the need arises. The resulting conglomeration of rooms and spaces is invariably never quite satisfactory either from the point of view of appearance or for practical purposes.

A garden design allows you to take all the features and elements you want to include and organize them in a harmonious way. You will effectively be combining a number of ideas that not only work well on their own but which will relate to one another in terms of both form and function. Proceeding with a design will at the same time give you the opportunity to check out the availability of the materials, ensure that they are suitable for your intended purpose and, of course, to ascertain their likely cost.

Another beneficial aspect of a well thought-out design is that it will enable you to build your garden in stages if you wish, in the knowledge that the end result will always be a coherent whole.

The scope and scale of your design will depend on the money and time available. Once you have a worked-out idea in place, you can zone the areas you wish to create (see p.27). It will pay to do the section closest to the house first.

Transforming a garden

The key to a successful transformation is to retain useful and important features, such as shade-giving trees or shrubs that screen a boundary, while incorporating new ones – for instance, a patio area near the house. To decide what to keep, you should take some time to assess the relative merits of each major element of the garden. It is a good idea to observe the garden for several months before making major changes, such as removing a tree that gives the site character. When planning where to sit and what to plant, note the incidence of sun and shade at different times of the day and in different seasons. Deciduous trees that cast heavy shade in summer can let in welcome light when leafless in winter.

A change of scene
The small, neglected and featureless garden (inset) has been given a facelift with a neatly shaped lawn, a paved patio near the house and well-ordered borders around the perimeter.

Basic design rules

The use of simple shapes and forms, whether two dimensional like flower beds and paved areas, or three dimensional structures such as pergolas and summerhouses, will not only make your garden design more effective, but will have the added benefit of making the garden easier and less expensive to build and look after subsequently.

In small gardens especially, it is easy to let a design run away with you and become overcomplicated in an effort to include all your requirements. Avoid falling into this trap by including in your garden only those features that have a high priority, such as a patio, lawn, outdoor storage and maybe a play area for the children.

Limit your choice of materials for paved areas to two or, at most, three different sorts. Similarly, structures such as fences, trellis, pergolas and the like, will all blend together much more successfully if they are built from the same material, whether it be timber, wrought iron or something else.

Resist the temptation to include many different varieties of plants and choose a few good structural plants instead. These will give the garden its shape even in winter, and should be supplemented by a limited range of other varieties planted in groups of three or five. This will be much more effective than using a wider range of plants all planted singly.

Informal plantsman's garden

A simple brick path and patio laid in a straightforward herringbone pattern create the 'holding' element for a diverse selection of shrubs and perennials.

Creating a theme

A single theme provides vital unity in a garden design. It can bring together and harmonize a mixture of features and ideas. Major themes can be based on a colour, on the use of a particular material, or on a geometric shape, form, or pattern.

Colour

Colour can be used in several ways. One is to make all the 'hard' elements (paving, walls, fences and so on) the same colour, or a combination of colours, such as warm grey with terracotta.

Another is to have a colour theme in the planting. This might be a single colour such as white or red (although this approach can be very restrictive, especially in a small garden) or perhaps a combination of complementary shades, such as pale yellow, soft pink and light blue. A third way would be to have a colour theme reflected in both the hard and soft elements.

Materials

This approach is most suited to the hard elements of a garden. For example you could build walls, patio, paths and raised beds using the same brick throughout, or maybe in a combination of brick and stone. Or you could make all the vertical structures such as fences and screens from the same wood, in one particular style – perhaps rustic.

Unity of shape, form and pattern

If you want to include materials and ideas that do not harmonize naturally, the use of a particular geometric shape can provide a theme. Two-dimensional elements, for example a patio, lawn or pool, can all be made circular or semi-circular. Extend this idea to the three-dimensional features, maybe using trees and shrubs that are naturally more or less spherical in shape, or that can be trained to be so, such as box or yew. Another approach might be simply to divide your garden into a series of equal squares or rectangles, each one fulfilling a different purpose – lawn, patio, kitchen garden and so on.

Formal patio

Minor changes of level and matched pairs of containers help to prevent a largely paved area from looking monotonous.

Introducing the third dimension

It is important when designing a garden to remember that it will be three-dimensional. The plants and structures that you mark out on your plan need to be thought of not only as occupying a certain amount of space on the ground, but also in terms of their height and density.

A weeping birch will produce a very different effect from, say, a conical evergreen, whereas an ornamental stone ball could be imitated by a ball of clipped box. The garden's basic framework – whether of living plants, man-made, or a combination of the two – gives the underlying structure of the three-dimensional effect,

and this can be greatly enhanced by the judicious use of vertical elements, such as arches, arbours, fences, walls and hedges, which form screening barriers or offer glimpses of what lies beyond.

In the garden plans on the following pages, as much thought has been given to these details as to the rest of the design. Boundary walls have been clothed with climbers, pergolas and arches beckon the onlooker into other parts of the garden, single specimen shrubs or trees act as focal points, and raised beds, steps and other features have been used to prevent large expanses of lawn or hard surfacing from looking flat.

Using vertical elements

By the careful selection and positioning of such verticals as fences, hedges, garden structures, trees and tall shrubs, it is possible to achieve a number of desirable effects in your garden.

Screening is useful for masking views of unsightly objects both within and outside the garden. Frequently, complete screening is almost impossible: however, planting just a tree or group of tall

shrubs to break up the outline of the unwanted view is often enough to have the desired effect.

Framing is the opposite of screening. Use it to draw

Enhancing a sloping garden
Three-dimensional elements accentuate the gentle slope of this garden: steps, the pergola and repeat planting of spiky, architectural foliage plants.

attention to a particular view within, or maybe outside, the garden, or to an object or focal point such as a statue or pond. While an arch is a classic example of a frame through which to look at an object or view, even the suggestion of an arch, for example the view between the trunks of two trees with mingling canopies, can be equally effective.

Both sun and shade are important and any reasonably sized vertical object, whether man-made or natural, can be

positioned to create sun-traps or areas of shade to suit.

Division of space is another key factor. Many gardens can be given an added dimension by subdividing them into smaller individual spaces. Often it is better to achieve this with objects such as tall shrubs than with walls or fences.

Screening buildings
Trellis and climbing plants together with leaf canopies afford privacy from the neighbouring block of flats.

The garden framework

Just as a building has a concrete or steel framework beneath its brick or glass facade, so a garden needs a framework or basic structure to build on. This framework can serve, if necessary, to break the garden down into different spaces according to the needs of the owner – for example to give an area for children's play, or an area for growing vegetables. Paradoxically, gardens that are subdivided into smaller areas often seem larger and more complex.

The framework can consist of man-made structures or plants, but is usually a combination of both, as the gardens on the following pages show.

Such a framework is necessary so that at any time of the year, particularly where the climate is temperate and many plants are deciduous, the essential shape of the garden is always present, even if only in a skeletal form. Without this, most gardens would appear flat and uninteresting, especially during the winter months.

Framework plants such as trees and large shrubs, both deciduous and evergreen, should be selected not only for their individual beauty but also for the way in which their scale and form act as foils to smaller flowering and foliage plants. Large evergreen shrubs and trees in particular are, by their nature, ideal for the purpose,

Organizing space
A raised trellis screen not only divides the garden, but with the rose-covered arch beyond and a meandering path, creates a vista down it.

even if their flowers are insignificant. Similarly, man-made structures, such as fences, trellises, pergolas and arbours, while having their own intrinsic attractions, must also be designed and detailed so that again, whatever the time of year, they will always be interesting.

Shrubs for framework
Neat, low-level hedges of clipped dwarf box (above) can firmly contain a wide variety of more exuberant plant forms.

Trees for framework
A group of Robinia pseudoacacia 'Frisia' forms a deciduous canopy over garden furniture, while an evergreen hedge provides a year-round backdrop.

Planning the garden

One of the most fascinating aspects of gardening is that every garden is unique, because every owner is also unique. This means that everyone's expectations of how a garden should be laid out to satisfy their own needs is going to be different from the next person's – sometimes only in the tiniest of ways, but at other times in major respects.

When looked at from the point of view of a single individual, planning a garden can be comparatively straightforward. If, for instance, you like growing vegetables, then the whole garden can be put down to vegetables! However, when a garden is going to be used by more than one individual, the choice of what goes in it, and where, suddenly becomes far more difficult and can often be quite challenging.

The first step in tackling the challenge is to draw up a list of what you (and perhaps other members of your family) want from the garden. Next you need to assess what you already have in terms of the garden's size and aspect and, in the case of an established garden, in terms of the plants and features that are already there. Finally, you will be ready to think about where to put the features you want, bearing in mind the need for ease of access around the garden and safety.

Existing garden plan
Make a sketch plan of your garden with any existing features. Decide which of these are worth retaining in the light of your list. Here, we could keep the mature cherry tree and the old concrete paving to use it to lay stone flags and build an arch.

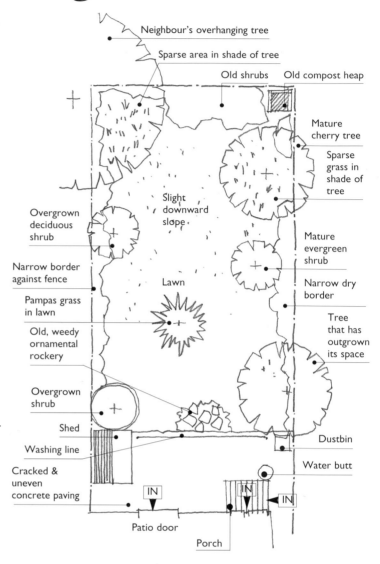

Neighbour's overhanging tree
Sparse area in shade of tree
Old shrubs   Old compost heap
Mature cherry tree
Sparse grass in shade of tree
Slight downward slope
Overgrown deciduous shrub
Mature evergreen shrub
Narrow border against fence
Narrow dry border
Lawn
Pampas grass in lawn
Tree that has outgrown its space
Old, weedy ornamental rockery
Overgrown shrub
Shed
Dustbin
Washing line
Water butt
Cracked & uneven concrete paving
IN   IN   IN
Patio door
Porch

Your requirements

Make a list of your requirements in order of priority. The list here includes features for a family garden.

Be careful not to become involved with small details at this stage. Once the basic structure of the garden and the size, shape and position of major elements are established, then you can work out the detailing, such as plant varieties or the colour of the brick.

Utility
Line or rotary drier for washing
Paths
Shed for lawnmower, bicycles, tools
Screening for oil tank
Compost box
Lighting
Greenhouse
Higher boundaries
Bin store
Fuel store - coal, wood

Recreation
Patio or sitting area
  1 shaded, for summer
  2 sunny
Seating
Lawn

Play area
Water feature
Arch or pergola
Summerhouse
Ornaments/statues

Ornamental planting
Trees
Shrubs
Roses
Herbaceous border
Containers
Annual bed
Raised beds
Rockery/scree garden
Bog garden

Other planting
Fruit trees
Herb bed
Vegetable plot or area
Soft fruit cage

Safety
Safety, particularly in a garden used by children or old people, must be considered early in the planning stage.

Steps should be regular (see p.47) and, if using a dark material, could be edged with lighter coloured material. Consider lighting them at night. If the garden is to include a play area for children, you could use wood or bark chippings as a surface (see p.40) to cushion falls.

Avoid planting poisonous or potentially dangerous plants such as yew (*Taxus baccata*) and monkshood (*Aconitum*).

Assessing the space

There will be some things in your garden over which you have little or no control – its size, the direction it faces, the effect of neighbouring buildings or trees on the amount of sun or shade it receives, the presence of particularly damp or exposed spots, the type of soil. You will usually have to work with, not against these factors, so be prepared to make some compromises. It will help if you have prioritized your list of requirements.

With a small garden, for instance, the greenhouse might be low on the list, and if there were no space, it would have to go. However, a compromise might be to find room for a small cold or heated frame instead. Fruit trees, such as apples and pears, could be used in mixed borders in place of ornamental trees, while salad crops might be grown in spaces at the front of borders or in pots on the patio. Or, why not plant pergolas and trellises with climbing beans or a thornless blackberry which can be practical as well as attractive?

Finally, especially in a small garden, it pays to group all the utilitarian elements, such as the shed and bin store, in one place.

Zoning the garden

The plan of the garden with new areas dedicated to specific features, some features moved and removed, others added.

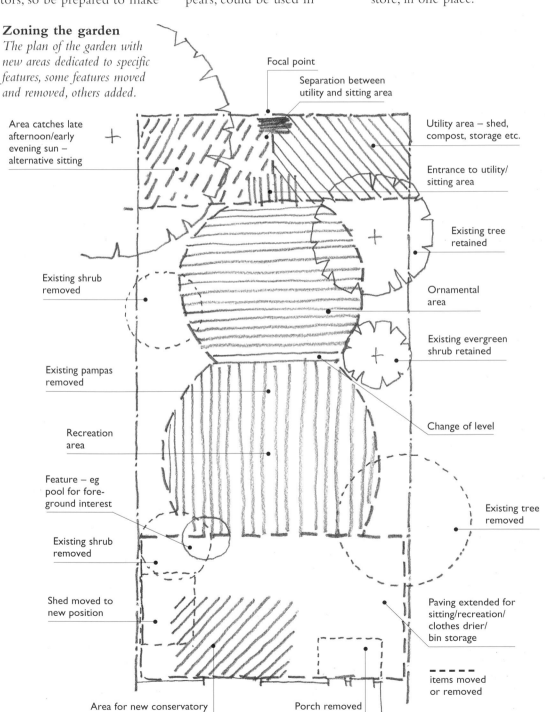

Focal point

Separation between utility and sitting area

Utility area – shed, compost, storage etc.

Entrance to utility/sitting area

Existing tree retained

Ornamental area

Existing evergreen shrub retained

Change of level

Existing tree removed

Paving extended for sitting/recreation/clothes drier/bin storage

Area catches late afternoon/early evening sun – alternative sitting

Existing shrub removed

Existing pampas removed

Recreation area

Feature – eg pool for foreground interest

Existing shrub removed

Shed moved to new position

Area for new conservatory

Porch removed

- - - - items moved or removed

Access around the garden

The position and size of paths are essentially predetermined because they have to provide the links between different parts of the garden.

Especially important are the routes between the house and features such as a rear entrance, garage or tool store. The first priority in designing paths like these is to make them functional round-the-clock and all through the year. Other garden paths also need to provide safe, efficient access for foot traffic and wheelbarrows, but the way they are laid out depends on personal taste.

The design of paths and other surfaces, such as lawns, will considerably influence the appearance and feel of the garden. A regular, straight path gives a long, open vista, while a curving, informal path, partly hidden by planting, will suggest an air of mystery.

Remember, too, that a broad grass path or stretch of lawn invites a leisurely stroll, while a narrow, twisting path of diagonal brickwork will suggest a more hurried pace.

Angular pathways
Gravel paths meander slowly around the beds in this formal garden, inviting an unhurried pace and close inspection of the planting.

Drawing up the plan

So far you have been considering the garden in fairly general terms, working from sketch plans. Now is the time to measure the garden accurately and draw a scale plan of it. This will form the basis of your finished plan. With an accurate scale plan, you can start to finalize the location of your garden features. Remember that looks need to be combined with practicality. If you want a lawn for sunbathing, you will need to make sure it is located so that it receives enough sun. If a children's play area is required, it is not a good idea to put it in a far corner of the garden where the children cannot be watched over. The location of a patio, which ideally needs to be near the house for ease of access when entertaining, can be quite critical. If the area near the house is hot and sunny, a second sitting area in a shadier part of the garden may be worth considering. Also, to avoid glare on your patio, steer clear of light-coloured surface materials and gleaming white patio furniture.

Making a scale plan

A scale plan is simply an overhead view of the garden, reduced to a size that is convenient for you to copy onto a sheet of paper. Most plans are drawn to a scale of 1:50 or 1:100.

With a scale of 1:50, for example, every dimension you measure in the garden, such as the length of a fence, is divided by 50 before being drawn on the plan. Therefore, a 10m (30ft) long fence would be 20cm (8in) on the plan. Conversely, multiplying a dimension marked on the plan by 50, let us say a 6cm (2in) wide patio, will give you the patio's actual width – 3m (10ft).

Using this technique you can recreate the shape of your garden on paper, and then add the different features you want, all drawn to the same scale.

You should also add an indication of the garden's aspect – whether it faces north, south, east or west – as aspect can determine where some features should go.

Taking measurements
The arrowed lines give the dimensions you need to measure, including those of trees and shrubs to be retained. The diagonal measurement of the plot is necessary as your garden may not be exactly rectangular.

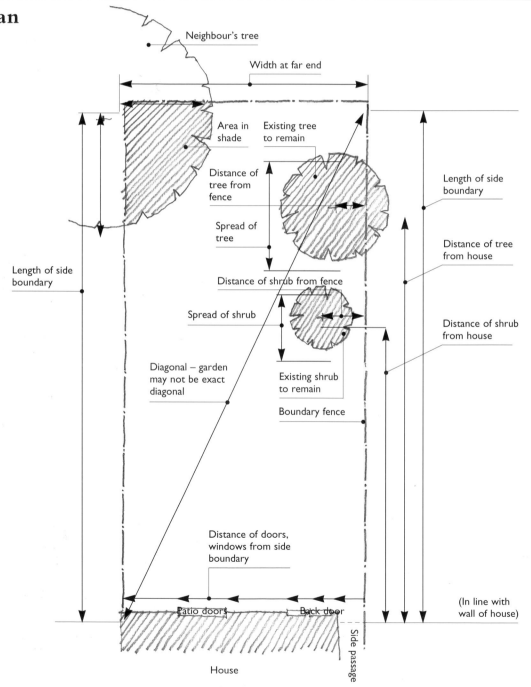

Neighbour's tree

Width at far end

Area in shade

Existing tree to remain

Distance of tree from fence

Spread of tree

Length of side boundary

Length of side boundary

Distance of tree from house

Distance of shrub from fence

Spread of shrub

Distance of shrub from house

Diagonal – garden may not be exact diagonal

Existing shrub to remain

Boundary fence

Distance of doors, windows from side boundary

Patio doors

Back door

(In line with wall of house)

House

Side passage

The finished plan

This plan of a family garden incorporates features listed on p.26. Needing relatively little maintenance, the result is both practical and good-looking. The large area of simply shaped lawn that almost reaches to the boundaries is much more practical than one or more small or oddly shaped areas, and is easier to mow.

The lawn is in the sunniest part of the garden and is connected to the patio to provide a useful overspill area for the occasional outdoor party or summer barbecue. There is a second, shaded area in the far corner, providing seclusion beneath the canopy of a neighbouring tree.

An alternative to the circular fountain in the ornamental gravel area might be a statue or sundial, a specimen shrub in a container, or perhaps a raised circular bed with planting.

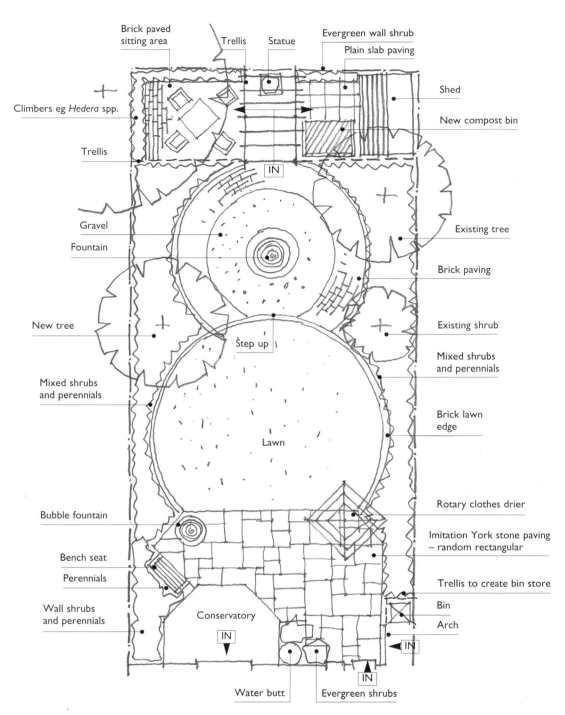

Brick paved sitting area · Trellis · Statue · Evergreen wall shrub · Plain slab paving · Shed · New compost bin · Climbers eg *Hedera* spp. · Trellis · Gravel · Fountain · New tree · Mixed shrubs and perennials · Existing tree · Brick paving · Existing shrub · Mixed shrubs and perennials · Brick lawn edge · Lawn · Step up · IN · Bubble fountain · Bench seat · Perennials · Wall shrubs and perennials · Conservatory · IN · Rotary clothes drier · Imitation York stone paving – random rectangular · Trellis to create bin store · Bin · Arch · IN · IN · Water butt · Evergreen shrubs

Estimating sizes

Measuring out sizes of features is an important element in design. To check that you have left enough space for a seating area, you should first check the patio is of a shape and size to accommodate your garden furniture and still leave room for people to walk around it.

Draw a rough sketch of your garden furniture set out as it usually would be, and seen from above. Mark its dimensions. This plan shows that the patio will need to be a minimum of 3.6 x 3.3m (12 x 14ft). These dimensions are based on a patio for a rectangular table and seating for six.

Use canes, pegs and string to mark out the various elements on the ground prior to construction. For marking out paths push a wheelbarrow along a 'path' of canes to see if it is wide enough and that it is possible to get round corners or sharp bends comfortably.

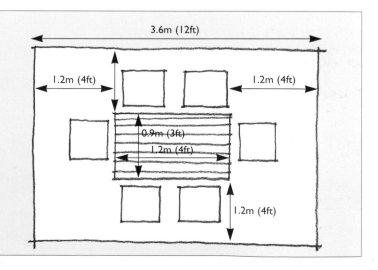

3.6m (12ft) · 1.2m (4ft) · 1.2m (4ft) · 0.9m (3ft) · 1.2m (4ft) · 1.2m (4ft)

Constructing the garden

Having finalized your garden design, your next decision will be whether to carry out all or some of the work yourself, or whether to employ professionals. The advantages of doing it yourself are that it is less expensive, and you have complete control over all stages of the job. On the down side, you may find that you do not have enough free time to finish the work within your chosen time-scale, or that you do not possess all the necessary skills, particularly in specialized areas such as bricklaying. Even if you decide to pay for a professional, do not forget that you still need to take responsibility for ensuring that he or she is fully briefed and knows what standards you expect. Whether you decide to use a professional or not, one of the advantages of having drawn up a plan is that it will enable you to phase the work. This obviously helps if you are doing it yourself, but it can also be useful if you are employing someone else as it will enable you to stagger the cost if you wish. Another factor you need to consider is the timing of the various stages of work. Certain seasons are more suited to certain jobs than others.

And finally, if you are doing the work yourself, you need to know how to deal with uneven ground, if necessary even terracing it.

Phasing the work

There are several different approaches to phasing the work. One that is useful for larger gardens is to identify a particular part of the garden and complete it in all respects from paving through to planting. The rest of the garden could then be put down to grass, used for vegetables or even kept bare. In year two a second area could be tackled and so on. Another option is to divide the work according to different elements or types of construction and complete several each year. In year one you might build the patio, paths and other hard landscape features such as a summerhouse base and a shed, and perhaps plant trees and a few shrubs that take a long time to mature. Year two could also see construction of a pergola or arch, a water feature, basic shrub planting and the completion of areas of grass. Finally, in year three, you could incorporate the finishing touches – ornaments, trellis, and climbers, a fountain in the pond and perhaps the summerhouse.

A three-year plan
This plan shows construction of the family garden (on p.32), with the work colour coded for each year. First priority is given to establishing permanent planting and laying hard surfaces near the house.
Year 1 (Yellow)
Patio, path, shed, rotary clothes drier, trees, hedge around kitchen garden, climbers on fences and walls.
Year 2 (Green)
Lawn, play area, hedge around play area, mixed shrub border, shrubs to screen shed, prepare soil in kitchen garden, compost bin.
Year 3 (Red)
Bubble fountain, arch, climbers on arch, greenhouse, heathers/herbs/cut flower border, bin store, ornaments, pots and tubs, climbing frame etc in play area.

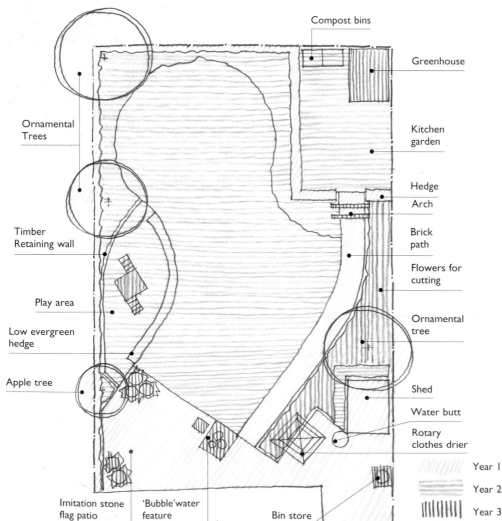

Compost bins
Greenhouse
Ornamental Trees
Kitchen garden
Hedge
Arch
Timber Retaining wall
Brick path
Play area
Flowers for cutting
Low evergreen hedge
Ornamental tree
Apple tree
Shed
Water butt
Rotary clothes drier
Imitation stone flag patio
'Bubble' water feature
Bin store

Year 1
Year 2
Year 3

Timing the work

Although most hard land-scaping can be carried out more or less all year round, it is particularly inadvisable to use wet concrete or mortars when the temperature is at or near freezing point, or when it is so hot as to dry them out rapidly. Also, if the ground is frozen solid then a lot of work becomes difficult or near impossible to carry out, so working during the depths of winter should be avoided.

Preparing the soil requires planning to achieve the best results. The ground should not be dug when it is frozen or so wet that the soil sticks to your boots and spade. If the soil contains either weed seeds or pieces of perennial weed root, these will need to be eliminated as far as possible before planting. For this to happen, the weeds must first be visible so you can hoe or treat them in some other way, and the obvious time to do this is when they are active, between spring and autumn.

Heavy clay soils benefit from being roughly dug in the autumn and left to weather in winter frost and ice. You will then need to decide whether to plant next spring and risk weed infestation, or wait until the following autumn by which time you should have eradicated the weeds.

Planting is traditionally carried out between autumn and spring when most plants are dormant, that is to say not actively growing. The planting season can, however, be extended almost all year round where container-grown plants are used, as long as they are adequately watered, particularly during long, hot spells. Obtaining the plants for your garden may require some planning, too. Once a nursery or garden centre has sold out of a particular line, it may not stock it again until the following spring or autumn. Advance ordering is therefore recommended if you do not want to have gaps in your borders.

Tackling major jobs
Avoid using wet concrete or mortar when the temperature is near, or at, freezing point, or if the conditions are very wet.

Levelling uneven ground

There are occasions when, even with a seemingly flat garden, you will need to ensure that the ground is level – for instance when laying a lawn, patio or other area of paving. Similarly, if you have a slightly sloping site, you will almost certainly want some level areas for lawn or sitting out.

Alternatively, you may decide to add interest to such a site by making a raised bed or terrace. Steep slopes are very difficult to manage without terracing, and may need professionally built retaining walls. It is often better to plan two small terraces rather than one big one. Unless you already have an abundance of good topsoil, remember that when you excavate an area it is always worth conserving the topsoil for use elsewhere (for a lawn, for example). Store it in small heaps to prevent it from deteriorating through becoming compacted.

Excavating for terracing
Roughly mark out the area to be dug using canes, pegs and string. Then estimate the depth of the excavation. You will need pegs or stakes longer than this depth and a long straightedge and spirit level. If the straightedge is not long enough, you will need to use intermediate pegs as well.

Drive a peg into the ground at the top of the slope and a longer peg at the bottom, where your proposed terrace is to start. Lay a straightedge and spirit level between the two. Excavate the fall to depth 'A' (see right) to create a flat, even terrace.

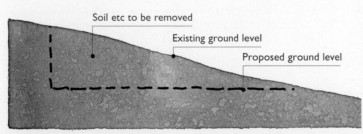

Soil etc to be removed
Existing ground level
Proposed ground level

Marking out the ground
Mark out the area to be dug and estimate the depth of the excavation.

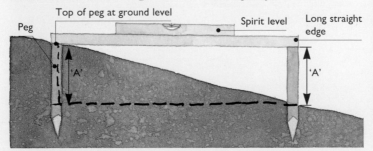

Top of peg at ground level
Peg
Spirit level
Long straight edge
'A'
'A'

Positioning the pegs
Use a spirit level and straightedge to ensure the tops of the pegs are even.

Terraced garden
Raised beds and a seating area enhance this attractive multi-level garden.

Family gardens

A family garden needs a design that will be compatible with a family's needs, while still making sure the garden looks good for as much of the year as possible. For families with small children, time is at a premium, so maintenance should be kept to a minimum. With children, open space is a priority, and so in each of these three designs the patio is generous and links directly to the lawn. In the rectangular garden, the patio extends into a paved utility area, with a shed, bin store and rotary clothes drier, all conveniently placed near the back door.

Year-round practicality
Mature shrub borders require relatively little maintenance to look good all year round. Here they successfully 'frame' an expanse of lawn which provides plenty of open space for energetic children.

The rectangular garden

A small kitchen garden with greenhouse is in the far corner, diagonally opposite the patio. This arrangement allows more space for the lawn and makes the garden appear larger. A brick path provides a practical, all-weather link between the house and kitchen garden and contrasts in colour and style with the square flags of the patio and utility area.

In addition to the generous lawn and patio, there is a separate play area for small children which is ideally located for supervision from the house or elsewhere in the garden. A bubble water feature makes a focal point at the corner of the patio, and acts as a divider between the patio and the utility area. At the far end of the gently curving path, a rustic arch makes an attractive feature and marks the entrance to the kitchen garden.

The planting consists of trees, shrubs and perennials, carefully selected to give year round interest with minimum work, and including varieties that can be used for cut or dried flowers. There is also a small herb bed situated in the sun, with convenient access to the kitchen.

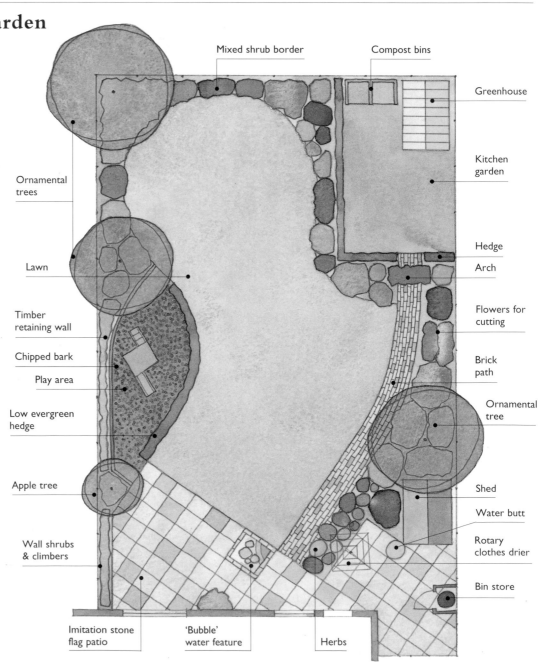

Mixed shrub border
Compost bins
Greenhouse
Kitchen garden
Hedge
Arch
Flowers for cutting
Brick path
Ornamental tree
Shed
Water butt
Rotary clothes drier
Bin store
Ornamental trees
Lawn
Timber retaining wall
Chipped bark
Play area
Low evergreen hedge
Apple tree
Wall shrubs & climbers
Imitation stone flag patio
'Bubble' water feature
Herbs

Long narrow plot

Here, the relative positions of the key elements are more or less unchanged, but by placing the patio, path and kitchen garden at an angle, and dividing the lawn by a change in the direction of the path, the narrowness of the plot is effectively disguised.

Very narrow plot
On a long, narrow plot, you can grow vegetables, for example, on either side of the path rather than in conventional rows.

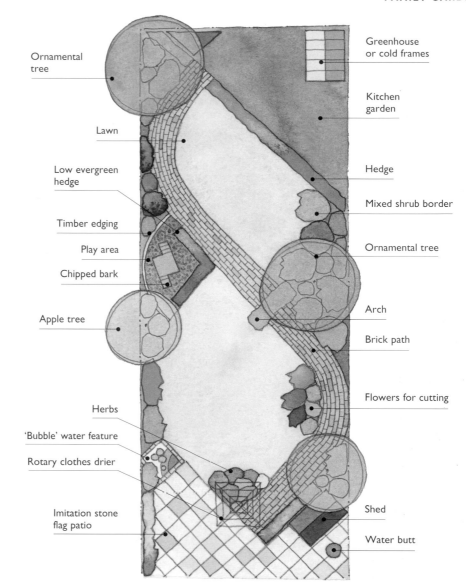

Ornamental tree

Greenhouse or cold frames

Kitchen garden

Lawn

Hedge

Low evergreen hedge

Mixed shrub border

Timber edging

Ornamental tree

Play area

Chipped bark

Arch

Apple tree

Brick path

Flowers for cutting

Herbs

'Bubble' water feature

Rotary clothes drier

Imitation stone flag patio

Shed

Water butt

Triangular plot

In this variation, the corners of the plot are taken up by the kitchen garden, screened from view by a hedge, and the play area surrounded with generous tree and shrub planting. This arrangement not only gets over the problem of narrow, awkward corners, but also maximizes the space available for the lawn and patio.

Ornamental tree

Play area

Ornamental tree

Shrubs

Chipped bark

Mixed shrub border

Timber edging

Boundary fence

Low evergreen hedge

Shed

Rotary clothes drier

Greenhouse or cold frames

Kitchen garden

Apple tree

Wall shrubs

Compost bins

'Bubble' water feature

Imitation stone flag patio

Brick path   Arch   Flowers for cutting   Herbs

Divisions in the garden
If the contours permit, a change of level between the patio and the rest of the garden helps to create a more 'private' feel to the sitting area.

Patio gardens

Enclosed by high walls or buildings, patio gardens can be small, angular, claustrophobic and bleak. But do not be deterred. There are many tricks to disguise these problems. Firstly, use planting to soften walls and disguise corners. With the boundaries partly concealed, the garden will appear larger. Secondly, any sense of squareness or angularity can be minimized by choosing a strong ground plan with a circular or curving theme, while any darkness may be overcome by painting the enclosing walls of the garden white, cream or another pale colour. On the plus side, patio gardens are relatively sheltered, so take advantage of this fact to grow more unusual and perhaps less hardy plants.

Secluded town courtyard
At the height of summer, a planting of cream and white flowers softens the boundaries of this patio, while the white garden furniture also helps to make the space appear larger than it really is.

Square plot

Here, the strong, circular ground plan helps to camouflage the squareness of the plot. Access to the pool and seat is via a brick path that reflects the circular theme, and matches the brick edging around the gravel area. The contrast between the brick path and surrounding gravel helps to disguise the fact that most of the garden is finished in hard surfacing. Any tendency towards this looking flat is avoided by the careful positioning of terracotta and stone containers filled with striking annuals, succulents and foliage plants.

Circular design
Used for beds, paving and furniture, circles form the theme of a square, walled garden.

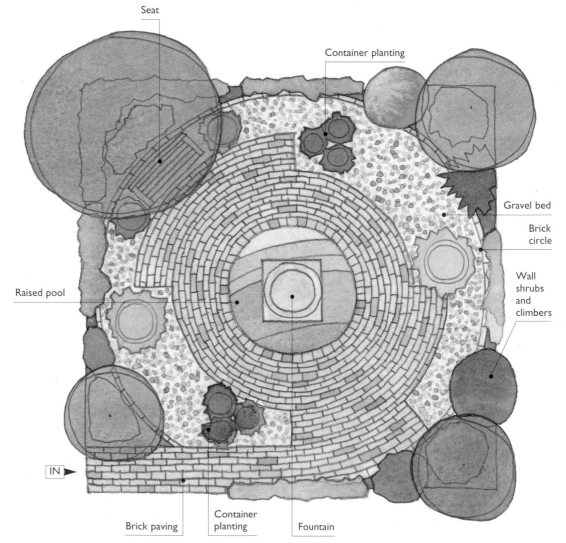

Seat

Container planting

Gravel bed

Brick circle

Wall shrubs and climbers

Raised pool

IN

Brick paving

Container planting

Fountain

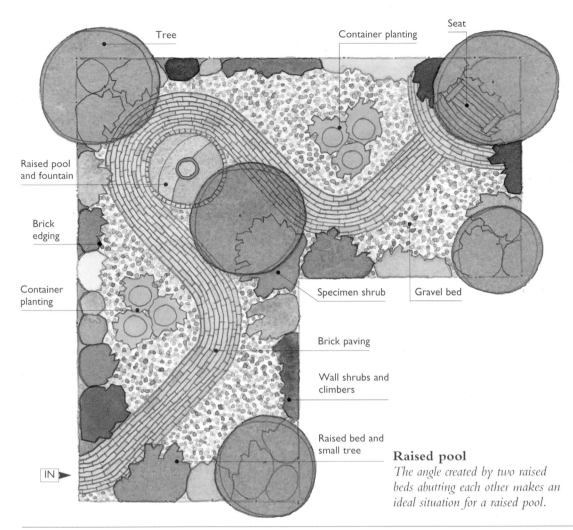

Tree

Container planting

Seat

Raised pool and fountain

Brick edging

Container planting

Specimen shrub

Gravel bed

Brick paving

Wall shrubs and climbers

Raised bed and small tree

IN ▶

L-shaped plot

In this awkwardly shaped garden, the circular theme is retained as far as possible, enhanced by the sweeping curves of the brick path and perimeter border.

The raised pool is now positioned so that it effectively links the two halves of the garden, and an additional raised bed planted with a small tree and ground cover shrubs acts as a focal point near the entrance.

Raised pool
The angle created by two raised beds abutting each other makes an ideal situation for a raised pool.

Rectangular plot

In this rectangular plot, the seating area is shifted to the far corner of the garden, the sweeping, curved path through the middle increasing the feeling of space.

The circular theme is retained in the shapes of the brick-paved seating area and the raised pool and fountain.

Seating areas
These can be positioned so that they get the benefit of shade or sun, whichever is appropriate. Enough space needs to be allocated to them to allow chairs to be drawn back from the table.

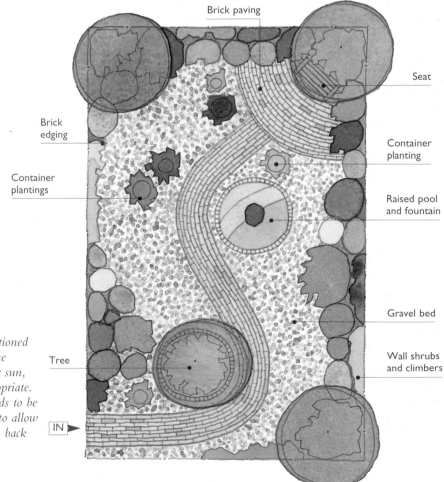

Brick paving

Seat

Container planting

Raised pool and fountain

Gravel bed

Wall shrubs and climbers

Brick edging

Container plantings

Tree

IN

Low maintenance gardens

One way to reduce maintenance in a garden, especially in small gardens, is to use gravel or paving rather than grass. You should also avoid over-fussy designs with squiggly borders and individual trees or shrubs planted in lawns. Instead choose simple shapes with long, flowing curves. Rather than struggle to keep a lawn looking good, or having to constantly water plants in pots and containers, choose plants that will grow well in the conditions available, are reliable and long-lived, have a habit which requires little maintenance and cover the ground well.

Trouble-free wood and paving
This garden requires very little work other than sweeping, applying an annual coat of preservative to furniture and planting containers.

Long narrow plot

To keep it low-maintenance, much of this garden is devoted to the decking terrace, paths and water feature, and gravel is used as a mulch. The plot's narrowness is disguised by taking the decking almost full width across it. The change of direction of the stepping stone path between the pool and seating area, plus the tree half-way down the boundary wall break up the garden's tunnel-like effect.

Tree
Shrub border
Gravel bed
Stepping stones
Bark mulch in shrub border
Raised bed (shrubs and perennials)
Shrub border

Seat
Flag patio
Climbers on pergola posts
Raised bed (shrubs and perennials)
Water feature
Shrub border
Decking terrace

Rectangular plot

Here, the central space of the garden is covered in relatively maintenance-free gravel as opposed to being put down to lawn.

It is separated from the perimeter planting by a brick edge, which matches the coping of the two raised beds while keeping the gravel in place. Planting is of shrubs and perennials selected not only for their flower and foliage but also for their relative ease of maintenance and ground-covering abilities. A generous mulch of ornamental-grade bark over the surface of the planted area keeps in moisture and also helps to discourage weeds.

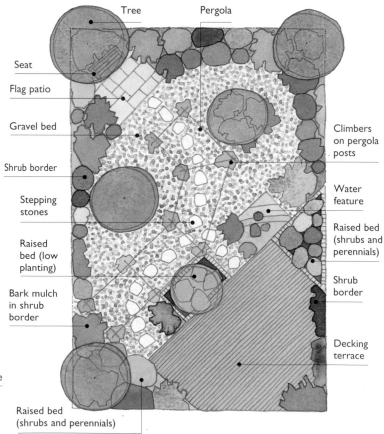

Tree
Pergola
Seat
Flag patio
Gravel bed
Shrub border
Stepping stones
Raised bed (low planting)
Bark mulch in shrub border
Raised bed (shrubs and perennials)

Climbers on pergola posts
Water feature
Raised bed (shrubs and perennials)
Shrub border
Decking terrace

Square plot

In this square variation, the design is simply 'clocked' 45°. By twisting the angle in this way, the garden appears less short and squat than it actually is. The pergola over the stepping stones will also deflect attention from the end boundaries.

Having the pool in the foreground provides a visual balance to the sitting area and ornamental tree in the opposite corner. The spaces for planting created by this arrangement are comparatively generous for such a small garden and help to disguise its squareness.

The design would suit plant enthusiasts without small children.

Oriental garden

A bamboo water spout and grasses on a bed of pebbles bring maintenance-free interest to a dull corner.

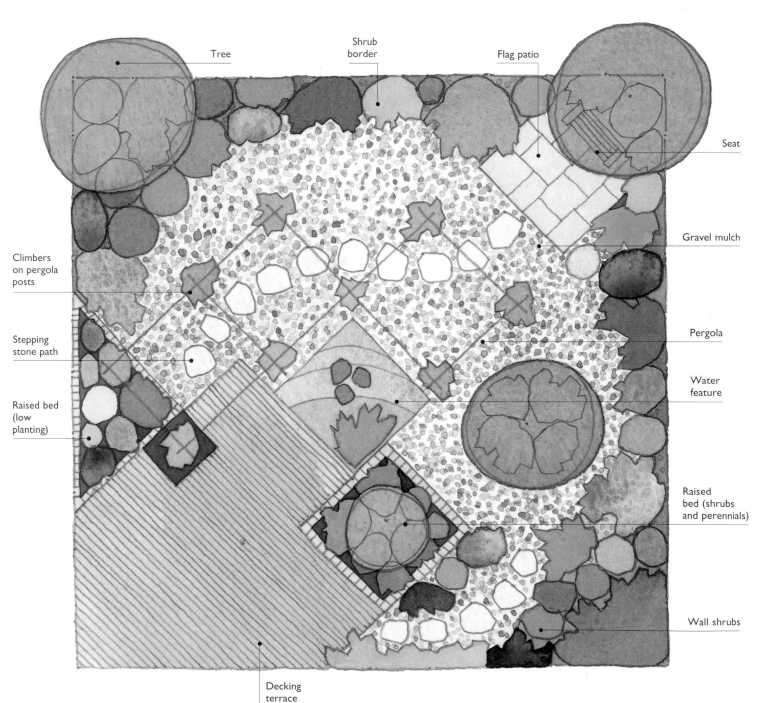

Tree

Shrub border

Flag patio

Seat

Gravel mulch

Climbers on pergola posts

Pergola

Stepping stone path

Water feature

Raised bed (low planting)

Raised bed (shrubs and perennials)

Wall shrubs

Decking terrace

Large gardens

Large gardens naturally provide more opportunities for a variety of garden features and ideas, both because of their size, and because they have fewer limitations or restrictions, such as shading from tall buildings, or being overlooked. There may be room to tuck away all the utility areas in their own separate space, leaving whole sections of the garden free for purely ornamental or recreational use. Similarly, a whole area could be devoted to fruit and vegetables without impinging on the rest of the garden. Within the ornamental garden you could opt for one theme throughout, or incorporate a variety of ideas. An effective way to do this is to gradually change style as you move from one end of the garden to the other.

Exuberant borders
A larger garden may need a lot of work but it does allow plenty of scope for massed plantings on a grand scale.

Wide, shallow plot

To effectively disguise the shape of this plot, the terrace and gravel garden are turned through an angle to focus the view diagonally into the two far corners of the garden.

Rather than being tucked away, as it might be in a smaller garden, the gazebo becomes a prominent feature, and the character of the garden changes from formal to natural across its width, rather than from end to end which is more usual. This means that the pond is situated in the corner beyond the gravel garden, but is still separated from the traditionally mown lawn by a wild-flower meadow area, as in the other designs here. The perimeter border is irregularly shaped, with room for generous planting of taller shrubs and perennials to further disguise the awkward shape of the boundaries.

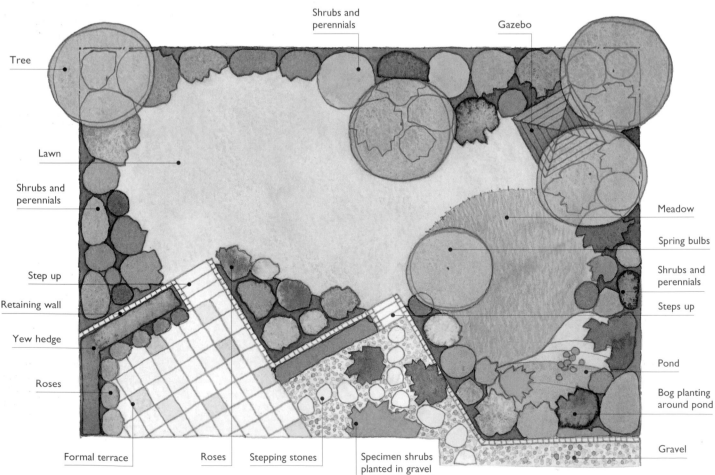

Labels: Tree, Lawn, Shrubs and perennials, Step up, Retaining wall, Yew hedge, Roses, Shrubs and perennials, Gazebo, Meadow, Spring bulbs, Shrubs and perennials, Steps up, Pond, Bog planting around pond, Gravel, Formal terrace, Roses, Stepping stones, Specimen shrubs planted in gravel

Long narrow plot

Here, the terrace runs across the full width of the garden, and the gravel area is brought into the foreground. This, the lawn and the wildflower meadow are all roughly circular and the junction of these is marked by trees and tall shrub planting which interrupts the view towards the far end of the garden and loosely divides the plot into smaller spaces. The glimpses of lawn visible from the area nearest the house entice exploration.

A mown path borders the longer grass of the wildflower meadow and carries the eye as well as the feet towards the gazebo in the far corner. The furthermost third of the garden has a wilder character. The natural-looking pond is brought away from the corner to form a focal point when viewed from the gazebo. Moisture-loving planting in the damp ground beside the pond makes it look part of the landscape.

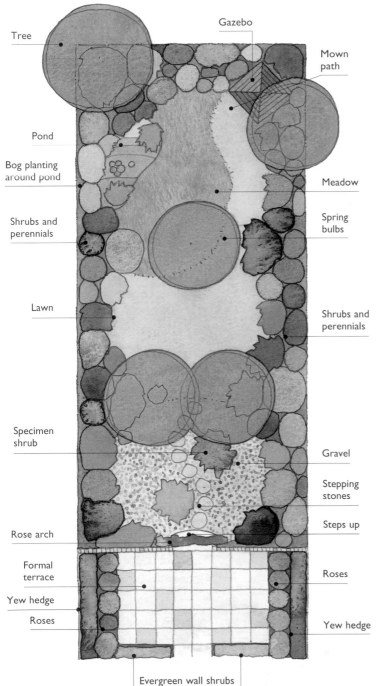

Tree

Pond

Bog planting around pond

Shrubs and perennials

Lawn

Specimen shrub

Rose arch

Formal terrace

Yew hedge

Roses

Gazebo

Mown path

Meadow

Spring bulbs

Shrubs and perennials

Gravel

Stepping stones

Steps up

Roses

Yew hedge

Evergreen wall shrubs

Rectangular plot

The extra width allows the terrace and gravel garden to be side by side, both dropping down to the lawn by way of stone steps.

The generous expanse of lawn gives a luxurious, spacious feel, while its irregular margins blur the boundaries and carry the eye into the distance. On the left, a meadow area is left uncut until the wild flowers that make it colourful in early summer have set their seed. The character of the garden changes gradually from formal to almost natural with the pond and gazebo partially screened from the house by a small copse of trees underplanted with spring flowering bulbs. Water-loving

gardeners with enough space might devote a larger area to the natural pond, or introduce a more formal water feature closer to the house.

Water-loving plants
A pond is the ideal habitat for plants such as Stratiotes, Menyanthes *and* Carex.

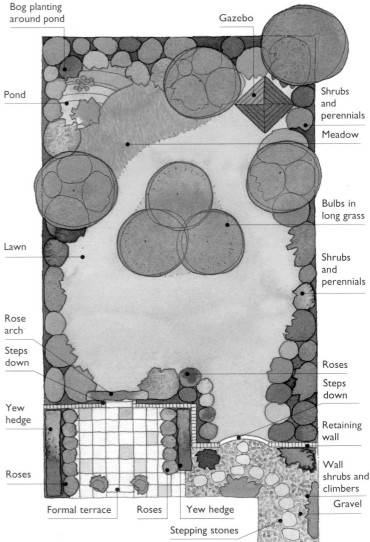

Bog planting around pond

Pond

Lawn

Rose arch

Steps down

Yew hedge

Roses

Formal terrace

Roses

Yew hedge

Stepping stones

Gazebo

Shrubs and perennials

Meadow

Bulbs in long grass

Shrubs and perennials

Roses

Steps down

Retaining wall

Wall shrubs and climbers

Gravel

Creating surface designs

Although in theory it is perfectly feasible to create a garden without any form of paving or hard surfacing, in reality it is needed in the vast majority of gardens to allow year-round, all-weather access, and to prevent wear and tear to soft elements such as lawns. Horizontal surfaces not only give access to other areas, but provide messages about how the garden is to be utilized. These should be comfortable to use, whether they are for a sitting area, for a path providing access around borders, or for steps up to a patio. The choice of surfacing will be determined partly by its function and how this relates to your overall garden design, and partly by the suitability of the material for its intended purpose.

Choosing the appropriate surface
Flat areas of curving lawn and gravel paths are relieved by islands of ground cover planting, while chipped bark, kept in place with timber edging, makes an excellent softer covering for the children's play area.

Ground cover planting

Although grass is an obvious choice for covering large areas, an alternative is a dense covering of low-growing plants. This will prevent or greatly reduce weed growth and act as an insulating layer to minimize wasteful evaporation of water from the soil's surface, keeping it cool in hot weather. Planting also absorbs the energy of heavy rainfall and in so doing protects the soil from erosion.

However, a lawn of closely mown grass will always have appeal, not least for its important visual role in both delineating and linking parts of the garden, but also for the delight we take in a cool green sward. A lawn is ideal for light recreational use and for more passive activities such as just sitting out. But concentrated or intense use can lead to wear and tear, particularly in wet conditions or when the grass is dormant in winter and unable to recover. Traditional lawns also require a fairly high degree of regular maintenance to keep them in shape and looking good, not forgetting that you may have to wait anything from a few weeks to several months before a newly seeded or turfed lawn can be used.

Timber decking

As an alternative to lawn or paving or gravel surfaces, timber planks and boards make excellent decking or walkways. They look and feel good, and blend in well with most other materials. If you use softwood, costs can compare quite favourably with good quality unit paving, though hardwood will usually be more expensive.

A fair degree of skill is required in both planning and constructing timber features and regular treatment against rot is necessary in all but the driest conditions. In damp, shady situations, wood surfaces may develop algal growths which, though not detrimental to the fabric of the construction, can become slippery and therefore potentially dangerous. So where possible, site your timber path or area in an open, dry, sunny position. Leave narrow joints between the boards to allow air to circulate and water to drain away quickly. If this is not possible you must be prepared to either scrub the surface clean on a regular basis or else treat it with a proprietary algicide to discourage algal growth.

Diagonal decking
Set in contrasting directions, these diagonal raised blocks provide a lively alternative surface material. Wood can be slippery when wet, but has a comforting, warm feel in mild, dry weather.

Gravel and bark chippings

These are not only cheaper and easier to put down than paving, but need little advance preparation. For small gardens, gravel is often more practicable than lawns. Obtainable in bulk or handy-sized bags, it can provide an instant paving solution, although it is best laid on a hardcore base, as it will gradually disappear into soft ground.

There are various types of gravel, but the one most suited to paths consists of small angular stones not larger than 25mm (1in) across. Shingle and larger cobbles are naturally worn rounded pebbles, uncomfortable to walk on but ideal for ornamental use. A surface of bark (or wood) chippings is a good protective mulch, pleasant to walk or play on and blending in well with landscape features. Fine bark can become soggy when wet, or blow away when dry. For paths, it is best laid over a hardcore base.

Paving

For rigid surfaces, paving units in the form of slabs, bricks, pavers, setts and tiles are hardwearing and long-lasting, and suitable for areas of constant use, all year round. The range of materials is extensive, and includes natural or reconstituted stone, and cement-based products often with a textured or 'weathered' finish.

The beauty of this type of surface is that it can be in use almost as soon as it is completed. Compared to grass or gravel, paving is more expensive and, for best results, more skill and effort is required in both preparation and laying.

Good paving should be reasonably smooth and be made from a non-slip material

Informal setting

Small paving slabs are excellent for informal settings as they can easily be laid to form curves or bends. The weatherbeaten grey stone blends well with the relaxed feel of this garden.

(so beware of using marble or slate). Even stone can become mossy and slippery in damp corners. Paving should be laid with a slight fall to throw off

water. It needs a firm, prepared base to prevent long-term settlement or damage which could cause it to become unsafe.

Combining materials

Used imaginatively, most surface materials can be successfully teamed with others for practical or aesthetic purposes. For example, paving flags laid as stepping stones across a lawn will cut down on grass wear and tear, or they can be laid in similar style amidst gravel to make walking easier.

To keep costs down, use a few contrasting bricks, tiles or cobbles to liven up plain,

Stones, brick and timber

A variety of materials has been used at the meeting place of brick and timber-and-gravel paths. The shingle-filled circle echoing the round stone ewer catches water from a Japanese-style trickle fountain, and self-seeded ground covers have crept in amongst the gravel.

grey concrete slabs. Or use them as edging to retain an area of gravel. Where old timbers are plentiful, use them in conjunction with gravel or

bark chippings to form path surfaces, or as the front edges to steps, where a contrasting edging material is a useful safety feature.

Pavings and cobbles

Red bricks turn plain concrete paving into a lively but even path surface, while the different-sized cobbles provide a good link with the planting, their rounded forms echoing those of the ground level leaf shapes.

Hard surfaces

As a general rule, all paving materials, whether gravel, slabs, bricks or tarmacadam, will perform better and last longer if laid on a properly prepared base, rather than straight onto soil. Bare earth can be prone to movement, settlement and other problems caused by tree roots or a high water table. For gravel, paving, bricks, setts and concrete or stone flags, a layer of sand over a hardcore base is usually more than adequate for most garden situations. However, on exceptionally soft or disturbed ground, or where the paving you are using is very thin, such as quarry tiles or slate, a rigid concrete base may be necessary (see p.44). In either case, the object is to create a sufficiently solid base that will not settle or move to the detriment of the paving laid on it.

In laying most hard surfaces, you will need first to remove soil. How much and how deep is primarily determined by the depth of hardcore base required (which in turn depends on its purpose), plus the bed of sand or mortar on which the paving is to be laid, and the thickness of the paving itself.

Mixing materials
Reconstituted stone slabs, brick and timber decking are used to create an attractive terrace overlooking a pebble-lined water feature.

Preparing a hardcore base

All hard surfaces in the garden will usually require soil to be replaced by compacted hardcore. This can consist of crushed or broken bricks, pieces of concrete, stone or large flints, which is then laid in a bed about 4–6in (10–15cm) thick.

You will need a mix of less coarse hardcore and a finer material such as coarse sand, ash or brick dust to 'blind', that is, fill in, any voids between the large hardcore chunks, to leave a relatively smooth and level surface on which to

Datum peg
Used to indicate:
• *depth of the excavation*
• *level of the hardcore*
• *level of the finished paving*

lay your gravel or paving. Hardcore must be well-compacted to make it firm. Use a square hand tamp for small areas, but for large areas over 10sq m (30ft), such as a driveway, you will probably need to hire a plate vibrator (a much larger machine used for levelling, available from tool hire companies

Excavate the area for your path, patio or paved area by removing the topsoil to the required depth. This will be the depth of the hardcore, plus the thickness of the paving, setts or brick surface.

Place a datum peg (left) to indicate the different levels of excavated base, hardcore and paving, measuring from here with a spirit level. If the area is dug from soft soil, you will need to shutter it with timber boards (see p.44), sawn to the correct length. Hammer in

pegs for the shuttering around the edge of the area to a common level and then attach the wooden planks to them with nails. Backfill outside with spare soil (or hardcore) so that the boards will stay firm as the base is infilled. Begin adding the hardcore and compact (tamp) it as you go. Cover coarse hardcore with finer materials and tamp again until the surface is firm and level.

1 *The excavated and shuttered area is 15cm (6in) deep. The top of the datum peg is level with the surrounding soil.*

2 *Shovel in hardcore (this is quite fine) to a depth of 10cm (4in), as indicated by marks on the datum peg.*

3 *Use a hand tamp to compact small areas. Because this hardcore is fine it needs no infill, and is ready for the sand bed.*

Bricks

Both the colour and durability of bricks vary considerably and it is important that any bricks you buy match those of your house, or other features, such as a garden wall. For example, extra-tough engineering bricks in a blue-grey colour would not suit an informal cottage garden. Nowadays, the choice of bricks for surface materials has been extended to include pavers, available in similar sizes as well as in squares or wedge shapes for curved areas or edgings. Granite setts, small square stones, are similar to old-fashioned cobbles, and laid as for bricks.

Bricks for a sitting area
Small unit pavings such as bricks, setts and pavers are extremely useful where paths or patios are to be curved rather than rectangular.

Laying bricks on a sand base

When laying paths and patios of brick or other units on a layer of sand over the hardcore base rather than mortaring them onto a concrete base, you will need some sort of edging to hold them in position. Here the same bricks are used. For greater stability this edging is laid on a concrete footing. Calculate the path or patio area carefully so that the brick pattern you want can be achieved with as many whole bricks as possible. A simple pattern based on rightangles, such as basket weave, (see right) is an example. Here, provided that the area is calculated as an exact multiple of brick lengths, no cutting will be needed. To make up some patterns, however, you will have to cut bricks in half, and designs with a diagonal bias call for triangular shapes to be cut. Having to do this makes the work more time-consuming and also requires extra skills and equipment.

1 *Edging bricks (here laid flat on) are placed along a string guide onto sand; the trowel is used to neaten the edge.*

2 *At the end of the path, lay another retaining edge of bricks at a precise right-angle to the first, to form a corner.*

3 *Use a notched screed board (cut at each end) to level the bed of sand before laying the infill bricks.*

4 *A half-brick completes the pattern. Split bricks with a hammer and bolster chisel, or a stone cutter or angle grinder.*

5 *Sprinkle sand over the bricks and brush in well until it fills the gaps.*

6 *Tamp the bricks down using a club hammer on a wooden block placed diagonally. Finally, brush in more sand.*

Brick patterns
Rectangular bricks can be laid in many patterns, either flat (the wider face) or on edge (the narrower side). The patterns below all use whole bricks with half or diagonally cut bricks to complete the work at the ends or sides.

Stretcher bond
Strongly linear, this design will make a path seem wider.

Diagonal herringbone
More difficult to lay, this suggests rapid movement.

Horizontal herringbone
A lively pattern, popular in Tudor times.

Basket weave
A variation on stretcher bond, using whole bricks.

Concrete

For rigid surfaces, especially those expected to take heavy use, unit paving should be set onto a concrete base. The same applies to edgings, retaining walls, steps and any construction – such as a shed – needing the long-term stability of a base or footing.

As well as acting as a base, an area of concrete laid in place can look attractive as a surface material in its own right. Surface texture can be varied by a number of means – by tamping with a wooden plank to give a textured linear pattern (see opposite) or with a metal hand tamp to give a smooth finish. Use a brush for a surface that gives some grip. For an even but weathered look, wash and gently brush away some of the surface cement to expose the aggregate, before the concrete quite sets.

When laying areas of concrete it is vital to work in small sections, both for ease of working and for laying the cement mix smoothly. This allows for gaps between each section to cope with natural shrinkage and expansion. Called 'thermal movement joints', these can be worked into the overall design, either as straight lines (using wood shuttering) or in curves using plastic strips for shuttering. Like any other material, a concrete surface also needs its own concrete base to prevent movement and cracks.

Concrete surface

With a little planning, concrete laid in situ can be made to look very attractive.

Creating shuttering

Before the hardcore base and concrete can be laid in the excavated area, it is essential to place shuttering around it. Wet concrete needs strong timber shuttering (or formwork), because it is not only very heavy but will tend to spread sideways unless prevented from doing so.

Fix the shuttering to small stakes or pegs each about 1m (3ft) apart. The top edge of the formwork should reach the same height as the intended level of concrete.

The exact depth of the hardcore base and concrete layer will depend on the type of surface or structure the foundation will support. As a rough guide:
• **paths, patios or greenhouse:** 15cm (6in) of hardcore plus 10–15cm (4–6in) of concrete.
• **driveways, car port, etc:** 15cm (6in) of hardcore plus 15–20cm/6–8in concrete.

To gauge the depth of each layer correctly, use a datum peg, driven into the ground with its top at surrounding soil level (see p.43), marked with the depth of excavation, the depth of the hardcore bed, and of the concrete foundation and/or surface material.

One datum peg, placed centrally, will do for a small area, but for areas larger than 1sq m (3sq ft) place pegs at intervals of not more than 1m (3ft) apart.

1 *After digging out and tamping the bed, insert the datum peg and check that its top is level with the surrounding soil.*

2 *Use some of the excavated soil to fill the pit to just above the bottom mark on the peg, and tamp well with the feet.*

3 *Place pegs for attaching the shuttering around the edge and level them to the datum peg with hammer and spirit level.*

4 *Wooden planks (shuttering) are first sawn to the correct length and height before they are nailed to the pegs.*

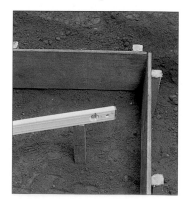

5 *Check with a spirit level that the shuttering is level all round, and then backfill outside the shuttering with soil to contain the weight of the hardcore and concrete.*

Laying a concrete base

Where the ground is soft, or under heavy use perhaps by vehicles, a concrete base should be laid on top of a minimum of 10cm (4in) thickness of compacted and blinded hardcore.

The area of concrete to be laid at any one time must be easily manageable – for an experienced person an absolute maximum would be 4.5m (15ft) in any direction. Apart from the difficulty of handling larger areas, a continuous surface will crack more easily.

After tamping to release air bubbles, wet concrete needs to be roughened with a plank as shown in order to key well with the mortar holding the final surface material in place.

Once the bed has been infilled with hardcore and concrete, the shuttering can be removed.

1 *Fill the shuttered area with loose hardcore and firm down well, using a square tamp as shown, or a plate vibrator.*

2 *Remove the datum peg and infill the hole. Note the markings on the peg indicating the different levels of the layers.*

3 *After mixing the cement mixture on a suitable surface or board, shovel it in, and level it with the shovel as you go.*

4 *Use a wooden plank to 'saw off' and smooth the surface of the cement, moving it from left to right and then dragging it back towards you.*

5 *Move a short-handled wooden tamp up and down (or left to right) in a regular chopping motion to bring air and surplus water to the top.*

6 *Repeat the sawing and smoothing of the concrete's surface, finally leaving a linear pattern to help the surface material adhere to the concrete.*

Concrete mixes

Different surfaces and foundations need different ratios of ingredients. A mix of 1:6 cement: sand/gravel (1 part cement to 6 parts ballast) is 'leaner' than one of 1:4.

Measure the quantities by volume (eg in a bucket). Add water until the mortar is just firm enough to hold its shape. If you need to spread the cement mix fast to level it, use a sloppier mix that almost flows.

• **concrete base/foundation** 1:2:4 cement: sand: gravel. If you are using all-in ballast (where sand and gravel are premixed), use 1:6 cement: ballast.

• **mortar pads under slabs** 1:4 or 1:5 cement: builders' sand (on hardcore or cement base)

• **stepping stones** 1:6 cement: sharp sand (a pad under each stone; no hardcore base)

• **concrete footing for steps or a brick retaining edge** 1:6 cement: sharp sand (onto hardcore base)

• **pointing for paving slabs** 1:3 or 1:4 cement: builders' sand.

Lean mortar mix
This is the correct consistency for mortaring paving slabs onto a hardcore or concrete base.

Cement for pointing

Finishing off areas of paving with mortar neatens their appearance and prevents weeds growing between the cracks. An alternative to using wet mortar is to brush a mix of dry cement and sand into the cracks between pavings and then water it in.

If you use sand instead of mortar, you will be able to grow creeping plants between the stones. Small tough perennials, such as creeping thyme (*Thymus* spp.) and Baby's Tears (*Soleirolia soleirolii*) are ideal.

In this case, you should make the joints slightly further apart than normal – a couple of centimetres (around an inch) is normal. It will, however, mean that weeds will also germinate in the cracks!

Pointing paving slabs
A stiff mortar mix of 1:3 or 1:4 cement: sand avoids staining.

Neatening off
Use a smaller trowel to neaten the mortar between the slabs.

Paving

Apart from practicality, any paving materials you select for your garden should reflect the theme of its design in style and colour. They should complement the fabric of the house, and be a low-key background to your planting. And, of course, they must be cost-effective.

Pavings should be made from a strong, durable and preferably non-slip material. Popular and not too costly are pre-cast concrete slabs in a range of sizes, colours and textures. Paved paths and patios must be laid on a firm, prepared foundation of hard-core or even concrete.

Near the house, especially, paving should have a slight fall to allow water to drain off into planting, a lawn or a drainage channel. For smooth surfaces such as concrete slabs, a fall of about 1 in 100 is adequate, but for rougher pavings, such as natural riven stone, it might need to be 1 in 80 or even 1 in 60.

If there is a manhole or drain within the area to be paved, make sure this is not covered over. So that the look of the area is not spoiled, most pavings can be fitted into a special metal frame to disguise the drain or cover.

An invitation to relax

Flat areas of concrete paving slabs are interspersed with large cobble stones, gravel and low planting, to give texture, variety and a relaxed, harmonious feel to this small patio.

Laying paving

Accurately setting out the shape and level of your patio using shuttering and string guides will make laying the flags or pavings much easier. (If you have not used shuttering for the hardcore base, you can use taut string between the edging pegs to indicate the area to be paved.)

Start off with the row nearest to the house and work from there. The flag-stones are lowered onto dabs of soft mortar (for the correct mix, see p.45) on top of the hardcore base.

Make sure that at this stage they are slightly higher than the finished level – they can then be tapped down until they line up with the guide strings and pegs. Once the mortar has set ('gone off'), the flags will remain at that level.

For a completely water-proof finish, leave a 13mm ($\frac{1}{2}$in) gap between flags, and point by filling the gap with a stiff mix of strong mortar when laying is completed (see p.45).

1 *Position a trial paving on the hardcore bed to indicate the placing of the string. Remove.*

2 *Put down dabs of mortar for the corners and centre. Repos-ition the first slab along the string.*

3 *All the while checking levels, knock the slab down to the correct height with the hammer.*

4 *Complete the row and then reposition the string for the second row. When you have placed two pavings in the second row, check the level diagonally across four slabs.*

The completed patio
The cracks between the pavings can be left or pointed with wet or dry mortar to prevent weeds from growing.

Steps

Gardens are rarely level and when laying paths, for example, you will need to take account of this – especially on sloping sites. A slope of 1 in 12 is about the maximum gradient that is comfortable to walk on. Anything steeper than this will require steps.

These might be in flights of two or more at a single point, or they could be well-spaced so that you climb one, walk two or three paces and then climb a second flight, and so on. Steps can be purely functional – just terraced ground edged with timber risers – or they can be a formal feature in their own right, perhaps enhanced with planted pots. The important thing is that they should fit in with their surroundings in both scale and materials, and be wide enough for the user to feel relaxed. Steps that are too narrow will have the opposite effect.

The height of a step, its 'riser', must feel safe and comfortable and, as a general rule, should be not less than 7.5cm (3in), or more than 17.5cm (7in) – not as high as stairs indoors. For similar reasons, the depth, or 'tread', should ideally be not less than 30cm (1ft).

Informal planting to enhance brick and stone

Steps can add to the charm of a small garden, especially when the same materials are used for connecting paths. The informal planting complements the harmonious feel.

Making paving slab steps

As well as allowing easier access, adding a flight of steps to a bank makes a strong design element. Plain concrete flags can be softened with low planting.

Work out the height of the bank (see p.31) and divide into the number of steps required. The shorter the riser, the deeper the tread needs to be. Insert canes to mark the position of each step. Excavate all the treads, roughly – but not so much that the bank collapses!

The first tread is supported on bricks and hardcore set on a concrete footing. Dig out a 5cm (2in) trench beneath the front and sides of the first flag position, allowing for a 2.5cm (1in) overlap of the flag's front edge.

Use a concrete mix of 1:5 or 1:6 cement: sharp sand for the footing, adding water until it is quite stiff. Leave overnight to set.

Lay prepared mortar on the footing. Make a fishbone pattern with the trowel so that the mortar can spread easily. On top of this lay four bricks, two at the front, one on each side, mortaring the joints as you go. (If you need to use more than four bricks, mortar them individually). Tamp the bricks into place with the trowel handle, and check with a spirit level.

Infill the space with hardcore and firm, using a piece of timber and a club-hammer handle. Lay a 2.5cm (1in) thick mortar bed along the top of the bricks and at the back edge of the hardcore. Add a mortar pad in the centre. Lower the flagstone into position, allowing a 2.5cm (1in) overhang at the front. Tamp with the hammer handle and check levels. Neaten the sides and mortar with a pointing trowel, sloping the pointing so that water will run off. Fill any space behind the tread with hardcore. Continue the process until all the steps are complete.

1 *Mortar the first brick risers in position on the footing, two at the front and one at each side.*

2 *The mortar and hardcore bed, ready for the first flag, to overhang by 2.5cm (1in) in front.*

3 *Put mortar along the back of the first tread to secure the two bricks as risers for the second tread. Infill again with hardcore.*

4 *Firm the hardcore, mortar the sides and bricks with a dab in the centre. Allow 2.5cm (1in) overhang for the second flag.*

5 *As a final touch, a flag tread has been placed at the bottom of the steps on a mortar bed and mortared against the footing.*

Gravel

A useful and economical substitute for paving is gravel, available in a choice of colours, textures and sizes, from almost round, river-worn pebbles to small, angular chips of mechanically crushed granite or sandstone.

There are three points to consider when using gravel. First, loose gravel tends to disperse and needs a slightly raised edge to retain it. Second, if gravel is laid too deep it can be difficult to walk on – particularly if it is smooth and round. Finally, constant foot or car traffic may push gravel into the base below, so you will have to top it up. How much and often will depend on whether the base is soft topsoil or firm, blinded hardcore. One way of taking these factors into account is to combine the gravel with concrete, stone flags or bricks laid like stepping stones, so that you actually walk on them rather than on the gravel itself. If you wish, you can plant into gravel to create a garden that is maintenance-free, as the gravel will suppress weeds.

Plants in gravel
An area of gravel will attract plants that enjoy the mulch-like quality of the dry stones.

Laying gravel

You will need to decide how you want to retain the gravel – with tiles, bricks or wood. Here, the shuttering round the path or gravel area stays to serve as edging. For a brick retaining edge, see p.43. Begin by excavating a trench or bed for the base, 7.5cm (3in) deep, and see p. 44 for setting up the formwork. With a shovel and and tamp, spread, level and compact a hardcore layer to within 2.5cm (1in) of the formwork top. This gap will leave room for quite enough gravel – there is no need to be extravagant with it. Check the level and lay the gravel with the shovel. Finish by tamping gently.

1 *Tamp the surface down well and check that it is even with a spirit level.*

2 *Use a sand layer for blinding if the hardcore is fairly coarse as this will hold the gravel better.*

Laying stepping stones

Begin by digging out the area, and tamping the earth base. Fix string guides for the paving levels (see p.46).

Mix up a stiff mortar in the ratio 1:6 cement: ballast for the footing pad. Gauge its depth by the thickness of the paving. Use the string guide to set the slabs at the correct height, but set them higher at first, so that they can be gently tamped down. Infill round the slabs with fairly fine hardcore such as crushed brick, and tamp so that the level is about 2.5cm (1in) below the top of the slabs. Then spread the gravel layer.

Bredon gravel, used here, is 'self-binding'. It has a layer of clay particles around the granite chips which eventually washes off in the rain to reveal its true, dark colour.

1 *Lay each slab on a pad of stiff mortar, directly onto the earth – no need for hardcore.*

3 *Infill around the slab with hardcore and sand, then tamp to just below the slab top.*

2 *Taut string guides indicate the alignment, height and level of the slab.*

4 *Add the gravel layer and smooth it, so it is flush with the top of the slab.*

Neat path with plantings
Stepping stones sit within the now-weathered gravel. The whole can then be framed by border plantings to rich effect.

Decking

With some forethought and a little long-term care, wood can make a very worthwhile alternative to traditional paving materials. It is one of the most versatile of natural materials, and timber features will enhance any garden.

Softwoods, predominantly from coniferous forest trees, are readily available in temperate climates. Less durable than hardwoods, they generally need some form of treatment with paints or stains. Hardwoods, coming from broad-leaved trees from other parts of the world, are more expensive; always check that the wood comes from a sustainable forest planting. They can frequently be used without additional treatment, though stains or natural oils may be necessary to maintain an attractive appearance.

However, all wood is vulnerable to rot when in contact with damp soil so, in any construction, it will pay you to treat even hardwood against this, and ensure there is plenty of air space under and around the decking.

Warmth of wood surfaces
Timber decking has a warm feel in sunny weather and teams well with the jungle-like planting, terracotta pots and pebbles.

Laying a raised timber deck

When designing layouts for small or awkward spaces, decking offers a great deal more flexibility than, for example, stone flags or pavings which have fixed dimensions. Decking can be laid at ground level or as a raised platform, as a straight rectangle for a simple path, or staggered in an intricate pattern over a large area.

The joists should be heavy treated timber, and the planks should be pressure treated. Sawn timber will provide a more textured surface than planed, though you might need to give sawn softwood a precautionary rub over with coarse glasspaper to remove any serious splinters.

To help protect the joists from rot it is a good idea to raise them above soil level by laying them across a base of bricks on concrete pads. If you want to deck a large area, the construction is best done in stages.

For decking at ground level, the depth of the excavation needs to equal the height of all the materials. This will be the height of the concrete pad and brick (or concrete block), the joist, the rafter and the plank surface.

1 *The holes for the concrete pads should be about 45 x 45cm (17 x 17in) and 15cm (6in) deep, with their centres 1m (3ft) apart. Dig out, tamp soil and place shuttering for each one (see p.44). Check heights are uniform with string and a spirit level, and lay the cement mix.*

2 *Decide which way you want the planks to run – they will follow the joists (with the rafters at right angles in between). Set up two string guides, 10cm (4in) apart, in the same direction as the planks, along the centre of the pads, and lay the bricks within them.*

3 *The joists can now be laid along the bricks. The timber should overlap the pads and bricks at each end by at least 30cm (1ft), to conceal them.*

4 *Lay rafters 15cm (6in) in from the joist ends. The gap between the rafters should not be more than half the length of the planks they will support. Fix the rafters to the joists using galvanized nails (screws for heavy use) inserted at an angle.*

5 *Set a string down the middle of each rafter as a guide for nailing the planks. Use galvanized nails that are twice as long as the planks are thick. Note that the planks are the same length as the joists.*

6 *To conceal the joists of raised decking you can attach boards to the ends and sides. A soffit board 1.5cm (½in) thick is used here. Nail the board to the joist ends so that it lies flush with the edges of the planks.*

Soft ground cover

The term ground cover can be applied to any method of covering bare soil in a garden whether using living plants or inanimate natural or artificial materials, or indeed a combination of both. Ground covers, from coloured stone chippings to prostrate roses, are the very essence of low-maintenance gardening – unless of course you include lawns, which are for the most part particularly labour-intensive. A mulch is generally a form of ground cover that utilizes inanimate materials to do the job, regardless of whether they are natural, such as gravel, bark chippings or grass clippings, or artificial, like polythene.

The right choice of ground cover can add much to the overall appearance of a garden, especially in covering awkward places such as dry shade under trees or steep banks, and also in hiding unattractive features such as concrete path edges or manhole covers.

Ground-hugging plants and bark mulch
Plants that cover ground and need little attention are a bonus. Here, mounds of santolina (S. rosmarinifolia) *and purple French lavender* (Lavandula stoechas) *harmonize with stones and bark chippings.*

Designing with ground cover

For plants to be successful as ground cover, their foliage needs to be attractive and to provide cover over a long season. Their habit needs to be either clump-forming, prostrate, creeping or trailing – but their spread should not be so rapid that they them-selves become invasive weeds. Beware, too, of plants that are excessive self-seeders.

Some creeping variegated plants, including vincas, ivies (*Hedera*) and bugle (*Ajuga*) fit this category, but many plants with colourful flowers that are not so ground-hugging also serve the purpose, among them geraniums, lamiums, low-growing cotoneaster and ceanothus, prostrate junipers such as *Juniperus horizontalis* and *J. procumbens*, heucheras, alchemilla, heathers and *Stachys byzantina*. Some species of flowering orna-mental grasses, too, spread quickly into clumps, such as miscanthus, stipa and *Carex stricta* 'Aurea'. Even bulbs, such as cyclamens, snowdrops and bluebells can be left to spread under deciduous trees.

Ground cover plants form a permanent planting so you should prepare soil with care, eliminating all perennial weeds (contrary to popular belief, ground cover planting will not in itself get rid of an existing perennial weed problem). Until all the bare soil is covered by planting, the bed should be kept weed-free by hoeing or by mulching with a 25-50mm thick layer of organic matter.

Ivies for shady places
Variegated ivy is a good choice beneath a thick evergreen hedge of Lonicera 'Baggesen's Gold'.

A cover of flowers under trees
Spring flowers like white Spanish bluebells (Hyacinthoides his-panica) *are excellent under trees. By the time the tree canopy casts heavy shade, the flowers and foliage will have died down.*

Grassed surfaces

It is tempting to think of lawns merely in terms of the demands they make – as grass that needs cutting on a regular basis during spring and summer, or from which the autumn leaves must be cleared. But a well-thought-out and cared-for lawn is an asset and can mean the difference between an acceptable garden and a brilliant one.

A cool, soft green sward is the perfect place for relaxation on a hot day, as well as the best companion to bright flower and foliage colours. The initial outlay is far less than for most hard surfaces, and the amount of time you devote to it depends on where you live and how much of a perfectionist you are. It is important to choose grass that is appropriate to the amount of wear and tear it is likely to experience, and

always take mowing requirements into account. You also need to ensure the lawn is sensibly sited: grass needs some sunshine and should be laid on level ground.

A successful lawn need not be a perfectly uniform, outdoor carpet with parallel, mowed lines. Some gardeners are perfectly happy to allow in flowers, or even 'weeds'. Clover, which is a satisfying deep green colour, will actually improve the nutrient value of a lawn! And either simple daisies or more deliberate plantings, like spring bulbs or wild flowers, will embellish a lawn.

Lawns can define space
In this formal garden the mown lines lead the eye to a focal point beyond the steps and a second lawn, increasing the sense of distance.

Flowering lawns

Creating a wild flower meadow in a part of the garden where wear and tear are light is many people's idea of a country haven. Wildflower seeds are available in various mixtures to suit different soil types and drainage. Sow seed onto prepared ground (not lawn) but don't add compost or fertilizer – the majority of desirable wild flowers need low-nutrient soils to thrive.

Mix the wildflower seed with a large volume of grass seed selected from slow-growing, fine-leaved varieties. This will provide the basic sward through which the wild flowers will grow, and help prevent coarser grasses

and weed seeds from germinating. Alternatively, plant very small plants or bulbs into an existing lawn. (A bulb planter will make this easier.)

Such lawns work best when the flowers share similar flowering times, because they should not be cut until after flowering, when seeds for next year's plants will have formed, or for bulbs, when the leaves that restore the plant's energy have died

down. A mown path either through or around the meadow helps provide definition as well as access and makes the area look deliberately part of a designed garden rather than simply a neglected area.

Tall daisies and flowering grasses
A clipped grass path through a sunny meadow planting of long grasses and oxeye daisies meanders into a hidden area – perhaps to a surprise, cool woodland glade.

A flowery meadow
Spring anemones, wild tulips (T. tarda) and emerging orchids have turned this stretch of lawn into a carpet of flowers. The spring flowering means that the grass can be cut by midsummer, before it becomes too long.

Lawns

As when choosing a carpet or other floor covering, creating a lawn involves consideration of wear and tear and cost as well as appearance.

Grass seed may be sown in autumn or spring. An autumn sowing will mean the lawn will be ready for use the following summer, whereas a spring-sown lawn cannot be used until the end of summer. Laying turf is quicker but more expensive. Different grass seed mixes are available; some produce a resilient turf, ideal for heavy wear or children's play areas, while others give a finer lawn which looks more manicured but is less hardwearing. A fine lawn also requires more care – during the summer it will need to be mown every two or three days whereas ordinary turf only has to be cut about once a week.

Wildflower meadow
Studded with wild flowers, grass cut only once or twice a year forms a natural meadow.

Sowing a lawn

The key to success lies in the preparation of the ground prior to seeding or turfing. Prepare the soil by thorough cultivation to at least 25cm (10in). Improve poor soils with compost or organic matter and heavy, clay soils with sharp sand or grit. Add suitable fertilizer and rake it in.

All perennial weeds should be eradicated as they will persist even when the ground is turfed over, while annual weeds will quickly infest newly seeded areas of grass unless the ground is cleaned before sowing. Rake and roll the proposed lawn area or alternatively firm using your heels, to achieve a smooth, firm, level bed, removing any stones and other debris. Seed is best sown in the spring or early autumn when soil temperatures and moisture are at their best for germination. Scatter the seed thinly over the ground before lightly raking it into the top 5mm ($\frac{1}{4}$in) of soil. Germination is often aided by rolling the ground again just after sowing.

1 *Once the soil has been thoroughly cultivated, cleared and improved, rake it to a fine tilth, levelling as you go and removing all except the smallest stones.*

2 *Marked out metre (3ft) squares help you apply the right amounts of fertilizer to provide short and long-term nutrition for new grass. Rake in.*

3 *Sow half the appropriate seed quantity evenly within each metre square. Then sow the remainder at right angles to the first sowing and rake in.*

Laying turf

Turf can be laid at any time of year, if it is available, but avoid the depths of winter when the ground is frozen or waterlogged, and hot summer months unless you can water every day for up to three or four weeks. The turves must be kept moist until they have rooted, or they will shrink.

Take care never to disturb your prepared ground, and always stand on a plank. First lay a row of turves around the lawn perimeter (if rectangular), or along a straight edge. Fill in the area in rows with staggered joints, much like a brick wall. Settle the turf into position by tamping

Placing a roll of turf
Once the perimeter is laid, infill the area in a staggered pattern of closely butted turf rolls. Kneel on a board placed on previously laid turf.

it gently with the back of a rake head or a broom. Finish off by lightly brushing in sieved topsoil, filling in any gaps along the joins. Then water in well.

Shaping irregular lawns
Shape the turf around an informal flowerbed using a length of hosepipe as a template for cutting curves. Stand on a board and cut with a half-moon cutter (as here), a sharpened lawn-edger, or an old carving knife.

Edgings

As ground level boundaries, edgings play an important role in the garden layout. Whether of hard materials or planted, they help define and give emphasis to a lawn, path or border and often enhance a dull driveway. An edging is essential where loose materials meet, such as where gravel adjoins a flower bed. Without some form of definition, the gravel and soil will quickly become mixed and unattractive. The solution is to provide a rigid edge to separate them.

Provided that it is durable or can be maintained, virtually any material can be used as edging. Bricks, setts, concrete pavers and cobbles can all be used loose or set into mortar and concrete for a stronger, more permanent edge. Bricks can be placed horizontally along their long or short edges, set at different heights for a crenellated look, or positioned at an angle to give a zigzag effect. Large pieces of slate or paving flags buried on edge to half their depth are particularly useful for creating a retaining wall for a mini raised bed or to prevent soil washing down a bank.

For planted edgings, ground spreading plants such as bugle (ajuga), violas and hostas are all suitable, as well as taller flowering plants such as lavender and a variety of other aromatic shrubs or herbs – parsley, rosemary, sage

Soft and hard edgings
A twisting 'plait' of cobbles contains but also complements an informal planting of carmine pinks by a path of granite setts.

and thyme – can also make good edging plants. Allowing these plants to flop over onto the pathway softens the divide between a hard and soft edging for a pleasing informal effect.

Formal planted edgings
Clipped dwarf box hedges are a traditional edging for vegetable gardens and flower beds. They are especially useful where controlled flowing lines are called for, such as in knot gardens.

Lawn edgings

Lawns should have a neat, defined edge; this can be achieved with a special tool called a half-moon blade which slices through the long grass vertically.

Where a lawn butts up against a wall, fence or terrace path, it is almost always impossible to mow right up to the edge, without leaving an unsightly strip of long grass or needing to cut with hand shears. By laying a level edge of bricks or paving stones, about 10mm ($^1/_2$ in) below the height of the lawn, you will be able to cut right to the edge of the grass and not damage the blades of your mower. This principle of a mowing edge can be used wherever lawn edges prove difficult to trim because of adjacent obstructions. Defining the edges of a lawn in this way also helps to give the garden a neat appearance and helps to make a clear distinction between grass and borders. Curved lawn edgings can be formed from thin, treated timber planks or plastic strips, which are unobtrusive and easy to lay. As an

A mowing edge
A neat brick edge protects silvery Stachys byzantina *from the mower's blades.*

alternative to hard edgings, the boundary of a lawn could be defined with a border of shrubby plants, such as *santolina,* which stand clear of the grass, leaving space for the mower to cut up to the edges.

Tall lavender for a low hedge
A continuous planting of shrubby lavender forms the boundary between a lawn and a dense flower border that includes fruit trees.

Creating vertical structures

Apart from giving height to a garden, vertical structures give width or depth, divide the garden, screen and provide seclusion, and act as focal points and backdrops. They can be used to frame or accentuate other structures or parts of the garden as well as views beyond the garden boundaries.

The size or height of a structure does not need to be great to create an effect in a garden setting – even a simple change of level of only one or two steps can make an otherwise flat garden seem more interesting. Nor does it have to be solid to achieve its intentions, and in some instances this can be a distinct disadvantage. If, for example, you screen an oil tank with a fence panel, you may actually draw attention to it, whereas it might be more effective to break up the outline with a trellis panel, or a group of shrubs.

Depending on where you live, the pattern of sunlight in your garden during the day will vary according to the time of year, and you should try and take this into account when planning your structures – you probably won't want to place a summerhouse in a position that casts a large shadow over your patio for much of the day. Also, do not forget that trees are generally long-lived and will continue to increase in size, so what may have started out as a neat dome could grow to dominate a whole garden in years to come.

Shelter and shade

The introduction of vertical structures will not only have an effect on the appearance of the garden, but also on the amount of light, and sometimes moisture, reaching different parts of the garden.

In some cases, such as the position of a boundary fence or the aspect of your garden, these areas of shade or shadow will be pre-determined and you will have no control over them. However, there are instances where you can choose the location of your structure deliberately to create a sunny or shady place, and also manipulate space in such a way as to form an area for plants or for sitting out that is sheltered from prevailing winds or draughts. Creating draught-free spaces is particularly useful in mild climates where you want to take advantage of any winter sunshine. Conversely, on a hot summer's day, and especially in small town gardens, introducing one or two trees not only provides precious shade but encourages welcome light breezes. Use canes and thick strings to define the heights and gauge the shapes of your intended structures, firstly to see how they will appear to the eye and secondly to try and ascertain their effect on sunlight entering the garden so that you can make adjustments that may avoid future problems.

The higher the structure, the smaller the space it encloses will appear. Larger built structures, such as summerhouses, gazebos and conservatories, may require planning permission, so it is a good idea to seek advice first.

Hedges as windbreaks
A thick hedge is excellent for creating shelter for plants as it filters the wind. A more solid structure, such as a fence or wall, tends to deflect wind, causing strong downward airflow.

Verticals of varying heights
As well as providing screening, open timberwork above the fence supports climbing plants. The continuous low retaining wall acts as both raised flowerbed and sheltered seat.

Linking vertical elements

Repeating a colour, material or style in your vertical structures is a good way of developing a common theme in a garden and this approach can be extended to include horizontal surfaces such as paths and paving, resulting in a much more unified effect than would be the case with a random approach.

At the same time, creating a surprise as you turn a corner, with careful placing of a garden seat or statue, adds interest without detracting from the overall design. A simple way of achieving a sense of order and pattern is to repeat plantings, or terracotta or other decorative containers, so that they stand out from the background as strategic focal points, not necessarily all visible at the same time.

Evergreen and foliage plants are particularly useful in creating links, whether in a continuous planting, such as a hedge or screen, or individual plantings, particularly of specimens with strong architectural shapes or large leaves.

Using planting to unify
Tall foliage plants are used to partly screen and soften the outline of a greenhouse. The restrained flower colours, mainly acid greens and yellows, further unify the scene.

Man-made structures

A host of plants can be trained to grow up and over garden structures, whether fences and trelliswork, walls, old tree stumps, living trees or hedges, and of course arches, pergolas and arbours made for the purpose.

Plants will both furnish and soften, or even disguise – which is an effect you can put to good use with other large garden structures such as a new summerhouse or garden shed, whose impact will be lessened if climbing plants are allowed to clamber over them.

Planting with a theme
A bold planting of architectural shrubs with contrasting foliage complements the oriental look of this grey-green wooden gazebo.

Space-creating devices
Various tactics can be used in gardens to give an illusion of more depth and space. One way is by using plant colour. Misty blues and silvery greens at the end of a vista suggest distance, especially in contrast with a foreground planting of sharp reds, oranges and yellows.

Other devices use perspective to exaggerate space and depth. For example, when a path gradually narrows in width as it recedes away from the house or point of view, it will appear longer than it is. Small openings that give views through otherwise solid fences or doors, and trellis wall 'arches' or painted murals are other tricks that can be used to open out space and give a less hemmed in feel, especially to small gardens. In a courtyard or patio garden, a cleverly placed wall mirror will reflect any planting – perhaps also the surface of a small pool – again giving a feeling of more space.

Peephole in a fence
The small window gives a view through this otherwise solid fence.

Trellis wall niche
The slats are placed to form an 'arch', partly hidden by clematis.

Boundaries

Garden boundaries, as with any other land boundaries, are a means of defining the extent of a particular parcel of land, and in most instances they have a legal significance.

Assuming that you know where they are, how you treat the boundaries of your own garden will depend partly on cost but also on your personal preferences. If you are a private person you might wish to conceal your garden with a high, solid wall or fence above eye level. On the other hand, a low, knee-high hedge might be all that you need. Security and safety must influence your selection, particularly if you have small children or dogs. You might need to strengthen a hedge with a wire mesh fence, or make sure that a fence or wall is built in such a way that it cannot be climbed easily. As well as practical aspects of garden boundaries, you should remember that they are an integral part of any garden design. You may therefore need to decide whether your boundaries are to become decorative garden features in their own right, or treated in a very low-key manner so that they are tucked away in the background. The general ambience or atmosphere of a garden can also be affected by the size and nature of any boundary enclosure. Think of the different effect you would create with a dense 3m (10ft) high conifer hedge and a 1m (3ft) high slender picket fence, in two otherwise identical gardens.

Fencing

Instant privacy is certainly one major reason why fences are popular and are often preferred to hedges, which can take several years to achieve the same effect. They are invariably cheaper to erect than walls of similar height, particularly if built from soft wood as opposed to hard wood. They do not require the same skill to construct, but may need periodic treatment with preservative to prevent rot.

As a way of demarcating two or more areas, there is nothing simpler than a fence of plain wooden posts with a couple of wires strung between them. But in most gardens, fences can serve more than one purpose and therefore their design and construction can become increasingly complex or ornate, depending on budget.

Rustic fencing
A criss-cross fence of rounded timber staves provides an informal boundary that allows plants behind to peep through.

Hedges

For most gardeners, hedges conveniently divide into formal and informal types, each of which may then be subdivided according to whether they are evergreen or deciduous. Though perhaps not requiring much money to maintain, hedges still need to be trimmed, therefore requiring a commitment of time.

Informal hedge
The flowing shape of this flowering hedge, aided by the conifer, obscures the solid outline of the next-door property to give a cheerful, relaxed boundary.

Walls

A brick, stone or concrete block wall will initially cost more than other barriers but if well built, should last more or less indefinitely and need little maintenance during its extensive lifetime.

Such a wall is relatively expensive, though, and the level of skill required to build even the simplest may be beyond the reach of the vast majority of gardeners.

However, on sloping sites a fairly easily built, low, retaining wall will hold back soil while creating terracing and changes of level.

A not-so-solid wall
A brick wall need not be entirely solid. Here an arched window, framed by climbing roses, gives a view of the lawn beyond.

Exits and entrances

Entrances to gardens are frequently treated almost as an afterthought in a design, nothing more than a way in or out. However there is lots of potential to make them something more than just a simple gap in a fence, wall or hedge. First, of course, you must consider any practical aspects, as you would for a boundary, which in most instances is what an entrance forms part of. So whether it is an open archway for example, or a gate in a wall, will depend on how secure you wish the garden to be.

From the outside, entrances can be used to give clues as to the garden within, either by the way they are used, perhaps framing a view of a small part of the garden beyond, or by their nature, such as an old brick path and honeysuckle-covered rustic arch leading into a cottage garden. Of course you might decide to keep the garden a secret until the last minute by making the entrance via a solid oak door in a high brick wall, or else you could create a way in down a narrow gravel path, hemmed in by tall plants either side and overhanging trees before it turns a corner into a wide open, light and airy garden as a complete contrast.

Romantic entrance
Rosa 'Adelaide d'Orléans' smothers an archway leading into an informal country garden.

Front entrances and garden gates

As with all garden design, simplicity and unity are the keynotes for the design of front entrances.

Their style needs to be in keeping with that of the house and any adjacent garden structures. A gate that matches a low picket fence will look in place and inviting, but a contrasting gate, say in black railings or solid wood set in a wall or thick prickly hedge, will make a much stronger 'keep out' statement, particularly if the gate happens to match the wall in height.

Welcoming garden gate
The open structure of this white gate set in a wall, the neat brick path and array of informal cottage plants – roses, delphiniums, hollyhocks and violas – sets a friendly tone.

Linking internal divisions

Your garden design may divide the garden, particularly if it is long and narrow or odd-shaped, into two or more separate spaces, each with their own boundaries.

A useful way of demarcating these areas is to use trellis, which screens without creating a totally enclosed feeling. The areas will need to be linked at some point, perhaps by an arch or gateway, which will allow the opportunity for contrast and similarity, secrecy and openness, to add yet another dimension to the garden.

Connecting arch
Looking through an arch of honeysuckle allows a glimpse of shrub roses and catmint, while the two garden areas are linked and unified by the continuous lawn surface.

Fences

Choice of fencing style and material depends partly on the purpose of the fence, partly on the design of the garden itself, and on cost. A 1.8m (6ft) high fence of posts with woven or lapped panels ensures complete privacy, for example, but may not be the most sympathetic backdrop to planting. A post and rail fence, to which vertical boards or palings are nailed, is a strong, attractive, but more costly partition.

Where privacy is not essential, the vertical boards may be spaced out (palisade or picket) or fixed at an angle (chevron), making the fence more economical and adding interest. These open fences (including trellis) are better for nearby plants as they allow air, light and rain onto them, as well as filtering the wind. Apart from timber, metal in the form of plain railings or wrought iron is extremely popular, and even plastic fences have their place.

Subtle partition
This simple yet attractive post and rail fence draws attention to the planting while allowing air and sunlight to filter through.

Trellis fences

To increase the height of an existing fence, or wall, either for privacy or security, you can use trellis fencing.

Made from lightweight timber battens, nailed in square or diamond patterns, it is the ideal solution for adding some extra height to an existing fence. Plants can then be grown against it, or,

indeed, twining climbers, such as honeysuckle, can be encouraged to grow through it, which will eventually more or less obscure the actual construction.

It pays to choose stoutly made trellis. Ideally, the timbers should be at least 2.5cm (1in) in section, and they should be treated with preservative. Trellis can be bought in ready-made panels, which are then nailed to the supporting structure, or it can be constructed by a carpenter to your own design. (It can also be used to screen parts of the garden, see p.6l).

If you wish, you can stain or paint the trellis, which will help to preserve it. Soft colours, such as sage greens, dove greys and dusky blues, are the most successful.

Using trellis to extend a solid fence
A trellis supporting climbing plants is a compromise that ensures privacy while not cutting out too much light.

Erecting wooden fence posts

Set the posts in concrete, or use metal fence post supports. For most fencing, use 7.5cm (3in) square posts of pressure-treated timber. Coat the section to go into the ground with a bitumastic compound. To calculate the length of the posts, add 2.5cm (1in) to the height of the fence panels, allowing for any capping or base board, plus the length of post going into the ground, about 60cm (24in) if it is to be set in concrete. Mark the post 2.5cm (1in) from the top; mark the height from here of the fence panels and also ground level (if different from the bottom of panels).

Concreting in a post
Place a string marker along the ground on the forward edge of the fence line. Dig a hole 35cm (14in) square, so the string lies one-third the way across the hole. A layer of small stones will assist drainage, so make the hole about 6-8cm (2½-3in) deeper than required. Fill with mortar to 5cm (2in) below ground level, checking that the post is plumb with a spirit level. Compact the mortar and leave to set.

1 *Check the post's ground level marker is at the correct height and its forward edge lies against the string marker.*

2 *Infill with mortar, using a spirit level to keep post vertical and a strut to keep it in position while the concrete sets.*

Constructing a panel fence

With panel fencing, the panels are nailed to the posts while the mortar is still wet. Mark the top and bottom of the panel. The top should come 2.5cm (1in) below the top of the posts.

To measure between the posts, place a panel on the ground, on the string line of the fence and against the foot of the first upright post. Insert a stick in the ground where the centre of the second post front will be. Remove the panel, mark and dig out the hole for the post. Fill with mortar and insert the post.

To position the panel, tap nails horizontally into the inside edges of both posts at the lower (ground) marker and place the panel on the supporting nails. Check with a spirit level that the panel is level, and nail into position.

For a 1.5m (5ft) fence panel, five nails are used for fixing the panel: starting from the back of the panel, insert three evenly spaced nails at the top, centre and bottom and, from the front of the panel, insert two in between.

1 *Measure the distance of the first post from the second by laying the panel flat against the foot of the first upright post.*

2 *The panel lowered onto the supporting nails on the lower marker, and (inset) using 5cm (2in) nails to affix the panel.*

3 *A completed section of panel fence. Once the fence is in position, it will need an annual coat of preservative to protect it.*

Constructing a picket fence

Here the mortar is left to set overnight before the pickets or pales are fixed to the rails.

The post height should be that of the vertical pale *minus* the pointed tip, plus 60cm (24in) to be inserted into the ground. Once the first post is set in concrete, calculate the distance between the posts and thus the length of the crossrails, which should be at most 3m (10ft). The rails, 5cm (2in) wide and 2.5cm (1in) thick, overlap the endposts. Concrete in all the uprights (the two endposts first) using a string guide to ensure all the posts align correctly.

Mark the position of the upper rail, 12cm (5in) from the post top, and the lower, 15cm (6in) from the ground. Fix the upper rail (have someone hold the other end), and position it fully across the endpost and half-way across the in-between post. Repeat for the lower rail. Use nails (place diagonally for the end posts and horizontally for those in between) long enough to go 2.5cm (1in) into the posts. To affix the pales, secure a string guide between the tops of the endposts. Half insert nails in the first pale at the centre of the two crossrails. Hold the pointed top against the string and outer edge of the post, and hammer in the nails, checking the pale is vertical with a spirit level.

For the second pale, half insert the top nail, and, taking another pale as a spacer, place the two pales together against the first. Hammer nails into position. Repeat for the whole fence.

1 *Fixing the top rail to a post with two nails. The crossrails would overlap endposts completely.*

2 *Positioning a pale, showing the spacer pale used to determine the gap between pales.*

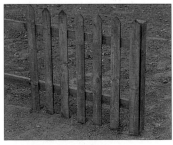

3 *The end post showing overlapping crossrail and pale. Use thinner spacers for greater privacy.*

Types of fence

All these panels are good for boundaries or internal screening. The first three are more wind resistant, so care is needed to ensure their posts are secure. The last two filter wind better, and because the pales have gaps in between, can easily support plants.

Interwoven

Lapboard (shiplap)

Closeboard (butted)

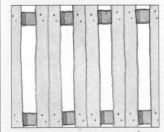

Double pickets or pales

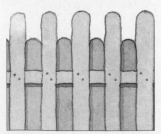

Hit-and-miss palisade

Hedges

To all intents and purposes, hedges are living walls or fences. They make just as good screens, and are often better as windbreaks and for blocking out noise. Formal hedges, almost always of a single variety, result from regular, close trimming, sometimes several times a year, to produce sharply defined straight lines or curves. For the more elaborate geometric shapes, small-leaved evergreen plants, such as yew (*Taxus baccata*) box (*Buxus sempervirens*), red cedar (*Thuja plicata*), privet (*Ligustrum*) and holly (*Ilex*), are best – but neat shapes can also be made from deciduous species, such as hawthorn (*Crataegus*), beech (*Fagus*) and hornbeam (*Carpinus*).

Informal hedges are trimmed infrequently, perhaps only once a year after flowering, and have a softer, more irregular outline. Berberis, cotoneaster, potentilla and roses are just some examples of suitable plants. For an attractive, and also traditional, hedgerow, you can mix different plant varieties, provided they are all roughly of the same vigour.

Formal hedging
Using a combination of tall and low hedging defines different areas in a formal garden. Here, a closely clipped yew (Taxus baccata) *hedge forms the backdrop to a chequerboard of box* (Buxus sempervirens).

Decorative hedging

If the effort of maintaining a formal, clipped hedge and even topiary shapes is not your particular hobby, there is a range of shrubby plants with fine leaf or flower colour, some of which are dense or prickly enough to put off possible two or four-footed intruders.

When selecting a plant variety for a hedge, make sure that its general growth rate and eventual height are compatible with the size of hedge you want to create. You will never achieve a 2-metre (6ft) high hedge with potentilla or hypericum because it is not capable of growing that tall. On the other hand, keeping a Leyland cypress (x *Cupressocyparis* spp.) at 50cm (20in) high would be like trying to stop a runaway train – you will be trimming it almost every week.

Alternating conifers
This unusual row makes a good backdrop for a perennial border.

Traditional box
The deserved favourite for formal low hedging for centuries.

Cheerful yellow flowers
Hypericum provides long-lasting colour in early summer.

Blazing berries and thorns
Autumn colour apart, pyracanthus makes an impenetrable barrier.

Rosa rugosa
Pink flowers are followed by huge hips lasting into late autumn.

Tapestry effect
For a country-style hedge, use two or more species mixed together.

Hedges and screens as dividers

Hedges are useful for dividing space within the garden as well as for boundaries. Most gardens, even small ones, benefit if the entire garden is not viewed in one glance. Different forms of hedging, and varying hedge heights, can be used for this purpose, as can various screening materials, such as trellis or bamboo.

For low-level hedges, box (*Buxus sempervirens*) is the most popular plant. It creates a dense, neat, evergreen hedge and, being slow-growing, needs infrequent clipping. Small flowering shrubs with small leaves, such as santolina and lavender, also make good low hedges. Larger screening can be created with taller hedges of yew or privet, whereas partial screening of a small area can be carried out with a 'hedge' of tall grasses or bamboos. Alternatively, trellis can be put up, through which plants, like clematis,

honeysuckle or campsis, are encouraged to twine.

It is important that the style of the hedge is in keeping with the design of the garden. Neatly clipped evergreens work well in small formal designs but they can also provide an effective backdrop to an informal border, providing a 'holding'

Dividing line
A clipped, low hedge separates areas of a large garden, allowing different design themes in each.

structure for the planting. Evergreen screening plants can be clipped into neat shapes to punctuate different areas in a formal garden.

Screening methods
Clipped shrubs act as small screening devices, lending an air of mystery to a small garden and making it appear larger than it is.

Planting a hedge

To look their best, hedges often need as much care, both in planting and subsequently, as most ornamental shrubs. Hedging plants are best bought small and in bulk. Once planted, keep the soil weed-free and water frequently during dry spells for at least the first season.

Conifer hedge
Mark the line of the hedge using canes and string (two canes for a straight hedge;

5 to 7 canes for a curve). Make a trench of well-worked soil, dug to at least 75cm (30in) depth, carefully forking out perennial weeds.

The trench should be made about 30cm (12in) wider overall than the expected hedge width. Dig as much well-rotted

Single row of conifers
To ensure an equal distance between the hedging plants, place a cane on the ground between the centres of the planting holes.

compost or organic matter into the lower spit of soil as you can. For even better results, sprinkle over and fork in slow-release or long term fertilizer before planting.

Conifers should be set in a single row at least 45–60cm (18–24in) apart (but 75cm/30in for Leyland cypress).

After placing the shrub in the hole, pack the root area with soil and gently firm in with the heel. Conifers do not need to be clipped after planting; simply clip lightly in the early years.

Deciduous hedge
For an impenetrable barrier, deciduous species are often planted in a double alternating row. Proceed as for planting conifers, but make the trench width the same as the intended hedge width.

Double row of deciduous plants
Allow 45cm (18in) between rows, and slightly more space between plants than for a single row. After planting clip back side shoots and the leader shoot by a third in late autumn.

Arches and pergolas

Pergolas and arches are desirable features to include in even the smallest garden. They create immediate height and vertical interest; they can frame a distant view of a statue, act as focal points themselves, or they divide a garden into spaces without the solidity of fences or hedges. Above all, they display plants.

A simple pergola can be turned into a cosy little arbour or sitting area by closing in three sides, perhaps with trellis panels covered with clematis and honeysuckle. Wood is a traditional material, whether simply sawn or extravagantly carved and moulded, but many other materials including metal, stone, brick and even light plastic-covered metal, can be used on their own or in combination. Brick and stone, for example, would be primarily used for building narrow columns or piers to support metal or wooden roof beams. All these materials have their own particular merits. Wood is relatively economical, whilst wrought iron, though more expensive, is tremendously flexible.

Arches and pergolas can be bought in kit form to create your own instant garden feature. But if you wanted something a little different from standard sizes and shapes, you would need either to make it yourself or have it tailor-made professionally.

A cool, airy pergola
Baskets of bright pink impatiens add a dash of colour to this all-green pergola. The greyish-green paint harmonizes well with the plants.

Ideal supports for plants

Pergolas and arches are ideal for a whole range of climbing plants. Vigorous, twining or self-clinging varieties such as honeysuckle (*Lonicera* spp.) and wisteria will quickly reach the top of the posts or columns with little help required. However, more delicate types like *Clematis alpina* or those with little or no ability to cling strongly, for example *Trachelospermum* may need some assistance at least to the top of any uprights.

Painted slender metal poles sometimes provide very little grip for climbers, which will continually slide down. In situations like this, some additional wires or strings wrapped around the uprights will provide that

extra hold for the plants until they reach the top and can become self-supporting.

If you wish to create a shaded area of the garden, you can use a series of arches or pergolas to cover a path, or perhaps use two to make a shady bower over a seat. Fruiting vines can be grown over pergolas or arches to create shade, and provide edible crops.

A flowery tunnel
A rose arch is an eye-catching feature, particularly at the height of its flowering season. Arches do not have to be used singly: place three or four at regular intervals to create a light and airy 'tunnel' of roses.

Constructing pergola posts

The pergola shown here is constructed along a newly laid brick path. Spacing between the uprights is roughly equal to the width of the pergola. For example, whether the span across the path is 1m (3ft) as here, or 1.8m (6ft), the distance between the posts should be the same.

The height will depend to a large extent on use: a thoroughfare will need to be 2.5m (8ft), a decorative arch or arbour can be lower.

The end posts of the pergola are positioned first. Dig a hole for each based on a square of the post size (7.5cm/3in) and about 60cm (24in) deep. Each post should be set in cement in a 1:4 to 1:6 proportion of cement to combined aggregate in a stiff mix (see p.45). Once the endposts have been positioned guidelines (string or canes) should be run between their tops so that the posts in between are set at a common level.

Two people are needed to position the posts: one to fill the hole with cement and the other to hold a spirit level against the upright post. Once the cement is hard, the supports and crossbeams can be fixed (see below).

1 *Using a spirit level, check throughout the operation that the post is exactly upright, from all angles.*

2 *As it is fed into the hole, the concrete is tamped down with the shovel and smoothed off. Make sure that it slopes so that water runs away from the post.*

3 *A strut nailed to the post at an angle keeps it in position until the concrete sets. A final smoothing off of the cement mix can be done with a metal tamp.*

Arch and pergola roofs

The fundamental structure of arches and pergolas doesn't vary, and in its simplest form consists of upright posts or columns linked together across their tops usually with horizontal rails or beams. So the simplest arch might just consist of two rustic poles set upright in the ground, joined across the top with a third pole nailed into place. From this starting point, all pergolas and tunnels evolve.

Crossbeams set flush
Supports and crossbeams are half-jointed, so they interlock fully. Here the support sits in a joist hanger attached to a wall.

Round rustic poles
The simplest roof with poles nailed together. Using untreated wood means that this arch's life will be short – however, the poles are fairly easily replaced.

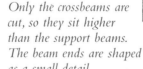

Raised crossbeams
Only the crossbeams are cut, so they sit higher than the support beams. The beam ends are shaped as a small detail.

Plants for pergolas and arches

These are just some of the many plants suitable for pergolas or other structures. Most have been chosen for their scent as well as for their flowers.

Actinidia kolomikta
Akebia quinata
Bougainvillea (*B. glabra*)
Clematis (*C. alpina, C. armandii, C. x durandii, C.* 'Gypsy Queen' and other large-flowered cvs, *C. montana* 'Elizabeth', *C. x macropetala, C. viticella*)
Golden hop (*Humulus lupulus* 'Aureus')
Honeysuckle (*Lonicera x americana, L. caprifolium,* *L. periclymenum)*
L. x tellmanniana)
Itea (*I. ilicifolia*)
Jasmine (*Jasminum nudiflorum, J. officinale*)
Laburnum x waterei
Passionflower (*Passiflora caerulea, P.c.* 'Constance Elliott'
Rose (many *Rosa* spp., e.g. 'Golden Showers', 'Madame Grégoire Staechelin', 'Spanish Beauty', 'Mermaid', 'Morning Jewel, 'New Dawn')
Solanum crispum
Sweet pea (*Lathyrus odoratus*)
Tropaeolum speciosum, T. tuberosum
Vitis coignetiae, V. vinifera 'Purpurea'
Wisteria (*W. floribunda, W. sinensis*)

Water features

There can be very few gardens that would not be enhanced by the addition of a small pool or water feature. Indeed in hot, dry climates where water is a valued resource, such features have often been central to garden design. The style of your chosen water feature should reflect the nature of your garden. Circular and square ponds are in keeping with formal features, while irregular shaped ponds and meandering streams might be more in keeping with wild or informal gardens.

The essence of any water feature, of course, is that it must hold an amount of water suitable for its intended purpose without leaking, or at least not noticeably, and this principle applies from the tiniest half-barrel pool to the largest lake.

Flowing or moving water is easily achieved by means of submersible pumps which can be used to create spouts or fountains, or else to carry water to a higher level from which it can return to the pool or other feature via a waterfall, stream or cascade.

Striking a balance
The strong architecture of this house is balanced by a formal, circular pool close by. The curved slabs of the pool's edge reflect the material used to pave the patio, serving as a link between house and garden.

Containing water

Though the traditional method of lining ponds with puddled clay still has its place, for the average garden owner there are other ways to create a water feature, whether for still or moving water:
• By lining a suitably pre-pared excavation with a flexible polythene, PVC or rubber-based liner.
• Using pre-formed ponds, usually made from fibreglass or plastic, or other rigid containers such as wood, metal and stone.
• Making a strong concrete shell rendered with water-proofed mortar.
• To provide a flexible waterproof layer, using *in-situ* fibreglass applied to a concrete or brick shell.

The first two methods are by far the most popular, partly by virtue of their relatively modest cost, and partly because only a modest degree of skill is required. The first method (see opposite) is also best for small features, such as bubble fountains.

Miniature fountain
The focal point of this courtyard garden is a pool and fountain enclosed by a raised brick edge and surrounding planting.

Trough with wall spout
Moving water transforms a solid stone trough into a delightful water feature. A low-power submersible pump, with careful concealment of the supply hose and wiring, is all that's required.

Wooden half barrel
This makes a perfectly adequate place for planting miniature waterlilies, which prefer still water, and rushes (here Nymphaea tetragona and Typha minima).

Making a lined pond

Flexible liners come in a range of materials and sizes, with cheaper PVC and polythene best suited to simple features. The heaviest-duty liners are used for reservoirs! In deciding the pond shape, remember it is easier to have shallow curves and gently sloping sides to avoid making large folds in the liner.

For marking out the pond you will need a supply of short canes, string and a datum peg (roughly as long as the pond depth – see p.43), marked 2.5cm (1in) from its top. Also mark a few short pegs in the same way.

Insert the datum peg near the centre of the pond area, so that the mark is at ground level. Place levelling pegs about 30cm (1ft) outside the pond circumference, using a spirit level from the datum peg to each in turn. In this way you can check that the sides are to a uniform level.

Excavate to one spade depth (spit) across the pond area. Dig out a second spit, and so on, until the required depth and shape are reached. To check the depth, remove the datum peg, place a straight edge above the hole, between two levelling pegs, and measure down.

Before installing the liner, remove all stones and roots.

Flatten the ground and line the bottom, sides and shelf with a layer of sand. Centre the liner over the pond and gently lower it in position, until it just touches the pond base. Hold the liner edges loosely in place with bricks or stones. Gradually fill the pond with water, easing the liner into place and making folds as you go. Once the liner is seen to be level all round – so no water spills – remove the holding stones.

1 *Use a spirit level to check that all levelling pegs outside the pond circumference are at the same height as the datum peg.*

2 *The pond is dug out to second spit depth; note the 30cm (12in) flat shelf left for marginal, shallow-water plants.*

3 *Line the sides, shelf and base with a 3-5cm (1-3in) layer of moist soft sand and level with a wooden float.*

4 *Lower the liner into position, using stones or bricks to secure edges. Fill with water, making folds in the liner as you go.*

5 *Position edging stones and trim the liner to 30cm (12in). Taking each slab in turn, tamp gently into position on a pad of mortar, using a 1:4 cement: soft sand mix. Point several slabs at a time.*

Calculating pond liner size

The major cost of the pond is the liner, so it is vital to work out how much liner you will need at the outset. Use four pegs to mark the *maximum* length and width of your proposed pond, be it a rectangle or an irregular shape.
liner width = max. pond width + (max. depth x 2)

liner length = max. pond length + (max. depth x 2)

The pond illustrated is 1.5m wide x 2.2m long x 0.75m deep, therefore:
liner width = 1.5m + (0.75m x 2) = 3m
liner length = 2.2m + (0.75m x 2) = 3.7m

The finished pond
In a short time the pond is transformed with marginal plants, waterlilies and pond edge planting. To secure and conceal the pond liner, you can use any type of paving material – as long as it reflects the style of the garden. The paving slabs should slightly overlap the pond edge. Cover the pond bottom and shelf with 3cm (1in) topsoil to help stabilize the water temperature, assist bacterial activity (if fish are to be kept in the pond), and provide nutrients for plants to grow.

Containers

Containers are the ideal solution for small-space gardening, permitting you to grow a surprisingly wide range of plants on patios, balconies, roof terraces and in window boxes and to group the displays successfully. Choosing an appropriate form and size of container is a key element in successful container gardening. The range of terracotta pots is now vast, and you can find almost any shape or size to suit your needs.

One of the great benefits of container gardening is that it allows you to move the plants around, so that those in flower are in the foreground and those out of flower are out of sight. Another bonus is that you can grow plants in specialized conditions, such as an acid-loving azalea in a pot of ericaceous compost. However, containers do need more attention than conventionally planted gardens, because they dry out so quickly and need frequent watering. You also need to provide nutrients for the plants on a regular basis, and repot the plants as they grow.

Creating a colourful environment
A small paved garden and timber-decked terrace is brought to life with the addition of a variety of containers. Vibrant greenery and interesting foliage are teamed with blue, lilac and yellow flowers.

Wall displays

In small gardens it pays to use the wall space as well as the floor space for planting. Groups of matching pots can be fixed to the wall on brackets or trellis to create vividly colourful displays on an otherwise blank canvas.

This is particularly useful for walls alongside narrow alleys which get very little light at the foot of the wall, narrowing the range of what you can grow. If you repeat a theme in several pots, it will give the area both visual interest and a strong sense of design unity. Many small flowering plants are ideal for this purpose, and you can replant the containers to give a year-long display.

Wall flowers
Small terracotta pots filled with blue pansies hang on a trellis-clad wall, with matching lavender in rectangular pots on top.

Planting a wall pot
1 *Place some stones for drainage at the base of the pot. Half fill the pot with compost and insert the first plant.*

2 *Fill with remaining plants, add compost to within 3cm (1in) of the rim and water well. Fix the pot to the wall.*

Free-standing containers

The choice of materials for containers is wonderfully varied, from simple unadorned terracotta to delicate and ornate wire. It is important to theme your containers in some way, either by colour or material, to prevent the display developing an unattractively 'bitty' look.

Make sure you have some big containers, perhaps containing one handsome feature plant, such as cordyline or a small tree. Square wooden tubs, known as 'Versailles' tubs, are ideal for formal displays of clipped box, often used in matching pairs either side of a doorway or flight of steps.

Window boxes can be of painted wood or terracotta, and you can create displays with, say, two round pots either side of a long rectangular area for greater visual interest, and to give some variety in the planting theme. Objects not intended as plant containers will sometimes serve the purpose very well, including old chimney pots, sinks or even wheelbarrows. Oil drums and plastic containers can be given a coat of paint and are surprisingly effective. Make sure any 'found' container has drainage holes created in the base, and use a layer of stones at the bottom to ensure the holes do not block with compost. Repot most plants every two years.

Wooden containers
Containers made of wood, even durable timber such as English oak, are best treated inside and underneath with a preservative – check that it is suitable for use near plants though.

Stone containers
Generally these need no treatment and can be planted straightaway. Be wary, however, of planting lime-hating plants, such as camellias or rhododendrons, in concrete tubs unless they are sealed inside, due to the presence of lime in the concrete.

Metal containers
Metals like iron and steel will rust, so may need treatment. So that the soil does not become contaminated by metals such as zinc or lead, found in antique or reproduction containers, paint the insides with latex-based paint or line them with heavy polythene.

Hanging baskets

For small spaces nothing beats a hanging basket as a show stopper since it is seen alone, and in the round. Some wonderfully vibrant displays can be achieved in baskets, but they do require very frequent watering since their exposure to drying winds causes moisture to evaporate rapidly. As with other container plantings, you could mix water-retentive granules with the compost. This will keep it moist for longer, although at the height of summer, daily watering is still essential, especially if the basket hangs in full sun. Feeding throughout the growing season is also a priority. Some slow-release fertilizer added to the compost when you plant the basket in late spring should supply the necessary nutrients. Hanging baskets look most effective if they have a limited colour scheme, either toning colours, two contrasting colours or a single colour. Any small trailing foliage or flowering plants can be used. Trailing forms of petunia, pelargonium, lobelia, nasturtium and ivy are popular.

Double the impact
When planting hanging baskets, sticking to a theme of just one or two colours often produces the best results, as these stunning displays of Pelargonium *and* Lobelia *demonstrate.*

Planting a hanging basket
1 *Place moss around the sides of the basket and then line it with a pierced plastic liner. Half-fill the basket with compost.*

2 *Start to add the plants, pushing some of them into the sides so that the whole basket is eventually covered.*

Structural planting

Structural planting is a phrase that often appears in discussions of garden design, and while it is a vital aspect to consider when planning a garden, it is actually quite difficult to define in precise terms. In essence, though, it could be described as a permanent framework of woody plants, that is to say trees and shrubs, which can be infilled with other smaller plants such as perennials, bulbs and grasses, and which results in a cohesive effect at all times of the year. Without such framework planting, most gardens would be very bitty and fragmented. At the same time, these trees and shrubs are used as one would use man-made garden features, to frame views, screen, divide or act as focal points. So the actual locations of trees and larger shrubs become more than just positions where they can be seen and appreciated as individual items of beauty: they are an intrinsic part of the garden design or scheme.

Some shrubs will assume almost tree-like proportions, which can be an advantage if your tree choice is otherwise limited, particularly in small gardens. Many large shrubs have distinctive growth habits, such as *Kerria japonica* 'Pleniflora' which is tall and upright, or *Viburnum plicatum* 'Mariesii', which is wide and spreading. Knowledge of plants' growth habits can be used to help you select shrubs, and indeed trees, that will serve a particular purpose in the framework of your garden.

Foliage composition
Here, trees and shrubs provide structure with dense evergreens giving contrasts of colour and height. The deciduous foreground trees will allow sunlight to filter through.

Tree and shrub forms

The natural form that trees and shrubs take creates a very positive design statement. The variation in these forms can be used to great effect in any design.

Small gardens, in particular, will benefit from the naturally columnar or conical shape of some trees, cypresses and conifers, for example. A small weeping tree is ideal as a focal point in a small formal garden. The forms of shrubs are equally varied. The tall sword-like leaves of yuccas and cordylines make a strong architectural statement, and, in handsome containers,

these make ideal punctuation plants to mark a transition in the design from one area to another. Shrubs with a spreading growth habit such as some cotoneasters and junipers, are useful where there are changes of level in the garden. A selection of some of the more popular forms of tree and shrub are shown right.

Try to suit the shape to the purpose. Columnar trees are ideal for small spaces while those with rounded canopies will help create areas of shade. When choosing shrubs, try to select as many different forms as possible to add interest to the planting.

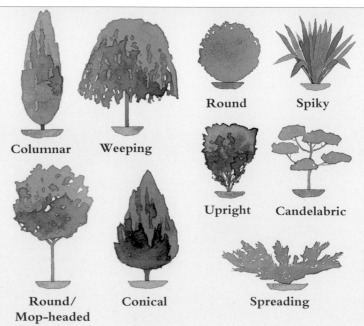

Columnar   Weeping   Round   Spiky

Round/Mop-headed   Conical   Upright   Candelabric   Spreading

Large-scale structure

Any garden will benefit from having a tree or two to provide vertical interest, and even quite small gardens can have at least two or three small trees or large shrubs.

Try to pick different forms, and a mixture of evergreen and deciduous types. Foliage colour and shape is important, too, and there are numerous colours and textures to choose from. Even the bare branches of deciduous trees add substance to the garden framework.

Because of their scale, trees assume probably the most important role in a garden and siting them carefully is critical. Avoid planting all the trees around the perimeter, and try to position one small tree as a focal point. Japanese maples are excellent feature trees for small gardens, and many have excellent autumn colour as well.

While evergreen trees are useful for year-round effect, remember that in the shorter days of winter, they may cast heavy shadows.

Tropical atmosphere
Palms, here surrounded by ferns and Cordyline, *can look very exotic when lit up at night.*

Small-scale structure

Shrubs provide the next level of the planting scheme, which the smaller perennials and annuals flesh out. Make sure that the shrubs have an interesting form. Many small-leaved evergreens that do not make naturally good shapes can be clipped or pruned to improve on nature.

It is a good idea to have a mixture of forms and foliage types in the garden. Look for varieties with interestingly marked foliage – many have gold or silver variegated leaves which will 'lighten' the effect of very dense foliage. At a lower level, mound-forming shrubs can be used to provide weed-suppressing ground cover. Heathers are particularly useful for this purpose. Aim to have a mixture of evergreen and deciduous shrubs – you will probably need one evergreen variety for every two or three deciduous ones to achieve a reasonable balance.

Bamboos and grasses
Tall bamboo above a low trickle fountain provides a focal point at the end of the path, its shape echoed by surrounding smaller clumps of grasses.

Foliage interest

Gardens need not be in flower to look good, and provided there is ample variety of form and foliage colour, will look interesting all year round.

Aim for a mixture of textures and leaf forms. Grasses, with their slender, often arching, leaves make a good contrast to the more typical oval leaf forms, throwing these into relief. In small gardens, a sense of unity can be created by concentrating on foliage rather than flowers, the colour being kept largely to one part of the garden, perhaps in a changing display of container plants. Remember, too, that there are many differently coloured leaves, not simply green. Plants with gold, purple and silver- and gold-variegation are worth looking out for and many plants turn attractive shades of scarlet, russet and gold in the autumn. Leaf shapes can vary from large hand-shaped leaves to neat ovals. Use plants with a wide range of attributes for the most interesting effects.

Contrasting foliage
The varied colours, textures and shapes of Salvia, Digitalis, grasses and Carpinus work well together in a small garden.

Trained ivy
A simple terracotta pot with variegated ivy – in this case trained in a spiral over wire – can act as a focal point.

Designing borders

Almost every gardener's dream is to create a brilliantly coloured border or bed for their garden, but orchestrating the whole is a complex task that requires a great deal of diligent research into plant sizes, flowering times and colour. The task is made more difficult if you wish to create a border or bed that looks good all year round. Generally, a mixed shrub and perennial border is easier to get right than a border made up solely of perennial plants, although the latter tend to give a more brilliant effect during a short season of the year. The greatest perennial borders are usually renowned for the season in which they are at their best – normally spring, summer or autumn. If you are fortunate in having a larger garden, you might plant up one border for spring, another for summer and a third for autumn.

Summer colour
Poppies (Papaver orientalis)*, Sambucus nigra and Spiraea japonica 'Goldflame' provide shades of red, orange and yellow that give this traditional summer mixed border a 'hot' colour theme.*

Shrub border for partial shade

Areas of the garden in partial shade are usually best given over to shrub borders, since there is a wide choice of shrubs that will do well in some shade, whereas many perennials prefer full sun.

The aim in a shrub border is to get a good mixture of foliage colours and textures, so the border looks attractive even when the shrubs are not in flower. A combination of evergreen and deciduous shrubs is normally the most effective, providing a shape and structure to the border even during the winter.

This predominantly shrub border features a few herbaceous perennials to give it variety and a little extra pace and colour – a geranium for a splash of lavender-blue in mid-summer, and rudbeckias for yellow highlights in late summer. The shrubs include a couple to add scent – the philadelphus and elaeagnus – plus a berberis for some purple-red contrast.

Plant list
The shrubs are all planted singly; perennials that act as infill in groups of three or five, according to size.
1 *Cotoneaster frigidus*
2 *Miscanthus sinensis* (such as 'Silver Feather' or another similar grass)
3 *Fuchsia riccartonii*
4 *Buddleja davidii* 'Black Knight' (deep purple flowers)
5 *Elaeagnus* x *ebbingei* 'Limelight'
6 *Philadelphus* 'Belle Etoile'
7 *Juniperus* x *media* 'Mint Julep'
8 *Hydrangea quercifolia* 'Snow Queen'
9 *Potentilla* 'Goldfinger'
10 *Spiraea* 'Goldflame'
11 *Berberis* 'Dart's Red Lady'
12 *Rudbeckia* 'Goldsturm'
13 *Weigela florida*
14 *Carex morrowii* 'Evergold'
15 *Acanthus spinosus*
16 *Geranium* 'Johnson's Blue'
17 *Thuja* 'Smaragd' (or similar small conical evergreen)
18 *Euonymus* 'Emerald 'n' Gold'

Colour and form
The colour scheme in this border is one of golds, purples, rusty oranges and blues. Foliage colour and form plays and important part, providing interest through most of the year.

Perennial border for full sun

A thriving perennial border in summer or autumn is something that all keen plantspeople hanker after.

The planning of such a border in terms of the heights and flowering times of the plants is very tricky. You also need some colour sense to make the finished result attractive.

If in doubt, go for a single colour (yellow or white are popular), or pick a range of pastels (pinks, mauves, blues and whites) or strong contrasts (yellows, oranges, purples and blues).

In this border, colour is introduced not just in the bright flower colours, such as the yellows of rudbeckias and the rusty oranges of heleniums, but in strong foliage colour too, for example the purple-tinged *Salvia officinalis* 'Purpurescens' and reddish purple *Sedum telephium*. A couple of shrubs, such as hydrangeas and euonymus, could also be added to help to give the border structure.

Summer brights

Purples, oranges, blues, yellows and whites make a vibrant mix in this exuberant and colourful sunny border. Foliage interest is provided by the likes of Carex striata *and* Festuca glauca.

Plant list
1 *Rudbeckia* 'Goldsturm'
2 *Deschampsia* spp. or *Carex striata*
3 Hybrid *Delphinium*
4 Bronze-flowered *Helenium* (such as *H.* 'Coppelia')
5 *Phlox paniculata* (such as *P.p.* 'Marlborough')
6 *Echinops ritro*
7 *Leucanthemum maximum* (such as 'Wirral Supreme')
8 *Sedum telephium*
9 *Salvia uliginosa*
10 *Gaillardia*
11 *Iris sibirica*
12 *Euphorbia griffithii* 'Fireglow'
13 *Aster amellus* 'Vanity'
14 *Hemerocallis* spp.
15 *Erysimum* spp.
16 *Helichrysum* spp.
17 *Penstemon* such as 'Sour Grapes'
18 *Coreopsis verticillata*
19 *Hemerocallis* 'Hyperion'
20 *Festuca glauca*
21 *Geranium magnificum*
22 *Salvia officinalis* 'Purpurascens'

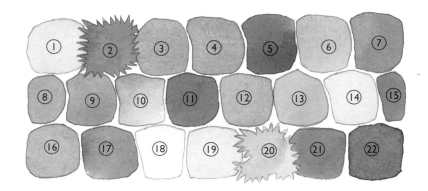

Spring borders

With their power to make us forget the starkness and cold of winter, the combination of spring-flowering shrubs and perennials with bulbs and corms is one of the delights of the garden. Whole beds can be filled with massed tulips and toning pansies, or with tulips and contrasting wallflowers. For a less labour-intensive display, you could try naturalizing grape hyacinths, squill and glory-of-the-snow.

The range of spring-flowering plants is huge, catering to any size of garden, any aspect and any colour scheme.

For shrubs and perennials, choose from forsythia, witch hazel, magnolias, rhododendrons, camellias and lilac, or from hellebores, bergenias, aubrietas and alyssums. Add to these the regular standbys such as daffodils, narcissi, tulips, muscari, and crocuses, or the more unusual fritillaries or erythroniums, and you can have borders that will look good from early spring until May. Also, because bulbs and corms vanish underground after flowering and can be over-planted with later-flowering perennials, you have the bonus of being able to double the usefulness of your border.

Traditional favourites
Narcissi, euphorbia, 'China Pink' tulips and geraniums mix in a traditional spring border.

On the wild side
'Spring Green' tulips and hyacinths are planted in a less formal arrangement.

Designing island beds

Although you can have borders composed entirely of shrubs, most people prefer to mix them with flowering plants for a more colourful and interesting display at any one time. Shrubs provide the backdrop for borders planted against boundary walls and form the centrepoint of the border if it is an 'island' bed – or one that you can walk right round. As a rule, an island bed should have a slightly asymmetric look, with the tallest plant slightly off-centre to avoid too 'bun-like' an appearance. Evergreens, like small conifers, or sword shaped plants, like cordylines, are good for providing this central backbone. Follow with medium-sized shrubs, scaling down towards sub-shrubs and tall perennials, with smaller perennials at the front of the border.

Individual displays
A lawn studded with several island beds provides a good opportunity to experiment with different plantings, as each bed is self-contained.

Creating a raised island bed

A small raised bed built as a retaining wall, or against an existing wall or freestanding, as here, is most useful, especially in a small patio garden.

This raised bed is built of an inner wall of cinder blocks and an outer wall of hand-made bricks, with a small gap in between (the width of the wall equals the length of a brick). The footing is 30cm (12in) wide, slightly wider than the wall, and 30cm (12in) deep. Using canes and string, mark out the site of the raised bed.

Calculate the width of the footing according to the width of the walling: here, one cinder block for the inner wall plus one hand-made brick for the outer = 23 cm (9in). Add 3.5cm (1½in) either side of the wall; total width 30cm (12in). Once the outside structure is complete, fill the base with stones or other drainage material to a depth of 3in (8cm) and fill with good garden soil or compost. (Acid-loving plants can be grown in a garden with alkaline soil by filling a raised bed with acid compost).

On a different level
Planting in and around a brick raised bed makes it a distinctive feature in the garden.

1 *The trench marked out with canes and string, with concrete footing in place. Leave to set overnight.*

2 *Building the inner cinder brick wall: each block is laid on a 10mm (¼in) layer of mortar, with one end 'buttered' with a triangular dab of mortar.*

3 *Lay each corner of the outer wall, then construct outwards. After three or four courses, set a string guideline between each corner. Infill with bricks, inserting a butterfly tie at intervals to bond inner and outer walls.*

4 *The wall is finished with a course of coping bricks laid lengthways across the inner and outer walls.*

Design for an all-seasons island bed

The prominent position of an island bed demands that it look good all year round, and it is of key importance to create a planting plan that takes this into account. What you sacrifice in impact during one specific season, you gain in all-year-round value. It is important, therefore, that you pick your plants with care for maximum show – ideally they should have flower colour in one season, and perhaps offer good autumn leaf colour or attractive seedheads in another. The use of spring- and autumn-flowering bulbs – tulips, narcissi, autumn-flowering crocuses – extends the season further, and these have the advantage of not taking up a lot of space. As they die down, their foliage will be concealed by the herbaceous perennials. Finally, a few evergreens are also necessary, to ensure that the planting retains some of its shape in winter. When choosing your plants, remember too that they will be viewed from all sides. Plants of varying heights with an even growth habit will give the best effect.

Plant list

Large-feature plants are planted singly, smaller plants in groups of three or five, depending on size.

1 *Festuca glauca*
2 *Doronicum orientale* 'Spring Bouquet'
3 *Aster novi-belgii* 'Jenny'
4 *Phlox paniculata* ('Fujiyama')
5 *Phlox* 'David'
6 *Tulipa* 'White Triumphator'
7 *Hemerocallis* 'Pink Damask'
8 *Stipa gigantea*
9 *Penstemon* 'Sour Grapes'
10 *Juniper chinensis* 'Pyramidalis'
11 *Geranium phaeum*
12 New Zealand flax (*Phormium* spp.)
13 *Agapanthus* 'Bressingham Blue'
14 *Euphorbia amygdaloides*
15 *Coreopsis* 'Moonbeam'
16 *Hosta* 'Halcyon'
17 *Artemisia* 'Lambrook Silver'
18 *Scabiosa caucasia* 'Butterfly Blue'
19 *Liatris spicata*
20 *Iris pallida* 'Argentea Variegata'
21 *Helleborus orientalis* 'Heartsease'
22 *Alchemilla mollis*
23 *Berberis thunbergii atropurpurea*

Island bed in spring
With a wealth of foliage interest (including juniper, berberis, phormium, festuca and euphorbia) in winter, colour is added in spring with tulips, doronicum and hellebores.

Island bed in summer
By summer the bed is in full swing, as the scabious (Scabiosa), penstemons, irises geraniums, asters and phlox come into flower. An attractive mix of foliage helps to flesh out the planting with hostas and alchemilla.

Design for pond-side planting

Water is a great asset in any garden. You can take advantage of a damp area to grow plants especially suited to moist soil and so create plantings in the form of a bog garden, with or without a pond.

Some of the most handsome plants come from moist soils and climates, their large lush leaves making a valuable contribution to any garden, as well as providing a respite from busy flower colour. Plants to use include ornamental rhubarb, large-leaved rodgersias, some of the big-leaved hostas and bamboos. It is a good idea to create the planting at one edge of the pond, rather than scattering it around the edges. Grouping the plants creates a more lush look to the pond, and the effect is more natural. If the pond is deep enough, include at least one floating aquatic (they require 90cm/3ft of water).

Bog garden
A damp area can be made to look very lush, with touches of colour from moisture-loving plants such as primulas and iris.

Plant list
Planted in groups of three, except *Glyceria* (1) and *Aponogeton* (1)
1. *Glyceria maxima* 'Variegata'
2 *Polygonum bistorta* 'Superbum'
3 *Rodgersia podophylla*
4 *Iris sibirica* 'Persimmon'
5 *Hosta* 'Francee'
6 *Astilbe* 'Elizabeth Bloom'
7 *Aponogeton distachyos*

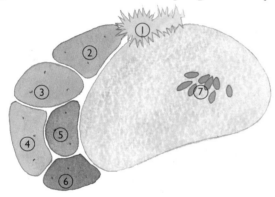

Leafy pond edges
Concentrate the marginal and poolside planting at one end of the pond for the best effect. Good foliage plants include Glyceria maxima.

Design for damp, shady corners

Many gardens have a damp, boggy area, often shaded by trees. There are a number of handsome foliage plants such as hostas and grasses that do well in these conditions and would create a small area of considerable planting interest. Damp shade also suits peat-loving plants like rhododendrons and ferns as well as plants like *Cimicifuga simplex* that dislike full sun. Other flowering perennials for damp shade are some of the euphorbias, monkshood (*Aconitum*), polygonum, thalictrum and veratrum.

Cool, shady group
This little group of perennials, ferns, grasses and shrubs all enjoy damp shade. Many shade plants have white flowers, creating a predominantly cool green and white colour scheme.

Plant list
Planted in groups of three, except for the hydrangea (1).
1 *Carex elatior* 'Aurea'
2. *Anemone japonica* 'Louise Whink'
3. *Hydrangea quercifolia*
4. *Hosta* 'Frances Williams'
5. *Polystichum setiferum*
6. *Polygonum amplexicaule atrosanguineum*

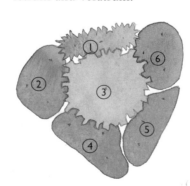

Design for dry, sunny borders

The plants for dry sunny conditions are often highly colourful, many of them with small silvery leaves that withstand drought conditions better than the larger, lusher leaves most often found in moisture-loving plants.

Big thistles do well in these conditions, as do the silver-leaved perennials such as lamb's ears (*Stachys byzantina* spp.), wormwood (*Artemisia* spp.) and senecio. Many geraniums, helianthemums and helichrysums, do well in hot sun, as do dianthus, hebe and small forms of phlox and penstemon. Try to aim for a good balance between large, medium and small perennials that like sunny conditions, and limit the theme to two colours (or toning colours), to give the area a feeling of unity.

Sun worshippers
Astromeria ligtu, Genista aetnensis *and* Lychnis *provide vibrant colour in a dry border.*

Plant list
Planted in groups of three, except for *Cistus* (1) and *Yucca* (1).
1 *Eryngium* x *oliverianum*
2 *Cistus* x *purpureus*
3 *Hemerocallis hyperion*
4 *Euphorbia amygdaloides* 'Rubra'
5 *Yucca filamentosa*
6 *Aster ameleus* 'Violet Queen'

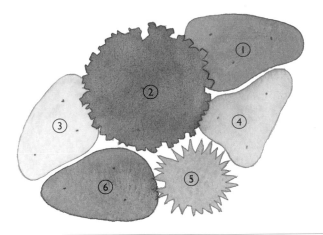

Mediterranean corner
This corner features plants that enjoy hot, sunny conditions. The yucca provides structure while the cistus counterbalances its form with brilliant flower colour.

Design for dry, shady corners

Dry shade is a common problem in small gardens with high walls, where the soil at the foot of the wall lies in the rain shadow area. It can be difficult to deal with this situation unless you turn to plants that naturally cope with dry shade. Among the larger plants that do well are foxgloves, alchemilla, pulmonarias and hellebores.

Dry, shady group
Good foliage plants that cope well with dry shade include the attractively variegated euonymus and ground-covering bugle (Ajuga reptans).

Plant list
Planted in groups of three, except mahonia (1).
1. *Dryopteris filix-mas*
2 *Euonymus* 'Emerald 'n' Gold'
3 *Mahonia* 'Charity'
4 *Ajuga reptans* 'Catlin's Giant'
5 *Iris foetidissima* 'Carina'
6 *Alchemilla mollis*

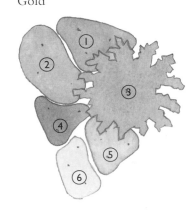

Planting designs for small spaces

If you have limited space, you are probably going to need to plant in containers and even if your garden is large, there will be areas, such as a patio, which will benefit from the occasional group of plants in pots. The aim in design terms is much the same as when planning larger borders and beds. Try to use foliage as well as flowers to create an impact, but ensure that the containers you choose are well suited to the plants, and enhance their attributes and qualities. It will pay to group the containers for maximum impact.

Many plants will do as well in containers as in the ground, but in their limited circumstances will demand a greater amount of care. They dry out notoriously quickly and need to be supplied with regular food and water. Most will also need repotting (depending on how vigorous they are) at least every two years.

Roof garden
A rooftop is lined with containers of plants on different levels, such as Rosa 'Scneewittchen and umbrella bamboo (Fargesia murieliae).

Design for a balcony

On a balcony, you usually need to get the most from a very limited space, so avoid plants with a spreading habit and go instead for conical plants, or those that will trail attractively over the edge of a wall or railing.

Make the most of the wall space for climbers, and try to leave an area free for a chair or two, or a small table. Placing a cluster of pots at one end looks better than scattering them randomly. The planting scheme here could be extended or reduced, depending on the size of the balcony. It has a mixture of architectural plants (bamboos and phormium), climbers (clematis and akebia), an evergreen shrub or two (*Choisya ternata* and *juniperus*) and colourful perennials. Including scented plants, like the lavender (*Lavandula angustifolia*), is also a good idea.

Plant list
These are all planted singly, except lavender (*Lavandula*), which has five plants to a trough, agapanthus (3) and sedum (3).
1 *Pleioblastus auricomus*
2 *Akebia quinata*
3 *Choisya ternata*
4 *Rosa* 'Happy Child'
5 *Helichrysum angustifolium*
6 *Solanum crispum*
7 *Agapanthus* 'Headbourne Hybrids'
8 *Fuchsia* 'Mrs Popple'
9 *Sedum* 'Vera Jameson'
10 *Hedera helix* 'Glacier'
11 *Lavandula angustifolia* 'Hidcote'
12 *Juniperus virginiana* 'Sulphur Spray'
13 *Clematis* 'Gipsy Queen'
14 *Phormium tenax purpureum*
15 *Akebia quinata*
16 *Hebe* 'Midsummer Beauty'
17 *Hosta* 'Halcyon'

A year-round balcony
A combination of perennials grown in pots, troughs and up a trellis provides year-round interest requiring little maintenance for a sheltered balcony.

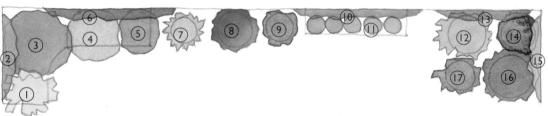

Designs for roof gardens

For a roof garden or small patio, you should concentrate the planting around the edges to leave space for seating and perhaps a table. A good mixture of evergreens for shelter, flowering shrubs and perennials for colour, and climbers and trailers is important, and plants included must be able to cope with the dry, sunny conditions of most patios and roof gardens. A good variety of container sizes and shapes widens the scope of your planting.

Plant list
1 *Campanula portenschlagiana*
2 *Pleioblastus auricomus*
3 *Clematis macropetala*
4 *Choisya* 'Aztec Pearl'
5 *Anthemis cupiana*
6 *Weigela* 'Victoria'
7 *Clematis* 'Gipsy Queen'
8 *Agapanthus* Headbourne Hybrids
9 *Juniperus* 'Sulphur Spray'
10 *Sedum* spp.
11 *Fuchsia* 'Mrs Popple'
12 *Rosa*'
13 *Phormium tenax purpureum*
14 *Salvia officinalis* 'Purpurascens'
15 *Elaeagnus ebbingei*
16 *Choisya* 'Sundance'
17 *Parthenocissus tricuspidata*
18 *Thuja plicata* 'Atrovirens'
19 *Ceanothus* 'Blue Mound'
20 *Hedera helix* 'Glacier'
21 *Thuja plicata* 'Atrovirens'
22 *Juniperus* 'Gold Sovereign'
23 *Parthenocissus tricuspidata*
24 *Philadelphus* 'Belle Etoile'
25 *Humulus lupus* 'Aureus'
26 *Hebe* 'Mrs Winder'
27 *Helichrysum angustifolium*
28 *Lonicera* x *americana*
29 *Potentilla fruticosa* 'Kobold'
30 *Aster* 'Violet Queen'
31 *Rosa* 'Evelyn'
32 *Stipa calamagrostis*
33 *Akebia quinata*
34 *Hydrangea quercifolia* 'Snow Queen'
35 *Campanula portenschlagiana*

A rooftop haven
This formally arranged combination of containers leaves plenty of room for a table and chairs or just for seating, so the owner can make the most of the sunshine.

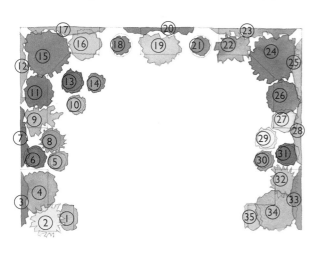

Designs for corners

A small group of pots can do wonders for a dull corner of a patio. Brought together in an artful arrangement, they will provide a burst of colour. The two groups shown here are intended for differing conditions: sun or shade. In either arrangement, the pots containing summer-flowering herbaceous perennials could be replaced with containers of spring bulbs to extend the interest.

Sun or shade
Two imaginative plantings show how to liven up a 'dead' corner. Watering and feeding are essential for a healthy display.

Plants for semi shade
1 *Clematis macropetala*
2 *Vitis cognetiae*
3 *Hydrangea serrata* 'Preziosa'
4 *Acer palmatum dissectum atropurpureum*
5 *Agapanthus* Headbourne Hybrids
6 *Alchemilla mollis*
7 *Euonymus fortunei* 'Emerald 'n' Gold'

Plants for sun
1 *Rosa* 'Alfred Carriere'
2 *Clematis* 'Elsa Spath'
3 *Elaeagnus x ebbingei* 'Limelight'
4 *Phormium tenax purpureum*
5 *Lilium regale*
6 *Ceanothus* 'Blue Mound'
7 *Sedum* 'Vera Jameson'
8 *Pinus* 'Hugo Ophir'

Problem areas

Apart from the main borders and beds that form the major elements of any garden planting, there are other areas where plants can add greatly to the atmosphere. They will enhance small corners and boundary walls, and special focal points, be they ponds, raised beds or alcoves. It is important to ensure that planting schemes in all parts of the garden are planned and considered in relation to each other. You can, of course, opt for several different themes, from a Mediterranean dry garden near a sunny patio to a shady, woodland garden under trees, but sudden, jarring transitions between one kind of planting and another need to be avoided. Colour is an important consideration, since an area of very strong colours – hot reds, yellows and vibrant purples – would make a pastel scheme look washed out in comparison if the two can be viewed simultaneously.

Creating a tranquil mood
A water feature blends in with the brick wall behind, allowing moisture-loving plants and climbers to grow together in a small space.

Disguising walls and fences

The vertical architecture of the garden – house walls, boundary walls and fences – provide a useful support for some plants and can be a great asset for the garden.

Flowering climbers greatly increase the number of flowering plants you can cram into the smallest garden, and many will grow successfully in close proximity, so that roses and clematis, for example, can be intertwined, extending the flowering season and the colour value over a longer period. It pays to include some evergreen and foliage climbers so that the walls and fences are clothed in autumn and winter as well as summer. Climbing hydrangeas, ornamental vines and some of the creepers are ideal for this. Remember that some good climbers, like wisteria, are exceptionally vigorous – so be prepared to prune them regularly to contain them and encourage flowering.

Green wall
Pots of herbs sit on a ledge between a wall and fence that are camouflaged by ivy.

Awkward spots

In many gardens, there are odd corners that are difficult to deal with, often because they are heavily shaded. Any desire to plant a sun-loving perennial border on this kind of site is doomed to instant failure. However, a quieter, no-less effective planting solution can be achieved if you opt for foliage texture and colour instead of flower power.

Once you establish whether the area is dry or damp, you can select suitable shade-loving plants that will thrive in these conditions. Very dry shade will limit your choices, although ivies do well in this environment, and a few carefully chosen varieties, with a judiciously placed statue or handsome pot, can turn a dull, dark corner into one of mystery and excitement.

Hostas, ferns and even busy lizzies (impatiens) also cope very well with shade, while dicentra, tiarella and heuchera do well in semi-shade. Plants in pots are especially useful for these difficult corners. If necessary, you can occasionally move the containers into sunnier positions. In areas where nothing much will grow, use hard materials such as beach pebbles to create surface interest, and perhaps include a interesting ornament – a statue or a well-shaped piece of driftwood.

Secluded spot
Climbers adorn a high fence and trellis, obscuring the view of a nearby house and allowing space for shade-loving plants beneath.

Hiding eyesores

To hide an unattractive view within the garden or beyond its boundaries, you may want to provide a screen clothed in plants. You need to be careful, however, as although some plants will quickly mask the unwanted view, they may present problems of control at a later date.

Plants such as quick-growing elaeagnus with its silvery, evergreen leaves, will put on nearly as much growth per year as the notoriously fast-growing conifer, x *cupressocyparis leylandii*, but will stop at around 5m (15ft) – a much more useful proposition for a small garden.

Although the Russian vine (*Fallopia baldschuanica*) is often recommended as a quick screening plant, which it undoubtedly is, it is a real bruiser in its determination to swamp every plant (and structure) in the vicinity. Unless you are prepared to control it with equal vigour and determination, you would be wise to avoid it.

Trellis, against which a variety of twining climbers can be grown, makes an excellent screen for masking a work area or a vegetable plot, for example. As it allows the wind through rather than creating a barrier, you will not suffer from problems caused by wind tunnels.

Trellis is also a useful means of providing privacy and shelter around a sitting area. Equally useful for screening or shelter are large pots, in which shrubs can be grouped in different places at various times of the year, depending on your needs.

Under cover
A facade of trellis and plants is a good way to hide eyesores – from a work area to ugly drainpipes.

Large pots are best moved on a series of small metal rollers; do not try to move them otherwise, as they are extremely heavy.

Remember that almost any plant will survive in a pot, even a smallish tree, providing it is well-watered during dry spells and fed throughout the growing season. Some plants to consider for this purpose are bamboos, yuccas, lilies, rhododendrons, box, yew and climbing roses.

Far corners

Many gardens have distant parts that are awaiting development. By planting naturally occurring species such as the humble nettle or cow parsley, you can turn such areas into wildlife havens, which will attract and bene-

Wildlife bonus
Naturally occurring flowers and grasses can turn a corner of the garden into a wildlife haven.

fit bees, butterflies and insects. Even in a much smaller garden you may still be able to find some space for a wildlife area, for instance by turning the end of a formal lawn into a wild-flower meadow.

This is also a useful labour-saving device in a large garden, as the grass will only need cutting twice a year, if native flowering plants and grasses are to be encouraged. A path can then be mown through the area, when the remainder of the grass is cut, to provide access. This looks very natural and appropriate.

In shadier, undeveloped corners, a tapestry of ground cover plants which require very little attention is the ideal solution. Your best bet is to choose plants that are naturally vigorous, but be prepared, once a year to remove any that are becoming too invasive.

Gravel corner
A gravel garden in a shady corner can be used to grow plants that like free-draining soil such as Centranthus *and some species of* Campanula.

PLANTS FOR THE GARDEN

To enable the different elements of a garden to blend comfortably and attractively, there has to be balance, which can to a large degree be dictated by the trees, shrubs and flowers that you choose. By opting for plants that complement and harmonize with other aspects of the garden, such as the paving or lawn, and its overall size and shape, you can create a framework in which art and nature reach a happy equilibrium. To help you choose plants to suit your garden's needs, concise descriptions of a wide range of trees, shrubs, roses, climbers, perennials, ground cover, bamboos, grasses, bulbs, annuals and biennials have been included. Each entry provides vital details as to what the plant looks like, how high it will grow, what kind of growing conditions it prefers, how hardy it is and when it flowers, if appropriate. This section also provides a host of helpful ideas on where to position plants, how to use and combine flower colours, design borders and incorporate different styles.

Principles of planting

'Harmony' is perhaps the most important word in making a garden. You want somewhere that is relaxing but also stimulating to the senses, where art and nature have reached a happy equilibrium. Creating a balance between the different elements of a garden, such as the paving, lawn, trees, shrubs and flowers, is crucial to the end result.

Colour is an essential design element, but because flowers are relatively fleeting, it can be difficult to maintain interest all year long. The stronger the framework of the garden, with plenty of 'architectural' plants (those with strong and distinct shapes), the less vital it will be to have flowers all year round.

Small gardens are especially difficult to plan. All plants are highly visible, so there is no room for the spectacular flowering plant that looks messy for the rest of the year. Good foliage and flowers with a long season are vital.

Creating a design core
This cottage garden has a formal plan. The gravel paths provide the 'bones' of the design while the planting is sympathetically unstructured.

Creating a structure

It is the larger or more upright plants that do most to develop the garden framework, dividing it into sections and serving as a guide as you walk or look round. Trees or shrubs with a narrow, vertical, columnar habit have lots of impact, but are useful in that they take up little space. Trees, under whose branches you can walk, hedges that act as green walls, or plants with strong shapes, all provide the visual 'bones' for the garden. The softer, more formless shrubs and flowering perennials are the 'flesh'. Some of the most successful gardens are those that balance the formality of clearly designed shapes, such as clipped hedges and topiary, with the informality of burgeoning borders of flowers and shrubs.

Informal design
This simple garden has all the ingredients for success: an enclosing structure of trees and hedges, space for relaxation and an impeded view so that the garden appears larger, and more inviting.

Year-round interest

Some gardeners are happy to have most of their garden flowering at once. They like to see a spring garden with lots of bulbs, or an early summer garden with roses and perennials, and they are happy to let it rest for the remainder of the year. Most gardeners, though, prefer to attempt a long season of interest, which involves trying to interweave plants so that there is always something, or some part, that looks good.

A garden takes time to develop, and never stands still. Planning planting for the short, medium and long term helps avoid the great gaps that can try the patience of even the most dedicated. Trees, needless to say, are the most long term, often maturing long after we have gone.

Shrubs, too, can take many years to look their best, which can mean that a garden that is heavily reliant on them may take rather a while to develop. Herbaceous perennials look established with remarkable speed, whereas annuals fulfil their promise and disappear within a year. It makes good sense, then, to include all these different plant forms in a garden.

Spring colour
An unusual contrasting bedding scheme with magenta tulips and yellow wallflowers brings strong colour to the garden in spring.

Autumn foliage
A dramatic canopy of foliage can provide both colour and interest in the garden, as the contrasting golds of this Liquidambar orientalis *and (behind) the reds of Japanese maple (*Acer palmatum *'Osakazuki') demonstrate.*

Harmony and contrast in the garden

Making a garden is an intensely personal business. What one person loves, another may hate. Such varying reactions are often to do with the level of harmony and contrast in the planting. Very harmonious gardens, where all the colours match, and clashes or surprises are avoided, are soothing, restful places. Those who like more stimulation may prefer gardens with lots of vivid, contrasting colours, or a wide and dramatic range of leaf shapes and plant forms.

Harmony in gardens is relatively easy to achieve with single colour schemes. 'White gardens' are particularly rewarding and straightforward. Plantings based on colour contrast are more difficult to get right, and are much more personal. Mixing strong colours can create results that are vibrant to some, but too obtrusive and clashing to others.

Mixing colours and shapes
Big, bold shapes, like this spiky variegated agave (left), make a striking feature against softer planting. Vibrant colour contrast is also provided by the yellow/green agave and the pink sedum.

Soft harmonies
The delicate blues, mauves and pinks and the softly billowing shapes of a herbaceous perennial border in summer (right) are a study in gentle harmony.

Plants for particular situations

To make a successful garden it is crucial to choose plants that are suitable for the prevailing conditions. All plants have preferences: moist or dry soils, acid or limey, warm climates or cold. Traditionally, gardeners have expended energy on making conditions suit particular plants, in places where they would not naturally grow, by changing the nature of the soil or using copious quantities of water. However, water shortages, and the pollutant effects of chemicals have compelled people to think in terms of a more natural approach. Instead of changing conditions to suit plants, today the trend is towards choosing plants to suit the place.

Sympathetic planting
Damp areas of the garden, in particular water features, need to be planted sympathetically. Moisture-loving plants have large lush foliage at the expense of brilliant flower colour. Use features, like this little bridge, to create colour accents instead.

What grows best?

Before you select plants for your garden, it is advisable to learn as much as you can about the area in which you live, as this will determine what you can grow. A good way of finding out which plants will grow well is to visit local parks and gardens that are open to the public. An area where everyone seems to have rhododendrons means that you can grow these acid-lovers, too, as well as azaleas, camellias and many more.

Keep a notebook handy to record plants that you like and that thrive in gardens with similar conditions to yours. It is a good way of building up your own body of knowledge. Once you have a clear idea of what the area can or cannot offer, you will be in a position to select plants that will succeed with little effort on your part.

Climate is the place to start. Is your area one that regularly experiences cold winters or hot, dry summers? If it is, then the hardiness of plants or their drought tolerance are two important limiting factors. Then there is the 'microclimate', which refers to factors that affect the overall climate on a small scale and of your garden in particular.

A wall or hedge that protects the garden from the prevailing wind may mean you are able to grow a range of more tender plants than anyone else in your neighbourhood. On the other hand, being in an exposed position, or in a frost hollow, where cold, heavy air gathers, can mean the opposite.

Sheltered spots
If you are lucky enough to have a walled garden, you can grow more tender plants that require protection from cold winds. Your perennial borders will flower earlier than your neighbour's in these conditions.

Light is yet another very important factor. Is your garden shaded by trees, or is it on the sunless side of a hill or your house? If it is, then you will need to concentrate your efforts on growing shade-tolerant plants.

The soil is the other major consideration. Is it generally damp or even wet, or is it very free-draining and so liable to dry out in summer? Is it fertile, or acid, or rich in lime? You may not require a soil-testing kit to find out – gardening neighbours can often supply the answers.

Hardiness ratings
In the following plant directory pages, plants that will not survive temperatures less than 5°C (40°F) are described as 'tender' in individual entries. Other plants are hardier, and are given ratings as follows:

★ will survive 4 to -1°C (30–40°F)
★★ will survive -1 to -7°C (20–30°F)
★★★ will survive -7 to -17°C (0–20°F)
★★★★ will survive -17 to -30°C (0 to -20°F)

Choosing your plants

Any garden benefits from having a good mixture of plants, both in terms of height and shape, and in the variety of foliage and flower form and colour. However, it is surprising how much diversity and interest you can create without flower colour.

Plants for shady parts of the garden will inevitably major on leaf form and shape; plants for full sun will have more flower power. Make sure that you choose those that do well for these differing situations, and look, too, at the soil conditions. Some plants prefer acid soil, others alkaline. Rhododendrons and azaleas, for example, refuse to grow on alkaline soil but will quickly provide useful ground cover for large gardens on peaty soil.

Hopefully, the differing habitats in your garden will allow you to choose a variety of plants from dry-loving to damp-loving, sun-loving to shade-loving.

Plants for dry sun

Many grasses like dry, sunny conditions. Big, clump-forming Miscanthus sinensis 'Variegatus' (right) is a handsome architectural plant for a dry border.

Plants for shade

Some euphorbias (left), and most dicentras, cope well with partial shade. Among the many plants that enjoy shady conditions are those that grow naturally in woodland. Some prefer damp, while others prefer dry shade (see list below).

Natural planting

The next time you take a country walk, or go on holiday, look at the plants around you. Notice how those that grow in exposed places usually have tiny, closely packed leaves, how those in hot, dry areas have a tendency to grey foliage or succulent leaves, and how woodland plants are often evergreen or dormant in the summer. All these are adaptations plants have evolved over millions of years to enable them to grow successfully in different environments.

It makes sense to take advantage of this, and select plants for our gardens that are naturally adapted to our particular type of soil and climate, whatever it is.

Gardeners often complain of bad drainage, or of dry, or clay, or limestone soil. They never seem satisfied, and are prone to label anything that is not a perfect loam as a 'problem garden'. However,

the fact is that nature has developed a wonderful and beautiful flora for every 'problem', at least those that are of natural origin.

A good start is to consider growing more wild plants native to your region. They are often very beautiful, but underrated for being wild, and at least they are perfectly adapted and will not have

difficulty growing. If there are no local nurseries selling local wild plants, you can collect seed (but *never* dig up the plants) and propagate them yourself.

Natural planting

A woodland edge provides the ideal habitat for shade-loving perennials, including geraniums, ferns and these foxgloves.

Dry or damp shade?

A number of plants enjoy shady conditions, but some prefer it dry, others damp. The shade created by walls, for example, is often dry as a rain shadow area is formed as a result. Damp shade is likely in a naturally damp garden, overshadowed by a few large trees.

Plants for damp shade

Brunnera macrophylla
Dicentra formosa
Geranium phaeum
Hosta sieboldiana
Pachysandra terminalis
Trillium spp.

Plants for dry shade

Alchemilla conjuncta, A. mollis
Anemone nemorosa
Epimedium spp.
Euphorbia amygdaloides
Hedera spp.
Humulus lupulus 'Aureus'
Hypericum spp.
Lonicera (some)
Pulmonaria spp.
Symphytum spp.

Trees for the framework

Trees and large shrubs are an essential part of most landscapes, and by planting trees you are not only planting for the future, but also contributing to the appearance of the whole neighbourhood for generations to come – which means that it is very important to get it right!

There are plenty of trees that are suitable even for small gardens, although their mature shape can vary considerably. Some are very narrow, columnar varieties, which will cast little shade but form a striking part of the garden framework. Others may not reach a great height, but develop a broad canopy which requires a fair bit of space. Trees with fine, elegant forms make a great contribution to the overall structure of the garden.

Achieving a balance
Trees surround this country garden, giving it shelter and privacy. Choose carefully to create different forms and colours, and mix evergreens and deciduous trees to give the garden balance.

Choosing trees

It is of fundamental importance to know the eventual size of any tree that you plant, not only for the effect it will have on your own garden, but on the neighbours' too. Also bear in mind the kind of shade it will cast: light like a birch, or so heavy that little will grow beneath it,

Siting trees
This old apple tree, carefully sited at the corner of a perennial border, is just the right size and scale for this garden and also offers the bonus of delicious fruit in late summer.

such as with a beech. There are safety considerations, too. Any tree right next to a house may undermine foundations. Some, such as willows and poplars, may cause damage from a distance. If strong winds are frequent, you need to ensure that whatever you plant is wind resistant, or cannot blow over onto someone's home. You should also consider whether it will block anyone's view or light when it matures.

Since a tree will have an effect on the wider landscape, consider what this might be. Country districts can be depressingly suburbanized by

trees that are not characteristic of the local area, but which are mass planted in towns and industrial sites. Conversely, you can contribute positively to your local landscape by planting native trees.

A tree may be chosen simply for its shape or the play of its branches. However, good foliage is particularly important if we have to look at the tree a lot. This may mean coloured foliage, such as purple or yellow-tinged, or simply quietly attractive green leaves. Evergreens are popular, many considering them essential for providing interest

and structure in the winter. However they have drawbacks. One is that very little will grow beneath them, and the other is that their never-changing quality can become boring after a while.

Perhaps even more than with deciduous trees, it is extremely important not to choose evergreens that will become too large in time.

Shady places
Small and large trees have their place in the garden. Shade provided by larger trees is ideal for creating a secluded sitting area. Smaller trees can act as punctuation points at the end of a border.

Planting a tree

Young trees need support in windy areas. Hammer a stake into the base of the planting hole before inserting the tree, to avoid damaging roots, and tie the tree to the stake about 50cm (20in) above ground level. Use an angled stake (right) for container or root-balled trees, place at a 45° angle and secure with a tie. When filling the hole, look for the soil mark on the base of the trunk and plant at the same depth as it was before transplanting. Remove or loosen the tie around the trunk as the tree grows.

1 *In autumn or spring, dig a large hole, roughly two and half times the width of the root-ball, and deep enough so that the base of the trunk is just below the surface of the soil. Add a general purpose fertilizer to the base of the hole.*

2 *For container-grown or root-balled trees, insert a stake at a 45° angle and secure loosely with a tie. Spread the roots out well to enable the tree to get off to a good start. Make sure that the earth around the hole has been well dug and is friable.*

3 *Backfill the hole, and firm the tree in by treading down around the base carefully. Pull the stem gently to ensure it is firmly fixed. (Windrock will damage the tree and stunt its eventual growth). Water well and regularly.*

Hedging

Sometimes we need to plant trees for purely functional reasons, such as for screening or for hedging. Fast-growing, upright trees are useful for the former, and those with a dense, twiggy habit are ideal for the latter.

However, there is a temptation to plant fast-growing trees for these purposes, such as poplars for screening and Leyland cypress (x *Cupressocyparis leylandii*) for hedging. Both of these can rapidly become too large, shading you and your neighbours and robbing gardens of light, moisture and nutrients. It is therefore often better to be patient and stick to less aggressive, slower-growing alternatives. Hedges are often a useful backdrop against which borders and groups of containers can be displayed. Not only do they provide a visual context, they also give much-needed shelter from cold or damaging winds.

Yew (*Taxus baccata*), although slow growing, is ideal for this purpose as it forms a thick, impenetrable hedge that needs only infrequent clipping.

Private view

A hedge can form a useful backdrop for groups of containers as well as providing a secluded, sheltered area for seating.

Trees and shrubs for colour

Flowering trees are understandably popular, with flowering cherries and plums (*Prunus* spp.) among the most widely planted. Ornamental apples (*Malus* spp.) and rowans and whitebeams (*Sorbus* spp.) are well-loved, too, because they have a dual season; flowers in spring and coloured fruit in the autumn.

However, if you want to plant a flowering tree, why not plant a culinary one? An apple or cherry tree will produce fruit you can eat and flowers that are every bit as good as the purely ornamental varieties.

Autumn colour is a good basis on which to select trees; after all, at its best it can rival flowers for sheer impact. It is as well to remember, though, that good autumn colour largely depends on there being sharp frosts at the right time in autumn, so areas with mild climates rarely see a good show of colour.

Many of the best trees are large, but there are smaller ones, such as amelanchiers, and several shrubs, like *Euonymus alatus* and species of rhus. Remember, too, that it is worth having at least one tree for winter colour. A little witch-hazel (*Hamamelis mollis*), with its bright yellow flowers on bare, midwinter branches, or the winter-flowering cherry, *Prunus* x *subhirtella* 'Autumnalis', are a source of great joy in what would otherwise be a flowerless period.

Foliage colour

For dramatic colour in autumn, Japanese maples (Acer palmatum) are hard to beat, with their beautiful filigree leaves which turn a range of russet tones from scarlet to burnt orange.

Trees

A mixture of evergreen and deciduous trees provides the best framework for a garden. Even a small garden needs at least one small tree for vertical interest. The trees here include evergreens, deciduous trees and conifers. A few are magnificent large trees, appropriate only for large gardens. Most are medium or small trees that can be grown in an average sized-garden. Trees are a permanent feature of the landscape, so plant them sensibly. Do not site them near buildings, and consider their height when full grown, even though some may take years to mature. Take care when pruning, as poor cuts lead to disease. The pruning of large trees is best left to experts.

Acer pseudoplatanus **'Brilliantissimum'**

Aesculus x *neglecta* **'Erythroblastos'**

Amelanchier lamarckii

Betula utilis var. *jacquemontii*

ACER DAVIDII
H 10–15m (30–48ft) ★★★★
Useful, small deciduous tree, known as Snake-bark Maple, with whitish-striped, green to dull-red bark. Leaves oval, mid-green, yellow to orange-flushed in autumn. Grow in any reasonably moist soil, sheltered from strongest winds in sun or partial shade. *A. palmatum,* Japanese Maple, has rounded leaves with 5 to 9 pointed lobes turning bright red to orange or yellow in autumn. H 6–8m (18–24ft). Best in neutral to acid soil. The variety 'Dissectum' has finely cut leaf-lobes and a mound-forming habit, H 2m (6½ft). *A. pseudoplatanus* 'Brilliantissimum', has 5-lobed leaves, bright pink when young, turning yellow then green, H 6m (18ft).

AESCULUS x CARNEA 'BRIOTII'
H 10–20m (30–64ft) ★★★★
Known as Red Horse Chestnut, this handsome, round-headed, deciduous flowering tree has deep green leaves. Flowers dark red in panicles in early summer. Fruits globular, smooth to sparsely spiny. Grow in fairly fertile, moist soil in sun or partial shade. *A.* x *neglecta* 'Erythroblastos', Sunrise Horse Chestnut is a conical tree, the leaves unfolding cream and bright pink on red leaf-stalks, becoming yellow then green with age. Flowers are yellow, flushed with red.

AMELANCHIER LAMARCKII
H 6–10m (18–32ft) ★★★★
Attractive, small deciduous flowering tree, also called Shadbush or Snowy Mespilus, is suitable for the small garden. Leaves oval, often bronze-tinted when young, becoming green then turning red to orange in autumn. Flowers 5-petalled, white, freely produced in loose spikes in late spring followed by edible, sweet, juicy fruits ripening purple-black. Grow in moderately fertile, moist soil in sun or partial shade. 'Ballerina' H 6m (18ft) is a more spreading tree, the leaves broadly elliptic, emerging bronze-tinted but becoming green by mid-summer, turning red and purple in mid-autumn. Flowers in arching spikes in mid- to late spring.

BETULA PENDULA
H 18m (60ft) ★★★★
An elegant, deciduous, medium-sized tree, the Silver Birch is erect with pendulous branchlets and a trunk covered with peeling white bark. Its triangular, mid-green leaves turn yellow in autumn. Catkins before the leaves, yellowish to brownish yellow. Grow in fertile soil in sun or partial shade. 'Laciniata' (often labelled 'Dalecarlica' by nurseries), H 15-18m (48-60ft), differs in having deeply lobed and toothed leaves. *B. nigra,* Black or River Birch, has more spreading branches and red-brown, peeling bark.

Leaves are diamond-shaped, glossy above, deep green, yellow in autumn. *B. utilis* var. *jacquemontii,* Himalayan Birch, H 15-18m (48-60ft), has white, peeling bark and oval leaves. Catkins are yellow, and red-tinted.

CARAGANA ARBORESCENS
H 6m (20ft) ★★★★

Known as the Pea Tree, this deciduous, hardy, small tree makes a good windbreak. It has spiny branches, attractive light green leaves of up to l2 leaflets, and pale yellow, pea-like flowers in late spring. Prefers well-drained soil and full sun. 'Nana' is a dwarf form, H l.5m (5ft).

CARPINUS BETULUS
H 20–25m (64–80ft) ★★★★

A handsome, deciduous specimen tree, the Hornbeam is grown for its habit and foliage, but is only suitable for larger gardens. Broadly pyramidal when young, later rounded with a smooth, fluted bark. Leaves are mid-green turning yellow or orange-yellow in autumn. Yellowish male catkins in spring, female ones followed by pendent spikes of winged nutlets. Grow in moist garden soil in sun or partial shade. 'Fastigiata' ('Pyramidalis'), H 12-15m (38-48ft), erect and narrowly pyramidal when young, broadens with age.

CERCIDIPHYLLUM JAPONICUM
H 18–20m (60–64ft) ★★★★

Also known as Kadsura, this is an attractive, deciduous specimen tree for the larger garden, pyramidal when young, later broadening and becoming rounded. It is grown for its foliage. Oval to rounded leaves emerge bronze and mature to mid- to bluish green, turning yellow, orange and red in autumn, particularly on acid soil. Grow in reasonably moist, neutral to acid soil in sun or partial shade.

CERCIS SILIQUASTRUM
H 8–10m (24–30ft) ★★★★

The flowering Judas Tree is a beautiful, rounded to spreading, deciduous tree suitable for smaller gardens. Flowers pea-shaped, magenta to pink or white, in profuse clusters on bare stems before the leaves which are kidney-shaped to inversely heart-shaped, bronze when young, usually changing to yellow in autumn. Grow in any reasonably moist soil, sheltered from cold winds, in full sun. *C. canadensis,* Eastern Redbud, has heart-shaped, pointed leaves. Flowers purple or pink, occasionally white. 'Forest Pansy' has red-purple leaves.

CORNUS KOUSA
H 5–7m (15–21ft) ★★★★

Showy, deciduous, flowering tree suitable for smaller gardens. Broadly conical to rounded, erect when young, with flaking bark. Leaves oval, wavy-margined, usually turning crimson-purple in autumn. Flowers in greenish, button-like clusters surrounded by four, large, conspicuous white, petal-like bracts, followed by strawberry-like fleshy, red fruits. Grow in fertile, moist soil, ideally sheltered from cold winds, in sun or partial shade. The variety *chinensis* has leaves with flat margins and floral bracts which age pink. 'China Girl' is free-flowering when young.

CRATAEGUS LAEVIGATA (C. OXYACANTHA)
H 6–8m (18–24ft) ★★★★

Attractive, small- to medium-sized flowering and fruiting deciduous tree, also known as Midland Hawthorn, of erect to spreading habit. Leaves oval, mid-glossy green, bearing 3-5 broad lobes. Flowers 5-petalled, white to red in clusters in spring, followed by globular, red fruits. Grow in ordinary garden soil in sun or partial shade. 'Paul's Scarlet' or

Caragana arborescens

Craetaegus laevigata **'Paul's Scarlet'**

'Coccinea Plena', bears fully double, reddish-pink flowers. *C. persimilis* 'Prunifolia' (*C.* x *prunifolia*), H6–8m (18–24ft) is a thorny-stemmed, bushy-headed tree. Leaves glossy deep-green, often turning orange to red in the autumn. White flowers followed by rounded, bright red fruits.

DAVIDIA INVOLUCRATA
H 10–15m (30–48ft) ★★★★

An outstanding deciduous specimen tree for larger gardens, also known as the Dove, or Handkerchief Tree. Broadly pyramidal, spreading with age. Leaves heart-shaped, mid- to deep green above, downy beneath. Flowers tiny, petal-less in clusters enclosed by two large, unequal-sized creamy white pendent bracts, followed by green, plum-like fruits. Grow in fertile, moist soil, sheltered from cold winds in sun or partial shade. The variety *vilmoriniana* has smooth, paler green leaves.

Cercis siliquastrum

Flowers of *Davidia involucrata*

Eucalyptus gunnii

EUCALYPTUS GUNNII
H 15–25m (48–64ft) ★★

An evergreen specimen tree, also called Cider Gum, with attractive, flaking, whitish-green bark. Leaves are blue-white and rounded on young plants, lance-shaped and green with maturity. (If plants are cut back annually they become bushy and retain their juvenile leaves). Grow in any well-drained garden soil in full sun, sheltered from cold winds. *E. pauciflora* ssp. *niphophila* (*E.*

Gleditsia triacanthos **'Sunburst'**

Laurus nobilis

Magnolia **x** *soulangeana*

Prunus **'Taihaku'**

niphophila), the Snow Gum, H 6m (18ft), is a rather bushy, spreading tree with waxy-white twigs and peeling white to pale brown bark. The hardiest eucalpyt.

GLEDITSIA TRIACANTHOS **'SUNBURST'**
H 10–12m (30–38ft) ★★★★

Also called Golden Honeylocust, this is a fast-growing, deciduous tree, conical when young, spreading with age. It is grown for its striking, ferny and colourful foliage, the long yellow leaves divided into 15 to 25 narrow, oval leaflets. The greenish-white flowers are insignificant. Grow in reasonably moist garden soil in full sun.

LABURNUM ALPINUM
H 6m (18ft) ★★★★

A colourful, deciduous tree for the smaller garden, also called Scotch Laburnum. It has smooth bark and trifoliate leaves, which are rich green and glossy. The bright yellow, pea-shaped flowers hang in pendent chains in late spring, followed by beanlike seed pods which are poisonous if eaten. Grow in moist, well-drained soil, sheltered from strong winds in sun or partial shade. Remove suckers from the stem and base. *L. anagyroides* (*L. vulgare*), Common Laburnum, has a spreading habit and hairy shoots. The leaves, with dark green elliptic leaflets, are silky haired beneath. *L.*

x *watereri* 'Vossii', Golden Rain, is similiar but has chains of bright yellow flowers to 60cm (2ft) long.

LAURUS NOBILIS
H 12m (40ft) ★★

Commonly known as Sweet Bay, this evergreen is grown for its aromatic glossy, dark green leaves (which are used as a flavouring in cooking). It bears clusters of insignificant flowers in spring and female plants bear small black berries after flowering. It prefers full sun and partial shade, and some shelter from cold winds. 'Aurea' has golden foliage.

LIQUIDAMBAR STYRACIFLUA
H 20–25m (64–80ft) ★★★★

Known as Sweet Gum, this deciduous tree often has richly coloured autumn foliage. Broadly conical in habit, spreading with age, the young stems often have corky wings. Leaves rounded, cut into 5 to 7 glossy, mid-green, pointed lobes turning orange red and purple in autumn. Flowers inconspicuous, yellow-green in small globular clusters which ripen into spiky seed pods. Grow in moist, neutral to acid soils for best autumn colour, in full sun, sheltered from strongest winds.

MAGNOLIA **x** *SOULANGEANA*
H 6m (18ft) ★★★★

This Magnolia is a small specimen tree is grown for its large, showy, goblet-shaped, many-petalled flowers which vary from deep purplish-pink to white and which are borne with or before the leaves. Leaves oval, often somewhat broader near the tip, medium-green above, paler beneath. Grow in fertile, reasonably moist soil with shelter from strong, cold winds. 'Brozzoni' has pure white flowers. 'Lennei' bears dark purple-pink flowers. 'San José' has white flowers flushed deep pink. *M. kobus*, H 10–12m (30–38ft), is a

broadly conical, deciduous tree. Leaves oval, usually broader at the tip, often turning yellow in autumn. Flowers saucer-shaped, white, profusely borne on bare twigs in spring.

MALUS FLORIBUNDA
H 8–10m (24–30ft) ★★★★

This beautiful, small, flowering deciduous tree, also called Japanese Crab-apple, is for medium-sized gardens. Leaves oval, toothed. Flowers 5-petalled, pale pink from red buds in profuse clusters, in late spring followed by globular yellow fruits. Grow in ordinary garden soil in full sun. 'Golden Hornet' H 8–10m (24–30ft) is a rounded- to oval-headed tree with white flowers from pink buds in late spring followed by a profusion of ovoid, golden yellow fruits which often last through winter. 'Profusion' is a spreading tree with bronze-green leaves. Flowers are purplish-pink in late spring, followed by glossy reddish-purple fruits.

PRUNUS **(SYN.** *AMYGDALUS*)
H 5–10m (15–40ft) ★★★★

Also known as Ornamental Cherry, there are more than 200 species in this genus of deciduous or evergreen, small garden trees. They are highly decorative with clusters of white or pink flowers in spring; there are single, semi-double and double forms. Certain species are grown for their edible fruits (plums, almonds and peaches among them). Among the popular ornamental hybrids, grown for their spring blossom, are 'Kanzan', H 10m (30ft), with double, deep-pink, large flowers, and 'Taihaku', H 8m (25ft), with large, bowl shaped, single white flowers.

ROBINIA PSEUDOACACIA **'FRISIA'**
H 15m (48ft) ★★★★

Also known as False Acacia, this is a popular, goldenfoliaged, deciduous tree of elegant habit. The leaves age to yellow-green, turning orange-yellow in autumn. Insignificant flowers in summer. Grow in moist, well-drained soil in full sun.

SORBUS AUCUPARIA
H 10–15m (32–48ft) ★★★★
Deciduous small tree, also called Mountain Ash, of broadly conical to rounded habit. Leaves dark green, composed of several oblong to lance-shaped, toothed leaflets turning yellow or red in autumn. Flattened heads of small white flowers in late spring, followed by orange-red berries. Grow in well-drained soil in sun or partial shade. 'Aspleniifolia' has deep, dissected leaflets. 'Fastigiata' has a conical to columnar habit. *S. aria*, Whitebeam, is broadly columnar to rounded in habit with oval, leaves dark green above and downy white below. 'Lutescens' has narrower, grey-green leaves.

TAMARIX RAMOSISSIMA
H 5m (15ft) ★★★★
Also known as Tamarisk, this deciduous small tree does well in coastal areas. It is grown for its graceful feathery foliage and plumes of 5-petalled pink flowers in late summer and early autumn. Grow in well-drained soil in full sun. Prune hard after planting for a more shrub-like form. *T. tetrandra* has 4-petalled pale pink flowers.

Conifers

ABIES KOREANA
H 8–10m (24–30ft) ★★★★
Also known as Korean Fir, this striking conical conifer has glossy, deep green needle-like leaves which are silver beneath. The erect, cylindrical violet-blue cones are produced on the upper branches, often on young trees. Grow in moist, well-drained, ideally neutral to acid soil, in full sun.

CHAMAECYPARIS LAWSONIANA
H 15–25m (48–80ft) ★★★★
One of the best-known conifers, also called Lawson Cypress, of columnar habit composed of minute, bright green, scale leaves in flattened sprays. The tiny male cones are crimson in spring. Grow in moist, well-drained soil in sun or light shade. 'Chilworth Silver' is slow-growing, with awl-shaped, blue-green leaves. 'Pembury Blue' is conical with sprays of blue-grey leaves. 'Ellwoodii' is dense and conical with blue-grey young leaves. 'Winston Churchill' is narrowly conical with golden foliage. *C. obtusa* Hinoki Cypress, shorter and slower-growing, has deep green leaves, white banded beneath.

CRYPTOMERIA JAPONICA
H 15–25m (48–80ft) ★★★
Also called Japanese Cedar, this handsome, large specimen tree of conical to columnar habit has mid- to deep green, awl-shaped leaves and small, prickly cones. Grow in fertile, moist but well-drained, humus-rich soil in sun or partial shade. 'Bandai-sugi' H 2m (6½ft), forms an irregularly rounded shrub with dense foliage turning bronze in winter. 'Elegans', H 6–10m (18–30ft), has a dense, conical habit, with bluish-green foliage turning bronze to reddish-brown in winter.

PICEA PUNGENS
H 15m (48ft) ★★★★
Also known as Colorado Spruce, this small, broadly columnar tree has upward-pointing orange-brown shoots covered in glaucous bluish-grey, sharply pointed leaves, arranged radially, and cylindrical long cones. It prefers a slightly acid soil and full sun. Other varieties include those with bluish-white and silvery blue foliage, and there are also dwarf forms, like 'Mrs Cesarini' which is only 2m (6½ft) tall.

Robinia pseudoacacia 'Frisia'

Tamarix tetranda

Chamaecyparis lawsoniana

Picea pungens 'Koster'

Using shrubs

For many gardeners, shrubs are the most important part of the garden. Quite apart from whatever intrinsic beauty of flower or foliage they may have, they create a sense of fullness, smoothing the rough edges of corners and walls and making the garden feel occupied. They enable the gardener to 'sculpt space', so that particular views through the garden can be shut off.

It is important to choose shrubs with different forms of growth, to give a variety of shapes. Some form neat, low mounds (such as *Skimmia japonica*), while others have a tall arching habit (like many of the buddlejas). Many of the evergreen shrubs can be clipped (below) into predetermined shapes, or trained to form standards, bushing out at the top of a slender stem.

Using shrub forms
Different forms of shrub have been used to create a change of pace where two compartments of the garden join.

Size and scale

The majority of shrubs can become quite substantial in time. Many small gardens become thickets as shrubs grow and get tangled up in each other. Since they take many years to reach their full size, there is also a tendency to plant too many together. It is vital to find out the eventual sizes of any shrubs you are considering planting, and plan accordingly. Large gaps between young shrubs can be filled with perennials, to be gradually displaced as the shrubs grow. One reason for the popularity of shrubs is their supposed low maintenance. This is true, if you have space to let them grow and grow. But if you have a small garden and several vigorous shrub species you may end up spending a lot of time pruning. Those with small gardens should look at using dwarf shrubs and perennials more extensively.

Shrubs in variety
This garden shows how varied shrubs can be in form, size and colour. Dogwoods (cornus), elaeagnus and viburnum grow to different sizes, in different forms, to add interest, even without flower colour.

Improving shape

Although shrubs are principally bought for their foliage form or flower colour or shape, their habit or form is important, too. Certain shrubs, many of them evergreen, have a naturally interesting form. *Viburnum davidii*, for example, makes a neat mound shape, as does *Skimmia japonica*. Others are notable for their arching shape, like *Buddleja alternifolia* or *Forsythia suspensa*.

However, most popular shrubs have an informal, rather amorphous, shape, yet this is easily overcome by clipping. Many gardeners train shrubs as standards, or clip them into shapes, so that they can be made part of a classically formal garden. Their primary appeal is sculptural and architectural rather than floral.

Historically, certain species have been used extensively for this, such as box (*Buxus sempervirens*). Yet most species can be clipped or trained, the only drawback being that such shaping reduces flowering.

Formal shapes
Many evergreen shrubs can be clipped to create formal shapes, as this little parterre with its clipped box demonstrates.

Using shrubs for colour

It is for their flowers that most shrubs are grown, which allows you to have something blooming at most times of the year.

Start in late winter with the brilliant yellow of forsythia, progress through spring with viburnums and camellias, through early summer with rhododendrons and ceanothus and end with roses, many of which flower until autumn. Apart from roses, though, there are few shrubs that flower in summer, which is something to bear in mind when planning. Indeed, many shrubs with beautiful flowers look dull after flowering, thus limiting their use in smaller gardens.

Autumn, again, sees certain shrubs come into their own. Many species bear brightly coloured berries; pyracanthas are notably dramatic with clusters of golden-yellow berries throughout winter. Some have good texture, too, such as amelanchiers and deciduous *Euonymus* varieties. Evergreen shrubs are very valuable for their attractive foliage and golden variegated plants, such as varieties of *elaeagnus* or the evergreen *euonymus*, remind us in winter of summer sunshine.

Those with coloured foliage can be a great asset in colour-schemed borders, their long season enhancing the look of any flowers. For example, yellow leaves go well with blue and purple flowers, and silver foliage sets

Colourful foliage
Shrubs like euonymus, holly (ilex) and elaeagnus are evergreens with the bonus of interesting coloured foliage. Species with variegated leaves, such as Euonymus 'Emerald 'n' Gold' are worth looking out for.

off pink flowers. Varieties with silver, grey or white variegated foliage provide flashes of light in the garden, especially against a dark evergreen backdrop. You will add to the variety and interest of the garden if you consider these various different attributes when choosing which shrubs. Ideally, a good mixture of leaf forms and colours should be chosen, as well as varying habits and sizes.

Dwarfs and heathers

Dwarf, often ground-hugging, shrubs are characteristic of harsh environments. Think of aromatic-leaved lavenders and herbs of Mediterranean climates, or the heathers (*Calluna* and *Erica* spp.) of windswept moorlands. These plants are obviously useful in gardens in such areas, but as they are so versatile, they can be used in any unshaded garden where low-maintenance ground cover is needed.

The vast majority of these low-growing shrubs are evergreen, often with attractive foliage, making them very useful garden plants indeed. Those from drought-prone habitats tend to be grey or

Heather beds
For gardens with acid soil, heather beds are a good source of colour and, since they cover the ground well with very little maintenance, are an excellent solution for large gardens.

silver, those from cooler areas green, although many of the latter have golden-leaved varieties. Among good small shrubs for dry gardens are hebes, lavenders and santolinas, all with a mound-forming habit and tough, small leaves. For example, they can be used to create a low edging to a path, softening its harder outlines.

Acid soils
Another difficult environment for many plants is any area that has infertile, acid soil, where very few herbaceous perennials grow well, leaving certain distinctive, shrubby plants as the dominant vegetation. Chief amongst these are rhododendrons and azaleas. They make so-called 'problem soil' into something of an asset, as they are surely the most varied and striking group of garden shrubs.

Rhododendron yakushimanum

Large shrubs

Buddleja alternifolia

Buddleja globosa

Camellia japonica
'Debutante'

Cotinus coggygria

Choisya ternata

Elaeagnus commutata

AUCUBA JAPONICA
H 3m (10ft) or more ★★★

Useful, very shade-tolerant, rounded, evergreen shrub with large, oval, glossy, mid- to deep green leaves. Insignificant male and female flowers are borne on separate plants and both are needed to produce the glossy red berries. Grow in moist, well-drained soil. Propagate by semi-hardwood cuttings in late summer or by seed sown in a cold frame when ripe. 'Crassifolia', male, has large, deep green leaves. 'Salicifolia', female, has narrow, rich green leaves. 'Gold Dust', female, has leaves dusted with golden yellow.

BUDDLEJA DAVIDII
H 3–5m (10–15ft) ★★★★

Also known as Butterfly Bush, this popular deciduous shrub has arching stems and slender, lance-shaped, grey-green leaves. Long spikes of small, fragrant, lilac flowers are borne in succession from summer to autumn. Grow in ordinary soil in full sun. Cut back hard in late winter. Propagate by semi-hardwood cuttings in late summer or hardwood cuttings in autumn. 'Black Knight' is dark purple-blue; 'White Profusion' has white flowers with yellow eyes in panicles. *B. globosa*, Orange Ball Tree, has clusters of orange to yellow flowers. *B. alternifolia* bears dense, rounded clusters of intensely fragrant lilac flowers.

CAMELLIA JAPONICA
H 3m (15ft) or more ★★★

Beautiful, erect to spreading, usually rounded evergreen shrub, with very glossy, deep green, leathery leaves. Large, single to double rose-like flowers in shades of pink, red and white from early to late spring. Grow in partial shade in humus-rich, neutral to acid soil in a sheltered site. Propagate by semi-hardwood or leaf-bud cuttings in a frame from late summer to winter. Single, semi and fully-double cultivars are available in many shades including bicolours.

CHIMONANTHUS PRAECOX
H 2.5–4m (8–12ft) ★★★

Also called Wintersweet, this is a delightful, strong-growing, erect to spreading deciduous shrub with slender pointed, lance-shaped, mid-green leaves. Sweetly fragrant, sulphur-yellow, brownish-purple centred, bell-shaped flowers wreathe the bare branches in late winter. Grow in fertile, well-drained soil in sun or partial shade, in a sheltered site. Propagate by softwood cuttings in a frame in summer or seed sown in a cold frame when ripe. 'Grandiflorus' has larger, richer yellow flowers. var. *luteus* is clear yellow.

CHOISYA TERNATA
H 2–2.5m (6½–8ft) ★★★

Charming, bushy, rounded evergreen shrub, also known as Mexican Orange Blossom, thickly set with glossy, deep green, rounded leaves divided into three oval leaflets. From late spring to late summer it bears terminal clusters of pure white, 5-petalled, fragrant flowers. Grow in well-drained soil, in sun, in a site sheltered from freezing winds. Propagate by semi-hardwood cuttings in summer. 'Sundance' has bright yellow foliage, particularly when young.

COTINUS COGGYGRIA
H 3–5m (10–15ft) ★★★★

Also known as Smoke Bush, this bushy, erect, deciduous shrub has mid-green, oval leaves that turn orange or red in autumn. Insignificant flowers give way to smoke-like clusters of downy filaments and seeds. Grow in any fairly fertile, well-drained soil in a sunny site. Propagate by softwood cuttings in summer or by layering in late winter. 'Royal Purple' has dark purple foliage, turning red in autumn.

ELAEAGNUS COMMUTATA
H 4m (12ft) ★★★★

Also known as Silver Berry, this hardy, evergreen shrub is useful for hedging and bears very fragrant, tiny flowers in autumn, followed by silvery red fruit. It has small downy mid-green leaves. Does well in sun or partial shade, and will cope with salt spray and dry soil, but not lime. Propagate from semi-ripe cuttings in summer.

HIBISCUS SYRIACUS
H 2–3m (6½–10ft) ★★★★

Ornamental, erect, deciduous shrub with oval leaves, usually shallowly to deeply three-lobed, coarsely toothed and mid- to deep green. Large, funnel-shaped, pink flowers open in succession from late summer to autumn. Grow in fertile, moist, well-drained soil in full sun. Propagate by semi-hardwood cuttings in a frame in summer or by layering in late winter. Colour forms occur in shades of blue, purple, pink and white.

KOLKWITZIA AMABILIS
H 2.5–3m (8–10ft) ★★★★
Also known as Beauty Bush, this lovely, erect then spreading, deciduous shrub has arching stems and broadly oval, slender pointed mid- to deep green leaves. The shoots are wreathed with clusters of bell-shaped, pale to deep pink flowers with yellow-flushed throats from late spring to early summer. Grow in fertile, moist, but well-drained soil in full sun. Propagate by semi-hardwood cuttings in summer.

MAGNOLIA STELLATA
H 2–3m (6½–10ft) ★★★★
Delightful, compact, spreading, deciduous shrub with oblong to narrowly paddle-shaped mid-green leaves. The silky-white buds open to pure white, star-shaped flowers before the leaves in early- to mid-spring. Grow in sun or partial shade in fertile, moist, but well-drained soil, ideally neutral to acid. 'Royal Star' has pink buds. 'Rubra' has flowers opening red.

OSMANTHUS HETEROPHYLLUS
H 2.5–4m (8–15ft) ★★★
Intriguing, holly-like evergreen shrub of dense, rounded habit with oval to elliptic, spine-toothed, leathery, deep green leaves. Small, tubular, fragrant white flowers open in small clusters from late summer to autumn, followed by blue-black berries. Grow in fertile, moist but well-drained soil in sun or partial shade. Propagate by semi-hardwood cuttings in summer or layering in autumn or winter. 'Aureomarginatus' has yellow margined leaves.

PHILADELPHUS CORONARIUS
H 2–2.5m (6½–8ft) ★★★★
Also known as Mock Orange, this is an appealing, rounded, deciduous, hardy shrub with somewhat arching stems and narrow, pointed, mid-green leaves. Small clusters of fairly large, fragrant, white bowl-shaped flowers in early summer. Grow in well-drained soil in sun or partial shade. Propagate by softwood cuttings in summer or hardwood cuttings in autumn. P.c. 'Aureus' has golden leaves, 'Variegatus' has leaves with white markings.

PYRACANTHA
H 2.5–3m (8–10ft) ★★★
This showy, erect, evergreen, hardy shrub has red-flushed young stems and broadly elliptic, glossy deep green leaves. In summer, a profusion of small white flowers is followed by masses of golden-yellow berries which can last all winter. Grow in fertile garden soil in sun. Propagate by semi-hardwood cuttings in late summer. 'Orange Glow' has orange-red berries. 'Mohave' has red berries. 'Mohave Silver' has white-variegated leaves.

SYRINGA VULGARIS
H 3–3.5m (10–11ft) ★★★★
Deservedly popular, often tree-like, hardy, deciduous shrub also known as Lilac. It bears mid- to bright green, smooth, heart-shaped leaves. Tubular, 4-petalled, very fragrant lilac flowers are produced in dense, conical clusters in late spring and early summer. Grow in moist but well-drained soil in sun or partial shade. Propagate by softwood cuttings in summer or by layering in autumn or winter. Many cultivars are available, some with larger flowers, others double, in shades of lilac, purple, white to creamy yellow and near red.

VIBURNUM TINUS
H 2–3m (6½–10ft) ★★★
Also known as Laurustinus, this hardy, winter-flowering shrub of bushy, rounded habit is thickly set with oblong to narrowly oval, deep green leaves. The small, somewhat starry, 5-petalled flowers are gathered into rounded, dense, flattened clusters, which open between late winter and spring. These may be followed by deep blue berry-like fruits. Grow in well-drained garden soil in sun or partial shade. Propagate by semi-hardwood cuttings in summer or by layering in winter. V. x burkwoodii is semi-evergreen with larger, fragrant, white flowers, often from pink buds, and has a looser habit. V. x bodnantense is an erect, robust, deciduous shrub with pendent clusters of longer, tubular, pink to white fragrant flowers.

Hibiscus syriacus 'Oiseau Bleu'

Kolkwitzia amabilis

Philadelphus coronarius 'Aureus'

Syringa vulgaris 'Vestale'

Viburnum x burkwoodii

Medium shrubs

Buxus sempervirens

Ceanothus thyrsiflorus **var.** *repens*

Chaenomeles **x** *superba*

Cornus alba 'Elegantissima'

BUXUS SEMPERVIRENS
H 5m (15ft) ★★★★

Also known as Box, this hardy, evergreen shrub has a bushy habit. The small, glossy dark green leaves are densely packed, making it ideal for topiary. It is also slow-growing. It prefers partial shade and fertile soil. Propagate from semi-ripe cuttings in summer. Some varieties have larger leaves, such as 'Handsworthiensis' which is good for hedging. 'Marginata' (syn. 'Aurea Marginata') has golden-margined leaves.

CEANOTHUS 'GLOIRE DE VERSAILLES'
H 1.5–2m (5–6½ft) ★★

This charming, deciduous shrub has finely toothed, mid- to deep green leaves and large trusses of tiny, 5-petalled, pale blue flowers from midsummer to autumn. Grow in fertile, well-drained garden soil in a sunny position. Propagate by semi-hardwood cuttings in late summer. *C.thyrsiflorus* var. *repens* is low and spreading.

CHAENOMELES X SUPERBA
H 1.5–2m (5–6½ft) ★★★★

Also called Flowering Quince, this is an attractive, bushy, rather rounded, deciduous shrub with spiny, wiry stems and oval, mid-green, glossy leaves. Cup-shaped, pink to red flowers appear on bare stems in spring, sometimes continuing into summer. Grow in fairly fertile, ideally neutral to acid, well-drained soil. It prefers a position in full sun. Propagate by semi-hardwood cuttings in a frame in late summer or layering in autumn. 'Crimson and Gold' has a compact habit and rich red flowers with golden stamens. 'Pink Lady' has early, deep pink flowers.

CORNUS ALBA
H 2m (6½ft) or more ★★★★

A very valuable, strong growing, erect, deciduous shrub, also known as Red-barked Dogwood, with red winter stems and smooth, elliptic to oval dark green leaves which may turn red or orange in autumn. The small white, starry flowers are carried in dense, flattish clusters from late spring to early summer. They are followed by white, sometimes blue-tinted berries. Grow in moist garden soil in sun or partial shade. Propagate by hardwood cuttings in autumn or semi-hardwood cuttings in summer. 'Elegantissima' has grey-green leaves which are variegated with white.

DEUTZIA 'MONT ROSE'
H 1.5m (5ft) or more ★★★★

This delightful, bushy, erect, deciduous shrub has narrowly oval, pointed, deep green leaves and attractive star-shaped, rose-pink flowers that appear in early summer. Grow in ordinary, well-drained soil in sun or partial shade. Propagate by hardwood cuttings in autumn. *D. scabra* has stems with peeling, brown bark and spikes of white or pink-tinted flowers in early to mid-summer. *D. s.* 'Candidissima' has double white flowers and 'Pride of Rochester' has double, pink-tinted flowers.

ESCALLONIA 'DONARD SEEDLING'
H 2m (6½ft) or more ★★★

This pretty, evergreen shrub has arching stems and narrow to spoon-shaped, glossy, toothed, rich green leaves. In summer, stems are wreathed with clusters of little, tubular, white, pink-tinted flowers opening from pink buds. Grow in fertile, well-drained soil in sun or partial shade. Propagate by semi-hardwood cuttings in a frame in late summer. 'Donard Radiance' is more compact with slightly larger, rich pink flowers.

EUONYMUS ALATUS
H 1.5–2m (5–6½ft) ★★★★

Interesting, bushy, spreading deciduous shrub, with mid- to deep green leaves that usually turn brilliant red in autumn. Insignificant greenish flowers give way to spherical, purplish-red fruits which split open to reveal bright orange seeds. Grow in moist, well-drained, preferably acid soil in either sun or partial shade. Propagate by semi-hardwood cuttings in summer.

EXOCHORDA X MACRANTHA
H 1.5–2m (5–6½ft) ★★★★

This beautiful, hummock-forming, dense, deciduous shrub has lots of spoon-shaped, light- to mid-green leaves. From late spring to early summer it is smothered with spikes of white flowers. Grow in fertile, moist but well-drained soil in full sun. Propagate by softwood cuttings in a frame in summer. *E. racemosa* bears slightly larger pure white flowers.

FORSYTHIA X INTERMEDIA
H 2m (6½ft) or more ★★★★

Showy, erect, bushy, deciduous shrub with oval to lance-shaped, sharp toothed mid-green leaves, occasionally with two basal lobes. From late winter to mid-spring bright

Exochorda racemosa

yellow, bell-shaped flowers appear on leafless stems. Grow in ordinary soil in sun or partial shade. Propagate by semi-hardwood cuttings in a frame in late summer.

HYDRANGEA MACROPHYLLA
H 1.5–2m (5–6½ft) ★★★★

Popular, rounded, deciduous shrub with robust, erect stems and large, broadly oval, toothed, glossy, rich-green leaves. From mid- to late summer, clusters of tiny, star-shaped blue, pink or white flowers are surrounded by a ring of larger, sterile ones: these are the Lace-caps. Grow in fertile, well-drained but moist soil in sun or partial shade. Propagate by softwood cuttings in early summer or semi-hardwood cuttings in late summer. Best-known Lace-cap is 'Mariesii Perfecta' (syn. 'Blue Wave') with rich blue or mauve flowers. Among the Hortensias (mop-head) are 'Deutschland' with large mauve heads, 'Europa' purple-blue and 'Madame Emile Mouillière' with white flowerheads which become pink-tinted with age.

MAHONIA JAPONICA
H 2m (6½ft) ★★★

Erect, evergreen, fragrant shrub with dark green, leathery leaves. From autumn to spring, small, pale yellow, bell-shaped flowers are produced in arching chains, often followed by purple-blue, white-bloomed berries. Grow in moist but well-drained, fertile soil in partial shade. Propagate by semi-hardwood or leaf-bud cuttings from late summer to autumn in a frame. *M. x media* 'Charity' is taller and more robust with richer yellow, denser flower spikes.

PIERIS JAPONICA
H 2m (6½ft) ★★★★

Striking, rounded, dense evergreen shrub, also known as Firecrest, with elliptic to narrow, spoon-shaped, toothed, leathery, mid-green leaves which are bright red when young. From late winter to spring, clusters of small, white, bell flowers appear. Grow in humus-rich, moist, acid soil in partial shade. Propagate by semi-hardwood cuttings in late summer.

RIBES SANGUINEUM
H 2–3m (6½–10ft) or more ★★★★

Popular, erect, deciduous shrub, also called Flowering Currant, with rounded, 3 to 5-lobed, toothed, curiously aromatic mid- to deep green leaves. In early spring tubular, 5-petalled, reddish-pink flowers are borne in dense, arching clusters. Grow in ordinary soil in sun or partial shade. Propagate by hardwood cuttings in autumn. 'Pulborough Scarlet' has rich red, white-centred flowers. 'Tydeman's White' has pure white flowers. 'Brocklebankii' is smaller and slower-growing with golden-green leaves.

SKIMMIA JAPONICA
H 1–2m (3–6½ft) or more ★★★

Attractive, rounded to hummock-forming, evergreen shrub with oval, slightly aromatic mid- to deep green leaves. The small, star-shaped, often fragrant, white flowers are carried in dense, terminal clusters from mid- to late spring. Male and female flowers are carried on separate plants. If both are grown together, the female plant will produce a crop of long-lasting bright-red berries. Grow in fertile, ideally humus-rich soil in partial shade. Propagate by semi-hardwood cuttings in late summer or by seed sown when ripe in a cold frame.

SPIRAEA 'ARGUTA'
H 2m (6½ft) ★★★

Also known as Bridal Wreath, this pretty, rounded, freely-branching, deciduous shrub has slim stems which tend to arch at the tips and are clad with lance-shaped to narrowly oblong, bright green leaves. The small, pure white, 5-petalled flowers are carried in flattened clusters in spring. Grow in well-drained soil in a sunny or partially shaded site. Propagate by semi-hardwood cuttings in summer or hardwood cuttings in autumn.

WEIGELA FLORIDA
H 2m (6½ft) ★★★★

This attractive, spreading, deciduous shrub has arching shoots and oval, toothed, mid-green leaves. The funnel-shaped flowers are pink and freely borne in clusters from late spring through until early summer. Grow in fertile garden soil in sun or partial shade. Propagate by semi-hardwood cuttings in late summer or by hardwood cuttings in autumn. There are many hybrid cultivars available which have larger flowers and leaves.

Hydrangea macrophylla

Mahonia x media 'Charity'

Skimmia japonica 'Tansley Gem'

Ribes sanguineum

Weigela 'Florida Variegata'

Small shrubs

Daphne mezereum

Euonymus fortunei 'Silver Queen'

Fuchsia magellanica

Genista hispanica 'Compacta'

BERBERIS CANDIDULA
H 60cm (2ft) ★★★★

Attractive, evergreen, densely hummock-forming shrub with oval, spine-tipped, glossy green leaves, waxy-white beneath. Bright yellow, bowl-shaped flowers open in late spring, followed by oval purple fruit. Grow in ordinary soil in sun or light shade. Propagate by suckers in winter. *B. wilsoniae* is mound-forming to 1m (3ft), semi-evergreen with small, spoon-shaped leaves and pale yellow flowers in summer followed by globular, pink fruits.

BUXUS SEMPERVIRENS 'SUFFRUTICOSA'
H 1.5m (5ft) ★★★★

This small, hardy evergreen variety of box is one of the best for low hedging, being dense, compact and slow-growing. The glossy green leaves are notched at the tips. Flowers are insignificant. Grow in fertile soil, ideally in partial shade as hot sun may scorch its leaves. Propagate from semi-ripe cuttings in summer. Many other varieties with yellow or variegated leaves are available.

CALLUNA VULGARIS
H 30–90cm (1–3ft) ★★★★

Popular, bushy, evergreen shrub, also known as Heather, with mid-to deep green, minute, sometimes hairy, scale-leaves and spikes of small bell-flowers in shades of pink, purple, red and white. Grow in moist but well-drained, acid soil in full sun. Propagate by semi-ripe cuttings in late summer in a cold frame or by layering in late winter. Hundreds of cultivars are available in many colours.

CISTUS SALVIIFOLIUS
H 60–75cm (24–28in) ★★★

Also known as Sun Rose, this attractive, dense, rounded evergreen shrub bears a profusion of white flowers with yellow centres that resemble species roses, in summer. The oval, deep green leaves are boldly veined. Hardy in all but the severerest of winters. Grow in well-drained soil in full sun. Propagate by semi-hardwood or softwood cuttings in summer.

COTONEASTER HORIZONTALIS
H 60–90cm (2–3ft) ★★★★

Intriguing, deciduous shrub with a neat herringbone branch formation and low arching habit. Stems are covered with small, rounded, glossy, deep green leaves usually turning red in autumn. Pinkish-white flowers in late spring are followed by bright red berries. Grow in ordinary soil in either sun or partial shade. Propagate by seed sown when ripe in a cold frame or by semi-ripe cuttings in late summer. *C. microphyllus* is more hummock-forming with narrower, glossy, evergreen leaves and larger, pinker fruits.

DAPHNE MEZEREUM
H 90–120cm (3–4ft) ★★★★

Showy, erect, deciduous shrub, also known as Mezereon, which in late winter and early spring becomes thickly wreathed with many, small, tubular, 4-petalled, pink to rose-purple fragrant flowers. They are followed by bright red, inedible berries. The lance-shaped to narrow spoon-shaped leaves are pale to greyish-green. Grow in fertile, well-drained, ideally limy soil in sun or partial shade. Propagate by seed sown as soon as ripe in a cold frame. 'Bowles' Variety' and f. *alba* varieties both have white flowers.

ERICA CARNEA
H 15–20cm (6–8in) ★★★★

Also known as Winter Heath, this is an invaluable, mat-forming, evergreen shrub smothered in winter and spring with short spikes of tiny, narrow bell-flowers in shades of pink to purple or white. The densely-borne leaves are deep green and needle-shaped. It prefers sun or light shade and a moist but well-drained, ideally neutral soil (though some lime is tolerated). Propagate by layering in winter or semi-hardwood cuttings in late summer. Many cultivars are available in many shades, some with the young foliage tinted yellow, bronze or red. *E. cinerea*, Bell Heather, is somewhat taller with broader bell-shaped flowers in summer, on some cultivars ranging to magenta and almost red. Some also have golden foliage. Requires neutral to acid soil to thrive.

EUONYMUS FORTUNEI
H 30–120cm (1–4ft) ★★★★

Hummock-forming evergreen shrub grown for its glossy, green leaves. The oval, toothed, glossy leaves are deep green and insignificant flowers give way to whitish globular fruits which burst to show orange seeds. Grow in ordinary soil in full sun. Propagate by semi-hardwood cuttings in late summer in a frame. 'Emerald 'n' Gold' has leaves with a broad, bright yellow margin. 'Silver Queen' is more erect in habit with white-margined leaves.

FUCHSIA MAGELLANICA
H 1–1.5m (3–5ft) ★★★
Attractive, erect, deciduous shrub producing many pendent flowers in shades of red and purple in summer. The oval, toothed leaves are mid- to deep green. Grow in ordinary garden soil in sun or partial shade. Prune hard annually in early spring. Propagate by softwood cuttings in summer in a frame. 'Tom Thumb' is a normally small hybrid which rarely exceeds 30cm (1ft). 'Riccartonii' is a hardier hybrid with somewhat more rounded flowers. There is a large number of cultivars in a variety of colours and forms, chiefly of hybrid origin.

GENISTA LYDIA
H 45–60cm (1½–2ft) ★★★
Also known as Lydian Broom, this bright, cheerful, domed deciduous shrub has numerous slender arching branches and very narrow blue-green leaves which are soon shed. In early summer it is smothered with clusters of small, bright yellow, pea-shaped flowers. Grow in a sunny position in well-drained, ideally limy soil. Propagate by semi-ripe cuttings in summer in a frame. *G. hispanica,* Spanish Gorse, is more rounded and denser in habit to 75cm (2½ft) tall with prickly foliage and equally profuse darker yellow flowers.

HEBE ALBICANS
H 45–60cm (1½–2ft) ★★★
Neat, rounded, dense evergreen shrub, thickly set with firm, oval, grey leaves. The small, tubular, 4-petalled white flowers are carried in dense, terminal spikes in summer. Grow in ordinary soil in sun or partial shade.

Propagate by cuttings in late summer in a cold frame. *H. pinguifolia* 'Pagei' is mat-forming, rarely above 15cm (6in) high with bright blue-grey leaves and white flowers in late spring.

HELIANTHEMUM NUMMULARIUM
H 10–15cm (4–6in) ★★★★
Also named Rock Rose, this showy, mat forming, evergreen shrub is closely set with small, elliptic, deep-green leaves. The flat, 5-petalled, freely produced, summer borne flowers are bright yellow with an orange eye. Grow in well-drained, ideally limy soil in a sunny position. Propagate by softwood cuttings in summer in a frame. The best known cultivars are of hybrid origin with a larger growth habit. The bigger flowers come in a range of colours from white to red and leaves which can also be grey or grey-green. The 'Ben' series of cultivars is recommended.

LAVANDULA ANGUSTIFOLIA
H 60–90cm (2–3ft) ★★★★
Much loved, compact, bushy shrub, also known as lavender, thickly set with small, strap-shaped, aromatic grey-green leaves. The dense spikes of small, tubular, purple flowers are borne on slender stems above the leaves. Grow in ordinary, ideally limy garden soil in full sun. Propagate by semi-hardwood cuttings in late summer in a frame or hardwood cuttings in the open garden. 'Hidcote' is more compact with greyer leaves and deeper flowers.

POTENTILLA FRUTICOSA
H 75–90cm (2½–3ft) ★★★★
Ornamental, rounded, bushy, deciduous shrub, also known as Shrubby Cinquefoil, with small, fingered deep green leaves. The 5-petalled flowers look like tiny wild roses and appear from late spring to autumn. Grow ideally in limy garden soil in sun or partial

Helianthemum 'Ben Heckla'

Lavandula angustifolia **'Hidcote'**

Potentilla fruticosa 'Primrose Beauty'

Santolina chamaecyparissus

shade. Propagate by semi-hardwood cuttings in summer or by seed sown in a cold frame when ripe. Many cultivars are available (some taller than 1.5m/5ft) with green to grey foliage and flowers primarily in shades of yellow, plus white, pink, orange and red.

RHODODENDRON WILLIAMSIANUM
H 90–150cm (3–5ft) ★★★
Beautiful, domed evergreen shrub with broadly oval to rounded, glossy rich green leaves which are grey beneath when mature. Rather large, bell-shaped flowers in shades of pink appear in late spring. Grow in humus-rich, acid soil in sun or partial shade. Propagate by semi-hardwood cuttings in a cold frame in late

summer. *R. impeditum* rarely exceeds 60cm (2ft) with much smaller, aromatic grey-green leaves and smaller, funnel-shaped lavender-blue flowers in mid to late spring.

SANTOLINA CHAMAECYPARISSUS (S. INCANA)
H 45–60cm (1–2ft) ★★★
Useful, rounded, evergreen shrub primarily grown for its densely borne, finely dissected grey-white leaves. In summer, bright yellow, button-shaped flowerheads are borne singly on slender stems above the foliage. Grow in well-drained soil in full sun. Propagate by semi-ripe cuttings in a frame in summer. 'Lemon Queen' has lemon-yellow flowerheads. 'Weston', H 15–20cm (6-8in) is dwarf and rarely flowers.

Roses

Favourites for several hundred years, today roses have never been more popular. Originally, only wild species were available, with single, five-petalled, usually fragrant flowers. Once attention had switched to the double-bloomed forms that occurred occasionally as natural mutations, man then took the lead with purposeful cross-breeding and selection which continues unabated today. Over the years many thousands of different roses have arisen, at least 2,000 of which are at present available.

Roses vary greatly in habit, from tall, thorny clinbers to miniature thornless bushes. The leaves are formed of several, oval, mid-green leaflets and the flowers range in size from 2.5–13cm (1–5in) across, usually semi- or fully double, in shades of pink, red, purple, yellow and white. All are hardy and like fertile, moist, well-drained soil in a sunny site, although some are shade-tolerant. Most roses need hard pruning after flowering or in early spring, or, in the case of climbers and ramblers, thinning out in autumn.

Rosa 'Maigold'

Rosa 'Alberic Barbier'

Rosa 'Peace'

Rosa 'Fragrant Cloud'

Rosa 'Iceberg'

CLIMBING
H 3–10m (10–30ft)

Generally vigorous, erect roses which extend almost indefinitely, though more slowly when older. The taller ones are best cascading from a redundant tree, the smaller ones on walls, pergolas and pillars. They prefer sun or partial shade. Pruning is mostly cutting out dead or weak stems in autumn or early spring, but to maintain vigour and curb ultimate size, thin out the oldest stems every two to four years. *R.* 'Mermaid' ★★★ H 6m (20ft) has deeper, glossy leaves and large, light yellow single flowers with reddish-amber stamens. *R.* 'Madame Grégoire Staechelin' ('Spanish Beauty') ★★★★ H 5–6m (15–20ft) has clusters of large, loosely double, pink flowers in early summer, followed by orange to red hips.

RAMBLER
H 2–5m (6½–15ft)

A group of freely-flowering cultivars producing strong stems from near the ground each year which bloom the next. The smallish, often double flowers are carried in large clusters in summer. Grow in full sun. Pruning consists of removing some or all of the flowered stems after blooming, just above strong new shoots. 'American Pillar' ★★★★ H 3–4m (10–12ft) is a vigorous, 1902 vintage that is still popular, with glossy leaves and freely-borne trusses of carmine-pink, white-eyed, single, almost scentless flowers. 'Veilchenblau' ★★★★ is almost as tall, with paler green leaves and double flowers in a unique dusky blue-violet. 'Goldfinch' ★★★★ H 2.5m (8ft) has plentiful, light green leaves and abundant, neat, yellow, double blooms that age to cream. 'Albéric Barbier' ★★★★ H 5m (15ft) has clusters of creamy white double flowers, which fade to white, set off against glossy, dark green leaves. *R. filipes* 'Kiftsgate' ★★★★ H 10m (30ft) has paler leaves and small, creamy white single flowers in late summer.

MINIATURE
H 15–45cm (6–18ins)

A group of very small, twiggy stemmed roses, freely producing small, double flowers from summer to autumn. Ideal for rock gardens or small borders in sunny sites. 'Angela Rippon' ★★★★ bears fully double, rose to salmon-pink flowers. 'Darling Flame' ★★★★ has glossy leaves and cup-shaped, orange-red flowers. 'Little Artist' ('Top Gear') ★★★★ has semi-double red flowers with white markings.

LARGE-FLOWERED BUSH
(Hybrid Tea)
H 54–90cm (1½–3ft)

Erect, thorny bushes with robust shoots and usually small clusters of large, double, often scented flowers. Prune by removing one-third of the oldest stems to the base each year and reduce the remaining stems by two-thirds. 'Fragrant Cloud' **** is strongly scented, with rich scarlet flowers. 'Pascali' **** is cup-shaped, double, creamy white flowers. 'Grandpa Dickson' **** fully double, large, pointed, primrose-yellow flowers. 'Blue Moon' **** fully double, fragrant, mauve-lilac flowers. Large-flowering 'Peace' **** H 1.2m (4ft) is very popular, with fully double, scented yellow flowers and a beautiful, old-fashioned rose shape.

CLUSTER-FLOWERED BUSH
(Floribunda)
H 45–90cm (1½–3ft)
Similar to Large-flowered Bush roses, but with larger clusters of smaller flowers, sometimes only semi-double. Prune by removing one-third of the oldest stems to the base each year and reduce the remaining stems by one-third. Grow in full sun. 'Elizabeth of Glamis' ('Irish Beauty') **** has elegant sprays of cupped, double, scented, orange-pink flowers. 'Iceberg' **** is tall-growing and vigorous, with large clusters of loosely double white flowers. 'Lilli Marlene' **** has loosely double, crimson flowers. 'Glenfiddich' **** rounded, loosely double, amber to yellow flowers. The modern Patio roses are dwarf, compact forms. 'Cider Cup' **** has glossy foliage and double, apricot-pink flowers. 'Tip Top' **** has glossy leaves and rich pink flowers. 'Wee Jock' has fully double, deep crimson flowers.

POLYANTHA
H 45cm–2m (1½–6½ft)
Similar to Cluster-flowered Bush roses but often somewhat smaller with a more twiggy growth habit and smaller, single to double, rarely scented flowers from summer to autumn. Prune by removing about one-third of old stems annually and short-

en the side stems by one-third to one-half. 'White Pet' **** H 45cm (1½ft) vigorous, spreading habit, with deep green leaves and fully double, rosetted, white flowers from red-flushed buds.

MODERN SHRUB (including Hybrid Musk)
H 1–2.5m (3–8ft) or more
A variable group of bushy roses, mostly of fairly recent origin with few- to many-flowered clusters of usually scented, single to double flowers, some followed by red hips. Little pruning is necessary, except to remove dead and weak stems and thin out congested ones. Grow in a sunny position. 'Ballerina' **** usually of dense and spreading habit, H 1-1.5m (3-5ft), with large clusters of bright, light pink, white-centred, single flowers. 'Cerise Bouquet', vigorous with arching habit, greyish leaves and semi-double, cherry-red flowers. 'Constance Spry' **** vigorous with arching habit, climbing if supported, greyish green leaves and large, fully double, glowing pink, richly fragrant flowers. 'Nevada', vigorous with spiny, arching red stems and flat, semi-double, glowing pink, richly fragrant flowers. 'Frühlingsgold' ****, strong growing, bristly stems, H 2.5m (8ft), with cupped, semi-double, fragrant, light yellow flowers. 'Graham Thomas' **** H 1.2m (4ft), quartered-rosette to cupped, fully double, fragrant, yellow flowers.

OLD-FASHIONED SHRUB
H 1–2.5m (3–8ft)
This name covers at least a dozen smaller groups of varied cultivars, most of which are 100 years old or more. All are erect to spreading shrubs with green to grey-green leaves and single to double, usually scented flowers, in shades of red, pink, purple and white. Grow in full sun. Pruning comprises cutting

Rosa 'Ballerina'

Rosa 'Louise Odier'

Rosa 'Graham Thomas'

Rosa xanthina 'Canary Bird'

out dead and weak stems and shortening back long ones by one-third to one-half. 'Alba Maxima' **** the White Rose of York, H 2.2m (7ft), vigorous, erect habit, greyish green leaves and loosely double, sweetly scented, white flowers. 'Charles de Mills' **** H 1.5m (5ft) or more, erect habit, densely petalled, bright magenta, fragrant flowers. 'Louise Odier' **** H 2m (6½ft), spreading habit with double, pink, scented flowers from summer to autumn. 'Mme Hardy' **** H 1.5m (5ft), erect habit, leathery, dark green leaves and very fully double, fragrant, white flowers with a green-button eye. 'William Lobb' **** vigorous, with arching stems to 2m (6½ft) and fully double, cupped, fragrant, purple-crimson flowers tinged lavender grey.

SPECIES
H 1–3m (3–10ft)
This includes all the cultivated wild roses ranging across the northern hemisphere. All have single flowers followed by hips in shades of purple-black to orange and red and some have autumn-tinted foliage. Little pruning other than removing dead stems and thinning crowded ones. *R. rugosa* **** H 2m (6½ft), sparingly branched, suckering stems, leathery, deep green leaves and large, single, scented carmine pink flowers followed by large, orange-red hips. Var *rosea* **** has rose pink flowers, var *rubra* **** has purplish red ones and 'Alba' **** is white. *R. xanthina* 'Canary Bird' **** H 2m (6½ft) or more, erect habit with red-flushed stems and ferny leaves. Flowers are yellow with a musky scent.

Using climbers and wall shrubs

Climbers have an innate flexibility, which makes them extremely useful to the gardener, who can bend and train them in all sorts of ways on a variety of supports. They also have different mechanisms by which they pull themselves up, which can determine how they are used in the garden. When considering climbers it is useful to look at 'wall shrubs' as well. These are grown against walls, either because they have a lax, floppy habit and need something to lean against, or because they are slightly tender and benefit from a wall's protection.

Climbers have a distinctly romantic appeal and are perfect for clothing eyesores, like outbuildings. They are a boon in small urban gardens, where they can do much to introduce a note of greenery and nature into a brick or concrete-dominated environment.

Vertical bonus
A high wall provides an opportunity to increase the capacity for flowering plants in the garden. Roses and clematis are an obvious choice, but it is worth mixing evergreens with deciduous climbers, and using the shelter of walls to grow tender wall shrubs.

Planting a climber

Most climbing garden plants climb by means of twining stems or tendrils, which means that they must have something to cling onto, and preferably not so wide that their tendrils cannot grip on. It is often necessary to attach wire to walls, or other structures, to help them to climb.

As with shrubs in the garden, it is important that the eventual size of any climber is understood. Several years' growth of stem and leaf can not only smother original supports, but exert a considerable amount of weight.

There are those, however, that are conveniently self-clinging, ivies (*Hedera* spp.) for example, which use aerial roots or suckers that emerge from the stems. They are especially useful for sending up big expanses of wall, to which they will tightly cling.

1 *Create a generous-sized planting hole 30-45cm (12-18in) away from a wall. Add fertilizer, tease out the roots of the plant and insert in the hole.*

2 *Backfill the hole, firm down and water well. As the plant grows, tie in the shoots, if necessary to a supporting structure of wire or trellis.*

Combining climbers

Where space is at a premium, you can greatly enhance the garden's visual beauty by combining climbers that will grow into one another.

Clematis and roses are the most commonly combined climbers, since both have a relatively short flowering season. By planting them together so that the clematis uses the rose as support, you extend the flowering value without actually adding to the space requirements.

When combining climbers in this way you need to be careful that the vigour of one does not completely overwhelm the growth of the other.

Macropetala type clematis are ideal companions for some of the less vigorous climbing roses. However, the big scrambling forms of the latter, such as *Rosa* 'Kiftsgate' or 'Bobbie James' should be left to strut their stuff alone.

Useful combinations
When combining climbers, it is important that they complement one another in terms of colour as well as scale and vigour. Roses and clematis, used to adorn this arch, make successful partners.

Knowing how far they go

Wall shrubs may be grown simply against a convenient wall, preferably one facing the sun, as most are sun lovers. The heat radiated by the wall will give protection from severe frosts and enhance the effect of summer sun, enabling you to grow species that might not be hardy elsewhere in the garden. The wall will also protect against damaging winds.

More creative, and useful in confined spaces, is training appropriate shrubs against walls. You can tie them to wires or trellis and cut back branches that thrust out too far, so that they are held close to the wall. This can be an effective way to treat, not only slightly tender species, but also certain other, bone-hardy, shrubs. Pyracantha, smothered in fiery, bright berries in autumn, looks stunning grown like this.

More difficult to guide in the right direction are plants, notably climbing roses, with strong stems that, in nature, can haul themselves up by means of sharp thorns. In the garden, their stems must be tied to supports at intervals, otherwise they will flop down and become an unmanageable mess.

Vigorous climbers
Wisteria is one of the most popular climbers for covering walls, but it is exceptionally vigorous and will need regular tying in and pruning to keep it in check.

Wall shrubs
Some shrubs, like winter-flowering jasmine (Jasminum nudiflorum) are not self-clinging, but can be trained to climb if a suitable supporting structure is provided.

Structures and supports

Given that in many gardens there is a limit to the amount of wall or fence space for climbers, various structures have been developed for supporting and displaying them. Pergolas, where supports carry the weight of an overhead structure with a walkway underneath, are suitable for medium-sized or larger gardens. Archways are more suited to the smaller garden, and are particularly useful as 'doors' between one part of the garden and another. Free-standing supports have recently become popular, enabling climbers to be grown in borders without having to rely on a convenient stretch of wall space. These vary from obelisks which are ideal for formal situations to 'wigwams' made from willow which are more rustic in feel. Established trees or shrubs can also be home to climbers. Using a late-flowering climber on an early-flowering shrub is a good way of capitalizing on space, although it is vital that the host plant is not smothered by too vigorous a choice of climber.

Overhead canopy
A pergola provides an ideal structure over which climbers can be grown to give shade in summer. Here, rustic wooden poles support a climbing rose.

Trellis arbour
Adding trellis to a garden fence or wall can create additional height, and provide a home for climbers. Here ivy has been grown over a trellis arbour in a shady city garden to give shelter and privacy.

Climbers and wall shrubs

Actinidia kolomikta

Campsis x tagliabuana

Garrya elliptica

Humulus lupulus 'Aureus'

Jasminum humile

ACTINIDIA KOLOMIKTA
H 5–7m (15–22ft) ★★★★

Deciduous, twining climber grown for its unique foliage. The oval to heart-shaped, mid-green leaves are flushed with white and pink for up to two-thirds of their surface. The bowl-shaped, white flowers appear in summer but are rather hidden by the foliage. Grow in moist but well-drained fertile soil in sun or partial shade. Propagate by semi-ripe cuttings in late summer.

CAMPSIS RADICANS
H 10m (30ft) or more ★★★★

Also known as Trumpet Creeper, this showy, deciduous, self-clinging climber has prominent clusters of tubular, 5-petalled, scarlet flowers in late summer. The dark green leaves are composed of several toothed, oval leaflets. Grow in moist but well-drained soil in a sunny site. Propagate by semi-ripe cuttings in summer or seed in spring. *C.* x *tagliabuana* 'Mme Galen' is a hybrid with orange-red flowers, which clings as vigorously as *C. radicans*.

CHIMONANTHUS PRAECOX
H 3–4m (10–12ft) ★★★

A deciduous, erect shrub, also called Wintersweet, grown for its very sweetly scented, sulphur-yellow, pendant bell-shaped flowers in winter. The large, rough-textured mid-green leaves are lance-shaped. Grow in moist but well-drained soil in a sunny position. Propagate by softwood cuttings in summer or by seed when ripe in a cold frame. Best trained out flat on a wall when young, then allowed to grow more freely. *C.p.* var. *luteus* has clearer, yellow flowers which open more widely.

CYTISUS BATTANDIERI
H 3–5m (10–15ft) ★★★

Also known as Pineapple or Moroccan Broom, this is a handsome, deciduous to semi-evergreen shrub bearing dense, erect spikes of strongly pineapple-scented, yellow pea flowers in summer. Leaves are composed of three oval, silky, silver-haired leaflets. Grow in well-drained, ideally limy soil in full sun. Propagate by semi-ripe cuttings in late summer. Best trained out flat on a wall when young, then allowed to grow more freely.

GARRYA ELLIPTICA
H 3–4m (10–12ft) ★★

Also called Silk Tassel Bush, this popular bushy, evergreen shrub or small tree is grown for its long, silvery grey, male catkins in winter. Female plants have shorter, less showy catkins and are seldom seen. The deep green, oval, leathery leaves have strongly waved margins. Grow in ordinary soil in sun or partial shade. Propagate by semi-ripe cuttings in summer. 'James Roof' bears clusters of longer, more silvery catkins.

HUMULUS LUPULUS
H 5–6m (15–20ft) ★★★★

Twining, herbaceous climber, also known as Hop, with striking foliage of large, 3 to 5-lobed, boldly toothed, rough-textured leaves. Female plants may bear soft, pale green, cone-like fruits (hops) in late summer. Grow in moist but well-drained fertile soil in sun or partial shade. Propagate by seed or softwood cuttings in spring. *H.l.* 'Aureus', with suffused golden yellow leaves, is most commonly grown but does not come true from seed.

HYDRANGEA ANOMALA
SSP. PETIOLARIS)
H 10–15m (30–50ft) ★★★★

Also known as Climbing Hydrangea, this attractive, self-clinging, deciduous climber has lacy, flat heads of small, white flowers in summer surrounded by larger, sterile florets. The rounded to broadly oval toothed leaves are mid- to deep green, turning yellow in autumn. Grow in moist but well-drained soil in sun or partial shade. Propagate by softwood cuttings in summer or hardwood cuttings in winter.

JASMINUM OFFICINALE
H 8–12m (25–40ft) ★★★

Twining climber, also known as Jasmine, with fragrant, white flowers in clusters from summer to early autumn. Grow in ordinary soil in sun or partial shade. Propagate by cuttings in summer or layering in autumn. The form *affine* has pink-tinted flowers. *J.* x *stephanense* is less vigorous with fragrant, pale pink flowers and matt green leaves, sometimes flushed with cream. *J. humile,* Yellow Jasmine, is semi-evergreen or evergreen with bright yellow, sometimes fragrant flowers. *J. nudiflorum,* Winter Jasmine, is a deciduous shrub with long, slender, arching green stems and bright yellow flowers in winter and early spring.

LONICERA PERICLYMENUM
H 5–8m (15–25ft) ★★★

Deciduous, vigorous, twining climber, also known as Common Honeysuckle, with clusters of tubular, fragrant flowers which open white and age to yellow. Broadly spoon-shaped leaves are mid-green. The flowers are followed by bright red berries. Grow in ordinary soil in sun or partial shade. Propagate by semi-ripe cuttings in summer. *L.p.* 'Belgica', Early Dutch Honeysuckle, has earlier flowers which are strongly suffused red. *L. caprifolium* is less vigorous with creamy white to yellow, pink-flushed, scented flowers in summer, borne at the stem tips in the centre of a cup-like leaf.

SOLANUM CRISPUM
H 4–6m (12–20ft) ★★★

Also known as Chilean Potato Tree, this showy, scrambling climber produces a profusion of starry, purple-blue flowers with cone-shaped, yellow centres in terminal clusters in summer. Grow in ordinary soil in full sun, sheltered from cold winds and secured to its support. Propagate by semi-ripe cuttings in summer. 'Glasnevin' ('Autumnale'), flowers freely from summer to autumn.

VITIS COIGNETIAE
H 10–15m (30–50ft) ★★★★

Vigorous, deciduous, woody, tendril climber with large, heart-shaped, deep-green leaves which turn bright red in autumn. Small flowers may be followed by blue-black, unpalatable grapes. Grow in moist, well-drained, fertile soil in full sun. Propagate by hardwood cuttings in winter, layering in autumn or by bud-cuttings in early spring.

WISTERIA FLORIBUNDA
H 8–10m (25–30ft) ★★★★

A vigorous, deciduous, twining climber bearing many loosely pendent spikes of fragrant, pea-shaped flowers in shades of lavender to purple and white. Long leaves consist of lance-shaped, mid-green leaflets. Grow in fertile, well-drained soil in sun. Propagate by softwood cuttings in summer or layering in autumn. 'Alba' has white flowers, 'Multijuga' ('Macrobotrys'), lilac-blue flowers in spikes 90-120cm (3–4ft) long. *W. sinensis* has lilac-blue to white flowers in denser spikes.

Jasminum nudiflorum

Lonicera periclymenum 'Belgica'

Solanum crispum 'Glasnevin'

Wisteria floribunda 'Multijuga'

Clematis

This large group of often fast-growing climbers comes in a wide variety of flower shapes and sizes. The leaves can be simple or dissected into three of more mid- to deep green leaflets, the stalks of which coil like tendrils around any available support. All clematis prefer a moist, but well-drained, rich soil where the roots are shaded and the top is in the sun. Propagate by layering in late winter, softwood cuttings in spring or semi-hardwood ones in summer. Prune the early, large-flowered cultivars by cutting the previous season's stems back to the highest and plumpest expanding bud. Cut late flowerers to 10–15cm (4–6in), above ground level, both in spring.

LARGE-FLOWERED – EARLY GROUP H 2.5–3.5m (8–11ft)

Moderately vigorous growers with 3 to 5 or more leaflets and 8-petalled, or more, flowers 15–25cm (6–10in) across in late spring and early summer and again in late summer. A wide range of excellent cultivars is available.

LARGE-FLOWERED – LATE GROUP H 2.6m (8½ft)

Vigorous growers with 1–3 or more leaflets and flowers 10–20cm (4–8in) across composed of six or more petals from midsummer to autumn. A wide range of excellent cultivars is available.

SPECIES H 2–15m (6½–48ft)

Some early flowering species are evergreen or semi-evergreen but the three listed here are deciduous.

C. macropetala ★★★★ H 2–3m (6–10ft), has a slender-stemmed, bushy habit with 6 to 9, coarsely toothed leaflets and nodding, bell-shaped, blue to violet, pink or white, 4-petalled flowers with a central boss of petaloid stamens from mid- to late spring, followed by decorative seedheads. *C. montana* ★★★★ H 7–15m (21–48ft) is very vigorous with trifoliate, lobed and toothed leaflets and many 4-petalled, white flowers in late spring to early summer. 'Elizabeth' has pink flowers and purple-flushed leaves. *C. tangutica* ★★★★ H 4–6m (12–20ft) is vigorous, with irregularly shaped, toothed leaflets and nodding, lantern-shaped flowers of pointed, yellow petals from midsummer to autumn followed by striking silvery seedheads.

Clematis montana 'Odorata'

Clematis 'Jackmanii'

Using perennials

Herbaceous perennials are, for most people, what gardening is all about: flowers and colour. They are generally long-lived, resilient species that die back every autumn to re-emerge the following spring (which is what is meant by the word 'herbaceous'). Quicker to establish than shrubs, they are invaluable for the impatient gardener. Being smaller, too, they suit restricted spaces.

The seasonal habit of growth of perennials gives them a strongly dynamic character, many being practically invisible over the winter, yet growing to over 2m (6½ft) by the end of the year. This creates a strong sense of change in the garden, quite different to one dominated by shrubs or conifers. Winter, when the majority are dormant, need not be dull, as many perennials have dead stems and seedheads that are attractive in a ghostly way, especially in low winter light.

Cottage-garden border
A perennial planting of cottage garden favourites – foxgloves (Digitalis), poppies (Papaver orientale), flax (Linum) and burning bush (Dictamnus albus) – is an ideal choice for a country garden.

Perennials for colour

In many gardens it is shrubs and, perhaps, trees that make up the framework, with perennials being the 'infill'. Given that they take up relatively little space, and flower over a long period, it makes

Perennials for colour
Bright summer border asters (Aster amellus 'King George') and Japanese anemones (Anemone x hybrida 'Prinz Heinrich') mingle in a vibrant late summer border (below).

sense to rely on perennials for the bulk of the garden's floral interest. The perennial year starts off in late winter with a limited number of extremely versatile plants, notably hellebores and pulmonarias, with their often strangely coloured flowers and attractive evergreen leaves. While there are certainly a number of attractive, spring-flowering perennials and plenty of spring-flowering bulbs, it is not until early summer that perennials really get into their stride, with the pinks and blues of the hardy geraniums ('cranesbills').

Because perennials have to renew all their above-ground growth every year, it is not, perhaps, surprising that the majority flower later in the

Naturalistic forms
Planting in large groups, or drifts, to echo the way that plants grow in the wild, gives the garden a natural appearance and reduces labour. Here grasses and perennials are grown in a relaxed border.

year. Numbers build up through midsummer to a peak in late summer and early autumn. Midsummer sees monardas in pinks, purples and mauves, later months

a huge variety of species from the daisy family, such as asters and rudbeckias. Yellow is the dominant late colour, although there are plenty of good blues and violets too.

Evergreens and architecturals

Although their growth is replaced every year, there are certain species that are effectively evergreen. These are usually rather statuesque plants, such as varieties of hellebore and euphorbia, whose attractive foliage alone is reason enough to grow them. They are vital in providing some interest for perennial plantings in winter, especially appreciated in smaller gardens.

While flowers are the main attraction for most gardeners, and good-looking leaves an additional boon, it is the habit of certain perennials that earns them a place in the garden, a quality best described as architectural. Examples include the eryngiums, upright growers with the atmosphere of refined thistles, and macleayas, large growers with a combination of bulk and elegance.

Grasses, too, play an extremely useful role in adding structure and form to a perennial border. Their slender leaves and arching habit make a welcome counterpoint to smaller flowering perennials.

Strong architecture
Giant thistles, such as Onopordum acanthium, *with their large, steely-blue leaves, make an eye-catching feature in any perennial border.*

Graceful elegance
The elegant shape and arching habit of the silver-leaved grass, Miscanthus sinensis *'Variegatus', gives a border striking architectural form.*

Naturalistic and border planting

The border may be the traditional place to grow perennials, but there is now interest in more innovative ways, such as alongside grasses in wildflower meadow or prairie plantings, or in naturalistic, wild garden drifts.

Such plantings are low maintenance once established, but need as much care and attention as any other planting for the first few years. The core idea of these naturalistic plantings is the selection of appropriate perennials (and grasses). They must be plants that are naturally adapted to the prevailing conditions, and which stand a reasonable chance of competing together.

Shady border
Restrained colour, in a variety of shades of blue, is the keynote of a shady perennial border where forget-me-nots (Myosotis), Lunaria rediviva *and grasses, such as this Bowles' golden grass* (Milium effusum) *predominate.*

Selecting for success

Selecting perennials suited to the environment of your garden is an important part of success. Herbaceous perennials have a reputation for needing a lot of maintenance. This is largely to do with the way they were grown in the past, when they were fed well and grown in distinct and separate clumps. They would become top heavy, as a result, and so needed staking. The choice of more robust, modern varieties or natural species helps to reduce the need for support, as does avoiding heavy feeding. The range of perennials available today is far more suited to mixed borders and informal styles of planting than those of the past. These are plants that are becoming increasingly important in modern gardening.

Damp lovers
Next to a gulley, various moisture-loving perennials do well, including irises, euphorbia, ferns, Heuchera *'Palace Purple' and* Alchemilla mollis.

Perennial borders

Given that most of us only have limited space in the garden, achieving a border with as long a period of interest as possible is crucial. Many gardeners decide to colour-scheme a border, by including only pink or only yellow flowers, for example, or a mix such as blue and white. Others simply want to include as many of the plants they like as possible. No matter how well colour-schemed, a border will never be an entire success unless there is also foliage interest. Leaves have a longer season, give the border structure and also make a contribution in terms of colour. Because most plants, perennials and shrubs tend to be fairly shapeless, a border will greatly benefit from the inclusion of clearly defined, contrasting shapes.

Vibrant summer border
Seen in early summer, this perennial border features a number of cottage garden perennials, including delphiniums, flax (Linum spp.), astrantia, inula and pyrethrums (Tanacetum coccineum).

Height in the border

A perennial border is normally organized with the tallest plants at the back, medium ones in the middle and smaller perennials at the front. Failure to plan your border in this way will mean that some plants are obscured by others as the seasons progress.

The perennials on the following pages therefore, are organized from the tallest to the smallest. It also helps to have a few punctuation points in the border created by larger plants, such as shrubs.

Punctuation points
Give the border shape and form by including a few shrubs to add height. A clipped yew (Taxus baccata) pyramid gives definition to a border of African lilies (agapanthus) and fuchsia.

Colour in the border

Planning a colour scheme for a border is a complex task, since you have to orchestrate the flowering times as well. Limiting the colour choices helps not only to produce greater impact but it means that you do not have to worry so much about what is flowering when.

You can therefore opt for a single colour theme border – all white flowers or all blue for example. This means that you do not have to worry about whether colours 'go' together. In general, when mixing colours in the border aim either for all pastel shades – pale pinks, blues, mauves, creamy yellows – or strong contrasting colours - red, yellows, strong blues or purples. Problems may arise when you mix strong colours with pastels as the bright colours will swamp or overwhelm the pale ones.

Single theme
Opting for a single colour theme, such as white, means that you do not have to worry about whether colours 'go' together.

Designing a border

It is all too easy to plant a border that becomes a jumbled collection of plants without a real theme. A few distinct 'theme plants' can make all the difference.

Dotting a few of the same variety through a border can do wonders in unifying it and developing a sense of rhythm. Such plants need to have a distinct colour and a reasonably long flowering season. If there is space, it is possible to use a particularly effective colour combination as a repeating element.

It pays when planning a border to go for simplicity. Repeat groups of plants at intervals, and keep the colour palette limited. The

Colour co-ordination
This backed border has been carefully designed with a yellow and blue colour theme. Delphiniums and catmint (Nepeta) create the blue areas; mulleins, helenium and thalictrum the yellow. Limiting the colour palette in this way greatly increases the impact.

border, below, is effective because it is created from blue and yellow plants only. The contrast gives interest without appearing either bitty or unstructured.

Plant small plants in odd-numbered groups – 3, 5 or 7. Use quick-growing annuals to fill those holes where

plants inevitaby die or fail. Busy lizzies (*Impatiens* spp.) or large annuals, such as *Nicotiana sylvestris* are excellent plants for this purpose.

Remember to have some plants in the border for foliage interest – big thistles, grasses, euphorbias, irises, and the large hellebores are ideal for this purpose – so that once the main flower-

ing period is over, there will still be something interesting to look at. An occasional evergreen will help give the border form in winter.

Remember that not all plants like the same soil conditions, or the same climate, so for the best results, it is advisable to choose those that enjoy the conditions you have.

Planning the planting

To create a border, mark the planting down on paper and plant in groups of at least three to give the border bulk. The plan, right, is for a similar blue and yellow border to that shown above, for an area about 2.4m (8ft) x 1.2m (4ft). Repeat the planting for a longer border.

1 *Verbascum* 'Gainsborough'
2 *Delphinium* x *belladonna* 'Blue Bees'
3 *Thalictrum flavum*
4 *Aster frikartii* 'Monch'
5 *Solidago* 'Laurin'
6 *Hosta* 'Gold Standard'
7 *Nepeta mussinii*
8 *Hemerocallis* 'Canary Glow'
9 *Salvia* x *sylvestris* 'Indigo'
10 *Helenium* 'Butterpat'
11 *Geranium* 'Johnson's Blue'

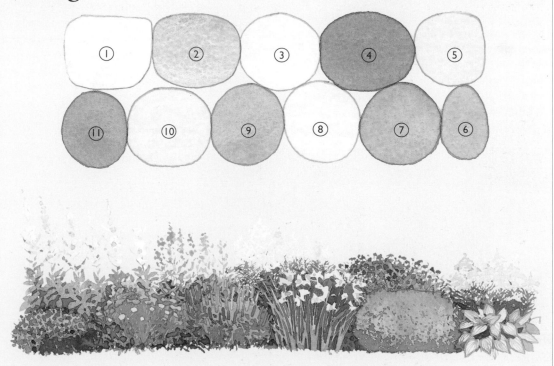

Water-loving perennials

Some plants thrive in very moist soil or with their feet in water itself. A few are actually aquatic plants, floating in deep water. It is important to ensure that the plants are grown in appropriate conditions if they are to survive. Some prefer full sun; others will cope well with partial shade, and while some are frost hardy, others, such as the big-leaved gunneras are not. Ideally a pond needs a range of water-loving perennials: a couple of deep water plants, a few in the shallow margins of the pond, and some which enjoy moist soil alongside the pond's edges.

Astilbe x *arendsii* 'Rotlicht'

Astilboides tabularis

Caltha palustris 'Flore Pleno'

Gunnera manicata

Iris ensata **Higo Hybrids**

ASTILBE X ARENDSII
H 50–120cm (1¾–4ft) ★★★★
Grown for its elegant plumes of tiny flowers in shades of white to red in summer. The dissected, mainly basal leaves are mid-green, sometimes bronze-tinted and coarsely fern-like. Grow in moist to wet soil in sun or partial shade. Propagate by division in autumn or early spring. 'Bressingham Beauty', H 90cm (3ft), has bronze-flushed leaves and bright pink flowers. 'Deutschland', H 50cm (1¾ft), has bright green leaves and pure white flowers.

ASTILBOIDES TABULARIS
H 90–120cm (3–4ft) ★★★★
Handsome, clump-forming, herbaceous perennial with thick rhizomes and large, stiff, but open clusters of numerous tiny white flowers in early to midsummer. The large, oval, softly hairy leaves are deeply veined and a shiny, deep green. Grow in permanently wet soil at the edge of a pond or watercourse in sun or partial shade. Propagate by division in autumn or early spring.

CALTHA PALUSTRIS
H 25–45cm (10–18in) ★★★★
Cheerful, herbaceous perennial, also known as Marsh Marigold, grown for its bowl-shaped, 5-petalled, bright yellow flowers in spring. The long-stalked, heart- to kidney-shaped leaves are toothed and rich, lustrous green. Grow in wet soil at the edge of a pond or watercourse in sun or partial shade. Propagate by division in early autumn or very early spring. Var. *alba* has white flowers, 'Flore Pleno' has double ones.

EUPHORBIA PALUSTRIS
H 70–90cm (2¼–3ft) ★★★★
Useful, clump-forming herbaceous perennial with erect, unbranched stems, topped by clusters of small, deep yellow flowers in late spring and surrounded by larger, paler, leaf-like bracts. The entirely stem-borne leaves are oblong to elliptic, bright green, with orange and yellow tones in autumn. Grow in any permanently moist soil or pond margins in a sunny position. Propagate by division in late winter or early spring or sow seeds when ripe in a cold frame.

GUNNERA MANICATA
H 2–2.5m (6½–8ft) or more ★★
Statuesque, half-hardy, herbaceous perennial forming loose clumps from large rhizomes. Grown for its huge, deeply-lobed, rounded, deep green leaves on robust, erect, prickly stalks. Grow in wet soil at the edge of a pond in sun or partial shade. Propagate by division, separating the rhizomes in spring, or sow seeds as soon as ripe in wet soil in a cold frame.

IRIS ENSATA (I. KAEMPFERI)
H 75–90cm (2½–3ft) ★★★★
Beautiful, herbaceous perennial forming loose clumps with large, round-petalled flowers in shades of purple, in summer. The erect, sword-like leaves are mid- to bright green. Grow in any permanently moist soil or pond margins in sun. Propagate by division in early spring or sow seeds when ripe, in wet soil in a cold frame. 'Alba' has white flowers. 'Moonlight Waves' has white flowers with lime-green centres. 'Rose Queen' is soft pink, 'Variegata' has green and white striped leaves and purple flowers. *I. laevigata* has

smaller, narrower-petalled flowers produced in larger numbers. *I. pseudacorus*, Yellow Flag, is very vigorous, forming wide clumps up to 1m (3ft) tall and has yellow flowers with violet to brownish markings. Variety *bastardii* has sulphur-yellow flowers.

LYSICHITON AMERICANUS
H 60–90cm (2–3ft) ★★★

Distinctive, herbaceous perennial, also known as Skunk Cabbage, grown for its large, hooded, bright yellow, arum-like, flowering spathes which appear in early spring before the leaves. The mature leaves are large, oval to oblong, boldly-veined, glossy mid- to deep green. Grow in wet soil at the edge of a pond or watercourse in sun or partial shade. Propagate by offsets in spring or by seed sown as soon as ripe in wet soil in a cold frame. *L. camtschatcensis* is slightly smaller with pure white flowering spathes.

LYTHRUM SALICARIA
H 90–120cm (3–4ft) ★★★★

An excellent, self-supporting perennial, also known as Purple Loosestrife, for moist soils with close spikes of rose-purple flowers from summer to early autumn. Leaves are mid- to deep green and lance-shaped. Grow in moist to wet soil in sun or partial shade. Propagate by division in early spring or basal cuttings in late spring. 'Feuerkerze' ('Firecandle') is intense rosered. 'Robert' is bright pink.

MYOSOTIS SCORPIOIDES
(M. PALUSTRIS)
H 15–30cm (6–12in) ★★★★

One of the few, true blue-flowered aquatics, Water Forget-me-not is a colony-former, producing a profusion of bright blue, rounded, 5-petalled flowers from early to late summer. The oblong to narrowly oval, mid-green leaves have bristly hairs.

Grow in permanently wet soil, planted either above or below shallow water, in sun or partial shade. Propagate by division in spring or seed when ripe in wet soil in a cold frame. 'Mermaid' is more erect and compact with darker green leaves.

PETASITES JAPONICUS
H 60–90cm (2–3ft) ★★★★

Colony-forming, herbaceous perennial spreading by thick rhizomes. The dense-clusters of white, groundsel-like flowerheads in early spring are surrounded by large, lime-green leaf-like bracts. The large, long-stalked, kidney-shaped, entirely basal leaves are bright to mid-green and arise after the flowers. Grow in damp soil in sun or partial shade. Can become invasive.

PONTEDERIA CORDATA
H 75–90cm (2½–3ft) or more ★★★

Attractive, dense, colony-forming, herbaceous perennial known as Pickerel Weed, slowly spreading by rhizomes and producing spikes of blue, tubular flowers in late summer. The long-stalked leaves, some of which may be floating when grown in water, are oval to triangular and a glossy, rich green. Grow in shallow water, rooted in the soil or in baskets, in sun or partial shade. Propagate by division in spring.

PRIMULA FLORINDAE
H 90–120cm (3–4ft) ★★★★

A splendid giant cowslip for permanently wet or moist soil with large, terminal clusters of nodding, yellow bell-flowers in summer. The entirely basal leaves are oval to oblong, bright green and long stalked. Grow in moist soil in sun or partial shade. Propagate by seed sown when ripe or in spring in a cold frame. *P. pulverulenta* has deep red or red-purple flowers, *P. japonica* is similar

but has green stems, larger leaves and magenta flowers. *P. denticulata* has tubular to trumpet- or bell-shaped, purple flowers with yellow eyes.

ZANTEDESCHIA AETHIOPICA
H 60–90cm (2–3ft) ★★★

Dramatic, tuberous-rooted perennial, also known as Arum Lily, with large, waxy white, erect, trumpet-shaped, flowering spathes, each with a central yellow spike which appear in summer. The long-stalked, arrowhead-shaped leaves are glossy, bright green. This plant will survive most winters if planted in at least 15cm (6in) of water. It prefers full sun. Propagate by removing offsets when dormant, or by division of large clumps in spring. 'Crowborough' is reputedly hardier than the ordinary species. 'Green Goddess' has green and white spathes and matt green leaves.

Lysichiton americanus

Petasites japonicus

Pontederia cordata

Primula denticulata

Zantedeschia aethiopica

Plants for sunny corners and containers

Abutilon 'Kentish Belle'

Plants from hotter, drier regions of the world, such as the Mediterranean, do well in warm, sunny parts of the garden. They are particularly suited to the drier conditions of containers, as they are drought tolerant, and will thrive in relatively poor soils. These sun-loving plants give exciting displays of colourful flowers and, sometimes, foliage. Those that are not frost-hardy should be brought indoors in winter in cold climates. Annuals will need to be planted from seed each spring.

Browallia speciosa

Plants listed below need more-or-less frost-free conditions in winter.

ABUTILON PICTUM (A. STRIATUM)
H 3–5m (10–15ft) ✶✶

Attractive, evergreen shrub with long-stalked, maple-like mid- to deep green leaves and bell-shaped, yellow to orange flowers on slender stalks from late spring to autumn. Grow in fertile, well-drained soil in sun or partial shade. Propagate by greenwood cuttings in summer. *A.* x *hybridum* is similar but with more rounded, bell-shaped flowers in shades of yellow, red, orange and white. *A. megapotamicum* is smaller with slender, arching stems and bi-coloured flowers with a large, bright red calyx from which protrudes a short skirt of yellow petals and a tuft of purple stamens. 'Kentish Belle' has pendent, bell-shaped apricot-yellow flowers and purple stamens protruding from red calyces.

BEGONIA X TUBERHYBRIDA
H 60cm (2ft) or more ✶

Colourful, tuberous-rooted perennial with thick, erect, mainly unbranched stems, topped by fully double, rose-like, male flowers in shades of white, pink, red, yellow and bi-colours. The large, basically oval, lop-sided leaves are mid- to deep glossy green. The Pendula Group is similar but with slimmer, arching to pendulous stems and smaller flowers. Grow in humus-rich, moist but well-drained soil in partial shade. Good for hanging baskets. Propagate by basal cuttings in spring or by seed in late winter.

BROWALLIA SPECIOSA
H 45–60cm (1½–2ft) ✶

Charming, bushy, woody-based perennial, clad with oval to elliptic, veined, matt green leaves which are slightly sticky. The tubular-based, 5-petalled, pansy-like flowers in shades of violet-blue are freely borne in summer. Grow in fertile, moist but well-drained soil in sun or partial shade. Propagate by seed sown in warmth in early spring or late summer. *B.s.* 'Blue Troll' does not exceed 25cm (10in). *B.s.* 'Heavenly Bells' has pale blue flowers.

BRUGMANSIA X CANDIDA (DATURA X CANDIDA)
H 2–5m (6½–15ft) ✶✶

Spectacular shrub, also known as Angels' Trumpets, with robust, sparingly branched stems and large, oval to elliptic, sometimes toothed, mid- to deep green leaves. The 25–30cm (10–12in) long, pendent, trumpet-shaped flowers are white to soft yellow, or (rarely) pink, from summer to autumn. Grow in fertile, moist, but well-drained soil in sun or partial shade. Propagate by semi-hardwood cuttings in summer. *B.* x *c.* 'Grand Marnier' has apricot flowers. *B.* x *c.* 'Knightii' has semi-double white ones.

CANNA X GENERALIS
H 1.5–2m (5–6½ft) ✶

This magnificent, clump-forming, rhizomatous perennial bears terminal spikes of orchid-like flowers in shades of red, orange, yellow and pink, sometimes bi-coloured or picotee. The handsome, stem-borne leaves are oval to elliptic, mid- to deep green, in some cultivars flushed with purple. Grow in fertile, moist soil in sun. Propagate by dividing established clumps or removing short sections of rhizome, in spring.

Canna 'General Eisenhower'

Cordyline australis

Felicia amelloides

Heliotropium arborescens 'Marine'

CORDYLINE AUSTRALIS
H 2–5m (6½–15ft) ★★

Also known as the New Zealand Cabbage Palm. An erect, sparingly branched tree, the stem tips bearing a palm-like head of lance-shaped, light- to mid-green leaves which may reach 1m (3ft) in length. Mature specimens bear huge, airy clusters of tiny, white, 6-petalled flowers followed by white or blue-tinted berries. Young plants make good non-flowering tub or pot plants. Grow in moist but well-drained soil in sun or partial shade. Propagate by seed in warmth or by removing rooted suckers, in spring. *C.a.* 'Purpurea' has its leaves heavily flushed with purple. *C.a.* 'Torbay Dazzler' has leaves striped with cream.

DIASCIA RIGESCENS
H 30cm (1ft) ★★

Delightful, bushy, erect to spreading, evergreen perennial with angular stems and heart-shaped, toothed, mid- to deep green leaves. Rich pink flowers are carried in dense, erect spikes throughout summer. Grow in fertile, well-drained soil in sun. Propagate by soft-wood cuttings in spring or late summer. *D. barberae* 'Ruby Field' is mat-forming, with heart-shaped leaves and salmon-pink flowers. *D.b.* 'Blackthorn Apricot' is similar with apricot flowers. *D.r.* 'Lilac Belle' is more compact with lilac-pink flowers.

FELICIA AMELLOIDES
H 35–45cm (14–18in) ★★

Dainty, bushy, semi-shrub with oval to narrow, spoon-shaped, deep green leaves and bright blue, yellow-centred, daisy flowers from summer to autumn. Grow in well-drained soil in sun. Propagate by seed in spring or softwood cuttings in summer. *F.a.* 'Read's Blue' is rich blue, *F.a.* 'Read's White' is white and *F.a.* 'Santa Anita Variegated' has white-patterned leaves.

LANTANA CAMARA
H 1m (3ft) or more ★

Colourful, evergreen, somewhat prickly-stemmed shrub with oval, finely corrugated, deep green leaves. The tubular flowers are freely produced in dense, rounded clusters in shades of purple, pink, yellow and white from late spring to autumn. Each flower opens paler and darkens with age, creating a bicoloured effect. Grow in ordinary, well-drained soil in sun. Propagate by semi-hardwood cuttings in summer or by seed in warmth in spring.

OSTEOSPERMUM JUCUNDUM (DIMORPHOTHECA BARBERAE)
H 30–60cm (1–2ft) ★★

Showy, mat-forming perennial with lance-shaped, somewhat greyish-green leaves. The daisy-like flower-heads are held well above the leaves in summer. Grow in well-drained soil in full sun. Propagate by soft cuttings in late summer. *O. ecklonis* has an erect habit to 60cm (2ft) or more, with white, blue-backed flowers. 'Pink Whirls' has spoon-shaped petals. 'Buttermilk' has yellow florets.

PELARGONIUM
H 30–75cm (1–2½ft) ★★

The most popular house and bedding geranium, an ever-green, shrubby perennial with fleshy, robust stems. In the Zonal Group, the long-stalked, rounded, shallowly-lobed, mid- to light green, aromatic leaves may have a ring-like bronze zone. The 5-petalled flowers, in shades of red, pink or white, are borne in dense, rounded clusters from spring to autumn. Hundreds of varieties are available in a wide colour range, some of them double or semi-double. Grow in well-drained soil in sun or partial shade. Propagate by stem-tip cuttings in summer. The Regal Group is similar but with toothed, rich green leaves and larger flowers, often bicoloured, in shades of red, pink, purple, orange and white. The Ivy-leaved Group has flexible, trailing stems, fleshy leaves shaped like those of the ivy, and smaller clusters of single or double flowers in a similar colour range. From the Scented-leaved Group, *P.* 'Lady Plymouth' has eucalyptus scented leaves and lavender pink flowers.

STREPTOSOLEN JAMESONII
H 2–4m (6½–12ft) ★

Dramatic, slender-stemmed shrub or semi-climber with elliptic, deep green leaves. The tubular flowers open yellow and turn bright orange and are carried in large, terminal clusters in profusion from spring to summer. Grow in fertile, moist but well-drained soil in sun or partial shade. May be kept to a smaller size by hard pruning after flowering. Propagate by softwood cuttings in early summer.

Lantana camara **'Mine d'Or'**

Osteospermum **'Buttermilk'**

Osteospermum **'Pink Whirls'**

Pelargonium **'Lady Plymouth'**

Regal Pelargonium

Streptosolen jamesonii

Large perennials

Aruncus dioicus

Campanula lactiflora

Crambe cordifolia

Delphinium **'Carl Topping'**

Euphorbia characias ssp. *wulfenii*

ARUNCUS DIOICUS (A. SYLVESTER)
H 1.5–2m (5–6½ft) ★★★★
Also known as Goatsbeard, this statuesque, self-support-ing perennial is grown for its large, frothy clusters of tiny, cream flowers from early to mid-summer. The large, fern-like leaves are composed of mid-green, toothed leaflets. Grow in moist garden soil in sun or partial shade. Propa-gate by division in autumn or early spring. *A.d.* 'Kneiffii' is smaller in all its parts with more finely divided leaves.

CAMPANULA LACTIFLORA
H 1.5–1.8m (5–6ft) ★★★★
Herbaceous perennial pro-ducing wide clusters of 5-petalled, upward-facing bells in shades of lavender-blue to lilac blue. The entirely stem-borne leaves are oval to oblong, toothed, mid- to light green. Grow in fertile, moisture-retentive soil in sun or partial shade. Propagate by division in autumn or early spring. *C.l.* 'Alba' is pure white. *C.l.* 'Loddon Anna' is lilac-pink.

CIMICIFUGA RACEMOSA
H 1.5–2.2m (5–7ft) ★★★★
Imposing, herbaceous peren-nial, also known as Black Snakeroot, with strong, wind-firm stems branching above and bearing numerous slender, tapered spikes of small, fluffy white flowers in summer. The broad leaves are dissected into oval, toothed, dark green leaflets. Grow in fertile, moist but well-drained soil in sun or partial shade. Propagate by seed when ripe in a cold frame or by division in early spring.

CRAMBE CORDIFOLIA
H 2–2.5m (6½–8ft) ★★★★
Striking, robust, herbaceous perennial with widely branching, erect stems bear-ing a profusion of tiny, 4-petalled, white flowers in early summer. The mainly basal leaves are large, long-stalked, kidney-shaped, dark green and often puckered and toothed. Grow in fertile, moist but well-drained and, ideally limy, soil in a sunny site. Propagate by division in early spring or by root cut-tings in early winter.

DELPHINIUM HYBRIDS
H 2m (6½ft) or more ★★★★
Beautiful, herbaceous peren-nials bearing long, tapering spires of bowl-shaped flowers in shades of blue, purple and white, rarely pink, pale yel-low and red. The long-stalked, rounded leaves are deeply cleft into several mid-green, toothed lobes. Grow in fertile, moist but well-drained soil in a sunny site.

Propagate by basal cuttings in spring or by seed sown in warmth in early spring. A wide variety of cultivars is available.

ECHINOPS SPHAEROCEPHALUS
H 2m (6½ft or more) ★★★★
Striking, herbaceous perenni-al, also known as Globe Thistle, bearing large, globu-lar heads of small, 5-petalled, tubular silvery blue flowers in late summer. The entirely stem-borne leaves are irregu-larly cut into jagged lobes, deep green above and grey beneath. Grow in any fertile, moist but well-drained soil in a sunny position. Propagate by division in autumn to spring or by seed in a seed-bed in spring. *E. ritro* is simi-lar but smaller, H 1.2m (4ft), with bright blue flowerheads.

EUPHORBIA CHARACIAS
H 1.2m (4ft) ★★★
This handsome, evergreen perennial (sometimes classed as a shrub) has large spread-ing mounds of bottle brush-like stems covered with long, slim, grey-green, waxy leaves. At their tips are borne green-ish flower bracts with brown centres from spring to early summer. Prefers well-drained soil in full sun. Propagate by division in spring. The sub-species *wulfenii* has green flower centres.

FILIPENDULA CAMTSCHATICA
H 2–3m (6½–10ft) ★★★★
Imposing, clump-forming perennial with strong, wind-proof stems and long leaves divided into several, rounded to oval, mid-green, toothed leaflets. From late summer to early autumn, tiny, fragrant white or pale pink flowers are carried in large, flattish, terminal heads. Grow in moist, fertile soil in sun or partial shade. Propagate by

division in winter and early spring. *F. rubra*, Queen of the Prairies, is a little shorter, with pink flowers and rounded leaflets.

HELIANTHUS SALICIFOLIUS
H 2–2.5m (6½–8ft) ★★★★
This striking, herbaceous perennial has daisy-like flowerheads with golden yellow petals and a brown, central disk from late summer to mid-autumn. The leaves are narrow, willow-shaped, deep green and arching. Grow in fertile, moist but well-drained soil in sun. Propagate by division in winter and early spring. *H. x laetiflorus* is shorter, with larger, entirely bright yellow flowers. *H. x l.* 'Miss Mellish' is semi-double and orange-yellow.

INULA MAGNIFICA
H 1.5–1.8m (5–6ft) ★★★★
This bold, self-supporting perennial bears large, golden yellow daisies in terminal clusters, in late summer. The basal and stem leaves are large, elliptic to oval, dark green and softly hairy beneath. Needs fertile, reasonably moist soil and sun or partial shade. Propagate by division in autumn or spring, or by seed sown in a cold frame in early spring.

LIGULARIA PRZEWALSKII
H 2m (6½ft) or more ★★★★
Dramatic, herbaceous perennial with clumps of purple-brown stems bearing airy spikes of small, bright yellow, daisy flowers from mid- to late summer. The basal and stem leaves are rounded, mid-green, deeply cut into long, jaggedly toothed lobes. Grow in moist, fertile soil in sun or partial shade. Propagate by division in early spring. *L. stenocephala* 'The Rocket' is slightly shorter with oval to triangular leaves bearing many large teeth and slightly darker yellow flowers. *L.* 'Gregynog Gold', with lighter green, heart-shaped leaves

and shorter, pyramidal spikes of larger, deep yellow flowers. *L. dentata* 'Desdemona' is smaller, H 1m (3ft), with deep orange flowers and rounded, brownish leaves.

MACLEAYA CORDATA (*BOCCONIA CORDATA*)
H 2.5m (8ft) ★★★★
A graceful, herbaceous perennial, known as Plume Poppy, with stems topped by large, airy plumes of tiny, creamy white flowers with many stamens from mid- to late summer. The long-stalked, rounded leaves are olive green above and downy white beneath. It prefers fertile, moist but well-drained soil in sun or partial shade. Propagate by division in winter to early spring. *M. microcarpa* 'Kelway's Coral Plume' has buff pink to coral-pink flowers.

PENSTEMON BARBATUS
H 1.2–1.8m (4–6ft) ★★★★
Grown for its wand-like spikes of tubular red flowers from summer to early autumn. The basal and stem leaves are lance- to strap-shaped, pointed, mid-green or slightly blue-tinted. Grow in well-drained, fertile soil in full sun. Propagate by softwood cuttings in early summer or division in spring.

RHEUM PALMATUM
H 2m (6½ft) or more ★★★★
Self-supporting perennial, also known as Chinese Rhubarb, with cream to red plumes of tiny flowers in summer and large, long-stalked, deep green leaves Grow in moist soil in sun or partial shade. Propagate by division in early spring or by seed when ripe. 'Bowles' Crimson', has dark red flowers and leaves which are flushed crimson beneath.

RODGERSIA AESCULIFOLIA
H 1.8m–2m (6–6½ft) or more ★★★
An impressive, widely clump-forming herbaceous perennial spreading by thick rhi-

zomes. The mainly basal leaves are large, long-stalked and rounded, bronze-flushed when young, then mid- to deep green. The tiny, white or pink flowers form fluffy, loose or pyramidal clusters in summer. Grow in moist, fertile soil in partial shade. Propagate by division in early autumn. *R. podophylla* has broader, jaggedly lobed, red-bronze leaflets and creamy white flowers.

THALICTRUM FLAVUM SSP. *GLAUCUM* (*T. SPECIOSISSIMUM*)
H 2m (6½ft) ★★★★
Charming, clump-forming, herbaceous perennial with airy clusters of tiny, bright yellow, many-stamened flowers in summer and rounded leaves cut into small, blue-grey leaflets. Grow in fertile, moist soil in sun. Propagate by division in early spring. *T. chelidonii* has clusters of fewer, larger purple-mauve flowers.

Inula magnifica

Ligularia 'The Rocket'

Macleaya microcarpa

Rheum palmatum

Rodgersia aesculifolia

Medium perennials

Agapanthus hybrid

Anemone x hybrida

Dicentra spectabilis 'Alba'

Dictamnus albus

Helenium 'Gartensonne'

AGAPANTHUS
HEADBOURNE HYBRIDS
H 60–120cm (2–4ft) ★★★
Striking, herbaceous perennial, also known as African Lily, bearing large, globular heads of 6-petalled, funnel-shaped flowers in shades of blue, purple and white. The strap-shaped leaves are mid- to deep green. Grow in fertile, moist but well-drained soil in sun or partial shade. Propagate by seeds sown when ripe or in spring in a cold frame, planting out when at least two years old, or by division in spring.

ANCHUSA AZUREA
(A. ITALICA)
H 90–150cm (3–5ft) ★★★★
Grown for its 5-petalled, gentian blue flowers in long, erect, loose sprays in early to mid-summer. The basal and stem-leaves are lance-shaped, mid- to deep green and coarsely hairy. Grow in fertile, moist but well-drained soil in a sunny position. Propagate by seed in spring or root cuttings in winter. 'Little John', H 40cm (16in), stays at this height, 'Loddon Royalist', H 90cm (3ft), seldom needs staking.

ANEMONE X HYBRIDA
(A. JAPONICA OF GARDENS)
H 1–1.5m (3–5ft) ★★★★
Outstanding, autumn-flowering perennial, also known as Japanese anemone, with bowl-shaped flowers ranging from white to shades of pink. The mainly basal leaves are divided into three broad leaflets, mid-green above and softly hairy beneath. Grow in moist soil in partial shade. Propagate by division in late autumn. 'Honorine Jobert' has pure white flowers with golden stamens.

DICENTRA SPECTABILIS
H 60–75cm (2–2½ft) ★★★★
Also known as Bleeding Heart, or Dutchman's Breeches, this intriguing plant has unique heart-shaped, pendent flowers produced in arching sprays in early summer. The leaves are large, pale green and cut into many small leaflets creating a fern-like effect. Grow in moist but well-drained soil in sun or partial shade.

Propagate by division in early autumn. 'Alba' produces pure white flowers.

DICTAMNUS ALBUS
H 60–90cm (2–3ft) ★★★★
Handsome, self-supporting perennial known also as Burning Bush or Dittany, grown for its fragrance and irregularly 5-petalled, white or pink summer flowers borne in stiff spikes. The stem-borne leaves are divided into leathery, mid- to deep-green, lemon-scented leaflets. Grow in ordinary soil in a sunny site. Propagate by seed when ripe, or by division in autumn or spring.

HELENIUM AUTUMNALE
H 90–150cm (3–5ft) ★★★★
Showy, clump-forming, herbaceous perennial, also known as Sneezeweed, freely producing large, terminal clusters of yellow daisy flowers with brown centres. The narrowly oval to lance-shaped, toothed leaves are mid-green. Grow in a fertile, moist but well-drained soil in a sunny position. Propagate by division in late winter to early spring. Several cultivars are available and are more popular than the species, being sturdier with flowers in shades of yellow to crimson.

LEUCANTHEMUM
X SUPERBUM (C. MAXIMUM)
H 75–90cm (2½–3ft) ★★★★
Also known as Shasta Daisy, the most striking of the garden daisies has large, single or double flowers in shades of white to pale yellow from early summer to early autumn. Stem-borne leaves are narrow, toothed and deep green. Grow in moist, fertile soil in a sunny site. Propagate by division in autumn or early spring, or by seed sown in spring. 'Wirral Pride' has white flower-heads with double centres.

LUPINUS POLYPHYLLUS HYBRIDS
H 60–90cm (2–3ft) ★★★★

Essential border perennial, also known as Russell Lupins, grown for its bold, colourful spikes of pea flowers in early to midsummer, occurring in a wide range of self and bicolours. The long-stalked stem and basal leaves are mid-green, circular, divided into several lance-shaped leaflets. Grow in good garden soil in a sunny position. Propagate by seed, sown in spring or autumn, or by basal cuttings in a cold frame in spring. The following cultivars are recommended: 'My Castle', deep rose-pink, 'The Chatelaine', bicoloured, pink and white, 'The Governor', blue and white.

MONARDA DIDYMA
H 75–90cm (2½–3ft) ★★★★

An intriguing, self-supporting aromatic perennial, also known as Bee Balm, or Oswego Tea, with whorls of slender, tubular, 2-lipped flowers and red-tinted bracts in mid- to late summer. The leaves are oval to lance-shaped, mid-green, toothed and hairy beneath. Grow in reasonably moist garden soil in sun or partial shade. Propagate by division in spring. 'Mahogany' has wine-red flowers with brownish bracts. The hybrid 'Prärienacht' ('Prairie Night') has purple-lilac flowers with green, red-tinted bracts, hybrid 'Schneewittchen' ('Snow White') has white flowers with green bracts.

PAEONIA LACTIFLORA (P. ALBIFLORA) ★★★★
H 55–75cm (1¾–2½ft)

Grown for its large, handsome bowl-shaped flowers in shades of pink and white in summer. The entirely stem leaves are mid- to deep green divided into several lance-shaped leaflets. Grow in moist, but well-drained, fertile soil in full sun.

Propagate by division in late winter. Cultivars include 'Globe of Light', which has fragrant, anemone-centred rose-pink flowers with yellow petaloids. 'Defender' is a hybrid, with deep crimson flowers and golden stamens.

PAPAVER ORIENTALE
H 60–90cm (2–3ft) ★★★★

This striking perennial is also known as Oriental Poppy, and has huge poppy flowers in mid-summer in shades of red and orange, often with a black basal blotch. The stems and rich green leaves are prominently bristly. Grow in ordinary soil in full sun. Propagate by division in early spring or by root cuttings in early winter. 'Allegro' has bright orange-scarlet flowers with black basal marks. 'Perry's White' has white flowers with maroon blotches.

PHLOX PANICULATA
H 90–120cm (3–4ft) ★★★★

A showy, attractive, self-supporting perennial which bears a profusion of fragrant flowers in a wide variety of colours. The leaves are lance-shaped, pointed and mid- to bright green. Grow in moist, reasonably fertile soil in either sun or partial shade. Propagate by division in autumn or spring or by root cuttings in winter. 'Balmoral' has large trusses of pink flowers, 'Eventide' has lavender-blue flowers. 'Harlequin' has ivory-white margined leaves and reddish-purple flowers, and 'Prince of Orange' has orange-red flowers.

POLYGONATUM x HYBRIDUM
H 90–120cm (3–4ft) ★★★★

Elegant, self-supporting perennial with arching stems and small, pendent green and white bells in spring. The oval- to broadly lance-shaped leaves are prominently ribbed and mid- to grey-

ish green. Grow in ordinary soil. Propagate by division of the rhizomes in winter. 'Striatum' has the leaves boldly striped with cream.

SIDALCEA MALVIFLORA
H 90–120cm (3–4ft) ★★★★

An elegant, usually self-supporting perennial, also known as Prairie Mallow, with erect spires of pink to lilac silky textured, bowl-shaped, 5-petalled flowers in summer. The basal leaves are rounded to kidney-shaped and long stalked, the stem leaves are deeply lobed and short stalked. Grow in well-drained soil in full sun. Propagate by division in autumn or by seed in spring. 'Puck' has deep pink flowers on 40cm (1¼ft) stems. 'Sussex Beauty' has satin-textured, clear pink flowers on 90cm (3ft) stems.

VERBASCUM PHOENICEUM
H 90–120cm (3–4ft) ★★★★

Also known as Purple Mullein, this striking, short-lived perennial has long spires of bowl-shaped flowers in shades of white, pink and purple in early summer. The basal leaves are large, oval, wrinkled and deep green, the stem leaves are smaller and narrower. Grow in ordinary soil in a sunny site. Propagate by sowing seed in spring. Among hybrid cultivars is the striking 'Pink Domino' with deep rose-pink flowers on 1.2m (4ft) stems.

Leucanthemum x superbum 'Esther Read'

Paeonia lactiflora **'Bowl of Beauty'**

Papaver orientale

Verbascum **hybrid**

Small perennials

Alyssum spinosum

Arenaria montana

Armeria maritima

Aubrieta hybrid

Campanula carpatica

Erigeron karvinskianus

ACHILLEA CLAVENNAE
H 15–20cm (6–8in) ★★★★
This handsome, silvery, hairy mat-former is usually grown for its flat clusters of small, white, daisy flowers, in summer. Leaves are narrowly spoon-shaped, usually toothed or lobed, silvery grey-green. Grow in well-drained soil in full sun. Propagate by division in late winter or soft cuttings in late spring.

ALCHEMILLA CONJUNCTA
H 15–25cm (6–10in) or more ★★★★
Useful, clump- and mat-forming perennial, also known as Lady's Mantle, with frothy clusters of tiny, greenish-yellow flowers in summer. The long-stalked, rounded leaves are dissected into 7 to 9 finger-shaped lobes, which are dark green above, silvery haired beneath. Grow in ordinary soil in sun or partial shade. Propagate by division in autumn or early spring.

ALYSSUM SPINOSUM (PTILOTRICHUM SPINOSUM)
H 10–15cm (4–6in) ★★★
Loosely hummock-forming, shrubby perennial with dense, wiry, sometimes spine-tipped stems and a profusion of small, 4-petalled, white to pink flowers in late spring. The tiny leaves are grey and oval to spoon-shaped. Grow in well-drained, ideally limy, soil in full sun. Propagate by greenwood cuttings in summer or seed in autumn or spring in a cold frame. The best forms of var. *roseum* have deep pink flowers.

ARENARIA BALEARICA
H 1–2cm (³⁄₈–³⁄₄in) ★★★
Charming Lilliputian carpeter, also known as Balearic Sandwort, with starry white flowers from late spring to late summer. The minute leaves are oval and light green. Grow in moist garden soil in partial shade. Propagate by division in spring. *A. montana* differs, being loosely mat-forming, H 10cm (4in) or more, with larger, white flowers and much larger, lance-shaped, dark greyish-green leaves. Best in a sunny site.

ARMERIA JUNIPERIFOLIA (A. CAESPITOSA)
H 5–8cm (2–3¼in) ★★★
A delightful, small, evergreen hummock-former, also known as Thrift, which is freely studded with globular pink to purple-pink flower-heads in spring and early summer. The grey-green leaves are short and bristle-like. Grow in well-drained soil in a sunny position. Propagate by semi-ripe cuttings in late summer. *A. maritima*, the Common Thrift, H 15–20cm (6-8in), is larger in all its parts with a 20-30cm (8-12in) spread. The grassy foliage is mid- to deep green. 'Bloodstone' is rich red and 'Vindictive' is rose pink.

AUBRIETA HYBRIDS
H 5–10cm (2–4in) ★★★★
Showy, mat-forming perennial producing abundant clusters of 4-petalled flowers in shades of mauve and purple in spring. The small, crowded leaves are oblong to spoon-shaped, mid- to deep green. Grow in well-drained, ideally limy soil in full sun. Propagate by seed in autumn or spring or by softwood cuttings in summer. *A.* 'Bressingham Pink' is double pink. *A.* 'Greencourt Purple' is rich purple.

AURINIA SAXATILIS (ALYSSUM SAXATILE)
H 15–25cm (6–10in) ★★★★
This plant is grown for its spectacular blaze of golden yellow, crowded clusters of small flowers in spring. The densely borne, grey-green, spoon-shaped leaves form low hummocks. Grow in well-drained, ideally limy soil in full sun. Propagate by seed in autumn or spring or softwood cuttings in summer. 'Citrina' has lemon-yellow flowers. 'Dudley Nevill' has yellowish-buff flowers. 'Variegata' bears leaves with irregularly cream margins.

CAMPANULA CARPATICA
H 30cm (12in) ★★★★
Beautiful clump-forming perennial grown for its profusion of large, upturned, bell flowers in shades of purple, blue and white. The basal leaves are heart-shaped, toothed and mid-green, the stem leaves somewhat smaller and narrower. Grow in well-drained soil in full sun. Propagate by seeds in a cold frame when ripe, or by

division in autumn or early spring. Var. *turbinata* has pale lavender-blue flowers on 10-15cm (3-4in) stems. *C. cochleariifolia*, Fairies' Thimbles, is creeping and tufted, H 8-10cm (4-6in), with small, thimble-shaped bells of white, lavender or slate blue. *C. glomerata*, Clustered Bell-flower, H 40cm (16in) or more, is a vigorous perennial with clusters of violet to pur-ple-blue bells in summer.

DIANTHUS DELTOIDES
H 20–25cm (8–10in) or more ★★★★

Attractive, mat-forming perennial, also called Maiden Pink, with a profusion of miniature 'pinks' in shades of white, pink to red, often with a darker eye. Leaves are small, narrow, deep green and densely borne. Grow in well-drained soil in sun. Propagate by seed in spring or by cut-tings in summer. *D. superbus* is a taller, tufted plant H 20-30cm (8-12in), spread with large, rose-purple flowers with more deeply fringed petals and mid-green leaves.

EPIMEDIUM GRANDIFLORUM
H 20–30cm (8–12in) or more ★★★★

Shade-tolerant perennial with white, pink or purple flowers, like tiny columbines, carried in short, arching spikes. Light green leaves, bronze-flushed when young, are divided into heart-shaped leaflets. Grow in moist but well-drained soil. Propagate by division in autumn or after flowering. 'White Queen' has pure white flowers. 'Rose Queen' has darker, bronze-green leaves and rose pink flowers.

ERIGERON AURANTIACUS
H 20–30cm (8–12in) ★★★★

Clump-forming perennial with bright orange, daisy-like flowerheads in summer. The basal, mid- to deep green leaves are elliptic to spoon-shaped, the velvety downed stem leaves are smaller and

narrower. Grow in ordinary soil in full sun. Propagate by division or basal cuttings in spring. *E. karvinskianus (E. mucronatus)* H 15-20cm (6-8in), is similar, with smaller flowerheads opening white and aging to pink and purple.

GENTIANA ACAULIS
H 7–10cm (2¾–4in) ★★★★

Perhaps the best-loved of the gentians, with large, trumpet-shaped flowers of pure deep blue, spotted green, in spring. The small, mid- to deep-green, lance-shaped, ever-green leaves are borne in dense hummocks. Grow in moist garden soil in sun or partial shade. Propagate by division in late winter or off-sets in spring. *G. verna* is like a miniature *G. acaulis* with broad, spreading lobes to its brilliant blue flowers.

GERANIUM X MAGNIFICUM
H 45–60cm (1½–2ft) ★★★★

Handsome and vigorous clump-forming perennial, also known as Cranesbill, with large, saucer-shaped, rich vio-let-blue flowers freely pro-duced in summer. The long-stalked, rounded, broadly-lobed leaves are downy, and colour well in autumn. Grow in ordinary soil in sun or par-tial shade. Propagate by divi-sion from autumn to early spring or by seed when ripe. *G. sanguineum* is a clump-forming perennial with saucer-shaped, magenta pink flowers in summer.

GEUM CHILOENSE (G. COCCINEUM)
H 40–60cm (16–24in) ★★★★

Valuable front of the border plant with saucer-shaped, 5-petalled, scarlet flowers from early to late summer. The mainly basal leaves are divided into heart to kidney-shaped, toothed, mid-green leaflets. Grow in moist, well-drained garden soil in sun or partial shade. Propagate by division in autumn or early spring or by seed sown in a cold frame

when ripe. *G. rivale* is similar to *G. chiloense* but of rather spreading habit with bell-shaped, nodding flowers of pink to orange-red. Of the hybrids, 'Fire Opal' has semi-double orange flowers. 'Lady Stratheden' has semi-double, rich yellow flowers.

HELICHRYSUM BELLIDIOIDES
H 10–15cm (4–6in) ★★★

Pleasant, evergreen mat-forming perennial with white-hairy stems and white, papery, daisy-like flowerheads in late spring and summer. The tiny, oval to spoon-shaped leaves are mid-green above and white felted beneath. Grow in any well drained soil. Propagate by careful division in spring or cuttings in summer.

HELLEBORUS NIGER
H 30–40cm (12–16in) ★★★★

Beautiful, winter-flowering, evergreen perennial, also known as Christmas Rose, bearing bowl-shaped white

Epimedium grandiflorum 'Rose Queen'

Geranium x magnificum

Geranium sanguineum

Geum 'Lady Stratheden'

Helleborus niger

Helleborus orientalis hybrid

Hosta fortunei var. *albopicta*

Lewisia cotyledon hybrids

flowers from early winter to early spring. The leathery, deep green leaves are composed of lance-shaped leaflets. Grow in moist but well drained soil in partial shade. Propagate by division after flowering or in late summer. Pink-flushed cultivars are available. *H. orientalis* hybrids, H45cm (18in), are more robust and free-flowering with nodding flowers in shades of white, pink and purple, often with darker spotting. *H. argutifolius* (*H. corsicus*), H 90cm (3ft), has biennial stems which bear large, dark green, trifoliate leaves. The bright yellow-green flowers are carried in trusses in late winter.

HOSTA FORTUNEI
H 50–60cm (20–24in) ★★★★
Handsome, long-lived perennial grown for its narrow, trumpet-shaped mauve flowers carried in loose spikes above the leaves. The leaves are heart-shaped, long-stalked and deep green. Grow in fertile soil in partial shade.

'Albomarginata' has the leaves edged with cream to white. *H. sieboldiana* is larger, H 1m (3ft), with rounded to heart-shaped, grey-green, strongly ribbed leaves. Flowers are lilac-grey, fading with age. Var. *elegans* has strongly blue-grey leaves.

LEWISIA COTYLEDON
H 25–30cm (10–12in) ★★★★
Attractive perennial grown for its freely produced showers of shallowly funnel-shaped flowers in shades of pink to purple or white, usually with darker stripes. The entirely basal leaves are fleshy and narrowly oblong, mid- to deep green. Best grown against a dry wall, it prefers a well-drained, humus-rich soil and thrives in either sun or partial shade. Propagate by seed sown when ripe in a cold frame or offsets as cuttings in late spring. The popular *L. cotyledon* hybrids are more robust and come in a wide colour range.

PHLOX DOUGLASII
H 8–12cm (3–5in) ★★★★
This evergreen mat-former produces many starry flowers in white to blue and pink. Its crowded, tiny, leaves are dark green. Grow in well-drained soil in sun. Propagate by softwood or semi-hardwood cuttings in summer. 'Iceberg' is white, 'Red Admiral' is crimson and 'Violet Queen' has violet-purple flowers. *P. subulata* is similar, but has a larger, looser habit, longer leaves and flowers in a wider variety of colours.

PRIMULA VULGARIS
H 15cm (6in) ★★★★
Also known as Primrose, this rosette and clump forming perennial has a profusion of circular, 5-petalled single and double flowers in pinks, yellows and white. The semi-evergreen, corrugated leaves are lance-shaped, mid- to deep green. Cultivars and hybrids are available in many

colours from purple-blue and red to pale cream. Grow in moist soil in partial shade. Propagate by seed when ripe, or in spring in a cold frame, or by division after flowering. *P. auricula* is distinctive, having short, wrinkled stems that bear clusters of deep-yellow, white-mealy flowers, often with banded petals, and spoon-shaped, pale to grey-green leaves in rosettes.

PULSATILLA VULGARIS
H 10–20cm (4–8in) ★★★★
This beautiful clump-forming perennial is also known as Pasque Flower. It is grown for its erect to nodding, 6-petalled, bell-shaped, purple flowers and its finely dissected, fern-like foliage. Grow in ordinary, preferably limy, soil in full sun. Propagate by seed when ripe or root cuttings in winter. 'Alba' is white, 'Eva Constance' is red, opening wide. Var. *rubra* is similar but with more bell-shaped, rich red flowers.

RUDBECKIA FULGIDA
H 60–90cm (2–3ft) ★★★★
Long-lived, clump-forming perennial, also known as Black-eyed Susan, with a profusion of bright orange-yellow, black-brown centred daisies from late summer to mid-autumn. The stalked, basal leaves are lance-shaped, toothed and veined. Grow in ordinary soil in sun or partial shade. Propagate by division in autumn or early spring. *R.f.* var. *deamii* is one of the best-known and most freely flowering forms, with hairy stems and long pointed leaves.

SAXIFRAGA X ANGLICA
H 2–5cm (¾–2in) ★★★★
One of the best of the silver-encrusted saxifrages, *S.* x *a.* 'Cranbourne' forms firm, low hummocks and bears many, cup-shaped, deep rose-pink flowers in early spring. The narrow, grey-green, white-dotted leaves are borne in

Phlox subulata '**Scarlet Flame**'

tiny rosettes. Grow in well-drained, limy soil in full sun. Propagate by single rosettes taken as cuttings in late spring or early summer. *S. x apiculata* 'Gregor Mendel' has larger hummocks and many clusters of starry, light yellow flowers. *S. fortunei* is a clump-forming, herbaceous perennial with slender stems to 30cm (12in) tall bearing loose clusters of white flowers with petals of irregular sizes in autumn.

SEDUM
H 10cm (4in) ★★★★
Huge genus of mostly mat- or hummock forming perennials, also known as Stonecrop, some of which are evergreen. They have rosettes of basal leaves and small, starry flowers. Grow in well-drained soil in full sun. Propagate by division in spring or cuttings in summer. *S. spurium* has reddish stems bearing flattened clusters of star-shaped, pinkish-purple flowers in late summer. 'Schorbuser Blut' ('Dragon's Blood') has deep reddish-pink flowers and purple-tinted leaves. *S. kamtschaticum* forms low clumps of deep golden yellow flowers. S. *kamtschaticum* 'Variegatum' has pink-tinted leaves with cream margins. *S. spectabile*, Ice Plant, a clump-forming, herbaceous perennial, H 45cm (18in), has large, flattened heads of starry, pink flowers in late summer.

SEMPERVIVUM TECTORUM
H 15–25cm (6–10in) ★★★
Popular hardy, succulent perennial grown for its handsome rosettes with a bonus of pink to red-purple star-shaped flowers in summer. The narrowly oblong, slender-pointed leaves are mid- to blue-green, often tipped with red-purple. Grow in well-drained soil in full sun. Propagate by offsets in spring or summer. *S. ciliosum* has smaller, hairy rosettes

with incurved leaves and green-yellow flowers. *S. arachnoideum* has even smaller rosettes, green to purple-flushed leaves tipped with long, white hairs that form a cobweb over the rosette and reddish-pink flowers.

THYMUS
H 3–20cm (1–8in) ★★★
Aromatic, mat-forming evergreen perennial, also known as Thyme, thickly set with dense heads of tiny, tubular, purple flowers in summer. The tiny leaves are hairy and mid-green. Grow in well-drained, ideally limy, soil in full sun. Propagate by cuttings in mid- to late summer or by division in spring. *T serpyllum* var. *coccineus* ('Coccineus') has red flowers and 'Pink Chintz' has pink flowers and grey-green leaves. *T. x citriodorus*, lemon-scented thyme, forms low, bushy plants bearing lavender-pink flowers and lemon-scented leaves. 'Aureus' has gold-dappled leaves. 'Golden King' is more erect with gold-margined leaves. 'Silver Queen' has creamy white variegated leaves.

VERONICA SPICATA
H 30–40cm (12–16in) ★★★
Colourful, clump- or mat-forming perennial bearing numerous, erect, slender dense spikes of small flowers in shades of blue in summer. The leaves are oval to oblong, toothed, mid- to bright green. Grow in ordinary, ideally limy, soil in full sun. Propagate by division in autumn or early spring or by seed when ripe. The cultivar 'Heidekind' has pink flowers and grey leaves, ssp. *incana* has silvery-grey leaves and rich purple-blue flowers, and 'Rotfuchs' ('Red Fox') has red flowers. 'Shirley Blue' bears vivid blue flowers, *V. prostrata* forms wide mats bearing short spikes of blue flowers in early summer.

Saxifraga x apiculata 'Gregor Mendel'

Saxifraga fortunei

VIOLA ODORATA
H 10cm (4in) ★★★★
This well-loved perennial is also known as Sweet Violet. It forms wide, loose clumps or mats bearing scented, purple-blue, 5-petalled flowers. The long-stalked leaves are heart-shaped and mid- to bright green. Grow in ordinary garden soil in a sunny position or in partial shade. Propagate by seed when ripe or by division in autumn or early spring. Forms in other shades of purple-blue, pink, red, apricot and white are grown. *V. riviniana* 'Purpurea' (*V. labradorica* of gardens) is like a less robust *odorata* with smaller, smooth leaves that are heavily flushed with purple. *V. cornuta*, Horned Violet, is a tufted to clump-forming perennial, H 15cm (6in), with long-spurred, purple-blue flowers from spring to autumn. Lilac and white forms are also grown.

Sempervivum

Thymus doerfleri 'Bressingham'

Viola cornuta

Bamboos, grasses and ferns

These plants are used, primarily, for the contribution that their foliage brings to the garden. Ferns do not flower, bamboos (which are giant grasses) effectively do not, whereas the flowers of grasses often have considerable ornamental value, but for their form rather than their colour. Generally, grasses prefer drier soil and sunnier conditions. Bamboos cope well with more moist soil, and bamboos and ferns generally do best in partial shade but will cope with some sun as well.

Phyllostachys aurea

Phyllostachys nigra

Pseudosasa japonica

Hakonechloa macra '**Aureola**'

Bamboos

FARGESIA MURIELIAE (ARUNDINARIA MURIELIAE)
H 3–4m (10–12ft) ★★★★

Graceful, densely clump-forming bamboo with many slender, erect then arching, yellow-green stems and very slender branches with small, lance-shaped, bright green leaves. Grow in ordinary garden soil in sun or partial shade. Propagate by division in spring.

PHYLLOSTACHYS AUREA
H 4–10m (12–30ft) ★★★★

Colourful, clump-forming bamboo, also known as Golden or Fishpole Bamboo, with stiffly erect, grooved canes which are bright green at first, then brownish-yellow. The branchlets bear narrowly lance-shaped, yellowish to golden green leaves. Grow in ordinary soil in sun or partial shade, sheltered from freezing winds. Propagate by division in spring. *P. nigra*, Black Bamboo, has more slender green canes that turn lustrous black in their second or third year.

PSEUDOSASA JAPONICA (ARUNDINARIA JAPONICA)
H 4–6m (12–20ft) ★★★

Very hardy bamboo, eventually forming thickets of erect, olive-green stems which mature to pale brown. The dark green, oblong to lance-shaped leaves are 30cm (12in) or more in length. Grow in moist soil in sun or partial shade. Propagate by division or by separating rooted canes in spring.

SASA PALMATA
H 2m (6½ft) or more ★★★

Handsome but vigorous bamboo which spreads widely by woody rhizomes and bears erect to slightly arching, green canes, sometimes purple streaked. The large, broadly elliptic leaves are glossy, bright, rich green with paler midribs. The leaf tips may turn brown in severe winters. Grow in ordinary, preferably moist, garden soil in either sun or shade. Propagate by division or by separating rooted canes in spring. *S. veitchii* has scarious, parchment-coloured leaves giving the effect of variegation.

YUSHANIA ANCEPS (ARUNDINARIA ANCEPS)
H 3–4m (10–12ft) ★★★★

Elegant, colony-forming bamboo with glossy, dark green canes, erect then arching. The slender branches bear numerous narrow, lance-shaped, mid-green leaves. Grow in ordinary garden soil in either sun or partial shade, ideally sheltered from freezing winds. Propagate by division or by separating individual, rooted canes in spring.

Grasses

CAREX ELATA 'AUREA'
H 60–70cm (2–2½ft) ★★★★

Attractive, clump-forming perennial, also known as Bowles' Golden Sedge, with arching, slender, yellow leaves and short, contrasting brown flower spikes in summer. Grow in ordinary, ideally moist soil in sun. Propagate by division in spring.

CORTADERIA SELLOANA
H 2.5–3m (8–10ft) ★★★

Familiar, spectacular evergreen, known as Pampas Grass. This is densely clump-forming, with arching mid- to grey-green, rough-edged leaves and erect stems bearing large, fluffy plumes of numerous, silvery florets in late summer to autumn. Grow in well-drained soil in sun. Propagate by division in spring. *C.s.* 'Pumila' H 1.5m (5ft) is much smaller. *C.s.* 'Rendatleri' has pinkish-purple florets.

HAKONECHLOA MACRA
H 30–40cm(1–1½ft) ★★★★

Striking, tufted to mound-forming, herbaceous grass with densely borne, arching, mid- to bright-green leaves. Pale green florets are carried in sparse, slender plumes in summer. Grow in ordinary, ideally moist, soil in sun or partial shade. Propagate by division in spring. Represented in gardens by one of its variegated forms, *H.m.* 'Alboaurea', with leaves striped white and gold, and *H.m.* 'Aureola' with yellow leaves narrowly striped with green.

MISCANTHUS SINENSIS
H 2m (6½ft) ★★★★

Handsome, ornamental, clump-forming herbaceous perennial bearing arching, narrow, matt to slightly bluish-green leaves topped by silk-haired, greyish florets in a sheaf of slender spikes which arch with age. Grow in ordinary, ideally moist, soil in sun. Propagate by division in spring. *M.s.* 'Silberfeder' ('Silver Feather') is a reliable, free-flowering cultivar. *M.s.* 'Zebrinus' has broader leaves with zones of white to cream and green.

MOLINIA CAERULEA
H 60–90cm (2–3ft) ★★★★
Also known as Purple Moor Grass, this densely tufted, herbaceous perennial has slender, arching, mid-green leaves and erect, yellow-flushed flowering stems bearing loose, narrow heads of tiny, purplish florets. Grow in moist soil in sun or partial shade. Propagate by division in spring.

STIPA ARUNDINACEA
H 1m (3ft) ★★★★
Elegant, tufted, evergreen also known as Pheasant's-tail Grass, producing slender, arching, dark green leaves turning orange-brown in autumn. The large, airy, flowering plumes are formed of many, purplish-green florets. Grow in well-drained soil in sun. Propagate by division in spring. *S. calamagrostis* has bluish green leaves and smaller, more compact, floral plumes of purple-tinted to buff spikelets. *S. gigantea* is a fine, large specimen grass, H 2m (6½ft) or more, with robust, erect stems bearing huge, loose plumes of purplish green florets which turn corn yellow when ripe.

Ferns

ADIANTUM PEDATUM
H 30–40cm (1–1¼ft) ★★★★
Also known as Maidenhair Fern, this elegant, herbaceous, clump-former has slender, purple-black leaf stalks and hand-shaped fronds made up of triangular to diamond-shaped leaflets, bright green, darkening with age. Grow in ordinary, ideally humus-rich, soil in partial shade. Propagate by division in early spring. *A. pedatum* var. *subpumilum* (*A. aleuticum*), H 20–30cm (8–12in), has tighter clumps of congested fronds. *A. venustum*, Himalayan Maidenhair, is a widely spreading fern with triangular, lacy fronds of small, fan-shaped leaflets which emerge bright bronze-pink and age to mid-green. The hardiest true Maidenhair Fern.

ASPLENIUM SCOLOPENDRIUM (PHYLITTIS SCOLOPENDRIUM)
H 40–60cm (1¼–2ft) ★★★★
Distinctive, evergreen, clump-former, also known as Hart's Tongue Fern, with leathery, bright green, strap-shaped fronds which have a heart-shaped base and a pointed tip. Grow in ordinary soil. Propagate by division in early spring. *A.s.* Crispum Group has boldly crimped leaves. *A.s.* Undulatum Group has less strong undulations.

DRYOPTERIS FILIX-MAS
H 60–90cm (2–3ft) ★★★★
The most familiar shuttlecock fern, also known as Male Fern, with lance-shaped, semi evergreen fronds dissected into oblong leaflets. Grow in moist, well-drained soil in full or partial shade. Propagate by division in early spring. *D. affinis* (*D. borreri*), Golden-scaled Male Fern, is larger and more erect, its leaf stalks and midribs covered in golden brown scales. *D. erythrosora*, H 60cm (24in), has coppery red fronds when young, aging to lustrous, deep green.

MATTEUCCIA STRUTHIOPTERIS
H 1.2m (4ft) – single rosette ★★★★
Handsome, colony-forming, herbaceous fern, also known as Ostrich Plume Fern, with shuttlecock-shaped rosettes of lance-shaped, bright green leaves The dark brown, fertile fronds are much shorter and borne in the centre of the rosette. As this fern can spread 1m (3ft) a year, it is only for large gardens or where roots can be restricted. Grow in moist soil in sun to full shade. Propagate by separating individual rosettes in late winter.

Miscanthus sinensis 'Silberspinne'

Stipa gigantea

Asplenium scolopendrium

POLYPODIUM VULGARE
H 30–40cm (12–16in) ★★★★
Decorative, evergreen fern with narrowly triangular to lance-shaped fronds, deeply dissected into bright green lobes. Grow in well-drained soil in sun or partial shade. Propagate by division in spring or early summer. *P. interjectum* is very similar. The vigorous 'Cornubiense' makes good ground cover.

POLYSTICHUM SETIFERUM
H 45–75cm (18–30in) ★★★★
Attractive, evergreen, clump-forming fern, also known as Soft Shield Fern, with low arching, soft-textured, lance-shaped fronds dissected into tiny, oval, toothed leaflets. Grow in well-drained soil in partial to full shade. Propagate by division in spring or by detaching plantlets from old fronds. Divisilobum Group includes cultivars with feathery, finely dissected fronds.

Polypodium interjectum

Polystichum setiferum

Using ground cover

Shady places
Ferns, bamboos and grasses are ideal choices for shady areas of the garden as they provide dense, weed-suppressing cover in low light conditions.

The most familiar ground cover, lawn grass, is very dependent upon regular mowing and irrigation. Unfortunately, not all of us have the time to mow grass and water is in increasingly short supply. There are also areas where grass does not do well, notably in shade. Although paving is sometimes used as an alternative, its hard surface detracts from the idea most of us have of a garden, and you cannot pave slopes.

Ground cover plants are another, more attractive, low-maintenance alternative to lawn grass, and their development and use is one of the fastest growing areas of horticulture. There are some that can even be walked upon, although none will stand as much foot traffic as lawn grass. One of these is chamomile, which has been used as a lawn plant for centuries, another is yarrow (*Achillea millefolium*). The majority, however, are decorative ground covers only.

Since the object is to cover the ground, plants used are invariably evergreen, most commonly those which develop quite a dense foliage canopy which protects the ground underneath from erosion and suppresses weeds.

Types of ground cover

It is conventional to use only one kind of ground cover in any area, but there is no reason to restrict them in this way. Taller plants, such as bergenias and alchemilla, with more distinctive foliage can be used amongst lower growing, more undisciplined, creeping species, like ajuga and *Lysimachia nummularia*. In this way, the number of more expensive, slower growing plants is minimized.

Ground cover plants can create excitingly different textures and colours when planted in distinct shapes, either geometrical, or 'organic' and curved. The only proviso here is that it will be necessary to separate the groups of plants, otherwise they will begin to merge with each other and blur the boundaries.

An unorthodox, but often successful, method of creating ground cover is to use climbers, allowing them to trail over the ground. Ivy (*Hedera* spp.) is one plant that in nature seems as happy to trail as to climb. Honeysuckles (*Lonicera* spp.) make good, strong-growing ground cover. It is even possible to use clematis.

Ribbon planting
Ferns (above and right) are an excellent choice for ground cover for the area at the foot of a wall or fence, as they are among the few plants that flourish in the low light levels.

Planting ground cover

When selecting plants for ground cover, check they will thrive in the conditions in which you plan to plant them. The most useful types are those that spread rapidly by creeping stems or runners.

The best way to plant ground cover is through black plastic, as this keeps weeds down until the plants are established. A large area may need a lot of plants, which can be prohibitively expensive. One answer is to propagate your own.

1 *Peg down black, plastic sheeting across the area to be planted. Then cut crosses in the black plastic to create planting holes for the plants at appropriate distances apart.*

2 *Dig planting holes through the cut areas of the plastic. Carefully insert the plant through the sheeting and backfill the hole. Water in well and keep watered in dry weather.*

3 *To disguise the black plastic, cover it with a layer of coarse bark chippings. Once the ground cover is well established and serving its purpose, you can remove the plastic sheeting.*

Places for ground cover

It is possible to use ground cover plants in a naturalistic way, intermingling them so that the end result resembles wild vegetation growing on a woodland floor. It is important, though, that plants of fairly equal vigour are chosen. Putting a rampant spreader like *Lamium galeobdolon* next to a less speedy grower like bergenia is asking for trouble. It will soon be swamped.

Most of the ground covers that are commonly used are for planting in shade, where grass does not flourish and where there is often little incentive to grow flowering plants. Some, like *Ajuga reptans*, grow relatively low and because of their habit of rooting from the base of their spreading stems, can be used to cover an area quite rapidly. Others like the bergenias, are considerably taller – up to 30 cms (12in) – and much more slow growing. Some of these larger plants have considerable decorative value, as they are evergreen, have attractive foliage and good flowers. Before planting ground

Ground cover carpet

A great advantage of ground cover is that it is very low maintenance. Plants like Pachysandra terminalis *and* Trillium luteum, *are ideal for shady conditions.*

cover, ensure all perennial weeds have been destroyed, as it will be difficult to remove them later. Weeds growing in between a smooth planting of ground cover will mar its otherwise regular appearance.

In some parts of the garden, particularly under the canopies of evergreen trees, very little will grow. *Hedera hibernia* or *H. colchica* are among the candidates for this kind of deep shade. There are many different species of ivy with markedly different sizes and shapes of leaf, so you could grow more than one kind to add interest.

Woodland garden

Primulas, meconopsis and ferns are intermingled to produce a carpet of flowers and foliage that resembles the wild vegetation of a woodland floor.

Ground cover

Ajuga reptans

Alchemilla mollis

Heuchera micrantha
'Palace Purple'

Lamium maculatum and *L.m.* 'Album'

AJUGA REPTANS
H 15–20cm (6–8in)
S 60cm (2ft) or more ★★★★
Vigorous, evergreen perennial, also called Bugle, with erect stems of tubular, deep blue flowers in late spring and summer. The dense, basal leaves are oblong to spoon-shaped, rich green and semi-glossy. Grow in ordinary soil in sun to full shade. Propagate by division in autumn to spring. *A.r.* 'Multicolor' ('Rainbow') has bronze green leaves marked cream and pink, 'Variegata' has grey-green leaves edged and splashed with creamy white.

ALCHEMILLA MOLLIS
H 40–60cm (1½–2ft)
S 60–75cm (2–2½ft) ★★★★
Also called Lady's Mantle, this plant has rounded, shallowly lobed, softly hairy, light green leaves to 15cm (6in) across that die down in late autumn and lime green clusters of tiny flowers in summer. Grow in ordinary soil in sun or partial shade. Propagate by division from autumn to late winter. Self-sown seedlings often occur.

BERGENIA CORDIFOLIA
H 45–60cm (1½–2ft)
S 75–90cm (2½–3ft) ★★★★
A valuable, evergreen perennial, also known as Elephant's Ears, forming spreading clumps from thick rhizomes which produce clusters of pink to red, 5-petalled, bell-shaped flowers in early spring. The large, rounded to heart-shaped mid- to deep green leaves are often purple-tinted in winter. Grow in well-drained, ideally humus-rich soil in sun or partial shade. Propagate by division in autumn. *B.c.* 'Purpurea' has red-purple flowers and redder winter leaves. *B. crassifolia* has narrower, paddle-shaped leaves and pink flowers.

BRUNNERA MACROPHYLLA
(SYN. *ANCHUSA*
MYOSOTIDIFLORA) ★★★★
H 45cm (18in) S 60cm (2ft)
Sprays of blue, forget-me-not-like flowers are produced from spring to early summer. The mainly basal leaves are bold, heart-shaped and mid- to deep green. Grow in ordinary soil in sun or partial shade. Propagate by division from late autumn to early spring or root cuttings in winter. *B.m.* 'Hadspen Cream' has leaves irregularly variegated with creamy white. *B.m.* 'Langtrees' has leaves spotted with silvery grey.

HEDERA HELIX
H 10m (30ft) S indefinite
★★★★
This self-clinging climber or trailing perennial is also known as Common Ivy. It has broadly oval to triangular, glossy dark green leaves. There are many variants and cultivars, which are more commonly grown. 'Angularis Aurea' has shallowly lobed, glossy mid-green leaves, becoming suffused and variegated with yellow as they age.

HEUCHERA SANGUINEA
H & S 30cm (12in) ★★★★
Dainty, clump-forming, evergreen perennial, known as Coral Bells, grown for its clouds of tiny, red, pink or white bells. The leaves are rounded to kidney-shaped, toothed, deep green, sometimes with paler marbling. Grow in ordinary soil in sun or partial shade. Propagate by seed when ripe or by division in autumn. Hybrids are *H.* 'Red Spangles' with crimson-scarlet flowers and *H.* 'Pearl Drops', pink tinged with white. *H. micrantha* 'Palace Purple' has jagged, bronzed-red leaves and greenish cream flowers with red anthers.

LAMIUM MACULATUM
H 15–20cm (6–8in)
S 60–90cm (2–3ft) ★★★★
Attractive, evergreen perennial with pink to red-purple, tubular, hooded flowers in early summer. The broadly oval to triangular leaves bear a central silvery-white zone. Grow in ordinary soil in sun or partial shade. Propagate by division in early spring or in autumn. *L.m.* 'Album' has white flowers. *L.m.* 'Aureum' has yellow-suffused leaves. *L.m.* 'White Nancy' has pure white flowers above silver green margined leaves.

LYSIMACHIA NUMMULARIA
H 3–5cm (1¼–2in)
S 45–60cm (1½–2ft) ★★★★
Also known as Creeping Jenny, this vigorous, evergreen perennial bears cup-shaped, 5-petalled flowers in summer. The broadly oval to rounded leaves are mid- to deep green. Grow in ordinary, ideally moist, soil in sun or partial shade. Propagate by division in autumn or spring. *L.n.* 'Aurea', Golden Creeping Jenny, has leaves suffused with golden yellow.

PACHYPHRAGMA
MACROPHYLLUM
H 25–35cm (10–14in)
S 60cm (2ft) or more ★★★★
Cheerful, evergreen to semi-evergreen perennial producing spikes of pure white,

4-petalled flowers from late winter to late spring. The oval to rounded, irregularly scalloped leaves are mid- to deep green. Grow in moisture-retentive, fertile soil in sun or partial shade. Propagate by division in autumn or early spring or sow seeds when ripe.

PACHYSANDRA TERMINALIS
H 15–20cm (6–8in)
S 45–90cm (1½–3ft) ★★★★
Useful, strong-growing evergreen perennial with glossy, deep green, coarsely toothed, spoon-shaped leaves. Petalless, white-stamened flowers are produced in short, terminal spikes in early summer. Grow in ordinary soil in sun or partial shade. Propagate by division in spring or softwood cuttings in summer. *P.t.* 'Variegata' has cream- to white-margined leaves and is less vigorous.

PULMONARIA SACCHARATA
H 30cm (12in) S 45–60cm (1½–2ft) ★★★★
This early-flowering perennial bears funnel-shaped, violet flowers from reddish buds in spring. Leaves large, evergreen, elliptic and silvery spotted. Plants of the Argentea Group have entirely silvered leaves. Grow in ordinary soil in partial shade. Propagate by division after flowering or by seed when ripe. *P. officinalis* differs in having heart-shaped leaves and violet to blue flowers. *P.o.* 'Sissinghurst White' has pure white flowers. *P.o.* 'Cambridge Blue' has pale blue flowers. *P. longifolia* has funnel-shaped, blue-purple flowers.

SAXIFRAGA X URBIUM
H 30cm (12in) or more
S 40–60cm (1¼–2ft) ★★★★
Vigorous, evergreen perennial, known as London Pride, with slender, erect, reddish stems and airy clusters of tiny, star-shaped, pink-flushed, white flowers from late spring to summer. Spoon-shaped, toothed, mid- to deep green leaves are produced in neat, round rosettes. Grow in ordinary, even poor, garden soil in sun or partial shade. Propagate by division in autumn.

STACHYS BYZANTINA (S. LANATA)
H 40–50cm (16–20in)
S 60cm (2ft) or more ★★★★
Also known as Lambs' Ears, this evergreen mat-former has densely grey-white, woolly, elliptic leaves. The small, tubular, two-lipped, purplish-pink flowers are borne in leafy spikes in summer. Grow in ordinary soil in sun. Propagate by division in autumn or spring. *S.b.* 'Cotton Boll' has flower clusters like cotton-wool balls. 'Silver Carpet' H15cm (6in) rarely flowers. *S.b.* 'Primrose Heron' has leaves suffused with yellow.

SYMPHYTUM IBERICUM (S. GRANDIFLORUM)
H 25cm (10in) or more
S 60cm (2ft) or more ★★★★
Fast-growing evergreen perennial, known as Comfrey, bearing narrowly bell-shaped, white to cream flowers from red-tipped buds. Elliptic to oval leaves are mid- to deep green. Grow in ordinary soil in sun or partial shade. Propagate by division in early spring. Large hybrids include *S.* 'Hidcote Blue' with pale blue flowers and *S.* 'Hidcote Pink', pale pink and white. *S. officinale* has purple-violet, pink or creamy yellow flowers.

TIARELLA CORDIFOLIA
H 20–30cm (8–12in)
S 40–60cm (1¼–2ft) or more ★★★★
Delightful, evergreen perennial, also known as Foam Flower, producing many slender stems which bear a foam-like mass of tiny, creamy white flowers in summer. The hairy, maple-like, 3 to 5-lobed leaves are light green, often with a flush or pattern of bronze. Grow in ordinary, ideally humus-enriched, soil in partial shade. Propagate by division in early spring. *T. wherryi* (*T. cordifolia* var. *collina*) is compact-growing, rarely spreading beyond 30cm (12in) across with mainly 3-lobed, maroon-patterned leaves. Flowers are sometimes pink tinted. Best in moist shade.

TRACHYSTEMON ORIENTALIS
H 45–60cm (1½–2ft)
S 1m (3ft) ★★★★
Robust, herbaceous ground-cover for the larger garden with long-stalked, oval to heart-shaped, coarse-textured, deep green leaves. The star-shaped, blue-purple flowers are borne in pendent clusters in spring. Grow in ordinary, ideally moist, soil in partial shade. Propagate by division in early spring. Will tolerate dry shade.

Lysimachia nummularia

Pulmonaria longifolia

Pulmonaria saccharata **'Dora Bielefeld'**

Stachys byzantina **'Silver Carpet'**

Symphytum ibericum

Using bulbs

Bulbs are nature's form of instant gardening, neatly packaged and able to spring to life within months. Plants have tended to evolve the bulb form as a way of surviving adverse conditions – they can either grow rapidly in spring, before trees overhead have sprouted leaves, or they can grow in hot, dry climates or mountain areas that have short growing seasons. Many bulbs are still dug up from their native countries, resulting in losses and local extinction. Rarely do they do as well as cultivated ones, so ensure you buy from companies who can assure you that all their bulbs are cultivated and propagated in nurseries. Bulbs are invaluable for bringing spring colour to gardens and are very easy to combine with other plants. Plan ahead and you can have bulbs all year round!

Spring colour
By planting bulbs, you can look forward to a flowering display within months. Here, plants including the distinctive orange Fritillaria imperialis*, grape hyacinth (*Muscari*) and tulips provide a show of colour.*

Bulbs for all seasons

The bulb year starts with snowdrops, aconites and crocuses which may be grown under trees or in grass.

Daffodils and narcissi come next, available in a great many varieties, both 'normal' size and dwarf. The larger daffodils are useful for 'naturalizing' in grass. Bluebells, scillas and chiono-doxas, most of which flourish in sun or light shade, can all be naturalized, too.

Wonderful shades of blue are very much a feature of spring bulbs. For example, grape hyacinths (*Muscari* spp.) are among those that come in good blues, although they prefer sunnier conditions. Tulips tend to flower later, as spring turns into summer. As well as the vast range of brightly coloured, stiffly upright hybrids, there are a large number of 'species' tulips, which are the wild ancestors of the hybrids. These are much smaller and more informal in habit, but just as cheerfully coloured. Lilies (*Lilium* spp.) are probably the best-known summer bulbs, but there are others, such as the rather statuesque *Galtonia candicans* and the robustly majestic *Crinum* x *powellii*, with its large, pink trumpets.

At the end of the year, the smaller bulbs come into their own again, with cyclamen flowering beneath trees and the 'autumn crocuses', which produce flowers before they grow leaves.

Seasonal flowering
Lilium regale *(above) is one of the best-known summer bulbs, while tulips, such as* Tulipa *'Blizzard' (left), are a popular choice for a late spring border.*

Planting a bulb

Bulbs need to be planted at roughly twice their own depth. A bulb 5cm (2in) deep should be planted at a depth of 10cm (4in). The depth is important, because if bulbs are planted too close to the soil surface, or too deep, it will affect their flowering performance and/or their form.

Tulips planted too close to the soil surface, for example, tend to flop unattractively. Spring-flowering bulbs are generally planted in the autumn, and summer- and autumn-flowering bulbs in early spring.

Bulbs are also very successful container plants, and can be grown in any good potting compost. They must be well-watered, including during the period after flowering when next year's storage system for flowering is being built up.

If you plant bulbs in containers, remember to label the containers after planting. It is only too easy to forget precisely what you have planted!

1 *Fill the container to the appropriate level with compost (using a layer of stones as drainage at the base) and place the bulbs growing point upwards on top.*

2 *Top up with compost to within 2.5cm (1in) of the container rim. Water and keep moist, but not wet, throughout the growing period, and after flowering.*

Places for bulbs

Bulbs can be planted underneath deciduous shrubs or around summer flowering perennials to bring colour to what would otherwise be bare ground. Try combining them with early perennials like primulas, pulmonarias and hellebores.

It is important, though, not to plant them in places where they might get dug up accidentally during the summer. Smaller bulbs can be interplanted with dwarf shrubs and alpines in rockeries. Species tulips make excellent rockery plants, and are good to combine with alpines in containers, too.

Buying bulbs

Buying bulbs is more fraught with problems than almost any other plant purchase. They are easily muddled for one thing, which makes buying them in pre-packs from garden centres the most reliable way of getting what you want. These, however, often contain sub-standard bulbs. The punier the bulb, the less well it will flower. The best way of buying them is from a reputable mail-order company that specializes in bulbs.

Many of the smaller bulbs need high summer temperatures to repeat flower, so they should not be grown where they can get covered by the growth of other plants that would insulate them from the sun's heat.

Bulbs easily become naturalized given the right conditions, which means that they spread themselves over the years. When they are grown in a lawn, it is important that the grass is not cut until the leaves have died back, otherwise they will not be able to build up enough food reserves to flower the year after.

Bulbs that are good for this kind of situation are daffodils and narcissi, snowdrops, crocuses, and small fritillaries, like the snakeshead fritillary (*Fritillaria meleagris*). You can plant bulbs directly into grassed areas with the help of a special bulb planter, which cuts through tough grass easily to create a planting hole. For shady borders, bluebells (*Hyacinthoides non-scripta*) or lily-of-the-valley (*Convallaria majalis*) are ideal.

Nearly all tulips need hot, dry conditions in summer to encourage them to flower again the next year. This does not pose too much of a problem with the species tulips

Bulbs for all situations

Chionodoxa *and* narcissus, *(above) easily become naturalised in grass, while many bulbs, such as* Hyacinthus *and* Viola *(right) make excellent spring or summer bedding plants.*

that thrive in rockeries, but many of the hybrids rarely get enough sun unless they are dug up and stored in a warm, dry place over the summer. Alternatively, they can be treated as annuals.

Bulbs

Allium karavatiense

Anemone coronaria

Chionodoxa lucilae

Colchicum speciosum 'Album'

Crinum x *powellii*

ALLIUM CHRISTOPHII (A. ALBOPILOSUM)
H to 60cm (2ft) ★★★★

Intriguing, ornamental onion with erect, ribbed stems topped by airy, globular clusters to 20cm (8in) across, formed of numerous star-shaped, metallic, pinkish purple flowers in early summer. The entirely basal leaves are grey green and strap-shaped. Grow in ordinary soil in full sun. Propagate by seeds sown when ripe or in spring, in a cold frame or by removing offsets when dormant. *A. hollandicum* is a little taller with smaller, denser heads of brighter, rose-purple flowers. *A. karavatiense* has pairs of elliptic, red-margined, grey-green or grey-purple leaves and star-shaped, pale mauve flowers with purple mid-ribs.

ANEMONE BLANDA
H 15cm (6in) ★★★★

Charming, clump-forming perennial with comparatively large, saucer-shaped, deep purple-blue flowers in spring. The mainly basal leaves are divided into three, mid- to deep green, irregularly lobed and toothed leaflets. Grow in ordinary, ideally humus-rich soil in sun or partial shade. Propagate by dividing the tubers when dormant. *A.b.* 'Atrocaerulea' is deep blue, *A.b.* 'Charmer', deep pink, and *A.b.* 'White Splendour' has large, white flowers. *A. nemorosa*, Wood Anemone, with white, often pink-backed or blue flowers, is similar but spreads more widely. *A. ranunculoides* is similar in habit but has bright yellow single or double flowers. *A. coronaria* has showy, single flowers in red, blue or white, in spring.

CHIONODOXA SARDENSIS
H to 10cm (4in) ★★★★

Delightful, easy-going plant, also known as Glory of the Snow, with small clusters of 6-petalled, star-shaped, rich blue flowers with a white eye appearing in early spring. The few, entirely basal leaves are mid-green and strap-shaped. Grow in ordinary garden soil in sun or partial shade. Propagate by offsets removed when dormant or by seed sown when ripe, ideally *in situ*. Will self-sow when happily situated. *C. luciliae* is somewhat larger in all its parts with lighter blue flowers having larger white centres.

COLCHICUM SPECIOSUM
H to 30cm (12in) ★★★★

Indispensible for the autumn garden, autumn crocus produces sturdy, goblet-shaped flowers up to 20cm (8in) long in shades of pale to deep rose-purple, often with white throats before the leaves. The spring-maturing leaves are glossy, mid- to deep green, lance-shaped to oblong, in sheafs of three or four, fading by midsummer. Grow in moist, well-drained soil in sun or partial shade. Propagate by removing offsets when dormant. *C.s.* 'Album' has shapely, pure white, firm-textured flowers. Several cultivars are derived from this species, like 'The Giant' with larger, violet-purple flowers and 'Waterlily' which has fully double, lilac-pink flowers.

CRINUM x POWELLII
H 1–1.5m (3–5ft) ★★★

Striking, lily-like plant with strong, erect stems bearing clusters of nodding, 5-petalled, trumpet-shaped, fragrant flowers in shades of pink and white. The entirely basal, mid-green, deciduous leaves are strap shaped and arching. Grow in fertile, well-drained soil in sun, best at the foot of a sheltered wall as not fully frost-hardy. Propagate by separating offsets in spring before growth starts. *C.* x *p.* 'Album' has pure white blooms.

CROCUS VERNUS
H 12–20cm (5–8in) ★★★★

Cheerful harbingers of spring with shapely, 6-petalled, goblet-shaped flowers in shades of lilac and purple. The entirely basal leaves are narrowly strap-shaped, mid- to deep green with a narrow, central silvery stripe. Grow in ordinary, well-drained soil in a sunny position. Propagate by separating offsets when dormant. *C.v.* 'Jeanne d'Arc' is white with deep purple base, *C.v.* 'Pickwick', purple and white striped and *C.v.* 'Purpureus Grandiflorus' rich violet with a dark base. *C. tommasinianus* is smaller and more slender, the silvery lilac to reddish-purple flowers appearing in late winter; it is good for naturalizing. *C. chrysanthus* flower at the same time but have broader petals in shades of cream to orange or golden yellow; outstanding is *C. x luteus* 'Golden Yellow'. Hybrids such as 'Blue Bird' or 'Blue Pearl' are shaded or marked with blue. *C. speciosus* has larger flowers in shades of purple-blue and white appearing in autumn before the leaves.

CYCLAMEN HEDERIFOLIUM (C. NEAPOLITANUM)
H 10–12cm (4–5in) ★★★★
Dainty, smaller version of the familiar pot-plant producing 5-petalled, shuttlecock-shaped flowers in shades of pink or white from late summer to late autumn, often before the leaves. The entirely basal, long-stalked, triangular to heart-shaped, mid- to deep green leaves bear silver markings. Grow in ordinary, ideally humus-rich, well-drained soil in partial shade. Propagate by seed sown when ripe in a cold frame or *in situ*; it sometimes self-sows. *C. coum* is smaller with rounded leaves, sometimes unmarked and with more rounded flowers in shades of pink to red or white in winter to early spring.

ERANTHIS HYEMALIS
H 10cm (4in) or more ★★★★
Cheerful, winter-flowering, clump-former, also known as Winter Aconite, with erect stems topped by a ruff of bright green dissected leaves centred by 6-petalled, buttercup-like, bright yellow flowers. Grow in ordinary, ideally humus-rich, soil in partial shade. Propagate by dividing the tubers when dormant or by sowing seeds when ripe in a cold frame. Often self-sows when happily situated.

ERYTHRONIUM DENS-CANIS
H 10–15cm (4–6in) ★★★★
Also known as Dog's Tooth Violet, charming, modestly clump-forming herbaceous,

bulbous perennial bearing 6-petalled flowers in spring in shades of pink, white or lilac which are star-shaped at first, then reflex into a Turk's-cap shape. The entirely basal, oblong to elliptic leaves are attractively marbled with purplish-brown. Grow in moist but well-drained, humus-rich soil in partial shade. Propagate by division of established clumps when dormant. 'White Splendour' is white with a brown eye. 'Pagoda', a hybrid cultivar, is a little taller and stronger growing with several light yellow flowers; in 'Kondo' these are darker.

FRITILLARIA IMPERIALIS
H 1–1.5m (3–5ft) ★★★★
Dramatic, robust bulb, also known as Crown Imperial, producing dark, erect stems thickly set with lance-shaped, glossy bright green leaves and topped by a cluster of large, pendent, orange to red, 6-petalled bells, each cluster crowned with a tuft of narrower leaves. Grow in fertile, well-drained soil in sun or partial shade. Propagate by separating offsets when dormant. *F.i.* 'Lutea' has bright yellow flowers and is easier to grow. *F. meleagris* H 30cm (12in) is very different, with a slender stem sparingly set with narrow leaves and topped by one or rarely two, large, chequered bells in shades of purple to white.

GALANTHUS NIVALIS
H 8–12cm (3¼–4½in) ★★★★
Also known as Snowdrop, this winter-flowering clump-former has pure white, bell-shaped, pendent flowers formed of three larger outer petals and three, much smaller, green-marked inner ones. The entirely basal leaves are narrowly strap-shaped and grey-green. Grow in moisture-retentive but well-drained soil in sun or partial shade. Propagate by separating clumps or by removing off-

Crocus x luteus 'Golden Yellow'

Cyclamen hederifolium

Eranthis hyemalis

sets when in leaf. Several variants are grown, including 'Flore Pleno', which has double flowers.

GALTONIA CANDICANS
H 1–1.2m (3–4ft) ★★★
Elegant, robust herbaceous plant, also called Summer Hyacinth, with sturdy, erect stems topped by a spire of white, 6-petalled, bell-shaped flowers which dangle from slender, green stalks in late summer. The entirely basal leaves are strap-shaped and grey-green. Grow in moist, well-drained soil in sun. Propagate by removing offsets when dormant.

GLADIOLUS COMMUNIS SSP. BYZANTINUS (G. BYZANTINUS)
H. 60–75cm (2–2½ft) ★★★
Showy clump-former producing stiff, one-sided spikes of curved, funnel-shaped magenta flowers with paler markings in the centre from

Erythronium 'Pagoda'

Galanthus nivalis

Gladiolus communis ssp. *byzantinus*

Iris danfordiae

Muscari armeniacum

late spring to early summer. The mid-green, sword-shaped leaves are arranged in a flattened sheaf. Grow in well-drained garden soil in a sunny position. Propagate by separating established clumps or by removing offsets when dormant. A wide range of hybrid cultivars in all colours of the rainbow is freely available.

HYACINTHUS ORIENTALIS
H 20–30cm (8–12in) ★★★★

Indispensible for the spring garden, producing erect, thick, fleshy stems topped by a dense spike of tubular, six-petalled, starry, highly blue to blue-purple fragrant flowers. The entirely basal, bright green glossy leaves are strap-shaped and slightly incurved. Many cultivars are available in shades of blue, pink, red, orange, yellow and white. Grow in fertile, moist but well-drained soil in sun or partial shade. Propagate by offsets when dormant.

IRIS XIPHIUM
H 40–60cm (1¼–2ft) ★★★★

Beautiful, herbaceous plant, also known as Spanish Iris, with a slender, wind-firm stem topped in early summer by several large, 6-petalled flowers in shades of blue and violet, rarely white or yellow, with an orange blotch at the tip of each of the three larger petals (falls). The arching, grassy, grey-green leaves have upturned edges. Grow in fertile, well-drained soil in sun. Propagate by offsets when dormant. Best-known as the parent of the similar but more sturdy Dutch iris that is available in a greater colour range. Very different are the dwarf, winter-flowering irises with erect, rush-like leaves and smaller flowers. *I. unguicularis* H 20cm (8in) has larger, scented, lilac flowers. *I. reticulata* H 10–15cm (4–6in) has flowers in shades of purple to blue. *I. histrioides* is purple-blue and *I. danfordiae* is yellow.

LEUCOJUM VERNUM
H 20–30cm (8–12in) ★★★★

This clump-forming, charming harbinger of spring is also known as Spring Snowflake. It has, in late winter and early spring, an erect stem bearing one or two, white, green-tipped bells like snowdrops but with six petals all the same size. The entirely basal leaves are strap-shaped, glossy deep green. Grow in ordinary soil, moist during the growing season. It prefers partial shade. Propagate by dividing clumps or by separating offsets when dormant. *L. aestivum*, Summer Snowflake, H up to 60cm (2ft), has clusters of flowers to each stem later in spring.

LILIUM REGALE
H 1–1.5m (3–5ft) ★★★★

Superb, popular, summer-flowering trumpet-lily with terminal clusters of large, fragrant, white flowers with yellow centres and stamens from brown-purple flushed buds. The leaves are narrowly lance-shaped and deep green. Grow in fertile, ideally humus-rich, moist but well-drained soil in sun or partial shade. Propagate by seed as soon as ripe or in spring in a cold frame. This is a classic trumpet-shaped lily, typical of a large group of species and hybrids which vary in height and flower colour and include the well-known pure-white *L. candidum*. Equally popular are species and hybrids with petals creating a Turk's-cap shaped flower, for example, *L. martagon* which has spikes of purplish-red to pink or white flowers. Also recommended are the Asiatic hybrids which have less recurved petals and larger flowers in many colours.

MUSCARI ARMENIACUM
H 15–20cm (6–8in) ★★★★

The most popular clump-forming grape hyacinth with smooth, erect stems topped by dense, oval spikes of small, bright blue bells with constricted white mouths. The entirely basal leaves are narrowly strap-shaped, grooved, bright to mid-green. Grow in well-drained soil in sun or partial shade. Propagate by dividing established clumps or by removing the freely produced bulblets when dormant. *M. comosum*, Tassel Hyacinth, is a little taller with loose spikes of fertile, brownish white flowers at the base and smaller, sterile, bright blue-violet ones in a tassel at the top. 'Plumosum' has airy spikes entirely formed of purple-blue, tassel-like flowers.

NARCISSUS PSEUDONARCISSUS
H 15–30cm (6–12in) ★★★★

The best known of the truly wild trumpet daffodils, each erect stem bearing six, creamy yellow outer petals and a darker shaded trumpet. The entirely basal, strap-shaped leaves are mid- to

***Narcissus* 'Peeping Tom'**

grey-green. Good for naturalizing. Grow in ordinary soil, ideally moist during the growing season. Propagate by separating clumps or removing offsets when dormant. Many hybrid cultivars are available, from white to yellow with contrastingly coloured trumpets, a few of them fully double. There are also cultivars with shorter trumpets (cups) which are generally known as narcissus, these also have a wide colour range and are freely available. *N. triandrus* H 25cm (10in) is very different, bearing two to six, small, short-cupped yellow to white flowers on each stem. There are many taller hybrid cultivars with this form of growth with larger flowers in shades of yellow to white, some of them with red to orange cups. These are better garden plants. 'Peeping Tom', H 30cm (12in), is a small, dainty bulb which is particularly good for naturalizing.

NERINE BOWDENII
H 45–60cm (1¼–2ft) ★★★
Striking, robust plant with erect stems topped with rounded clusters of 6-petalled, somewhat lily-like flowers formed of six narrow, arching, wavy, pink petals which open in autumn as the leaves die down. The entirely basal, strap-shaped leaves are mid- to bright green. Grow in well-drained soil in a sunny position. Propagate by separating offsets when dormant. *N.b.* 'Mark Fenwick' is a recommended cultivar with rich pink flowers on dark stems.

ORNITHOGALUM UMBELLATUM
H 15–25cm (6–8in) ★★★
Attractive clump-former, also known as Star of Bethlehem, producing slim, erect stems topped by clusters of erect, 6-petalled, starry, pure white flowers from green buds in late spring. The entirely basal

leaves are very narrowly strap-shaped with a silvery, central vein and wither just before or at flowering time. Grow in well-drained soil either in sun or partial shade. Propagate by dividing clumps or by separating the freely borne off-sets. In light soils this plant can be invasive. *O. nutans*, Drooping Star-of-Bethlehem, differs mainly in that it bears spikes of nodding green and silvery white bells.

SCILLA SIBERICA
H 10–20cm (4–8in) ★★★★
Pretty, dwarf clump-former, also known as Siberian Squill, each bulb producing several erect stems topped by 3 to 5 bell-shaped, 6-petalled, bright blue or white flowers in spring. The entirely basal leaves are strap-shaped and glossy, mid- to deep green. Grow in moist but well-drained soil in sun or partial shade. Propagate by dividing clumps or by separating offsets when dormant. 'Spring Beauty' ('Atrocaerulea'), is the most reliable cultivar with deep blue flowers. *S. mistschenkoana* (*S. tubergeniana*) blooms a little earlier with slightly larger, white, blue-striped flowers. *S. bifolia* has upward-facing, star-shaped deep blue flowers.

TULIPA KAUFMANNIANA
H 15–30cm (6–12in) ★★★★
Decorative, dwarf tulip, also called Water-lily Tulip, with long-tapered, pink-flushed, urn-shaped buds which open out flat in the sun to disclose the petals' yellow inner faces. Leaves are lance-shaped, smooth and grey-green. Of similar size is *T. clusiana*, having white petals striped deep pink. *T.* 'Giuseppe Verde' has golden yellow petals striped red. Grow in well-drained, garden soil in a sunny position. Propagate by removing offsets when dormant. Several hybrid cultivars are available, usually in a variety

Narcissus pseudonarcissus

Nerine bowdenii

Scilla siberica

Tulipa clusiana

Tulipa 'Giuseppe Verde'

of striking bicolours, some with purple-striped leaves. There are many other hybrid groups of tulips which vary in flowering time, shape, height and come in a wide colour range. Cultivars of the Single Early Group produce large, cup-shaped flowers from early to mid-spring, the Double Earlies have fully double flowers. Plants of the

Lily-flowered Group have pointed-petalled, goblet-shaped flowers in late spring and those of the Parrot Group have large, cup-shaped flowers, the petals sometimes striped or blotched with other colours. Tallest is the Darwin Hybrid Group with large, deep cup-shaped flowers in a range of bright colours from early to mid-spring.

Using annuals and biennials

Annuals are plants that complete their life cycle within one year – germinating, flowering, setting seed and dying. Hardy annuals can withstand late frosts and so can be sown in the ground in spring without danger. Half-hardy annuals are frost-sensitive, so are usually started off inside and planted out after the frosts. These include a certain number of plants, such as ageratum and antirrhinum, that are, in fact, perennials in frost-free climates. They are grown as annuals in cooler climes, as it is possible to bring them to flower from seed in only a few months. The half-hardies are often referred to as bedding plants. Biennials are plants that are started off as seed one year, to flower the next, either dying after flowering or being discarded. Hollyhocks (*Alcea* spp.) are an example.

Shade-loving biennials
Although we often think of annuals and biennials as being plants for sunny corners of the garden only, some, like the biennial foxglove (Digitalis) do best in partial shade and are ideal for adding colour to a shady spot in the garden or for woodland planting.

Fillers and bedding

The speed with which annuals grow and the intensity of their colours are the main reason for their popularity with gardeners. They usually start to flower in mid-summer, after the perennials of early summer but before the profusion of late-season perennials has started. For people wanting a practically instant garden, annuals are just what is needed.

Annuals are particularly useful in new gardens where there are considerable gaps between young plants. They provide temporary cover while you make your mind up about permanent plans.

In established gardens, annuals of either kind are ideal for combining with other plants as gap fillers among shrubs and perennials. They provide colour long after these bedfellows have finished flowering, or, in the case of late perennials, before they have got into their stride. They can even be grown over dormant spring bulbs, so long as there is no risk of the bulbs being uprooted when the annuals are removed at the end of the year.

While there are no true spring-flowering annuals available for gardens, there are certain plants, usually short-lived perennials, or biennials, that take their place as spring bedding, being discarded after they flower. These are generally started off as young plants, from seed, the year before and planted out in autumn or late winter. Wallflowers (*Erysimum cheiri* varieties) and pansies (*Viola* hybrids) are the best known.

Border colour
Wallflowers and tulips (above) are excellent for spring bedding, while plants such as dahlias, salvia, pelargonium and petunias (right) are combined to provide a spectacular burst of colour in early autumn.

Formal versus informal

There are two traditions of annual growing. One is the formal one, familiar from public parks the world over, with the emphasis on strong, contrasting colours and geometrical layouts, using a lot of half-hardy annuals. The other is the informal, cottage-garden tradition, which relies on cheaper hardy annuals that are sown where they are to grow. Here, the colours are more muted, many are fragrant and a certain amount of untidiness is acceptable. Both traditions are currently undergoing changes as both are now using a much wider range of plants than formerly.

French marigolds (*Tagetes* spp.) and petunias are typical of the first tradition, while cornflowers (*Centaurea cyanus*) and Pot Marigolds (*Calendula*

officinalis) are cottage garden staples. Formal planting also, increasingly, makes use of the kind of plants discussed under 'Perennials for sunny corners and containers'.

Planting contrasts
Formal borders (above) empha-size regular, tidy patterns and contrasting colours, while in informal borders (right) the colours are muted and plants are allowed to grow as they will.

Annuals in containers

Annuals, or plants grown as annuals, are a favourite for use in containers. Hanging baskets, tubs and windowbox-es are the most usual, but there is nothing to stop those imaginative people who make use of practically any-thing that holds soil. Given that most have been bred for compactness and a long flow-ering season, it is the half-hardy annuals, like petunias, lobelias, impatiens and pelargoniums, that often find their way into containers.

Just as foliage plants are used in the perennial border, so they can be used among annuals, too. Silver helichry-sum species are often found in hanging baskets, their foliage forming an attractive counterpoint to the flowers.

Long-lasting displays
Annuals, especially those that are half-hardy, are favourites for win-dow-boxes (left) and containers (right) because many have been bred for their compactness and long flowering seasons.

Effective containers have a lot of plants packed into them, which means that the com-post used must be very fer-tile. The best way to make sure that the plants never run short of nutrients is to use slow-release fertilizer pellets, which will gradually release nutrients over the whole summer. Plentiful and regular watering is essential too.

When it comes to design-ing container plantings, a few plants widely used have more impact than trying to use as many as possible. The same 'rules' that apply to mixing colours and using structural plants in borders can be applied to containers too.

Annuals and biennials

Ageratum houstonanium 'Blue Danube'

AGERATUM HOUSTONIANUM
H 15-45cm (6-18in) ★

Pretty, half-hardy annual with tiny, blue, powder-puff shaped flowerheads in dense terminal clusters in summer to autumn. The oval to heart-shaped, downy leaves are mid- to bright green. Grow in fertile, ideally moist soil. Propagate by seed sown in warmth in spring. Usually represented in gardens by the dwarf cultivars such as 'Adriatic', H 15-20cm (6-8in), which is mid-blue, and 'Bavaria', blue and white. 'Blue Danube' is lavender-blue and weather-resistant. 'Blue Mink', H 20-30cm (8-12in), is extra-vigorous and powder blue. 'Hawaii White', H 15cm (6in), is white. 'Blue Horizon' bears purple-blue flowers on long stems.

ALCEA ROSEA (ALTHAEA ROSEA)
H 2–3m (6½–10ft) ★★★★

Statuesque, short-lived, hardy perennial, also known as Hollyhock, grown as an annual and biennial for its shallowly funnel-shaped, 5-petalled flowers in a variety of colours. The mid- to light green, rounded leaves are shallowly 3 to 7-lobed and roughly hairy. Grow in fertile soil in sun. Propagate as annuals by sowing seed in warmth in late winter and as biennials or perennials *in situ* in late spring. Chater's Double Group has fully double, pompon-like flowers in shades of pink, red, yellow, lavender, purple and white. 'Nigra' has deep chocolate-maroon, single flowers. Summer Carnival Group has double flowers in a wide colour range.

ANTIRRHINUM MAJUS
H to 1.2m (4ft) or more
★★★

Colourful, short-lived perennial, also called Snapdragon, usually grown as an annual with spikes of tubular, broadly two-lipped flowers in shades of yellow, red, pink, purple, bronze and white from summer to autumn. The leaves are lance-shaped, glossy mid- to dark green. Grow in ordinary, fertile soil in sun. Propagate as annuals by sowing seed in warmth in late winter. Many cultivars are available in mixed or single colours. The Tahiti Series are dwarf and rust-resistant.

BEGONIA X CARRIEREI
(B. SEMPERFLORENS)
H 20–30cm (8–12in)

Showy, tender, evergreen perennials usually grown as annuals, bearing a profusion of waxy, 4-petalled flowers in shades of red, pink and white in mid- to late summer. The lopsidedly oval leaves are slightly fleshy and bright glossy green, flushed with reddish-bronze in some cultivars. Grow in fertile soil in sun or partial shade. Propagate by seed sown in late winter in warmth or by cuttings of non-flowering shoots in late summer. The Cocktail Series is a good, weather-resistant strain in a wide range of shades. 'Organdy' has a mixture of white, pink and red flowers and green and bronze leaves.

BELLIS PERENNIS
H 10–15cm (4–6in) ★★★★

Also known as Daisy, this perennial is grown as a biennial for its pompon-like, fully double daisies in shades of red, pink and white from late winter to late summer. The spoon-shaped, glossy leaves are mid- to bright green. Grow in ordinary soil in sun or partial shade. Propagate by seed sown in a nursery bed outside in summer or in warmth in late winter. Can be divided in autumn, early spring or after flowering. Habanera Series bears large flowerheads. Roggli Series produces semi-double flowers. Tasso Series has large flowerheads of quilled petals.

CALENDULA OFFICINALIS
H 30–60cm (1–2ft) ★★

Also known as Pot Marigold, these popular, hardy, orange and yellow daisies are produced over a long period in

Antirrhinum

Begonia semperflorens

Bellis perennis

summer to autumn. Spoon-shaped to oblong leaves are softly hairy, somewhat aromatic and mid-green. Grow in ordinary soil in sun. Propagate by seed sown *in situ* in spring or autumn. 'Orange King' is double, deep orange. Pacific Series has double flowers in shades of orange, yellow and cream and bicolours. 'Indian Prince' is taller and dark orange.

CAMPANULA MEDIUM
H 60–90cm (2–3ft) ★★★
Handsome biennial, also known as Canterbury Bells, producing substantial spikes of large, bellflowers in shades of blue, pink and white. The mainly basal, lance-shaped leaves are mid-green and hairy and arranged in a neat rosette. Grow in fertile soil in sun or partial shade. Propagate by seed sown in late spring in a nursery bed or in boxes. 'Bells of Holland' H 45cm (18in) does not grow any taller and 'Calycanthema', Cup and Saucer Canterbury Bells, has the bell sitting in a colourful, saucer-like calyx.

CENTAUREA CYANUS
H 30–75cm (1–2½ft) ★★★
Well-known, hardy annual, also known as Cornflower, grown for its pompon-like blue flowers in summer. The narrowly lance-shaped, sometimes lobed leaves are deep green and woolly haired beneath. Grow in fertile soil in sun. Propagate by seed sown *in situ* in spring. Cultivars are available in shades of pink, blue and white. The Florence Series are compact and well-branched to 35cm (14in). Baby Series are dwarf plants to 30cm (12in).

CHEIRANTHUS CHEIRI
(ERYSIMUM)
H 30–60cm (1–2ft) ★★★
Also known as Wallflower, this short-lived, hardy perennial grown as a biennial for its fragrant, colourful, 4-petalled flowers borne in

bold, terminal spikes in a variety of colours. The lance-shaped leaves are mid- to deep green and crowded along the stems. Grow in well-drained, ideally limy soil in sun. Propagate by seed sown in a nursery bed in late spring. 'Blood Red', deep red, 'Ivory White, creamy white. 'Harlequin' is a mixed strain in shades of red, orange, cream and bicolours.

CLARKIA ELEGANS
(C. UNGUICULATA)
H 30–90cm (2–3ft) ★★★
Popular, erect, self-supporting, hardy annual bearing spikes of 4-petalled flowers in shades of pink, red, lavender and white in summer. The oval to lance-shaped leaves are mid-green. Grow in fertile soil in sun. Propagate by seed sown *in situ* in autumn or spring. In cold areas, protect autumn-sown seedlings with cloches. Single and double-flowered cultivars and several colour mixes are available of which the dwarf ones such as *C.e.* 'Royal Bouquet' H 30cm (1ft) has particularly valuable double flowers. *C. amoena*, also known as godetia, is an erect, hardy, branching annual bearing clusters of cup-shaped, 4-petalled flowers. Single or double, tall and dwarf cultivars are available in single or mixed colours.

COSMOS BIPINNATUS
H 60–150cm (2–5ft) ★
Elegant, half-hardy, erect annual bearing large, daisy-like flowers with broad, notched-tipped petals in shades of red, pink and white in summer to autumn. The mid- to deep green leaves are finely cut into many filament-like segments. Grow in well-drained, fertile soil in sun. Propagate by seed sown in early to mid-spring in warmth or *in situ* in late spring. There are cultivars in a variety of colours and mixes, from *C.* 'Sensation',

H90cm (3ft) varying from bright pink to white, to dwarfs at 30cm (1ft). *C. sulphureus* has more coarsely cut leaves and slightly smaller, orange to yellow flowers.

DIANTHUS BARBATUS
H 45–60cm (1½–2ft) ★★★★
A hardy cottage garden plant, also known as Sweet William. It is a short-lived perennial grown as a biennial or annual bearing broad heads of small, 5-petalled, strongly fragrant flowers in shades of red, pink and white, often bicoloured. The mid- to deep green leaves are oval to lance-shaped. Grow in fertile soil in sun. Propagate as a biennial by sowing seed in a nursery bed in spring or as an annual. Several cultivars are available in single or mixed colours, some with bronze or purple-tinted foliage, others dwarf, such as 'Wee Willie', H 15cm (6in).

DIGITALIS PURPUREA
H 1–2m (3–6½ft) ★★★★
Unmistakable, hardy biennial, also known as Foxglove, grown for its long, one-sided spires of thimble-shaped bells in shades of rose-purple to white in early to mid-summer, often with darker spotting within. The large leaves are oval to lance-shaped, toothed and deep green, forming a handsome rosette the first year. Grow in ordinary soil in sun or shade. Propagate by seed sown in a nursery bed in late spring.

Calendula officinalis

Erysismum x allionii

Cosmos 'Sensation Mixed'

Dianthus barbatus 'Harbinger Mixed'

Digitalis purpurea Excelsior Group

Eschscholzia californica

Iberis umbellata 'Fairyland'

Impatiens 'Accent Salmon'

Several cultivars in single or mixed colours are available, some more dwarf, e.g.Foxy H 1.2m (4ft). The Excelsior Group have flowers arranged in cylindrical spikes.

ESCHSCHOLZIA CALIFORNICA
H 25–35cm (10–14in) ★★
Showy, hardy annual, also called Californian Poppy, grown for its brilliant orange, poppy-like flowers which open in long succession in summer. The grey-green leaves are cut into slender segments. Grow in well-drained soil in sun. Propagate by sowing seeds *in situ* in spring or autumn. Several cultivars are available in single colours or in mixtures in shades of reds, pinks and orange. 'Ballerina' has semi-double flowers.

GYPSOPHILA ELEGANS
H 45–60cm (1½–2ft) ★★★
Dainty, hardy annual grown for its large, airy clusters of small, 5-petalled, starry white to pink flowers in summer. The narrowly lance-shaped, pointed leaves are grey-green. Grow in well-drained, preferably limy soil in sun. Propagate by seeds sown *in situ* in spring. A useful flower for cutting. Cultivars are available in shades of pink, carmine and white.

HELICHRYSUM BRACTEATUM (BRACHTEANTHA BRACTEATA)
H 60–90cm (2–3ft) ★★
Distinctive, short-lived, half-hardy perennial, also known as Strawflower, grown as an annual for its daisy-like flowers with yellow, pink or red petals. The broadly lance-shaped leaves are mid- to grey-green. Grow in well-drained soil in sun. Propagate by seed sown in warmth in mid-spring. Cultivars come in single and mixed colours. The Monstrosa Series bear huge fully double flower-heads. Bikini Series, H 30cm (1ft), has papery, pink, orange or white flowers.

IBERIS AMARA
H 30–45cm (1–1½ft) ★★★
Bright, erect, hardy annual, also known as Candytuft, grown for its dense, rounded to shortly cylindrical clusters of 4-petalled white to purple-tinted, fragrant flowers in summer. The entirely stem-borne, lance-shaped to narrowly spoon-shaped leaves are mid- to deep green. Grow in fertile, well-drained soil in sun. Propagate by sowing seeds *in situ* in spring or autumn. *I. umbellata*, Common Candytuft, rarely exceeds 30cm and is more freely branching with smaller, clusters of white, lavender, pink, purple or crimson flowers. Several cultivars are available in the 15–23cm (6–9in) height range in a variety of mixed colours.

IMPATIENS WALLERIANA
H 40–60cm (1¼–2ft) ★
Showy, bushy, tender perennial, also called Busy Lizzie, grown as an annual producing a long succession of rounded, 5-petalled flowers in shades of pink, red, orange, purple, white and bicolours. The elliptic to lance-shaped, toothed leaves are bright green. Grow in fertile soil in sun or partial shade. Propagate by seeds sown in warmth in early spring. Numerous cultivars are available in a range of colours, most of them dwarf and compact and very free flowering, such as 'Florette Stars', H 15–20cm (6–8in).

LATHYRUS ODORATUS
H 2–2.5m (6½–8ft) ★★★★
Also known as Sweet Pea, this well-loved, hardy, climbing annual is grown for its rounded, very fragrant pea-shaped flowers in shades of red, pink, purple, lavender and white, sometimes bicoloured with picotee margins to the petals. The mid- to deep green leaves are formed of two oval leaflets and branched tendril by which the plant clings to its support. Grow in moist but well drained soil in sun. A support of netting, trellis or tall pea sticks is required. Propagate by seeds, ideally first soaked, sown in a cold frame in early spring.

LAVATERA TRIMESTRIS
H 90–120cm (3–4ft) ★★★
Decorative, erect, bushy, hardy annual grown for its profusion of large, shallowly funnel-shaped 5-petalled flowers in shades of luminous pink and white. The softly hairy, mid- to deep green, rounded leaves have three to five or sometimes seven lobes. Grow in fertile soil in sun. Propagate by sowing seeds *in situ* in mid-spring. *L.t.* 'Loveliness' is deep pink, *L.t.* 'Mont Blanc' is white. *L.t.* 'Ruby Regis' is reddish-pink.

LIMNANTHES DOUGLASII
H 10–15cm (4–6in) ★★★
Colourful, hardy annual, also known as Poached Egg Plant, grown for its mass of shallowly cup-shaped, 5-petalled flowers which are bright yellow with white edges. The dissected, finely toothed leaves are somewhat fleshy and bright yellow-green. Grow in ordinary soil in sun. Propagate by seed sown *in situ* in autumn or mid-spring.

LOBULARIA MARITIMA
H 10–20cm (4–8in) ★★★

Useful, low-growing, hardy bushy annual, also known as Sweet Alison, producing a profusion of tiny, 4-petalled, scented, white to purple flowers throughout the summer. The narrowly lance-shaped leaves are mid- to greyish green. Grow in ordinary soil in sun. Propagate by sowing seed *in situ* in mid- to late spring. 'Carpet of Snow' H 10cm (4in) has white flowers, 'New Purple' is very compact with purple flowers. Several cultivars are available.

MATTHIOLA INCANA
H 30–75cm (12–30in) ★★★★

Pretty, woody-based perennial, also called Stock, grown as annuals or biennials, with erect spikes of scented, 4-petalled flowers in shades of purple, pink and white. The white-hairy to grey-green leaves are lance-shaped to narrowly spoon-shaped. Grow in well-drained, ideally limy soil in sun. Propagate by seed. For growing as an annual sow in warmth in early spring, as a biennial sow in summer and over-winter in a frame or *in situ*. A variety of cultivars in mixed and single colours is available.

MYOSOTIS SYLVATICA
H 15–30cm (6–12in) ★★★★

Forget-me-not, perhaps the best known of all hardy biennial bedding plants, produces a profusion of a small, bright blue 5-petalled flowers from spring to midsummer. The oval to lance-shaped, coarsely hairy leaves are mid- to deep green. Grow in ordinary garden soil in sun or partial shade. Propagate by sowing seeds in summer in a seed bed. Several cultivars are available, some of them of hybrid origin, with *M. alpestris* smaller and more compact, like Ball Series, H 15cm (6in). Pink and white cultivars are also available.

NEMESIA STRUMOSA
H 20–30cm (8–12in) ★

Dainty, erect, branching, half-hardy annual bearing terminal spikes of two-lipped flowers in shades of pink, blue, purple, yellow, red and white, sometimes bicoloured. The lance-shaped leaves may be toothed or smooth-edged, mid- to bright green. Grow in fertile, well-drained soil in sun. Propagate by sowing seeds in warmth in early to mid-spring. Several cultivars in single and mixed colours are available, mostly under 20cm (8in) in height.

PETUNIA HYBRIDS
H 15–30cm (6–12in) ★

Popular, colourful annual grown for its long succession of funnel-shaped flowers in shades of pink, red, purple, yellow and white, some bicoloured and frilled. The oval to lance-shaped leaves are mid-green and sticky. Many cultivars in single and mixed shades are available, some are dwarf and compact, e.g. the Celebrity and Merlin Series, H 23cm (9in), others have a more spreading growth habit, e.g. the Super Cascade Series, which have branches up to 45cm (1½ft) long and are good for hanging baskets.

TAGETES ERECTA
H 45cm (1½ft) ★

Brilliantly coloured, half-hardy, erect annual, also known as African Marigold, bearing large, often double, daisy-like flowers with broad petals in shades of yellow and orange. The mid-to bright green leaves are cut into several lobes. Grow in ordinary soil in full sun. Propagate by sowing seed in early spring in warmth or late spring *in situ*. Many cultivars are available, e.g. the Lady Series, H 40–45cm (16–18in), in orange, primrose and golden yellow shades. *T. patula*, French Marigold, H 30cm (1ft), is smaller, sometimes with red-brown petals or

bicoloured. Cultivars of the Boy Series, H 15cm (6in), are compact with double flower-heads in shades of yellow, orange and mahogany, often bicoloured. 'Lemon Gem' has lemon-yellow flowerheads.

TROPAEOLUM MAJUS
H 30cm–2m (1–6½ft) ★

Striking, colourful, tender annual, known as Nasturtium, with large, 5-petalled, spurred flowers in shades of red, orange and yellow throughout summer. Smooth, rounded leaves are bright green. Grow in ordinary soil in sun. The normal species is a climbing plant, needing support. More popular are the bushy, non-climbing cultivars like Jewel Series. Propagate by sowing seed in mid-spring in warmth or late spring *in situ*.

VIOLA x WITTROCKIANA
H 10–25cm (4–10in) ★★★★

This short-lived, hardy evergreen perennial, also known as Garden Pansy, is often grown as an annual. It has the typical 5-petalled, flat, pansy flower in shades of purple, blue, yellow, red and white, often with a dark, face-like pattern in the centre. The oval, scalloped leaves are mid- to deep green. Grow in fertile soil in sun or partial shade. Propagate by seeds sown in spring or early autumn in a nursery bed or frame. Cultivars are available in single and mixed colours, e.g. the Clear Crystal Series which have self-coloured flowers with no markings.

Lavatera 'Parade'

Nemesia 'Carnival'

Petunia 'Vogue'

Tagetes 'Lemon Gem'

VEGETABLES, FRUIT AND HERBS

For many gardeners, being able to sample the freshness and taste of home-grown produce is hugely satisfying. The quest for maximum flavour, size, juiciness, sweetness or crispness, however, is not without its pitfalls, which makes this section of the book essential reading for the less-experienced grower! Explaining just how simple it can be to reap a sensational harvest, all year round, it tells you how to organize and maintain your plot to grow crops efficiently and keep them healthy and productive. A second section is dedicated to step-by-step instructions on how to sow, cultivate and harvest a wide range of vegetables, fruit and herbs. From crisp mangetouts and succulent Brussels sprouts to curly endive, juicy tomatoes and ripe raspberries, each entry is colourfully illustrated and easy to follow. And if you can save room for a few herbs, there is also all you need to know about how to grow and use them.

Getting started

Gardeners want to grow their own fruit, vegetables and herbs for a variety of reasons. You may, for example, wish to control what you eat, which means growing produce organically and avoiding the use of potentially harmful chemicals and fertilizers necessary for higher yields of commercial production. There is also the pleasure of eating garden-fresh produce, which has a fullness of flavour that is lost in shop-bought food. Another attraction is the opportunity to experiment by growing more exotic and unusual fruit and vegetables that are either not available in most shops or are expensive.

Growing your own
Fruit, vegetables and herbs not only taste good, they can also look good if they are well laid-out.

The ornamental potager

There is no reason why your vegetable garden should be any less attractive than the flower garden. A mixture of fruit, vegetables and herbs, laid out in a square design, with perhaps an edging of clipped box, will turn the edible garden into an object of beauty. You can make a very simple square design with just a few rows of vegetables or opt for a series of squares, with brick paths in between each square, to make a more elaborate potager. Herbs are ideally suited to this kind of design, and your potager could devote one or two squares to them. Site such a potager near the house, to make access easier. Soft fruit, like gooseberries, can be trained as ornamental standards, and tree fruit can be fan-trained on wire supports, taking up minimal space and adding to the attraction of the garden.

Planning an attractive kitchen garden
Growing edible crops can be as satisfying visually as it is in culinary terms, as this elegant kitchen garden demonstrates.

Room for all
A neatly laid-out herb garden can succeed in the tiniest of areas.

Good planning
Close cultivation of vegetables makes the best use of space.

Growing edible plants

The earliest gardens evolved out of a purely functional need to have useful plants (those needed for food and medicines) close at hand, rather than having to search and scavenge for them far and wide.

Today, a huge range of vegetables, fruit and herbs can be grown. New and vastly improved cultivars are continually being introduced by gardeners and plant breeders who have selected plants with qualities that gardeners desire. The parsnip cultivar 'Avonresister', for example, can tolerate canker disease, to which parsnips are vulnerable. Other vegetables have been bred and

introduced for their improved performance or yield, such as the Brussels sprout cultivar 'Peer Gynt', which has the ability to develop all its sprouts to an even size over a short period of time; or there are dwarfing cultivars that are ideal for growing in small spaces, such as the sweet pepper 'Baby Belle'. Cultivars are also chosen for their qualities of long storage life, flavour, or rapid maturity.

Many of today's vegetables are hybrids that are bred for a specific purpose. They are called F_1 hybrids. F_2 hybrids are the result of either cross-pollination or self-pollination of F_1-hybrid parents.

Growing in containers

Vegetables, fruit and herbs can be grown in containers in the most unlikely of places – on patios, balconies, fire escapes and landings, or on any small plot of ground where the light is good.

Although you will want to choose the most attractive container, for successful results the container's appearance is not as important as the contents. You need to fill it with fresh, well-balanced potting compost and a base dressing of fertilizer, adding further top-dressings of fertilizer throughout the growing

season. Long-rooted vegetables such as carrots and parsnips need deep containers (at least 45cm/18in deep) to grow well.

Tall crops tend to become unstable, especially if grown in small pots, and can blow over in strong winds, so protect these with stones or netting. Container-grown crops need to be watered frequently during warm or dry weather.

Vegetables in containers
You can grow vegetables in containers or growbags on any small plot where the light is good.

Keeping crops healthy

It is important to ensure that your crops are not damaged or reduced by pests and diseases. To do this you can use either chemical or organic methods.

Chemical methods
These can be very effective in pest and disease control, as long as they are used strictly according to the instructions on the container and are applied thoroughly. Their main drawbacks are:
• Some chemicals may kill beneficial insects as well as harmful ones.
• Certain chemicals are very long-lasting.
• Chemicals may taint the produce with residue.

Organic methods
Reaching for a chemical is not the only solution to an outbreak of pests or disease; there are many other preventive measures that can be

taken. The first step is to grow healthy, vigorous plants as these seem less susceptible to attack, especially when there is also good garden hygiene, and crop rotation is carried out (see p.144).

Physical barriers can be put in place to deny pests access to the crop: for example, lay mats around the bases of brassicas to keep cabbage root fly at bay, or cover your crops with fine nets, the edges of which should be buried in the soil to deter flying pests.

Traps of shallow dishes containing cola or beer can also be laid to entice crawling pests into them so they can be easily disposed of.

Organic sprays based on natural substances, such as derris, pyrethrum, insecticidal soaps and sulphur, are useful and very effective controls against a variety of pests and diseases.

Organic sprays
Brassica plants are treated with a solution of insecticidal soap to kill aphids.

Protective barriers
A layer of netting protects succulent young vegetable plants from marauding birds.

Baited traps
Fill a sunken dish with beer to catch slugs and snails. The sticks help any beetles to escape.

Wasp traps
Hanging from a plum tree, this jar full of sweet-smelling liquid attracts wasps.

Growing vegetables

Vegetables tend to be relatively short-term crops, because most grow rapidly and are harvested before they reach maturity. The ideal soil for growing vegetables is a loam (a mixture of clay, sand and silt in more or less equal proportions) containing humus and with a pH preferably between 6.5 and 7.0. Soils that vary from this ideal – that is, they are more sandy, or have little humus – may need more cultivation. Soil also needs to be fertile, which usually means adding fertilizers or well-rotted manure before sowing or planting.

Growing vegetables
Vegetables and herbs, like these cabbages, lettuces, chives and fennel, can be grown even in small gardens, packed a little tighter than usual.

Crop rotation

When groups of related vegetables are grown on a different plot from year to year, this is called crop rotation. One reason for moving crops from one part of the plot to another is to avoid the build-up of diseases and pests in the soil. Another benefit is that the soil's fertility can be improved by growing crops that add nitrogen, such as peas and most beans.

Start by making a list of the various vegetables you intend to grow, and then classify them into groups based on their needs and growth patterns (see p.149).

Allocate each rotation group to a plot of land, and draw up a month-by-month cropping timetable. This will keep the land fully occupied and provide continuity. For example, after Brussels sprouts and leeks are finished in early spring, follow with sowings of peas, carrots, lettuces or salad onions.

If you prefer, the vegetables can be from different crop groupings, which means that the rotation from one plot to another is a gradual process, rather than a wholesale changeover on a certain date.

If there is not enough space in a small garden to rotate entire blocks of crops, you could grow the plants in narrow strips and swop the groups between the strips.

Grouping the different types of vegetables together makes crop management easier. Leave at least two years before planting any vegetable from the same group on the same ground.

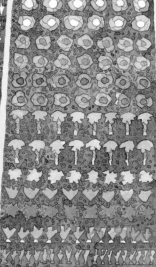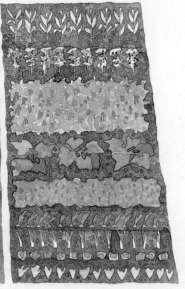

Crop rotation groups
This plot is divided into three groups: peas and beans (left), brassicas and leafy crops (middle) and roots and stems (right). A fourth, permanent, plot can be created for crops that are not shifted, such as asparagus (see p.146). Each group is moved each year onto a new strip of land.

Watering

Plants, whether they are seed-germinating or fruit-developing, must have water for growth. Vegetables will grow well only if they have enough water to replace that lost from the leaves. Most plants have critical periods when water is especially vital, so the skill in providing an optimum water supply is to know when and how to apply the water:
• At the seed and seedling stage, to aid establishment. Water the seed drills with a fine-rosed watering can until they have developed a deep root system.
• After transplanting, to aid re-establishment. Leave a slight depression in the soil at the base of each stem, then fill it with water.
• To produce crops. Fruiting crops such tomatoes and runner beans most need water while flowering and when the fruit starts to swell. Leafy crops need heavy watering about 15 days before harvesting. Root crops should have a steady supply of water from sowing through to cropping.

The best times to water are early mornings or evenings when the sun is less intense, reducing the amount of moisture lost to evaporation.

Feeding the soil

Soil that is intensively cultivated needs generous feeding for optimum results. This can be provided with organic or inorganic fertilizers. A great advantage of organic manures and fertilizers is that they encourage worm activity, which in turn aids soil fertility. Soil that has had no organic matter added is likely to have a worm count of 100–300 per sq m (sq yd) in the top 30cm (12in) of soil. This figure often increases to around 400–500 per sq m (sq yd) if organic matter is added on a regular basis.

Although quite adequate crops of vegetables can be grown in soils where only organic manure and fertilizers are used, higher yields are usually achieved where inorganic, 'chemical' fertilizers are incorporated. The amount of fertilizer needed will depend on the soil type, because light, sandy soils lose fertilizer quickly, whereas clay soils will hold nutrients for much longer. It is also affected by the kind of crop being grown: leafy crops, such as cabbages, need plenty of nitrogen, with one-third of this being provided when they are planted and the remaining two-thirds supplied while the plants are growing.

Vegetable crops growing through winter should get most of their nitrogen in spring rather than autumn, because nitrogen encourages soft growth and if large quantities of nitrogen are added in autumn, this could lead to the soft growth being killed by frost. Therefore, overwintering crops should be given a balanced fertilizer to toughen the leaves and stems. Fruiting crops such as tomatoes and peppers need regular feeding with phosphate and potash fertilizers as soon as the plants start to flower in order to encourage good flower and fruit development.

Preparing the soil

The aim of tasks such as digging and raking the soil is to get the soil into the best condition possible for growing vegetables. Digging is the most important of these operations, because it allows air into the soil. This encourages the biological activity so essential for soil fertility, as well as raising clods of earth so that they can be broken up by frost.

No-dig method

Growing methods involving little or no cultivation are very popular, especially on light soils where the soil structure is easily damaged or where natural fertility is low. The no-dig, or 'zero-cultivation', technique uses the resident worm population to cultivate the soil; layers of well-rotted organic matter are spread over the soil as a mulch and the worms incorporate this into the soil. Thus no digging is needed. Crop plants are inserted through the mulch, and when they have matured, the stalks are cut off at soil level and the new crop is planted between the rows of the previous crops, while the roots rot *in situ*.

Deep-dig method

The deep-digging method of soil preparation involves incorporating large amounts of compost or manure while double-digging a plot. This creates a deep, fertile rooting zone for the plants. Further dressings of organic matter are added at regular intervals, but there is no need for additional digging.

Difficult soils

The no-dig and deep-dig methods are ideal if you have a heavy soil that suffers from compaction when cultivated in wet conditions (although this problem may be overcome by working on wooden boards laid on the soil) or a light, sandy soil needing humus and fertility. These soils benefit from the lack of cultivation and the large amount of organic matter that is added.

Crops such as onions and lettuce, which can be planted close together, will usually do particularly well when they are cultivated in these kinds of soil.

The no-dig method
Young plants should be inserted into the soil through a thick layer of well-rotted organic matter.

The deep-dig method
1 *Spread a thick layer of well-rotted organic matter on to the soil surface.*

2 *Dig the bed, incorporating the manure. The final bed should have a slightly domed surface.*

Preparing a seedbed

Digging alone would leave the soil too uneven for growing most vegetables, so further cultivation is needed to produce a fine crumb structure, or 'tilth', on the soil surface. This usually involves raking the soil several times to break down any lumps, and removing any stones you find, to create a fairly level, even surface.

Well-raked seedbed
Seeds germinate more evenly in soil that has fine particles.

Getting the most from your plot

Many people grow vegetables only if they can find some spare room in the garden, while for others the challenge is to produce a year-round supply of home-grown food. The planning and layout of a vegetable plot and the types of vegetable chosen will be influenced by the number of people who want to eat home-grown vegetables, and the vegetables they like the most. It should be possible to keep a family of three supplied with vegetables all-year-round from a plot 7m x 4m (21ft x 12ft), but a good supply of produce can be grown on an area much smaller than this. Where space is limited, greater yields can be produced by plants that grow vertically rather than those that spread sideways.

Making the best use of available space
Summer and winter cabbages are interspersed in rows. As one row is harvested before the other, there is room for the remainder to grow on.

Planning the vegetable plot

It is important that you organize your vegetable plot as efficiently as possible, to ensure that the crops are rotated correctly (see p.144) and that you make the maximum use of the available sun and shelter.

Plant the tallest crops (such as Jerusalem artichokes or runner beans) so that they do not block the light from the smaller-growing vegetables. Use the walls or fences for shelter, and for supports for beans, peas, or cordon or espalier fruit trees.

Remember to leave yourself ample space to walk between the blocks or rows of vegetables. Trampling on the soil will destroy its structure, and reduce its potential yield.

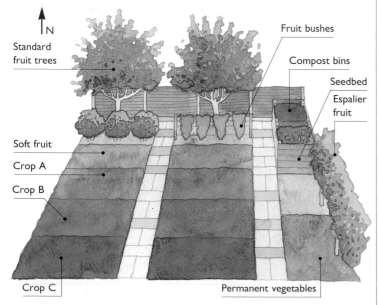

Designing your vegetable garden
An efficient vegetable garden should be planned to make the best use of sun, shelter and space. The vegetables should be planted in rotation groups (see p.144) to ensure pests do not build up.

Choosing a suitable site

The ideal site in which to grow vegetables is one that is warm and sunny during the growing season, and has plenty of light and good air circulation, while being sheltered from strong winds (as wind exposure can reduce plant growth by up to 30 per cent). The air flow is particularly important for wind-pollinated crops, such as sweetcorn, and to reduce the incidence of pests and diseases, which is worse in still air conditions. A gently sloping, sunny site is perfect for an early start in spring, because it will warm up slightly quicker than other aspects. On steeper slopes, plant across the slope rather than down it, as this will reduce soil erosion during heavy rain.

Hedging as a shelter
The hedge surrounding this vegetable plot protects it from the prevailing winds.

Spacing

Where space is limited, a special, multi-row bed system can be introduced. This has more, narrower beds than a conventional plot, and several rows of plants are grown more closely together than usual.

With this multi-row system, the beds are only 0.9–1.5m (3–5ft) wide and the centre of the bed can be reached from a path, so there is no need to walk on the soil and possibly crush it when tending plants. For several rows the plants are grown close together, with the distance between the rows being the same as the distance between the plants.

With such close spacing more plants can be grown per square metre (square yard) than by using a conventional system, where plants are usually grown 45–60cm (1–2ft) apart. In the multi-row system the pathways, at 60–75cm (2–2½ft) across, are slightly wider than those on the conventional system, which are generally about 45cm (1½ft) across.

By growing plants closer together, the competition for space between plants can be used to restrict the ultimate size of the individual vegetables. This can mean that having a small vegetable plot works as an advantage, and often the close spacing of plants reduces the amount of weeding necessary because the weeds are smothered.

However, such close planting does not work with all vegetables: lettuces, for example, will not form good hearts if grown at close spacings, unless a naturally small cultivar is chosen.

Extending the season

By making the most of your plot you can harvest crops all year round. This can be achieved by careful planning and successional sowings (see p.149), growing several types of the same crop and protecting the plants from frost. If protection is used, the growing season can be advanced in spring or run into autumn and winter.

For raising young plants, a cold frame with a glass or plastic top can be used to acclimatize them before they are planted out. Plastic sheeting, polytunnels and cloches warm the soil before planting and are invaluable for protecting young or overwintering plants. Floating mulches, such as fleece, laid over the crop or suspended on hoops will also protect early crops.

Forcing crops
Tuck in plastic sheeting with an edging iron over soil that needs warming before planting.

Hardening young plants
Gradually open the cold frame lid to harden off young plants.

Overwintering
Protect overwintering plants, such as broad beans, with a plastic tunnel in very cold weather.

Growing under glass
To establish early crops, a large number of vegetables, such as leeks and brassicas, can be sown in containers in a greenhouse. Other crops, like cucumbers and melons, need such a frost-free environment at all times.

Plants dislike very hot temperatures, so apply a shading paint to the glass in late spring and always ensure that the greenhouse is well ventilated during the day. Plants will require copious watering.

Intercropping

The space between crops that are slow-growing or need a wide spacing can be used to grow quick-maturing crops such as radishes, salad onions or turnips, which are harvested before the main crop is large enough to fill its allotted space.

Such gaps between crops within a bed can also prove invaluable as seedbeds for other vegetables, which will later need to be transplanted into permanent positions at much wider spacings elsewhere in the garden.

Maximum yields
Radishes and turnips make excellent catch crops when planted at the same time as later-maturing brassicas.

Planning through the year

How long crops take to grow, whether continuity is required, how much time is available and the skill of the gardener are all major considerations when planning a garden, as these will influence the time needed to tend the plot. Inexperienced gardeners should try not to be too ambitious at first and thus risk disappointment; they should start with fast-maturing salad crops, and gradually experiment with vegetables that are more difficult to grow as they gain more skill and experience. One advantage of short-term crops is that they often allow several cropping cycles in each year, which is a quick way to gain tangible results – and if something does go wrong, the mistakes will have no long-term implications.

Successional sowings

Some crops, particularly the short-term salad crops, are the most susceptible to gluts and gaps, but this can be avoided to a large extent by sowing batches of seed on a planned basis. Timing of sowings can be difficult to gauge, but a good guide is to choose the date when you hope to harvest the crop and count back from there the number of weeks needed for the plants to grow. Most of the information for this simple exercise will be given on the back of the seed packet.

To make the maximum use of the available soil, some vegetables, such as cabbages, cauliflowers and leeks, can be grown in a seedbed until they are large enough to transplant, and then they can be planted out into their cropping area. This is a very helpful technique that can be introduced on a wide range of vegetables, and is invaluable for plants that would otherwise occupy the ground for a long period of time at a wide plant spacing. The disadvantage of transplanting young plants is that the disruption may check their growth unless they are kept well watered so that they establish and grow quickly. This is particularly critical where the transplants are dug up from a seedbed and replanted; some roots will always be damaged by this process, and a good supply of water is essential to help these plants recover. If they are short of water, many vegetables will 'bolt': that is the plant will stop growing leaves and develop instead a flower-bearing stem in an attempt to produce seeds.

A timing guide to successional sowings is to make the next sowing when the previous sowing has germinated and emerged through the soil.

Fast-growing crops
Quick-maturing carrots and beetroot allow you to re-use the space within one growing year.

Slow-growing crops
Slower-maturing maincrop potatoes and onions occupy a section of the plot for most of the year.

Harvesting and storage

When to harvest vegetables and how to store them will depend on a number of factors, including the time of year and the type of storage organ that the vegetable consists of. Most vegetables are harvested when fully mature, but a few such as spinach can be cropped repeatedly as a cut-and-come-again crop.

Leafy vegetables, such as Brussels sprouts, are quite hardy and will survive outdoors in temperatures well below freezing point. Many root vegetables, however, have a high moisture content and are easily damaged in winter, even if left in the soil. Exceptions to this are carrots, parsnips and swedes, which are particularly hardy and can be allowed to overwinter in the ground until they are required for consumption.

The main causes of deterioration during storage are moisture loss from the plant tissue (with beetroot and carrots in particular drying out very quickly), or infection and rotting of damaged tissue caused by rough handling when the vegetables were being harvested. Onions and potatoes both tend to bruise particularly easily.

Some vegetables such as onions, chillis, peas, beans and garlic will keep quite well if stored in a dry condition. If they are not to deteriorate, they must be allowed to

Drying chillis
Bulbous vegetables and chillis should be hung up in an airy, frost-free place to dry.

dehydrate slowly in a cool dry place. Once dry, store beans and peas in airtight containers. Garlic, chillis and onions can be hung up in an airy place. Any storage area must be frost free.

Many vegetables also freeze well (see p.164). These should be blanched before being cooled rapidly and frozen in sealed, airtight boxes or bags.

Harvesting parsnips
Parsnips can be left to overwinter in the soil and dug up as required.

Vegetable chart

The chart below shows which conditions each vegetable needs and how long it is likely to occupy the ground.

	Crop rotation group	Ease of growing	pH range	Suitable for freezing	Length of growing season	Yield (kg per sq.m)	Tolerates frost
Asparagus (p.174)		D	6.0-7.5	✓	52	1.5	✓
Asparagus peas (p.151)	1	M	6.0-7.0	✕	16	1.0	✕
Aubergines (p.169)	3	D	5.5-6.5	✓	30	5.0	✕
Beetroot (p.164)	3	M	6.5-7.5	✓	26	2.0	✓
Broad beans (p.153)	1	M	6.5-7.5	✓	28	4.0	✓
Broccoli (p.157)	2	M	6.0-7.0	✓	45	2.0	✓
Brussels sprouts (p.155)	2	E	6.0-7.5	✓	52	1.5	✓
Cabbages (p.154)	2	E	6.5-7.5	✓	24	4.0	✓
Calabrese (p.156)	2	M	6.5-7.5	✓	45	2.0	✕
Carrots (p.162)	3	M	6.0-7.5	✓	36	2.0	✓
Cauliflowers (p.156)	2	D	7.0-7.5	✓	24	4.5	✓
Celeriac (p.173)	3	M	6.5-7.5	✓	28	3.0	✓
Celery (p.173)	3	D	6.5-7.5	✓	36	4.0	✓
Chicory (p.159)	2	D	6.5-7.5	✕	40	0.4	✓
Chinese cabbage (p.155)	2	E	6.5-7.5	✓	16	1.5	✕
Courgettes (p.170)	3	M	5.5-6.5	✓	20	2.0	✕
Cucumbers (p.170)	3	M	5.5-6.5	✕	20	3.0	✕
Dwarf beans (p.152)	1	D	6.5-7.5	✕	20	2.0	✕
Endive (p.159)	2	M	6.5-7.5	✕	12	1.5	✓
Florence fennel (p.174)	3	D	6.0-7.5	✕	16	3.0	✓
Garlic (p.167)	3	M	6.5-7.5	✕	40	2.0	✓
Globe artichokes (p.172)	3	D	6.5-7.5	✓	52	1.5	✓
Jerusalem artichokes (p.163)	3	E	6.5-7.5	✕	52	2.5	✓
Kale (p.155)	2	M	6.5-7.5	✓	40	1.5	✓
Kohl rabi (p.174)	2	M	6.5-7.0	✓	24	2.5	✓
Lamb's lettuces (p.159)	2	E	6.5-7.5	✕	24	1.0	✓
Lettuces (p.158)	2	E	6.5-7.5	✕	16	1.0	✕
Leeks (p.175)	3	M	6.5-7.5	✓	36	1.5	✓
Lima beans (p.153)	1	E	6.5-7.0	✓	20	2.5	✕

	Crop rotation group	Ease of growing	pH range	Suitable for freezing	Length of growing season	Yield (kg per sq.m)	Tolerates frost
Mangetouts (p.151)	1	M	6.0-7.0	✕	20	1.5	✕
Marrows (p.171)	3	M	5.5-6.5	✓	20	2.0	✕
Melons (p.171)	3	D	5.5-6.5	✕	28	1.5	✕
Okra (p.151)	1	M	6.5-7.0	✕	16	2.0	✕
Onions (p.166)	3	M	6.5-7.5	✓	32	1.5	✕
Parsnips (p.163)	3	M	6.5-7.5	✓	40	1.5	✓
Peas (p.150)	1	E	6.0-7.0	✓	28	3.0	✕
Peppers (p.169)	3	M	5.5-6.5	✓	28	1.5	✕
Potatoes (p.161)	3	E	5.5-6.5	✓	32	3.0	✕
Pumpkins (p.171)	3	E	5.5-6.5	✓	20	3.0	✕
Radishes (p.165)	3	E	6.0-7.0	✕	6	0.4	✓
Rocket (p.158)	2	E	6.5-7.5	✕	24	0.5	✓
Runner beans (p.152)	1	D	6.5-7.5	✓	20	4.0	✕
Salsify (p.164)	3	M	6.5-7.5	✕	40	1.5	✓
Scorzonera (p.165)	3	M	6.5-7.5	✕	40	2.0	✓
Shallots (p.167)	3	M	6.5-7.5	✕	40	2.0	✕
Sorrel (p.159)	2	E	6.5-7.5	✕	24	0.5	✓
Spinach (p.160)	2	M	6.5-7.5	✓	36	1.5	✓
Squashes (p.171)	3	M	5.5-6.5	✕	20	2.0	✕
Swedes (p.163)	3	E	6.0-7.0	✓	28	2.0	✓
Sweetcorn (p.172)	3	D	6.0-7.0	✓	20	0.5	✕
Swiss chard (p.160)	2	E	6.5-7.5	✕	40	1.0	✓
Tomatoes (p.168)	3	M	5.5-6.5	✓	24	2.5	✕
Turnips (p.162)	3	E	6.0-7.0	✓	30	1.5	✕

Crop rotation group = 1 Peas and beans, 2 Leaves and flowerheads, 3 Roots, stems and fruiting vegetables

Ease of growing = D difficult, M moderate, E easy

pH range = Preferred pH

Suitable for freezing = ✓ yes, ✕ no

Length of growing season in weeks

Yield = kilograms per square metre (double poundage for square yards)

Tolerates frost = ✓ yes, ✕ no

Pods and beans

These vegetables are grown for their succulent seedpods or seeds, although they can also be attractive plants in the border. Some, such as broad beans and peas, like cool temperatures, others including French beans and lima beans need high temperatures. All prefer soil that has previously been manured but they require no extra nitrogen during their growing season. Once the pods are forming, do not allow these plants to dry out: ensure they have good supplies of water – about 22 litres/sq m (5 gallons/sq yd) if conditions are dry.

Peas

Pisum sativum

Garden peas are grown for their sweet-tasting edible seeds, which are produced in green or (in a few cultivars) purple pods. The peas are generally round with a wrinkled or smooth skin, and can be eaten fresh – either cooked, or raw in salads – or dried and stored for use later.

Garden peas vary in height: the more recent, dwarf cultivars are only 18in (45cm) high, while the traditional types can grow to 5ft (1.5m). They are divided into three groups, according to when the peas are mature enough to eat, called earlies, second earlies and maincrop; the maincrop cultivars bear the heaviest crops and the earliest the lightest.

The time from sowing to harvesting varies with each type. If you sow early crop peas in mid-spring, they will be ready to harvest 12 weeks later in midsummer. Crops of

P.s. 'Holiday'

second early and maincrop cultivars will be ready to harvest about 10–12 weeks after sowing.

Sowing Sow seed in flat-bottomed drills 3–5cm (1–2in) deep. String foil across the rows to deter birds from taking the seeds or attacking the seedlings.

Cultivation The crop will be larger when the plants are supported by canes, sticks, or plastic or wire mesh. This is introduced as soon as two pairs of 'true' leaves develop.

If you are using a tent-like structure, a wide mesh will allow you to reach through to the pods. Keep the plants well watered from soon after flowering starts because this increases your yield appreciably, particularly with maincrop cultivars.

Harvesting Start harvesting the pods when they are well developed but before they become too tightly packed with peas. Keep picking regularly to encourage further flowering and the production of more pods.

Tip

The pods develop on the plant from the base up, so the bottom ones will be ready for harvesting first.

Peas have delicate rooting systems and, if you are not careful, you may pull up the whole plant by mistake if you tug at the pea pods when harvesting them, or you could break or damage the main stem. This will greatly reduce the available crop.

To avoid damaging the plant, hold the stem with one hand and the pod with the other, and gently pull the pod downwards and away from the stem.

Station sowing

First of all prepare the soil, removing large stones and raking it to a fine tilth. As a guide, for a cultivar growing to 60–75cm (24–30in), make the drills 60cm (24in) apart and 20cm (8in) wide, and scatter the seeds along them so that the seeds are spaced about 6cm (2½in) apart. Return the soil to the drills, covering the seeds, but do not firm it. Keep the seeds well-watered; do not let them dry out.

1 *Rake the soil to a fine tilth, then use a draw hoe to make a wide, flat seed drill in which to place the seeds.*

2 *Sow seeds at set spacings along the drill to produce a broad band of plants which are easier to support.*

Mangetouts

Pisum sativum var. *macrocarpon*

P.s. var. *macrocarpon*

Also known as sugar snap peas, sugar or snow peas, mangetouts are grown for their delicate, sweet-tasting pods, which are eaten young and whole. Alternatively, the peas can be harvested later, in the same way as garden peas. Mangetouts are much easier to grow than garden peas because they need very little care after the seeds have germinated. They will be ready to harvest eight weeks after sowing.

Sowing Sow seeds from mid-spring onwards at three-week intervals to provide a succession of crops throughout the summer. Sow in flat-bottomed drills 4cm (1½in) wide and 15cm (6in) apart, with 10cm (4in) between the seeds. For cropping purposes, sow in blocks of three drills, which can be separated from the next block by a 45cm (18in) path.

Cultivation The crop is larger when the plants are supported by canes, sticks, or plastic or wire mesh. With the three-row system, arrange the support over the rows in a tent-like structure, about 45–60cm (18–24in) tall at its highest point.

Harvesting The perfect stage for picking is when the peas are just visibly swelling in the pods. Harvest the pods by tugging them gently from the stem.

Growing tall/short peas
While sticks are sufficient to support shorter plants, wire mesh may be needed for taller ones.

Asparagus peas

Psophocarpus tetragonolobus

P. tetragonolobus

Asparagus peas are grown for their decorative scarlet to chocolate-brown flowers, delicate bluish-green foliage and triangular 'winged' pods that have an asparagus-like flavour. They are eaten whole.

The pods will be ready for picking about eight weeks after sowing. Do not expect large quantities of pods though: even a heavy yield will be only about half that of garden peas.

The plants have a dense, compact habit, reaching 45cm (18in) high and up to 60cm (24in) across, giving an almost hedge-like appearance to the rows. They grow best in a sunny position in a well-drained soil.

Sowing Sow seed in mid- to late spring, in drills about 2–3cm (1in) deep and 30cm (12in) apart, with 30cm (12in) between the seeds.

Cultivation Support the plants with canes, sticks, or plastic or wire mesh, or they will produce very few pods. Protection from pigeons is essential: suspending nets on canes above the crop is the best method.

Harvesting The pods are ready for picking from midsummer until early autumn. For the best flavour, harvest the pods while they are still immature and about 3–5cm (1–2in) long. Pick regularly to encourage further flowering and the production of more pods.

Okra

Abelmoschus esculentus

A. esculentus

Grown for its elegant edible pods, okra is nicknamed 'lady's finger' because of its resemblance in shape. This tender vegetable must have as long a growing season as possible because it will take at least 16 weeks from sowing until harvesting the pods. It grows to a height of 60–90cm (24–35in) and prefers a sunny, sheltered site.

Sowing In mid-spring, sow three seeds per 7.5cm (3in) pot at a temperature of 18–24°C (65–75°F). Thin out the seedlings, removing the two smallest seedlings from the pot.

Cultivation The plants should be 15–20cm (6–8in) high before they are planted out, usually from early summer onwards when all danger of frost has passed. Cover the planting area with black plastic for at least three weeks to warm the soil and insert the young plants into the soil through the plastic. Space them at 35cm (14in) all round to encourage strong, bushy plants. They must be sheltered from wind for the first week after planting.

Harvesting From midsummer until early autumn, harvest the pods while they are still immature and before the seeds have developed fully. Cut them from the stem with a sharp knife. Harvest the pods as they form, to encourage the plant to produce more.

Runner beans
Phaseolus coccineus

These easy-to-grow climbing plants were originally introduced as ornamentals. There are cultivars with red, white or pink flowers, as well as red-and-white bicolours such as 'Painted Lady' which would not look out of place in the garden border. Today, they are grown mainly for their long, edible pods which are produced prolifically until the first frosts.

Grown as annuals, runner beans require a sturdy support system, as they can reach heights of 2.5–3m (8–10ft) in a relatively short growing season of 18–20 weeks.

Sowing Sow seeds in late spring or early summer – runner beans grow better in warm soil. Using a dibber, station-sow 5cm (2in) deep in a double row spaced 60cm (2ft) apart and with 15cm (6in) between the seeds, to give the plants plenty of room as they grow. In colder areas, sow the beans indoors, two or three to a 15cm (6in) pot. Transplant when about 10cm (4in) tall.

Cultivation Insert the supports when the plants are about 15cm (6in) high, just as the twining stem starts to develop in the tip of the plant. Sturdy 2.4m (8ft) bamboo canes are ideal, inserted just outside the row and angled to form a tent-like structure so the plants grow up it. Water the roots well from soon after flowering and continue throughout the harvesting period, as this can

P. coccineus

increase the crop appreciably. Spray plants with water to disturb the flowers and thus aid pollination.

Harvesting The pods will be ready for picking from midsummer onwards and harvesting can continue until the first frosts, when the plants are killed. Begin picking when the pods are well developed and about 15cm (6in) long, with the seeds just visible as swellings along the pods. Keep picking

Tip
For an early start, from mid-spring sow seeds individually in 7.5cm (3in) pots. Grow seedlings in a greenhouse or cold frame and plant out when the danger of frost is past.

them regularly (large pods become tough and stringy); this also encourages further flowering and the production of more pods.

Watering
While the flowers are setting, keep the plant well watered.

Bean supports
Canes can be used as supports, either in the form of a wigwam or in a double row; in each case tie the tops of the cones together firmly. Or grow them over a decorative metal arch.

Wigwam supports
These are ideal for climbing vegetables, where space is limited.

Arch support
Growing beans over an arch is both decorative and productive.

Dwarf beans
Phaseolus vulgaris

P. vulgaris

Also known as French, string or kidney beans, dwarf beans are grown for their curved, green pods which are eaten whole and for their partially developed seeds, better known as 'flageolets'. Bush forms will grow 40–45cm (16–18in) high and 30–45cm (12–18in) wide. Climbing cultivars can be grown up supports. Harvest 12–14 weeks after sowing.

Sowing Station-sow seeds at three-week intervals from late spring until midsummer 5cm (2in) deep in double rows spaced 20cm (8in) apart, with 15cm (6in) between seeds. Stagger them to give plenty of room.

Cultivation Keep plants well-watered once flowering starts to increase the crop and delay the onset of stringiness.

Harvesting Pick regularly once the pods are about 10cm (4in) long and will snap cleanly in half.

Under cloche
A late crop of dwarf beans is protected by a cloche.

Lima beans
Phaseolus lunatus

P. lunatus

Also known as the 'butter bean', this plant is grown for its large white seeds, although the young pods can be eaten whole about eight weeks after sowing. The plants prefer a warm climate, and a well-drained soil.

There are both bush and climbing forms of the lima bean, the latter being useful in small gardens where space is at a premium. The bush forms will reach about 75cm (30in) high but have a spreading habit, while the climbing forms get up to about 1.8m (6ft) if they are well supported. The beans will be ready to harvest 14 weeks after sowing.

Sowing Sow seeds from late spring onwards 7.5cm (3in) deep and 30–45cm (12–18in) apart. Allow 75cm (30in) between the rows for climbing cultivars, slightly less for bush forms.

Cultivation Provide climbing cultivars with canes at least 1.8m (6ft) tall for adequate support. Once the plants reach 30cm (12in) high, supply a proprietary liquid feed at two-week intervals to ensure growth, but stop feeding when the plants start to flower.

Harvesting The beans will be ready to harvest when the swollen seeds are visible in the pods. Pull pods gently to prevent damage to the stems.

Broad beans
Vicia faba

V.f. **'The Sutton'**

Broad beans are very hardy plants, and will give a good crop with very little care and attention. They are grown mainly for their edible, greenish white seeds which develop inside thick, hairy pods, but the immature pods can be eaten when about 10cm (4in) long and the young shoots are also tasty. Those sown in autumn will take up to 24 weeks to harvest, spring-sown crops are ready in 16 weeks.

Sowing Sow in late autumn (this will discourage blackfly, to which broad beans are prone, since the plants will flower before the blackfly are out in force) or early spring, because the seeds germinate better at lower temperatures. Using a dibber, station-sow 5cm (2in) deep in a double row spaced at 30cm (12in), with 25cm (10in) between the seeds to give plenty of room.

Cultivation Most cultivars need support, and well-branched twigs 45cm (18in) tall will allow the plants to grow up through them. Insert the twigs after sowing to protect the seedlings from pigeons, especially if young plants are overwintered. Water the plants well once flowering starts and throughout harvest time.

Harvesting If you sow in autumn and spring, you should have broad beans for picking from late spring to mid-autumn. Begin picking when the swollen beans can be felt through the sides of the pods. Broad beans are delicious when young and tender, but as they age they become bitter and develop tough skins.

Tip
When the plants are in full flower, snap out the top 7.5cm (3in) to encourage the pods to develop and to discourage blackfly.

Types of bean
Grown for their pods, or the seeds inside them, or both, beans are in the main tender plants – broad beans being the exception.

Most beans are highly prized for their nutritious fibre and protein content, and many types have both bush and trailing forms to choose from.

Purple podded beans are coloured variants of French beans (*Phaseolus vulgaris*). They are available in both bush and climbing forms and can be eaten raw or cooked (when boiled the pod colour changes from purple to dark green). 'Royalty is a bush cultivar with a delicate flavour, and 'Climbing Purple' is a good climbing cultivar.

Bean varieties
French beans (left) including yellow and purple podded cultivars, broad bean (middle) and runner bean (right).

Bush forms
Broad bean 'Bonny Lad', 'Relon'
Dwarf bean 'Aramis', 'Tendergreen'
Lima bean 'Henderson', 'Fordhook'
Runner bean 'Gulliver', 'Pickwick'

Trailing forms
Dwarf bean 'Blue Lake', 'Purple Podded'
Lima bean 'Challenge', 'Florida Butter'
Runner bean 'Crusader', 'Liberty'

Leaves and flowerheads

Among vegetables grown for their leaves and flowerheads are brassicas (cabbages, cauliflowers, broccoli and calabrese), which prefer cool temperatures so are usually grown in winter and spring in warm regions. Brassicas must be planted in ground that has not been freshly manured as this promotes lush but easily damaged growth. Also grown for their leaves are lettuces, chicory, endive, and other salad vegetables. Most of these cannot tolerate consistently high temperatures – above 25°C (77°F) – without bolting (running to seed).

Cabbages

Brassica oleracea Capitata Group

The tightly packed leaves and growing point of the cabbage plant are often referred to as the 'head' or 'heart', and this varies in size and shape – from round, through pointed to almost flat – according to type and cultivar. Growing a selection of the many types on offer makes it possible to have fresh cabbage available to eat throughout the year, harvesting even through quite severe winter conditions.

All types of cabbage are cultivated in much the same way, with the timing of sowing and planting varying according to the season, the cultivars chosen and the time taken to reach maturity. The soil should be slightly alkaline to discourage a disease called club root, so apply lime if necessary (see p.157).

Sowing Sow seed thinly 2cm (¾in) deep in a well-

B.o. **'Red Drumhead'**

B.o. **'Wheeler's Imperial**

prepared seedbed outdoors from mid- to late spring through to midsummer, depending on the cabbage type. For many of the sowings, watering may be required to make sure the seedlings keep growing rapidly. If cabbages dry out, they will produce 'hearts' too easily or 'bolt' to produce seed.

Cultivation Transplant the seedlings (see box). Firm the soil well by treading it down before planting to encourage a strong root system which will support the plants. Plant out spring cabbages at a spacing of 30cm (12in) all round, summer and autumn types at 40 x 45cm (16 x 18in), and hardy winter cabbages at a spacing of 50 x 50cm (20 x 20in) apart.

Harvesting When the cabbage has developed a good-sized, solid heart, it is ready for harvesting. Using a sharp knife, cut through the main stem to remove the entire heart and a few outer leaves, leaving the oldest leaves and the stem in the soil (see below).

How to transplant brassicas

When the seedlings are at the fourth 'true' leaf stage, they are ready for transplanting into rows of about 30cm (12in) apart, with 45cm (18in) between the plants.

This crop matures quite rapidly and can take as little as 10 weeks from germination to harvest. However, as it is shallow-rooted, it is very important to keep the plants well watered.

1 *Before transplanting, check that the growing point on a young plant is undamaged.*

2 *Embed the seedling to the depth of the lowest 'true' leaves to stabilize the plants.*

3 *The plant is firmly enough planted if a leaf snaps or tears when tugged.*

Tip

With many cabbages, cross-cutting the surface of the stem which has been exposed after harvesting will encourage more edible green leaves to develop close to the cuts.

Brussels sprouts

Brassica oleracea Gemmifera Group

B.o. 'Topline'

These very hardy vegetables are grown for their edible flower buds, which form small, tight, 'cabbage-like' sprouts in the leaf joints of the plant's main stem. Tall cultivars are ideal if space is limited as they can be grown close together and produce a good 'vertical' crop.

The soil for Brussels sprouts should be slightly alkaline to discourage club root disease, so apply lime if necessary (see p.157). They take about 20 weeks from sowing to harvesting.

Sowing Sow seed thinly into a seedbed outdoors in mid- to late spring. Some watering may be required to make sure that the seedlings keep growing rapidly.

Cultivation Firm the soil well by treading it down before planting to encourage a strong root system which will hold the plants erect. When the seedlings have developed four or five 'true' leaves, transplant them into their cropping site with the rows 60cm (2ft) apart and 60cm (2ft) between the plants, firming each plant well into the soil.

Harvesting The sprouts will be ready to harvest from early autumn through to mid-spring, depending on the cultivar. To pick, pull the individual sprouts downwards so they snap from the stem. As the season ends, the tops of the plants can be snapped off and eaten as spring greens.

Stripping lower leaves
This allows light to reach the developing Brussels sprouts.

Kale

Brassica oleracea
Acephala Group

B.o. 'Dwarf Green Curled'

This is the hardiest of annual winter vegetables. The soil for kale should be slightly alkaline to discourage club root, so apply lime if necessary (see p.157).

Sowing Sow seed in late spring outdoors in a seedbed. You may need to protect the seedlings against birds.

Cultivation When the seedlings have developed four 'true' leaves, transplant them into their cropping site, spacing the rows 60cm (2ft) apart, with 45cm (18in) between the plants. Water well until established.

Harvesting Harvest on a cut-and-come-again basis from mid-autumn to mid-spring by snapping off young leaves from all the plants. This will prevent any leaves from maturing and becoming tough and 'stringy'.

Hoeing between rows
Hoeing between kale plants controls weeds as they emerge.

Chinese cabbage

Brassica rapa Chinensis Group

B.r. 'Harmony'

This annual plant is grown for its crisp, delicately flavoured leaves with white midribs which are used fresh in salads. It is relatively fast-growing and may be ready to harvest in as little as 10 weeks from germination.

Chinese cabbage resents root disturbance and is usually raised in pots. Transplant seedlings when three 'true' leaves are about 5cm (2in) high.

Sowing Sow seeds individually in plastic or peat pots 7.5cm (3in) square in mid-summer. Raise in a cold frame or unheated greenhouse as they need temperatures of 20–25°C (68–78°F) to germinate.

Cultivation When the seedlings have developed four 'true' leaves, transplant out-doors into rows about 30cm (12in) apart, with 45cm (18in) between the plants. Chinese cabbage is shallow-rooted and the plants must be kept well watered.

Harvesting Starting in late summer, harvesting can last for up to 14 weeks with successional sowings. Cut through the stem just above soil level to remove the heart. The remaining stalk will often sprout clusters of new leaves, which can be harvested later on.

Cauliflowers

Brassica oleracea Botrytis Group

Cauliflowers are grown for their edible flowerheads, which are harvested while they are in tight bud. Cauliflowers can be available for most of the year, and certainly from early spring through to midwinter. Autumn- and spring-heading cauliflowers are the easiest to grow, often producing curds (immature flowerheads) up to 30cm (1ft) across.

Cauliflowers are often judged on the whiteness and lack of blemishes on the curd – the 'yellow' curd types such as 'Marmalade' being the exception. There are also forms with green and purple heads, which have an outstanding flavour.

Cauliflowers are among the most difficult vegetables to grow well. They need plenty of water to ensure rapid growth and resent root disturbance, so should be transplanted as young as possible, certainly within six weeks of germination. If transplanted too late or allowed to dry out at this stage, they may produce small, premature, tight curds which are tough and woody.

The soil for cauliflowers should be slightly alkaline to discourage club root and because acid soils can

B.o. 'Idol'

promote some nutrient deficiencies, resulting in poor curds. (Apply lime if necessary; see opposite.)

Sowing Sow seed individually in plastic or peat pots 7.5cm (3in) square, and raise in a cold frame or unheated greenhouse. Sow early-summer cauliflowers in mid-autumn for harvest the following spring; autumn cauliflowers in late spring for harvest in autumn; winter cauliflowers in late spring for harvesting in winter the following year and sow spring cauliflowers in late spring for harvesting in early spring the following year.

Cultivation When the seedlings have developed four 'true' leaves, they are ready for transplanting to their cropping site. Spacing depends on the time of year: generally, the later the planting, the larger the cauliflower will grow and the greater the space needed for each plant. Early-summer cauliflowers, for example, should be planted at a spacing of 60 x 45cm (24 x 18in), winter cauliflowers at 75cm (30in) all round.

Harvesting When the covering leaves start to open and show the enclosed curd beneath, the cauliflower is ready to harvest. Using a sharp knife, cut through the main stem to remove the complete curd, together with a row of leaves around it to protect the curd from damage and marking.

Preparing the soil
Dig in plenty of well-rotted manure or compost in autumn to allow it to penetrate the soil.

Covering curds
Protect the curds from severe frost or sunlight by wrapping leaves over them.

Calabrese

Brassica oleracea Italica Group

Grown as an annual for its edible flowerheads, calabrese is similar to broccoli but less hardy, although it can be harvested in early spring if grown under protection. Many cultivars will mature within 12 weeks of sowing.

Well-grown calabrese is tasty eaten fresh and ideal for freezing, the main drawback being that the plant is very susceptible to mealy aphids, which are attracted to the flower spikes.

The soil for calabrese should be slightly alkaline in order to discourage club root, so apply lime if necessary. Calabrese resents root disturbance and often responds to transplanting by prematurely producing small, tight heads which can be tough and woody.

Sowing Sow seed thinly in drills 2.5cm (1in) deep and about 30cm (12in) apart, sowing three seeds 13mm (½in) apart in stations at 20cm (8in) intervals. Alternatively, sow seeds individually into 5cm (2in) diameter plastic or peat pots in a cold frame or unheated greenhouse if cold weather demands an earlier start.

Cultivation When the seedlings have developed three 'true' leaves, thin them to leave only the strongest and healthiest seedling at each station. Transplant pot-grown seedlings at this point. Watering is essential to keep the plants growing rapidly and to produce a good crop – critical times are the first month after sowing and the three-week period just before cropping commences.

Harvesting The main cropping season is from early summer to mid-autumn, but harvesting can continue until the plants are damaged by the first frosts. Cut the central spike first, before the flowers (usually yellow) start to open.

B.o. **Italica Group**

The slightly smaller spikes produced by the side shoots can be cut later. Main-season plantings will often yield up to four or five cuttings before the plants are discarded. (They make useful compost).

Applying lime

Lime can be applied at any time of year to raise the soil's pH but must be added alone, at least two to three months after manuring, or one month after fertilizing the soil. This is because lime and nitrogen react to release ammonia, which can harm plants.

If lime is used first however, fertilizers and manures can be added just one month later. It is also simpler to add lime before crops are sown or transplanted into the site. If lime is applied too often, plants may show signs of nutrient deficiency. Bear in mind that it is easier to raise the soil pH than it is to lower it.

Transplanting seedlings
If transplanting peat pots, ensure the rim is just below ground level.

Shattering stems
Bashing old brassica stems helps them rot and form compost.

Broccoli
Brassica oleracea Italica Group

B.o. **'Purple Sprouting'**

Grown for its edible flowerheads, which are harvested while in tight bud, sprouting broccoli is a very hardy, biennial, winter vegetable. There are both white- and purple-flowered forms.

The soil for broccoli should be slightly alkaline in order to discourage club root, so apply lime if necessary.
Sowing Sow seeds individually in 5cm (2in) square plastic or peat pots, in a cold frame or unheated greenhouse in spring.

Cultivation Plant out in early summer with 60cm (2ft) between the plants all round. Water is essential to produce a good crop, the critical time being the first month after sowing.
Harvesting Broccoli can be harvested from late winter until late spring and has a natural cut-and-come again habit. Cut the central spike first, before the flowers start to open; side shoots will also try to flower and these smaller spikes can be cut later.

Cropping
Harvest broccoli spears by cutting them with a sharp knife.

Providing protection
Surround young stems with extra soil to reduce windrock.

Lettuces
Lactuca sativa

There are many forms of this annual vegetable, grown for its fresh leaves which are a mainstay of summer salads. For best results, grow several types, such as crisp cos, butterhead and loose-leaf lettuces. Loose-leaf types are less likely to run to seed, and are tolerant of most growing conditions. Leaf colour can vary from pale green to reddish brown, and cultivars such as 'Salad Bowl' and 'Valeria Red' are quite deep rooting, making them ideal for dry soils. Harvesting can begin about 12 weeks after planting.

Sowing Sow seed thinly in drills 15mm (½in) deep and 35cm (14in) apart. Sowing at regular intervals from early spring through until midsummer will provide a succession of lettuces from early summer through to mid-autumn. During hot weather, sow in the late afternoon and water well immediately afterwards, to reduce the chance of poor germination caused by high soil temperatures.

Cultivation When the seedlings have developed two 'true' leaves, thin to 30cm

L. sativa **Lobjoits Green**

(12in) apart. In dry weather, keep the plants well watered in the last two weeks before harvesting, when they make the most growth.

Harvesting Loose-leaf lettuces should be harvested by pulling away the outer rows of leaves from one or two large plants on a regular basis. Cut off the entire heads of other types.

Transplanting lettuces
Seed sown indoors can be planted out when all danger of frost is past. Seedlings should be big enough to handle, with five or six leaves. Space them 30cm (12in) apart and keep watered.

Ready to handle
Transplant seedlings once they have five to six leaves.

Protection from birds
Black cotton suspended over the plants prevents them being eaten.

L.s. **'Fortune'**

L.s. **'Salad Bowl'**

Rocket
Eruca sativa

E. sativa

This tender-looking plant is actually quite hardy and will survive winter temperatures down to just above freezing. The leaves have a strong, tangy flavour which increases in strength when the plant matures or is kept too dry. Rocket can be eaten raw or cooked, and grown as individual plants or harvested regularly as a cut-and-come again crop. It makes an excellent addition to other leafy vegetables in a mixed salad.

Sowing Sow seed in succession at three-week intervals from mid-spring to early summer. Sow in broad drills to create a band of plants about 30cm (1ft) wide. If sown in such broad drills, weeds will be unable to establish themselves owing to the density of the plants.

Cultivation Keep the plants well watered to promote rapid growth.

Harvesting Either remove individual leaves from the plants, or cut the seedlings down to about 2.5cm (1in) above ground level, and wait for them to resprout before cutting again.

Lamb's lettuces
Valeriana locusta

V. locusta

Also known as corn salad, this very hardy annual salad crop is grown for its mild-flavoured leaves and will survive winter temperatures down to just above freezing. The erect-growing 'French' cultivars are the hardiest; the 'Dutch' and 'English' forms have a much laxer growth habit, but are more productive. As it takes up very little room, lamb's lettuce is ideal for intercropping between slow-growing or tall vegetable crops. It will do well in most soils and is easy to grow.

Sowing Sow seed in summer in drills 15cm (6in) apart, with 2.5cm (1in) between the seeds. For all-year-round cropping, make an additional sowing in spring.

Cultivation After germination, thin the seedlings to 10cm (4in) apart, and keep the seedbed well watered until they are about 2.5cm (1in) high.

Harvesting Either remove individual leaves from the plants, or cut the whole head down to about 2.5cm (1in) above ground level to encourage fresh growth to be made, which can then be cut again for a further crop.

Endive
Cichorium endivia

C.e. 'Batavian'

This relative of the lettuce is a popular salad vegetable. The leaves have a piquant, slightly bitter taste which can be modified by blanching.

Endive relishes a rich, fertile, well-drained soil.

Sowing Sow seed thinly in drills 13mm (½in) deep and 30cm (12in) apart, from mid-spring onwards.

Cultivation When the seedlings are about 2.5cm (1in) high, thin them to 30cm (12in) apart. Once the plants reach about 25cm (10in) across, place an upturned plate on the centre of each to 'blanch' the heart. Water well in dry weather or the plants will bolt.

Harvesting The plants will be ready to harvest about three weeks after blanching. Cut off the heads just above ground level.

Blanching endive
Cover endive with a blanching cap. This makes it less bitter.

Chicory
Cichorium intybus

C.i. 'Elmo'

This hardy, winter salad vegetable has tight, conical buds ('chicons') of creamy white leaves with a distinctive, bitter flavour.

Sowing In early summer, sow seed in drills 13mm (½in) deep and 30cm (12in) apart, with 2.5cm (1in) between the seeds.

Cultivation Thin the seedlings to about 20cm (8in) apart, and keep the plants well watered until autumn. In late autumn, cut off the leaves to about 2.5cm (1in) above the neck and mound up earth evenly over the plants to a height of 15cm (6in), or cover with a black plastic bucket. This will force the shoots to grow up through the mound or inside the bucket.

Harvesting The forced spears of chicory will be ready to pick in mid-spring, when the creamy white spikes are about 15cm (6in) high or just emerging through the mound of soil. Cut off the heads about 2.5cm (1in) above the neck. If they are re-covered, the roots will often produce two or three smaller secondary spears, about 10cm (4in) tall. In order to prevent the harvested spears from turning green and developing a bitter taste, keep them in the dark until required.

Sorrel
Rumex acetosa

R. acetosa

This versatile plant is an incredibly hardy perennial which is also very easy to grow. The tasty leaves have a sharp flavour and can be used fresh in salads or as a flavouring for soups.

Sorrel will grow on a range of soils, but prefers well-drained yet moisture-retentive, fertile conditions.

Sowing In autumn or spring, sow seed in drills 13mm (½in) deep and 30–40cm (12–16in) apart.

Cultivation Thin the seedlings to 25–30cm (10–12in) apart. Remove any flowers or seed heads as soon as they are spotted – this will preserve the plants' energy for leaf production – and replace the plants themselves every 4–5 years as their productivity declines.

Harvesting Remove the outer leaves for use as they develop, and new leaves will continue to emerge from the centre of the plant.

Spinach
Spinacia oleracea

S.o. 'Triathlon'

This reasonably hardy vegetable is renowned for its strongly flavoured, dark green leaves, which are rich in iron and vitamins.

Spinach prefers a well-drained but moisture-retentive, fertile soil which is high in nitrogen. It will tolerate light shade. Although it is a perennial plant, it is best grown as an annual in order to produce the most vigorous leaves. The plants will often 'bolt' (run to seed) and produce seed in the first year, especially during periods of hot, dry weather.

Spinach is usually ready for eating about 10 weeks after sowing. Individual leaves can be removed, or the whole plant cut back to produce new leaves for cut-and-come-again harvesting.

Sowing For a continuous supply, sow seed at three-week intervals from early spring to midsummer. Sow seed thinly in drills 2cm (³⁄₄in) deep and 30cm (12in) apart.

Cultivation When the seedlings are about 2.5cm (1in) high, thin them to 15cm (6in) apart. For cut-and-come-again crops, thin to 5cm (2in).

Harvesting Harvest the larger plants grown at wide spacings by cutting off the outer leaves at soil level. For a cut-and-come-again crop, cut down the whole plant to 2.5cm (1in) above soil level, leaving the stubs to produce another crop of young leaves.

Preparing the drill
With a cane tip, draw a shallow line in a well-prepared bed.

Sowing the seed
Sprinkle the seed thinly along the drill in the seedbed.

Swiss chard
Beta vulgaris Cicla Group

B. vulgaris

This hardy vegetable is grown for its large, glossy, succulent leaves, which can be up to 45cm (18in) long and 20cm (8in) wide. The brightly coloured leaf stalks are red or white, and the leaves range in colour from the deep green of 'Fordhook Giant' to the lime-green of 'Lucullus' or copper-green of 'Rhubarb Chard'. The best-known is 'Rhubarb Chard', more commonly known as 'Ruby Chard', which is easy to grow but prone to bolting, especially in hot, dry weather.

Swiss chard prefers a fertile, well-drained but moisture-retentive soil. The crop is usually ready for cutting (either by removing individual leaves or on a cut-and-come-again basis) 12 weeks after sowing, although the plants can be harvested through the winter and will usually occupy the ground for almost a year.

Sowing Incorporate plenty of organic matter into the soil before sowing. Sow seed for new plants at any time from early spring to midsummer into drills 2cm (³⁄₄in) deep and 45cm (18in) apart, with 15cm (6in) between the seeds.

Harvesting ruby chard
Select the older leaves and cut off just a few at a time from the base of each plant.

Cultivation When the seedlings are about 5cm (2in) high, thin them to 30cm (12in) apart – as a long-term crop, the plants need plenty of room or mildew may attack them. For cut-and-come-again crops, thin to 7.5cm (3in) apart.

Harvesting Harvest the plants grown at wider spacings by cutting off the outer leaves at soil level. For a cut-and-come-again crop, cut the whole plant down to 2.5cm (1in) above soil level, leaving the stubs to produce another crop of young leaves.

Roots

Vegetables that are grown for their swollen roots or tubers include potatoes, carrots, turnips, swedes, Jerusalem artichokes, parsnips, beetroot, radishes, scorzonera and salsify. Onions and shallots, as well as garlic, are grown for their strong-flavoured bulbs. These groups prefer cool temperatures (18°C/64°F) but will tolerate up to 24°C/75°F, especially in the early stages of growth, and all store well during winter.

Potatoes

Solanum tuberosum

This versatile vegetable is divided into three main groups: early season (quicker-growing cultivars); maincrop (slower-growing cultivars, producing heavier crops); and second earlies, which mature between the other two. Most early-season potatoes are ready to harvest from early summer onwards, and do not store well. Maincrop potatoes are available from midsummer through into winter and can be stored.

Tuber shapes vary considerably between cultivars and sometimes even on the same plant. Flesh texture is either 'floury' (suitable for baking) or 'waxy' (suitable for boiling).

Sowing 'Seed' is the term used for young potato tubers which are planted to produce the next crop. Purchase good-quality 'seed' in late winter and arrange the tubers in shallow trays to chit (see below) in early spring.

Cultivation In most areas, planting can commence from

S. tuberosum

mid-spring onwards for earlies, finishing with the last of the maincrop tubers by early to midsummer. A few days before planting, incorporate a generous dressing of general fertilizer into the topsoil to encourage rapid growth. Plant the tubers 40cm (16in) apart, in rows 60cm (2ft) apart. Use a trowel to make holes about 20cm (8in) deep and carefully place a tuber in each one, with the 'rose' end uppermost and at least 5cm (2in) below the soil surface. Cover with soil, taking care not to damage the delicate new shoots.

To increase the number of tubers produced, when the potato stems are 20–25cm (8–10in) high, use a draw hoe to mound up loose soil over the bottom 10–12cm (4–5in) of each stem ('earthing up'). The top of the ridge should be flat to allow rainwater to soak into it rather than run down the sides.

Harvesting Early potatoes are ready for lifting when the flowers start to open. Two or three weeks before harvesting maincrop potatoes, cut off the tops ('haulms') and remove them from the site (if left, they will encourage slugs); this will allow you to see where the tubers are.

To harvest, use a garden fork to dig under the ridge of earth and ease the tubers from the soil to avoid 'stabbing' them. If the weather is dry, leave the potatoes on top for an hour or so to allow the skins to dry and harden; in damp conditions, spread out the tubers on a hessian sack or newspaper under cover and leave to dry overnight.

Store maincrop potatoes in a cool, dark, frost-free place. Some cultivars will keep well until the following summer.

Chitting potatoes

Arrange the tubers in boxes with the 'rose' end (the area with the most 'eyes', or dormant shoots) upwards. Cut large tubers into two or three sections, dip cut surfaces in dry sand to prevent excessive bleeding, and then treat the sections as individual tubers. Place the boxes in a light, frost-free environment. This process causes the tubers to produce shoots ('chit'). With early cultivars, allow three or four shoots to develop; with maincrop cultivars, the aim is to have as many shoots as possible.

Chitted 'earlies'
Once the chits develop, remove all but three or four.

Spacing tubers
Use a piece of cane to measure spacing between tubers accurately.

Earthing up
Draw the soil up around each stem to maximize yields.

Carrots
Daucus carota

D. carota

This popular root vegetable is usually classified according to the shape of its orange-coloured root, which can be eaten either raw in salads or as a cooked vegetable.

Carrots need a deep, stone-free, well-drained, fertile soil which is high in nitrogen. Do not manure the soil just before growing carrots or much of the crop will develop forked roots. Early-maturing cultivars will be ready to harvest 8 weeks after sowing, maincrop types after 10–12 weeks.

Sowing Sow seed thinly in drills 1.5cm ($\frac{1}{2}$in) deep and 15–20cm (6–8in) apart, from late spring to midsummer.

Cultivation Thin the seedlings to 4–7cm ($1\frac{1}{2}$–$2\frac{1}{2}$in) apart for medium-sized carrots, 7–10cm ($2\frac{1}{2}$–4in) for larger carrots suitable for storing through the winter. Thinning is best done in the evening or in cool, dull conditions to deter carrot root fly. Hoe between the rows until the foliage shades the soil and reduces weed seed germination.

Harvesting Early carrots can be eased out with a fork and then pulled by hand. Dig up maincrop carrots with a fork for immediate use, freezing or storing. Twist off and then discard the foliage.

Thinning
Overcrowded plants will be weak, so allow plenty of space.

Digging carrots
Use a garden fork to reduce damage to the plants' roots.

Turnips
Brassica rapa Rapifera Group

B.r. 'Tokyo Cross'

Often regarded as winter vegetables, turnips can be available throughout the year if a range of cultivars are grown in succession. Some, such as 'Tokyo Cross', are large enough to eat within 6 weeks of sowing, others within 8–10 weeks. The strong-tasting flesh varies in colour from white through to yellow. Turnips require a neutral or slightly alkaline soil to discourage club root, so apply lime if necessary (see p.157). They prefer a light, fertile, well-drained but moisture-retentive soil which is high in nitrogen.

Sowing Sow seed thinly in drills 2cm ($\frac{3}{4}$in) deep and 25–30cm (10–12in) apart in a finely sieved, well-prepared seedbed and subsequently at three-week intervals from late spring until mid- to late summer.

Cultivation The soil should never be allowed to dry out, or much of the crop will develop forked roots and the plants may bolt. When seedlings are no higher than 2.5cm (1in), thin to 10cm (4in) apart for early-maturing cultivars, 15cm (6in) for later, hardy cultivars.

Harvesting Turnips will be ready to harvest from early to mid-autumn, but must be lifted by midwinter. (For storage tips see p.165.)

Ridged beds
To grow vegetables on heavy soils, create a ridged bed.

Harvesting young turnips
Turnips can be harvested when about the size of a golf ball.

Swedes

Brassica napus Napobrassica Group

B. napus

This vegetable is one of the hardiest of all root crops and is grown for its mild, sweet-tasting flesh, which can be creamy white ('Lizzy') or yellow ('Marian').

Swedes require similar soil conditions to turnips (see left). The roots will be ready to harvest about 24 weeks after sowing.

Sowing Sow seed thinly in drills 2cm (¾in) deep and 40cm (16in) apart in a finely sieved, well-prepared seed bed, from late spring onwards.

Cultivation The soil should not be allowed to dry out at any stage, or a large proportion of the crop will develop forked roots and the plants may bolt. When the seedlings are about 2.5cm (1in) high, thin them to 7–10cm (3–4in) apart, and then thin again three weeks later to leave the plants 25cm (10in) apart.

Harvesting Swedes are usually ready to harvest from early to mid-autumn onwards. Although they survive well outdoors through the winter, the low temperatures often give the flesh a fibrous or woody texture. It is therefore advisable to lift them and store indoors.

Jerusalem artichokes

Helianthus tuberosus

H. tuberosus

Grown for its edible root, the hardy Jerusalem artichoke is also used to help clear rough ground. A vigorous perennial and relative of the sunflower, it can grow to a height of 3m (10ft), although the cultivar 'Dwarf Sunray' will only reach about 2m (6ft).

Sowing Plant purchased tubers in spring, 10–15cm (4–6in) deep in soil which has been deeply cultivated. Plant in rows 60cm (24in) apart, with 30cm (12in) between the tubers. Large tubers can be divided up so that each piece has a separate shoot, and the sections planted individually.

Cultivation When the plants are about 30cm (12in) high, mound up the soil 15cm (6in) high around the base to keep the plants stable. In summer, cut the stems down to 1.5m (5ft) to encourage tuber formation. In dry weather, irrigate to keep the tubers swelling.

Harvesting The tubers are ready from mid-autumn onwards and should be dug up with a garden fork. In well-drained soils, the tubers can be overwintered in the growing site. When harvesting, remove all parts of the tubers from the soil, or they will resprout next season.

Separating tubers
Use a sharp knife to divide large artichoke tubers.

Planting
Tubers should be planted into holes at least 10cm (4in) deep.

Parsnips

Pastinaca sativa

P. sativa

These winter vegetables have a very distinctive flavour and are hardy enough to over-winter in the soil. Parsnips prefer a deep, stone-free, well-drained, fertile soil, but on shallow soils shorter-rooted cultivars can be used.

Sowing Sow seed thinly in drills 1.5cm (½in) deep and 30cm (12in) apart, in early spring. Fresh seed gives the best results.

Cultivation When the seedlings are about 2.5cm (1in) high, thin them to 7–10cm (2½–4in) apart to produce large roots suitable for overwintering.

Harvesting The roots will be ready to be lifted from mid-autumn onwards. Dig them up with a fork.

Creating a fine tilth
Before sowing parsnips, form a tilth along a string-marked line.

Beetroot
Beta vulgaris

This useful root vegetable is a biennial plant which is grown as an annual, and can be used at just about any time of year either fresh, stored or pickled.

Although the round beet is the most common, other shapes such as oval, flat and oblong are also grown. There is also a wide variation in colour, red being the most popular, but golden forms such as 'Burpee's Golden', and white ones are available. The leaves are also edible, and taste similar to spinach.

Beetroot prefers a well-drained, fertile soil which is high in nitrogen.

Sowing Beetroot seed is either natural, which is a fruit containing two or three seeds in a cluster, or 'mono-germ' in cultivars such as 'Cheltenham Mono' and 'Monopoly', which have been specially bred to produce one seedling only. Sow from mid-spring through to late summer. Soak the seed in warm water for half an hour before sowing to promote rapid germination, then sow thinly in drills 2cm (¾in) deep and 30cm (12in) apart.

Cultivation When the seedlings are about 2.5cm (1in) high, thin them to 7–10cm (3–4in) apart for large beets, and 4–5cm (1½–2in) to produce small, round beets for pickling.

Harvesting Harvesting usually runs from early summer to mid-autumn, although beetroot can be harvested at any stage of growth depending on the size of beets required. The plants are not fully hardy, however, and should all be lifted for storage by late autumn. Dig up the beets with a garden fork and twist off the leaves, then use immediately or store the roots in a box of moist sand in a cool, dry, frost-free place.

B.v. **'Boltardy'**

Covering seeds
After sowing, draw soil over the seed drill with the back of a rake.

Removing leaves
After digging up beetroot, twist off leaves before storing the roots.

Freezing produce

In addition to storing root vegetables in sand (see opposite), you can also freeze many vegetables. Not all lend themselves to this method of storage, as those with a large amount of water in their structure will freeze less well than those without.

The vegetables listed here will keep their flavour and structure if frozen in the manner suggested. To blanch vegetables, simply plunge them in boiling water for one minute. Drain and cool.

Blanched Asparagus, aubergines, beetroot, broad beans, broccoli, Brussels sprouts, calabrese, carrots, cauliflowers, cabbages, courgettes, French beans, kale, kohl rabi, marrows, parsnips, peas, potatoes, runner beans, spinach, spring onions, swedes, sweetcorn, tomatoes, turnips.

Shredded, pureed, diced or sliced Aubergines, cauliflowers, cabbages, celery, kohl rabi, marrows, swede, turnips.

Frozen when young Beetroot, carrots, parsnips, turnips.

Salsify
Tragopogon porrifolius

T.p. **'Sandwich Island'**

A hardy biennial plant, salsify is usually grown for its creamy white, fleshy roots, although its shoots are also edible. Because of its delicious flavour, it is often called the 'vegetable oyster'.

In order to achieve maximum growth, salsify requires a deep, well-drained, fertile soil.

Sowing Sow seed in drills 1cm (½in) deep and 15cm (6in) apart, in spring. Fresh seed gives the best results, as salsify seed loses viability very quickly.

Cultivation Thin the seedlings to 10cm (4in) apart soon after germination. To encourage rapid growth, keep the plants weed-free and well watered.

Harvesting The roots will be ready to harvest from late autumn onwards. In mild areas, the roots can be lifted and used as required, but in colder areas the roots should be lifted and stored in boxes of sand (see opposite) before winter frosts set in.

Radishes
Raphanus sativus

R.s. 'French Breakfast'

Although usually grown for their swollen roots, which have a 'hot' flavour, radish leaves and their crisp young seed pods also make a useful addition to salads. The swollen roots come in a range of colours, shapes and sizes, and if several types are grown it is possible to have radishes all year round.

Most radishes are ready for harvesting 14–21 days after sowing and are therefore good for growing as a catch crop or for intercropping between vegetables such as Brussels sprouts and leeks, which mature much more slowly. Their rapid germination and growth is ideal for covering the ground quickly, especially when sown broadcast, which makes radishes an ideal 'mulch crop' to smother out annual weeds. They prefer a light, well-drained, fertile soil.

Sowing Sow seed thinly in drills 13mm (½in) deep and about 15cm (6in) apart. For a continuous supply, sow seed in small batches at 10 day intervals from early spring to early autumn. The seed will keep for up to 10 years if kept cool and stored in an airtight container.

Cultivation Radishes produce poor plants if overcrowded, and ideally they should be about 3cm (1in) apart. Watering is essential: drought will make the roots woody or encourage the plants to bolt.

Harvesting Radishes are ready to harvest when the roots are about 3cm (1in) across at their widest point. Grip the plant firmly by its leaves and pull gently. If the soil is dry, water the plants the day before harvesting so that they will pull out of the ground easily.

Thinning
Radish seedlings should be thinned as they grow to keep them strong and healthy.

Scorzonera
Scorzonera hispanica

S.h. 'Russian Giant'

This hardy, perennial plant is usually grown as an annual, similar to carrots, for its thick, fleshy roots. These are about 20cm (8in) with a shiny, black skin, and have a distinctive flavour when cooked. The young shoots (chards) and flower buds are also edible. Scorzonera is a good source of iron and fairly easy to grow. It needs to have a deep, fertile soil in order to do well and produce a good crop.

Sowing Sow seed thinly in drills 1cm (½in) deep and 20cm (8in) apart, in spring.

Cultivation Thin the seedlings to 10cm (4in) apart soon after germination. In order to achieve maximum growth, keep the plants weed-free and make sure they are well watered.

Harvesting The roots will be ready to harvest from late autumn onwards. In mild areas, the roots can be lifted and used immediately, but in colder areas they should be lifted and stored in boxes of sand before the winter weather sets in.

The roots can be over-wintered in the ground and covered with straw in the early spring. The young shoots will emerge through the straw, and these (and the flower buds) can be harvested when they are about 10cm (4in) high.

Storing root vegetables

A traditional way to store root vegetables, such as turnips, carrots and beetroot, is in a wooden box, laid in a bed of loose straw or sand and then covered with straw or sand.

Place in a cool, dry, frost-free area, such as a garage. The length of time that vegetables may be stored will depend not only on the vegetable type and cultivar but also the conditions within the store. Generally, they will survive for a few months in reasonable shape.

Onions
Allium cepa

The strong-flavoured bulbs of onions are invaluable in the kitchen for a wide range of dishes. They are grown as annual plants, with the brown- or yellow-skinned cultivars being the most popular with gardeners.

Onions are tolerant of cool temperatures and even frost, especially in the early stages of development, with low temperatures often producing a better-quality crop. They have a long growing season, and for good skin quality and colour the bulbs need plenty of bright sunshine in the period just before harvesting. Onions prefer a well-drained, fertile soil, which has been well dug to encourage the plants to root deeply and enable them to grow well in dry conditions. Onions will be ready to harvest 14 weeks after spring sowing or 36 weeks after autumn sowing.

Sowing In early autumn or early spring, sow seed in drills 1.5cm (½in) deep and about 30cm (12in) apart, with 2.5cm (1in) between the seeds. These spacings should produce bulbs 7.5–10cm (3–4in) across at harvest time.

A. cepa

Cultivation Onions suffer from weed competition, and keeping the plants weed-free by hoeing between rows until they establish (this takes about 6 weeks) is critical. Remove any flower heads on the onions as soon as they are seen, or dig up the plant, to ensure the plant's efforts are concentrated on the bulb.

Harvesting Onions are ready for harvesting when the leaves turn yellow and the tops keel over. The process can be speeded up by bending over the tops by hand, but this must be done carefully or the bulb may be bruised and will start to rot when in store.

Lift the bulbs gently with a garden fork and allow them to dry naturally (see right) before storing in a cool, dry, frost-free place. Onions rarely store well beyond mid-spring, and will start to produce new top growth after this time.

Harvesting and storage

Once the onions have swelled to an appropriate size and the leaves have turned yellow, they can be harvested. Lift the bulbs carefully, to avoid damaging or bruising them, and spread them out to dry.

A raised, open-slatted rack covered with a plastic sheet supported on a cloche frame, will ensure the onions do not turn mouldy before they dry, as plenty of air must circulate around the bulbs. Spread the onions out to improve air circulation. Once dry, you can hang the onions on string indoors (see opposite).

Drying out
Onions left to dry in the sun may need protection from rain.

Bolted plants
Onions that have started to produce seed should be dug up and discarded.

Overwintering
Autumn-sown onions may need to be protected if the weather is very severe.

Bending leaves
Gently pushing over onion leaves when the tips start to turn yellow helps the tops die quickly.

Shallots

Allium cepa Aggregatum Group

A.c. 'Dutch Yellow'

These onion-like, yellow- or orange-skinned bulbs, which develop into a clump of up to 12, have a distinct flavour and are eaten raw or cooked.

Shallots like a fertile, well-drained, soil which has been well dug, as this encourages the plants to root deeply and grow well in dry conditions. For best results, the bulbs need lots of sunshine just before harvesting.

Sowing From late winter to early spring, shallowly plant virus-free sets 15cm (6in) apart, with 25cm (10in) between rows, into a soil with a seedbed-like tilth that has then been firmed down to discourage birds from disturbing the soil.

Cultivation Follow the same guidelines as for onions (see left).

Harvesting The bulbs are ready to harvest when the leaves have died down. Lift them with a garden fork.

Firming soil
Press on the soil to firm it down before planting the shallots.

Garlic

Allium sativum

This hardy vegetable, with its characteristic strong flavour that makes such a valuable contribution to both cooked dishes and salads, is far easier to grow than many gardeners realize. There are two distinct forms, one with white skin and the other with purple.

Garlic has a long growing period, but will survive outdoors throughout the winter if grown in a light, dry, well-drained soil. On wetter soils, the plants should be grown on ridges to improve drainage.

The best crops come from autumn plantings, because most garlic requires about 6 weeks of cool weather (at 0–10°C/32–50°F) to promote good growth the following season.

Sowing Dig over the soil deeply before planting in autumn. Split the bulbs into

Planting
Garlic cloves should be pushed into the soil, base first.

Drying
Hang up garlic in a cool, frost-free place to dry out naturally.

A. sativum

individual 'cloves' and push these into the soil, so that the top (pointed end) of the clove is approximately 2.5cm (1in) below the soil surface. For maximum yields and even bulb development, plant the cloves in a square arrangement at a spacing of 18cm (7in).

Cultivation As they develop, the bulbs will gradually work their way up to the surface of the soil.

Harvesting The bulbs will be ready to harvest as soon as the leaves begin to turn from green to yellow. A delay in harvesting will result in shrivelled bulbs – these will be usable in the kitchen, but will deteriorate in storage. Lift the bulbs gently with a garden fork and allow them to dry naturally before storing in a cool, dry, frost-free place. In these conditions, they will keep for up to 10 months.

Stringing onions and garlic

After harvesting, hang up onions and garlic to dry in a cool frost-free place.

To keep them tidy, you can hang the bulbs on a length of string. Simply knot a length of string or raffia and hang it from a hook so that it forms a loop. Weave the dried stem of the first onion (or garlic) through the base of the loop and then add each bulb in turn in the same way.

Finally, hang the string of bulbs from the wall or ceiling in a place that is cool and dry.

Securing the bulbs
Weave each bulb on to the string loop, as shown, pulling the stem taut to secure.

Fruiting vegetables

Many of these vegetables, such as peppers, aubergines, peppers and melons, originate from tropical and sub-tropical regions and need very warm or in some cases subtropical (21–30°C/70–86°F) temperatures to ripen. Despite this, they can be grown successfully outdoors in southern temperate regions, and inside or in a green-house in cooler northern areas. Other fruiting vegetables, such as globe artichokes, marrows, courgettes, pumpkins and sweetcorn can be germinated indoors but will ripen outdoors. With some plants (such as melons, marrows and pumpkins), fertilization can be a problem, and it is often best to pollinate by hand.

Tomatoes
Lycospersicon esculentum

This popular fruiting vegetable is grown as an annual and requires long, warm summers to really perform well. Given the right conditions, some cultivars can reach 2.5m (8ft) high. Bush tomatoes have no obvious main stem but produce several fruit-bearing branches of about the same size. Cordon tomatoes have a dominant main stem which carries fruit trusses along its length.

Tomatoes prefer a fertile, well-cultivated soil. They will also grow successfully in pots, troughs and growbags, but regular watering is essential to produce a good yield of larger fruit. Cropping usually starts within 12–14 weeks of transplanting.

Sowing For outdoor culti-vation, sow seed in late spring. Place individual seeds in 10cm (4in) pots and ger-minate at 15°C (60°F), hard-

L.e. **'Phyra'**

ening off in a cold frame for 10 days before planting out.
Cultivation The best growth is achieved at tem-peratures of 20–25°C (68–78°F), and the plants and their fruits can be dam-aged when temperatures fall below 10°C (50°F), so in colder climates tomatoes are usually grown under glass or in plastic tunnels. Plant out the young plants as the first flowers open.

Plant out bush types first, as they are the hardiest group. Space the plants about 90cm (3ft) apart: closer spacings will produce earlier crops, wider spacings a later but heavier yield. The plants can spread along the ground, per-haps on a mulch of straw or plastic. Plant cordon types at a spacing of 75cm (30in) and train them up canes. Remove any side shoots as they develop, so the plants' ener-gy goes into fruit produc-tion. As the fruits develop, apply a high-potash feed every two weeks to help them swell. When five fruit trusses have formed, remove the main stem at two leaves above this point, to encour-age even growth. Then remove the canes and lay the plants on straw to encourage quicker ripening. To extend the growing season, cloches or polythene tunnels can be used for protection.

Harvesting Pick the fruits as they ripen and remove any leaves covering the fruit to encourage more to do so. If frost threatens in autumn, uproot the plants and hang up in a dry, frost-free place to allow the remaining fruits to ripen.

Pinching out side shoots
Snap out any side shoots to channel the plant's energies into producing fruit.

Removing main shoot
Break off the main shoot two leaves above the fifth truss to encourage the fruits to develop.

Tomato types
Tomatoes come in many shapes and sizes, from the large, thick-skinned 'beef-steak' tomatoes, which hail from America, to the more traditional 'Marmande' types and small, multi-trussed 'cherry-' and 'currant-fruit-ed' cultivars. A vast range of fruit colours takes in shades of red, pink, orange and yellow, or even combinations of these, which show as striped flecks on the skin and flesh of the fruit.

'Beefsteak'

'Marmande'

Cherry

Tomato sizes
'Beefsteak' varieties are the largest, Cherry types smallest and 'Marmande' medium-sized.

Sweet peppers
Capsicum annuum Grassum Group

C.a. 'Mavras'

These annual plants are grown for their characteristic bell-shaped fruits. When ripe, the fruits can be red, yellow, orange and even bluish black, depending on which cultivars are grown.

Sweet peppers prefer a deeply cultivated soil, but also do well in growbags, pots and troughs; make sure the soil or compost is slightly acidic. They require an average temperature of around 21°C (70°F) and fairly high humidity.

Easy-to-grow cultivars such as 'Bell Boy' and 'Yellow Bell' will be ready to harvest as green fruits 14 weeks after planting out, and 3 weeks later for coloured fruits.

Sowing Sow seeds individually in peat pots in mid-spring and germinate at 18°C (64°F). Young plants will be ready to plant out 10 weeks later.

Cultivation Plant out 75cm (30in) apart. When the plants reach 75cm (30in) high, stake them individually and pinch out the growing point to encourage bushy growth. Spray them with water regularly to keep the humidity high. Once the fruits have started to develop, apply a high-potash feed every two weeks to encourage them to swell.

Harvesting Pick the ripe peppers by cutting through the stalk about 2cm (¾in) from the top of the fruit.

Chilli peppers
Capsicum frutescens

C.f. 'Apache'

These plants are grown for their small, thin tapering fruits which are green or red when mature, depending on the cultivars grown. The flavour is often very hot, with even the mildest increasing in strength as the fruits mature. The plants can grow up to 60cm (24in) high and 45cm (18in) across, while dwarf cultivars suit pots or growbags.

Chilli and cayenne peppers require an average temperature of around 21°C (70°F) and fairly high humidity, so are often grown under protection.

The easy-to-grow cultivars such as 'Apache' and 'Red Chilli' are ready to harvest about 17 weeks after planting out, but the riper the fruit, the hotter the flavour – the seeds being the hottest part.

Sowing Sow seeds individually in peat pots in mid-spring and germinate at 18°C (64°F).

Cultivation Plant out 45cm (18in) apart, and when the plants reach 45cm (18in) high pinch out the growing point to encourage bushy growth. Spray the plants with water regularly to keep the humidity high.

Harvesting When frost is imminent, pull up the plants and hang them upside down in a frost-free place, where they will continue to ripen and can be used as needed.

Aubergines
Solanum melongena

S.m. 'Slice Rite'

The 'eggplant' is grown for its egg-shaped fruits, which are usually a blackish purple but may be white flushed or completely white in cultivars such as 'Easter Egg'.

The plants can reach 75cm (30in) high and 60cm (2ft) across and have a deep root system. They therefore prefer a deep, fertile soil, but will also grow well in containers if fertilized and watered generously. Grow in a warm, sheltered spot, as aubergines are susceptible to wind damage. The fruits will be ready to harvest 16 weeks after planting out.

Sowing Sow seed in small pots in mid-spring, and

Harvesting aubergines
Cut through the stalk 2cm (¾in) from the fruit.

germinate at 25°C (78°F). After germination, you will need to lower the temperature to about 17°C (62°F) – if higher than this, the plants will become spindly and prone to falling over.

Cultivation Plant out as the first flowers start to open, but after all risk of frost has passed. Space the plants 75cm (30in) apart, and stake them individually to provide extra support. When the main stem reaches 45cm (18in) high, pinch out the growing point to encourage bushy growth. Once the fruits have started to develop, apply a high-potash feed every two weeks to help them swell. To grow large aubergines, allow about five fruits to develop on each plant, removing all other flowers.

Harvesting Pick the fruits when they are fully swollen, shiny and firm with a smooth skin, cutting the stalk about 2cm (¾in) from the top of the fruit. If left too long before picking, the flesh will become bitter.

Cucumbers
Cucumis sativa

C.s. 'Femdan'

These tender plants are grown for their characteristic fruits with a high water content. Some cultivars have a bushy, compact habit while others can trail over several metres. The latter can be trained vertically to save space in small gardens.

Outdoor cucumbers tend to be much easier to grow than indoor types as they are less susceptible to disease and do not have the same requirements for high temperatures and humidity.

Cucumbers will not tolerate temperatures below 10°C (50°F), so a frost-free environment is essential. The plants will do well in loam-less compost in growbags and, as they need lots of water, will also thrive using 'ring culture'. In this, the plants are grown in compost-filled, open-bottomed pots on a gravel bed where they develop two sets of roots, one within the compost for nourishment, the other growing into the gravel for water. The fruits will be ready to harvest about 16 weeks after sowing.

Sowing In mid-spring, sow seeds, individually in 7.5cm (3in) pots, at a temperature of 18–30°C (64–86°F).

Cultivation Once the risk of frost has passed and the seedlings are 30cm (12in) high, gradually harden off those to be grown outside. Plant at least 40–45cm (16–18in) apart, with 90cm (36in) between rows, to allow lots of light to reach the plants. Train trailing types vertically as cordons up nets or strings at least 2m (6ft) high. Twist support strings around the plants to hold them upright. As the main stem grows upwards, trim back the side shoots to two or three leaves.

Harvesting The fruits will be ready to harvest by late summer. Cut them from the plant, leaving a stalk of about 2.5cm (1in) on each fruit.

Planting seeds
To avoid root disturbance, cucumber seeds are sown into pots.

Courgettes and marrows
Curcubita pepo

C. pepo

Grown for their long, cylindrical fruits, marrows come in a range of colours from white, through yellow, to deep green; some cultivars, such as 'Tiger Cross', are a mixture of green and creamy white stripes. Marrow fruits will be ready to harvest about 16 weeks after sowing.

Courgettes are cultivars of marrows, but their fruits are harvested while they are still immature – about 6–8 weeks after sowing – and the skin is smooth and shiny. Numerous new courgette cultivars have been introduced, with fruit colours ranging from the dark green of 'Ambassador', through lighter shades, to the yellow of 'Taxi'.

Sowing In spring, soak the seeds overnight and then sow individually in 7.5cm (3in) peat pots at a temperature of 15°C (59°F).

Cultivation Harden off the young plants before planting out. Plant bush types 90cm (36in) apart; trailing cultivars will need at least 2m (6ft) all round unless trained vertically, when they can be planted at the same spacing as bush types. Immediately after planting out, make sure that the plants are protected from overnight frost.

Each plant needs a minimum of 13.5 litres (3 gallons) of water per week. Mulch with a layer of organic matter at least 10cm (4in) deep, to retain soil moisture. Cut away any leaves shading the fruits. As the fruits start to swell, remove any male flowers close by to prevent the fruits developing a bitter taste.

Harvesting Although they can grow much larger, marrows are usually harvested when the fruits are about 45cm (18in) long and 15cm (6in) in diameter. Such mature fruits, with their seeds formed, can be stored for several months in an airy, frost-free environment. Pick courgettes when they are 10–15cm (4–6in) long. Regular picking encourages the production of further flowers and fruits.

Removing growing tip
Cut out shoot tips later in the season to help fruit develop fully.

Storing marrows
Suspend produce from beams in loosely woven mesh sacks.

Squashes and pumpkins
Cucurbita pepo, C. maxima, C. moschata

C.p. 'Tivoli'

These tender plants are grown for their unusual fruits, which vary tremendously in shape and size – from the large, orange fruits of the traditional Hallowe'en pumpkin to the distinctive 'Turk's Turban' squash. They can weigh up to 227kg (500lb) each and come in a range of colours from yellow to grey-green.

Squashes and pumpkins grow best in a warm, sheltered position and are generally ready to harvest about 16–20 weeks after sowing. 'Gold Nugget' is a useful cultivar, producing fruits which can weigh as much as 1kg (2¼lb), even though this very compact plant is one of the earliest to mature.

Sowing In mid- to late spring, soak the seeds overnight in cold water and then sow individually in 7.5cm (3in) pots. Raise at 12–14°C (54–57°F).

Cultivation Harden off the young plants for 2–3 weeks before planting out once the danger of frost is minimal. However, if frost is forecast, make sure that the plants are protected with fleece. Plant bush types 90cm (36in) apart; trailing cultivars need at least 2m (6ft) all round.

Each plant requires a minimum of 13.5 litres (3 gallons) of water per week. Mulch with a layer of organic matter at least 10cm (4in) deep, to retain soil moisture. Cut away any leaves that shade the fruits. As the fruits start to swell, remove any male flowers that are close by to prevent the fruits developing a bitter taste.

Harvesting Although they can grow much larger, the fruits are usually harvested when about 20–25cm (8–10in) across, or when the foliage starts to turn yellow and the fruit stems start to crack. This is often just before the first hard frosts occur. After severing the fruit from the parent plant, dry it for about 10 days outdoors, using the warmth of the sun to improve storage quality. Place the fruit in a string or netting bag, and hang in an airy, frost-free place at a temperature of 10°C (50°F) for up to six months.

Melons
Cucurbita melo

C. melo

These tender tropical plants are grown as annuals and prefer temperatures of 25°C (77°F) or above. They need full sun to do well and are damaged by low temperatures (10°C/50°F), so must be in a sheltered position. They can be grown as horizontal bush plants or as cordons up canes.

There are three main types of sweet melon: cantaloupes have thick, rough, grey-green coloured skins, casabas have smooth green or yellow skins, and musk types produce the smallest fruit and have yellow or orange skins. The musk, or honeydew, melons are the easiest to grow.

Sowing Sow seeds two to a 7.5cm (3in) pot in a temperature of 18°C (64°F) in early spring. If both seedlings germinate, the weaker one should be removed after they have been transplanted, usually six weeks after germination.

Cultivation Space the young plants 1m (3ft) apart with 1.5m (5ft) between the rows on a slight mound about 10cm (4in) above the surrounding soil.

Harvesting Usually 12–15 weeks after transplanting, remove the fruits by cutting through the stalk.

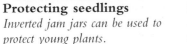

Protecting seedlings
Inverted jam jars can be used to protect young plants.

Ripening pumpkins
Lay black plastic sheeting underneath ripening pumpkins and squashes to keep them off the ground.

Sweetcorn
Zea mays

Z.m. 'Sweet Nugget'

Grown for its sweet-tasting yellow 'cobs', this tender annual crop must have as long a growing season as possible. This often means starting plants early under protection, before planting out from late spring onwards. The extra trouble is well worthwhile, because freshly picked cobs are the most nutritious and have by far the best flavour.

Sowing Sow seed under protection, with three seeds to a 7.5cm (3in) pot. Outdoors, sow seed from mid-spring onwards in a seedbed in a warm, sheltered spot.

Cultivation Sweetcorn relies on the wind to pollinate the plants later on. To facilitate this, plant in square or rectangular, 6-row blocks, with the plants spaced 35cm (14in) apart all round. Before transplanting seedlings grown in pots, cover the planting area with black plastic to warm the soil. When the seedlings are 15–20cm (6–8in) high, insert the young plants into the soil through the plastic and shelter them from wind for the first week after planting. Most of the plants will produce four or five cobs – to get large cobs, water the plants well as the cobs are developing.

Harvesting The cobs will be ready to harvest from late summer to mid-autumn. When the tassel ('silk') at the top of the cob starts to turn brown, snap the cob from the main stem.

Planting
Sweetcorn should be planted in a block in order to aid wind pollination.

Globe artichokes
Cynara cardunculus Scolymus Group

C.c. 'Green Globe'

These large, bushy perennials are grown for their greenish-purple flower bracts and have a cropping life of three years.

Sowing Sow seed 2.5cm (1in) deep in a seedbed in early spring in rows 30cm (12in) apart with 10cm (4in) between the seeds. Transplant the young plants into their cropping site in early summer. These plants will be variable, however, so division of named varieties is preferable. Remove well-rooted suckers from established plants in early spring and replant, leaving at least three shoots on the parent plant to produce new flower heads.

Cultivation Before planting, spread a 10cm (4in) layer of well-rotted manure and dig the ground to one spade's depth. Plant out young plants about 5cm (2in) deep and 90cm (36in) apart all round, and trim back the shoots by half their length to prevent wilting. After planting, spread a 10cm (4in) layer of manure around the plants to reduce weeds and moisture loss. Protect over winter with a layer of straw, until early spring, when each plant will produce two or three shoots to bear the flower heads.

Harvesting From early summer to early autumn, depending on the age of the plants, each stem will carry one primary flower head and several secondary ones. These should be cut when they are about 10cm (4in) across, removing each one with a 10cm (4in) section of stem.

Dividing artichokes
Dig around the plant's base to remove well-rooted side shoots.

Trimming tops
This will stop the leaves wilting and help plants establish quickly.

Stems

Stem vegetables such as celery, celeriac, kohl rabi, Florence fennel, leeks and rhubarb are cultivated for their edible, swollen stems. To grow successfully, almost all of them require cool temperatures (below 24°C/75°F) and a long growing season. Florence fennel, however, will tolerate temperatures up to 18–30°C (64-86°F) and has a short growing season, and kohl rabi also matures quickly.

Celery

Apium graveolens

Celery is grown for its crisp, blanched leaf stalks, which can be white, pink or red. Newer, self-blanching forms are easier to grow as they do not need to be artificially blanched. Celery needs a sunny, open site with deep, stone-free, well-drained, fertile soil that has had plenty of organic matter incorporated. To prevent plants from 'bolting' or producing stringy leaf stalks, it is important to keep them growing steadily.

Celery will be ready to harvest 7–8 months from sowing, by which time each plant will be about 45–60cm (1½–2ft) high.

Sowing Sow seed in trays or peat pots under protection from early to late spring to establish successional crops. Place seed on the surface of the compost, as it needs light to germinate. Self-blanching celery needs warmth to germinate – the temperature should be above 10°C (50°F).

Harvesting celery
The tops and roots of celery plants should be removed as soon as they have been dug up.

A. graveolens

Cultivation About eight weeks after sowing, harden off the seedlings in a cold frame. From late spring on, when the plants have developed five to six 'true' leaves, plant them out. Celery needs plenty of water to grow quickly and remain crisp. Celery that needs blanching should be planted 45cm (18in) apart, into trenches 30cm (12in) deep and 45cm (18in) wide. For self-blanching celery, plant closely, 25cm (10in) apart, with 25cm (10in) between rows. There is no need to trench. For trench celery, wrap a 25cm (10in) paper collar loosely around each plant when they reach 30–45cm (12–18in) high. Tie in position and half-fill the trench with soil to blanch the celery stalks. Three weeks later, fill the trench until the soil is level with the surrounding ground. Four weeks later, add another paper collar to each plant and 'earth up' with a further 15cm (6in) of soil.

Harvesting Harvesting for trench celery can begin in late autumn, when the leaf stalks are crunchy to eat; the pink and red forms are the hardiest and will be harvested last. Dig out the soil around each plant, lift the celery and remove the paper collars, then cut off the head and roots. Self-blanching celery can be harvested from late summer onwards. Celery can be left in the ground over winter.

Celeriac

Apium graveolens Rapaceum Group

A. g. Rapaceum Group

This vegetable is grown for its celery-flavoured, swollen stem, which takes six months to mature after sowing. It can be cooked or used raw.

Grow celeriac in a sunny, open site in free-draining soil. It may eventually reach 75cm (30in) high.

Sowing Sow seed in trays or modules under protection, at a temperature of 16°C (61°F) from early spring onwards for a continuous supply.

Cultivation About six weeks after sowing, harden off the seedlings in a cold frame. Plant them out in rows 30cm (12in) apart, with 40cm (16in) between the plants, with the stems just visible on the soil surface. In late autumn, remove the outer leaves to encourage the stems to swell, and mulch with straw to protect from severe frost.

Harvesting Harvest celeriac from early autumn until the following spring, digging up the plants with a garden fork. However, plants will survive in the ground in most sites.

Florence fennel
Foeniculum vulgare Azoricum Group

F.v. 'Zefa Fino'

Florence fennel is grown for its succulent bulb, which has a distinctive aniseed flavour, the edible part being the swollen bases of its decorative, feathery leaves.

It prefers well-drained but moisture-retentive, fertile soil which has had plenty of organic matter incorporated six to eight weeks before planting. The bulbs are ready to harvest about 15 weeks after sowing.

Sowing Sow seed in modules under protection from early spring onwards. Set in a temperature of 16°C (61°F) if growing in a greenhouse; seeds germinated in a polytunnel require 12–14°C (54–57°F), while those in a cold frame need 10°C (50°F).

Cultivation About six weeks after sowing, harden off the seedlings in a cold frame. Plant them out from early summer onwards, after two 'true' leaves have developed, in rows 30cm (12in) apart and with 40cm (16in) between plants. When the bulbs begin to swell, cover the lower half with soil to blanch them.

Harvesting The bulbs will be ready to harvest from late summer onwards, when they are about 10cm (4in) across. Cut them off at soil level and trim away the leaves. Fennel can withstand light frosts only, and does not store well.

Asparagus
Asparagus officinalis

A.o. 'Franklim'

This herbaceous perennial can produce crops of its delicious shoots ('spears') for up to 25 years, so requires a permanent site. If possible, plant only male cultivars such as 'Franklin' or 'Sorbonne', which produce much higher yields than female ones. The plants must be at least three years old before harvesting can begin.

Asparagus prefers deep, fertile, well-drained soil which has had plenty of organic matter incorporated into it 2–3 months before planting. In spring, before the spears emerge, the soil is often topdressed with salt, which controls weeds but does not harm the crop.

Cultivation Asparagus plants grown from seed give a variable crop, so it is best to purchase one-year-old asparagus crowns ready for planting. Plant crowns in early spring, 10–15cm (4–6in) deep and 45cm (18in) apart, in ridge-bottomed trenches 30cm (12in) apart. Cut down and remove all top-growth in late autumn as it turns yellow.

Harvesting Harvesting usually begins in mid-spring and lasts for eight weeks. When the spears are 15cm (6in) high, cut them off with a sharp knife, slicing through the stem 2–3cm (1–1½in) below soil level. Keep the cut spears covered to prevent them drying out.

Harvesting asparagus
Cut the young stems just below soil level with a sharp knife.

Maintaining the plants
Chop old stems down to ground level in autumn.

Kohl rabi
Brassica oleracea Gongylodes Group

B.o. 'Trero'

Kohl rabi is grown for its nutritious, globe-like, swollen stem. There are both green- and purple-skinned forms, both of which grow to a height of 60cm (24in). Kohl rabi thrives in hot, dry conditions, and at the height of summer, the stems will be ready to harvest eight weeks from sowing.

Sowing Sow seed thinly in drills 2cm (¾in) deep and 30cm (12in) apart, in a well-prepared, finely sieved seedbed. Sow the quicker-maturing, green-skinned types from mid-spring to midsummer, and the hardier, purple-skinned types from mid- to late summer.

Cultivation As the first 'true' leaf develops, thin seedlings to 20cm (8in) apart.

Harvesting The swollen stems are ready when they are about 8–10cm (3–4in) across. The newer cultivars can grow much larger, as they remain tender.

Harvesting kohl rabi
Cut through the tap-root just below the swollen stem.

Leeks

Allium porrum

A. porrum

One of the hardiest of winter vegetables, leeks have a long cropping season, from early autumn, through winter, and into late spring of the following year.

They are grown for their white, fleshy leaf bases, which form a stem-like shank or 'leg'. Early types take 28 weeks from sowing to harvest; late-season ones need up to 40 weeks to mature.

Leeks prefer light, loamy soil, and their fibrous root system also helps to improve soil structure.

Sowing In late spring sow seed thinly, 3cm (1in) apart, in drills 3cm (1in) deep and 30cm (12in) apart.

Cultivation Transplant seedlings when they are about 20cm (8in) high, the main planting season being midsummer. Incorporate a dressing of high-nitrogen fertilizer into the soil surface before planting. The best yields come from planting at a spacing of 15cm (6in), with 30cm (12in) between the rows. Quality is determined by the depth of planting, which blanches the shank: the aim is to obtain 15–20cm (6–8in) of white shank. Push a dibber into the ground to a depth of 15cm (6in), drop the plant into the hole and fill the hole with water so the soil will fall back into it.

Harvesting Harvest leeks when their leaves start to hang down, from early autumn onwards, by lifting them with a garden fork. Mid- and late-season cultivars will tolerate winter climes without protection.

Rhubarb

Rheum x *hybridum*, syn. *R.* x *cultorum*

R. x h. 'Timperley Early'

Often regarded as a fruit, but technically a vegetable, this herbaceous perennial is grown for its edible leaf stalks, which can be used for desserts and jam-making from mid-spring onwards.

Rhubarb, which matures to a height of 30cm (12in), can be grown in the same plot for many years, but the well-drained, fertile soil must be dug deeply and plenty of organic matter incorporated prior to planting.

Planting In late autumn or early winter plant one-year-old crowns about 1m (3ft) apart, with the young shoots ('eyes') just above soil level. If they are planted too deeply, the eyes will rot away.

Cultivation Mulch the crowns well, keep the soil moist, and provide a generous feed of balanced fertilizer after harvesting. Cut off any flowering spikes as they emerge in the spring and summer, and remove any spindly, unwanted leaves as they occur.

The crop can be advanced by as much as three weeks if covered with loose straw to protect the developing leaves and stalks from frost damage. Alternatively, cover with an upturned pot or bucket.

Harvesting Pick the rhubarb when the stalks are about 30cm (12in) long and deep pink in colour. Grip each stalk as close to its base as possible and and pull it gently from the crown with a twisting action. Cut off the leaves and discard, as these are not edible.

Transplanting leeks
If the soil is very dry, water each hole before planting seedlings.

Harvesting leeks
Use a garden fork to gently lift leeks from the soil.

Forcing rhubarb
Place an upturned pot over the crown to force young rhubarb.

Cutting flowering spikes
Remove any rhubarb flowers as soon as they appear.

Growing fruit

It is always possible to grow fruit, even in the smallest of gardens. For most people, 'fruit' conjures up trees in blossom, apple pies and strawberries and cream, which is not surprising, as one of the most satisfying aspects of gardening is picking ripe fruit straight from the plant and eating it at the peak of freshness. There is also a decorative value to fruit: not only is the blossom colourful but there are also the changing hues of the ripening fruit through summer and autumn.

For cultivation purposes, most fruits fall into two main categories: soft fruit (such as currants, raspberries and gooseberries) which grows on bushes or canes or as groundcover, and top fruit (such as apples, peaches, plums and cherries) which grows on trees. Some fruits fall into neither category: grapes and kiwi fruits, for example, are produced on long, trailing vines.

To cultivate fruit, you must first establish which varieties will grow successfully in your climate, although the range and growing season of fruiting plants can be extended by growing them in a greenhouse or conservatory. You should then decide on a suitable site in the garden. Most fruits will thrive if grown in a sunny but sheltered position, the sun being important for ripening and encouraging good fruit colour and flavour. Shelter is needed to keep plants warm and to reduce the risk of wind damage. On a windy site, insect activity is reduced, and this results in

Training fruit trees
Fruit trees can be trained against walls and fences, or along wires, giving good yields from relatively small spaces, like this espalier pear.

restricted pollination at flowering time, and a correspondingly poor crop. Any windbreak, however, must be carefully positioned to avoid cold air being trapped on the site and thus creating a frost pocket – the biggest enemy of most fruit-growing plants being the occurrence of late spring frosts, especially on a sunny slope.

Choosing fruit bushes and trees

Always buy healthy, sturdy bushes and trees that are certified free from virus, in order to minimize attacks from pests and diseases. The shape and cultivar of plant you select, however, will depend on the available space in your garden. Free-standing forms, such as spindle bushes or dwarf pyramids, generally take up far less room than branch-headed bushes, standards and half-standards. To save space, many fruits can also be trained as cordons, espaliers and fans against a wall or fence.

Most fruit trees tend to grow badly on their own roots, so when you buy a fruit tree it usually comprises two plants that have been grafted together. The top part, or scion, is the cultivar, which is grown for its fruit flavour and colour, while the bottom part, or rootstock, provides a ready-made root system that influences the size and vigour of the tree and the amount of fruit it will yield. Rootstocks are classified according to their vigour and are available from the extremely vigorous through to very dwarfing.

The main advantages of dwarf rootstocks are that fruit is much easier to pick, prune and spray than on larger rootstocks, and the trees fit easily even into the smallest gardens.

Fruit tree formations
The formations below are those most commonly found in gardens.

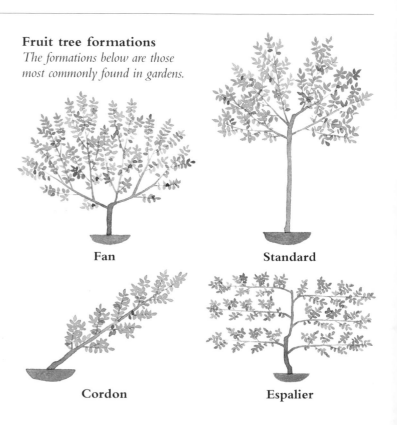

Fan

Standard

Cordon

Espalier

Planting

Most fruit bushes and trees are best planted in late autumn or early winter. If they are container-grown, they can be transplanted at any time, except in very cold, very wet or very dry weather.

Thorough preparation of the planting site is important, so dig the soil well, adding plenty of well-rotted garden compost or manure. The planting hole should be at least as wide as the root system and the plant should be inserted at the same depth as previously, so check for a soil mark on the stem.

All trees should be supported with a stake or, if trained against a wall or fence, they need to be tied to wires. For a tree with bare roots, drive a vertical stake into the planting hole before inserting the plant. For container-grown plants, add an angled stake after planting and then tie the plant to the stake or wires.

Planting a bareroot bush
Spread out the roots and plant so that the uppermost root is 5–7cm (2–3in) below soil level.

Planting a tree
Plant a container-grown tree so that the surface of the compost is 3–5cm (1–2in) below soil level.

Feeding

Most fruits need the essential nutrients of nitrogen, phosphate and potassium on a regular basis. However, nutrients incorporated during planting will only last for the first few years.

After this, topdressings should be applied around the base of trees or bushes during spring or summer. Before applying fertilizer, mark out the area where it should be applied. Using string and a peg, tie one end of the string around the trunk of the tree or bush. Pull the line taut to just beyond the spread of the branches and use the peg to mark a circle. Fertilizer scattered over this area will cover the entire span of the tree's root system.

Nitrogen-based fertilizers are usually given in spring to encourage shoot growth, while phosphate and potash are often needed in summer to encourage fruit development and flower formation for the next year.

Fruit pollination

The transfer of pollen grains from the male to the female parts of a flower is essential for fertilization, so that seeds and fruit can develop. If this occurs in the same flower on the same plant, it is called self-pollination. The transfer of pollen from the male parts of one flower to the female parts of the flower on a different but closely related plant is cross-pollination. Most tree fruits need cross-pollinating. This transfer of pollen is usually carried out by bees or other insects, but fruiting plants such as peaches – which flower in early spring before insects are very active – may need pollinating by hand.

It is possible to grow a single tree with more than one variety on it. These 'family' trees consist of three selected varieties of the same type of fruit, which flower at the same time. This enables them to pollinate one other and produce fruit.

Protecting your crop

At one time or another most fruit bushes and trees need to be protected against birds, other pests, diseases and frost.

Some birds can be a particular nuisance by eating flower buds and the fruit itself. A piece of netting draped over the plant at critical times may be all that is needed in the way of protection, although if the problem is bad or you have several plants, it may be worth investing in a fruit cage. This comprises metal supports covered in wire or plastic netting. However, the netting must be removed in winter, as it will be damaged by the weight of snow.

Unfortunately all fruit crops are prone to attacks from certain pests and diseases but chemical sprays can achieve a dramatic improvement in fruit quality, although they should be used sparingly. Where possible, avoid spraying fungicides and insecticides when the plants are in blossom, as some sprays may also kill or deter pollinating insects.

Flowers and fruits are also vulnerable to late-spring frosts, so early-flowering bushes such as gooseberries should be protected with fleece or heavy netting at night. Always remove netting during the day so that insects can pollinate the flowers.

Boughs bearing heavy crops may need supporting with a forked stick and sacking, especially if the site is particularly windy.

Beating the frost
During prolonged cold weather, strawberries, fruit bushes and fruit trees should be protected at night with fleece or similar material. Always remove again once the temperature has risen above 0°C (32°F).

Keeping birds at bay
Netting can be used to protect ripening fruit from marauders.

Sheltered site
A fan-trained tree grown against a fence for wind protection.

Pruning soft fruit

The aim of pruning soft fruit is to develop a healthy plant in optimum shape to produce a large quantity of fruit. Shoots that have already fruited should be removed, as should any diseased, damaged, dying or dead stems. Specific pruning techniques, however, depend on the growth habit of the plant, and soft fruits grow in three main ways: as canes, bushes and ground cover. Canes are very slender shrubs and their stems develop at ground level or slightly below. Bushes have a basic woody framework that starts at ground level, or just above, and they are generally as high as they are wide. The most popular ground-cover soft fruit is the strawberry, which is a low-growing bedding plant.

Making an impression
Soft fruit bushes can be of ornamental as well as practical value, as this standard gooseberry bush demonstrates.

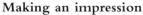

Pruning cane fruit

Cane fruits produce fruit only once on each cane, and should have all the old canes cut down to ground level in summer or autumn, after the fruit has been harvested.

Young cane fruit

To encourage new plants to establish quickly, and strong shoots to merge from soil level around their base, young plants should be pruned immediately after planting, in late autumn to early spring. The plants should be spaced at 30cm (12in) intervals in rows 30cm (12in) apart.

Cut the new canes back to 23cm (9in) above ground level. Tie young canes to their support wires as they develop and remove all flowers in the first season. If plants are to become well established, a fair amount of patience is required. It will be 18 months before a crop can be picked.

In late summer, cut out all canes that were shortened at the time of planting.

Securing new growth
Tie in young canes as they begin to develop.

Removing suckers
Pull up suckers along with any surplus new plants.

Mature cane fruit

Immediately after cropping, remove canes that have fruited, as well as damaged and weak ones. The old canes should be grey or dark brown, while new shoots are usually a light brown colour. Prompt clearance enables the remaining canes to grow unhindered. Also remove suckers and unwanted young plants as they develop and dead, damaged and diseased wood as soon as it is noticed.

To protect canes from wind damage, regularly tie new canes to their support wires, giving each cane equal room – usually one cane every 10cm (4in). The tops of vigorous canes can be further supported in autumn by looping them over the top wire and tying firmly with string.

Each spring, you will need to shorten the canes back to 15cm (6in) above the top support wire, and cut back canes that have frost-damaged tips. Remove some canes from overcrowded sections on the row, so that there is one every 10cm (4in).

Fruited canes
Remove old canes as soon as they have fruited, cutting them at ground level.

Tip pruning
Shorten all canes back to within 15cm (6in) of the top wire in spring.

Pruning bush fruit

Bush fruits, such as gooseberries and red and white currants, which develop branches above ground level, on a short leg, are most commonly grown as bushes with an open centre. They can also be trained as standards or cordons (see pp.180–181). Bush fruits, such as blackcurrants and blueberries, are pruned in a slightly different way because they produce shoots from ground level and fruit on one-year-old shoots. Red and white currants and gooseberries fruit on shoots that are one year old or more and these should be pruned to produce plenty of new wood. All these bush fruits are pruned in winter and early spring.

One-year-old currant bush
Cut back stems by one-half in late winter.

Young bush fruit

In autumn or winter, at the time of planting gooseberries and red and white currants, remove any shoots that are less than 30cm (12in) above ground level to produce a short leg, which will prevent any branches or fruit trailing on the ground. Shorten the remaining shoots by one-half in late winter. The following winter, cut back all new growth by one-half to form the framework of main branches. Prune back any side shoots growing into the centre of the bush or in a downward direction to a single bud. These form the basis of fruiting spurs later.

Two-year-old gooseberry bush
Cut back leaders by one-half and other side shoots back to just one bud in winter.

Black currants

With black currants the majority of fruit is produced on shoots formed the previous year, and, in order to promote the production of new shoots, regular hard pruning each winter is essential. Immediately after planting the new bushes, in autumn or winter, prune all stems to one bud above soil level. The following winter cut out any thin, weak or diseased shoots.

For established black currant bushes, renewal pruning in mid-winter is used. This involves cutting out up to one-third of the oldest, dark-coloured shoots, and removing all thin, weak or diseased ones. Using such a pruning system, the entire top growth of the bush is replaced over a three-year period and thus the full fruiting potential of the bush is utilized. Blueberries are pruned in a similar way except that they are not pruned for the first three years after planting.

Mature bush fruit

Established fruit bushes should have an open centre. This encourages good air circulation through the plants, allows the sun to ripen the fruit and helps to reduce the incidence of pests and diseases. Therefore any low-growing, overcrowded and crossing shoots should be removed in winter or early spring. Picking is easier when the fruit is produced on short spurs, so also shorten side shoots to one bud. Cut out any old, unproductive shoots and encourage strong, young shoots to grow into the available space. Completely remove any shoots on the stem, or leg, below the main framework of branches.

Old, neglected bushes that have not been regularly pruned need more drastic treatment. In late winter or early spring remove some or all the old wood and retain only healthy, new shoots. This process may need to be repeated the following winter until new stems have replaced all the older ones. To reduce competition, thin out some of the new shoots, retaining only the strongest.

Removing suckers
Removing competing suckers from the trunk of a gooseberry bush.

Renovating gooseberry
Thin out competing stems on neglected or overcrowded bushes.

Pruning strawberries

Strawberries are pruned in late summer or autumn, after the crop has been picked. Cut off the old leaves with secateurs or shears, leaving plenty of room for young, new leaves to emerge. Discarding these old leaves also removes any pests and diseases that might be resident on them.

At the same time cut away any runners, which will weaken the development of the plants (these runners can later be used to form the basis of a new crop). After three years, strawberry plants should be discarded as their fruiting capacity will be much reduced.

Pruning tree fruit

Apple, pear and sweet cherry trees mostly bear fruit on shoots that are two years old or more, and the aim of pruning these trees is to maintain a balance between the number of old, fruit-bearing shoots and the development of new growth, which will eventually produce fruit. Damson and plum trees, on the other hand, produce fruit on shoots that are one year old or more, and these should be pruned to produce plenty of new shoots. Fig and peach trees carry most of their fruit on one-year-old shoots, and these are pruned by removing the shoots that have just fruited.

Most pruning of tree, or top, fruit is done in winter and early spring, when the plants are dormant, although summer pruning can be used to encourage more fruit-bearing spurs to develop, especially with trained trees,

such as cordons, espaliers and fans. However, all stone tree fruits, such as plums, peaches, nectarines and cherries, should be pruned in summer whenever possible, to reduce the risk of infection from the silver leaf fungus *Chondrostereum purpureum*, which usually enters a tree through pruning wounds made in winter.

Before any pruning is done, it is important to establish whether the tree is a tip bearer (if it carries its fruit at, or near, the tips of young shoots) or a spur bearer (if it develops fruit along the full length of the young shoot). Tip bearers do not need much pruning and are best grown as bush fruits, standards and half-standards. Spur bearers respond well to pruning and are excellent for intensive forms of tree-fruit growing such as espaliers and cordons.

Encouraging better crops

Ideal weather at blossom time can lead to a larger than average number of flowers being fertilized.

If all of these juvenile fruits are allowed to develop, the tree may produce quantities of undersized and deformed fruits.

The sheer weight of the crop may also cause structural damage to some branches, and retard fruit-bud development for the following year.

To prevent these problems, you should thin out up to 40 per cent of juvenile fruit, if the tree does not naturally shed some itself, in the 'June drop'. This

will allow the remaining fruit to develop normally, to full size. Juvenile fruits should be removed by pulling off only the fruits, leaving the stalks behind on the tree.

To promote flower-bud and fruit-spur formation, and thus increase yields, tree fruits such as cordons, which have been trained for intensive fruit growing in a restricted space, can be pruned in midsummer, just before next year's flower buds are formed.

Woody-based side shoots are cut back to one leaf, while side shoots of the current season's growth are reduced to three leaves.

Spur thinning

The continual pruning to encourage the formation of fruiting spurs causes the spurs eventually to become entangled and carry small, poorly coloured and sized

fruit. When this occurs, the overcrowded spurs should be thinned in winter.

Remove the older wood, sawing off complete clusters of spur systems if necessary to allow more space for new spurs to develop.

Overcrowded spurs
Dense spur systems will produce large numbers of small fruits.

Spurs after thinning
Older, tangled growth and any thin, weak spurs are cut out.

Pruning standards

Standards, half-standards and bush fruit trees are the most commonly grown free-standing fruit trees. A standard has a clear stem of some 1.8m (6ft) before its branches radiate. A half-standard has about 1.35m (4½ft) of clear stem and bush fruit trees 75cm (2½ft) of clear stem. All are pruned in winter; the aim to maintain an open framework to aid ripening and picking.

Young standards
Remove dead, dying or diseased shoots and thin out congested ones to make the framework even. Shorten leaders by up to two-thirds, and well-spaced shoots arising from the branch framework by one-half, to an outward-facing bud. Tip bearers need no further pruning but spur bearers should have shoots that are not needed for the basic

framework shortened to four or five buds to encourage fruiting spurs to form.

Mature standards
Continue to prune as for young standards, stimulating some new growth and maintaining an open structure so that the tree crops well on a regular basis and the fruit is of good quality. The exact pruning needed will vary each year depending on the type, the growth, and the general habit of the tree.

Controlling vigour
Cut vigorous leading shoots by half to help lateral shoots develop.

How to prune cordons

Cordons are specially trained, angled trees that have been intensively pruned so that they have generally only one main stem. Because they are compact, having no major branches, they take up little space in the garden and they are convenient to manage. Pears, apples and some bush fruits (see p.179) are best suited to training as cordons.

Each cordon is grown at a 45° angle against wires, 60cm (2ft) apart, secured to a fence, wall or set of posts, 10cm (4in) by 10cm (4in) square and 2.1m (7ft) high. A bamboo cane, set at 45°, is tied to the wires and the cordon trained along it.

Young cordons

Training of young cordons starts immediately after planting, in winter, when each tree is positioned with the graft union uppermost on the stem, to reduce the risk of breakage. Immediately after planting, secure the main stem to the bamboo cane, in several places, and cut all side shoots back to 10cm (4in). To allow the tree to become fully established before it produces fruit, remove any flowers the first spring after planting.

Mature cordons

To ensure that cordon trees keep on producing a constant supply of fruit buds, and to suppress vigorous shoot growth, most pruning is carried out in summer, with shoots being pruned in succession as they mature.

Once young shoots have become woody at the base, all side shoots of the current season's growth on the main stem or branches are cut back to three leaves above the basal cluster of leaves. At the same time any new shoots growing from older side shoots and from spurs are shortened to just one leaf above the basal cluster.

Some spur thinning may be required in winter to prevent congestion.

Winter pruning
Cut all side shoots beack to 10cm (4in) in the first winter.

Disbudding
Remove flowers in the first spring, so the tree can establish itself.

Summer pruning
Cut back side shoots to within three leaves above the base cluster.

How to prune espaliers

The fruitfulness of a tree can be increased by training its branches horizontally, into an espalier, for example. This tree form has pairs of shoots – trained in two or three tiers – growing at right angles to the main stem. The tiers are trained along horizontal wires set about 40cm (16in) apart and secured to a wall, fence or set of posts, 10cm (4in) by 10cm (4in) square and 2.1m (7ft) high. This type of training is best suited to apple and pear trees.

Young espaliers

After planting a young espalier, in winter, cut back the main stem just above the bottom wire, ensuring there are two healthy buds below it. As it develops, tie the new leader to a vertical bamboo cane; also secure two vigorous side shoots to canes set at 45° to the wires. Shorten to two or three leaves or remove any other side shoots. In winter cut back the leader just above the second wire, ensuring there are two healthy buds below it.

In subsequent summers, repeat this process, treating the three new shoots arising from the vertical stem in the same way as those in the first year, until the required number of tiers has been achieved. Gradually lower each tier of side shoots until they are lying along the wires. Do not tie them into a horizontal position too early or extension growth will be checked.

Mature espaliers

Once established, espaliers are pruned in the same way as mature cordons (see above), except that any terminal growths on vertical and horizontal tiers of the espalier should also be kept pruned back. The whole idea of an espalier tree is to produce horizontal, spur-bearing platforms to carry the fruit – but on older trees, these spur formations may become complicated and overcrowded.

During the winter, when the fruit buds on the spurs are easy to see, relieve this overcrowding by cutting out any thin, weak or damaged spurs, as well as removing any spurs that are developing on the underside of the horizontal branches.

Young espalier
Removing side shoots on a two-year-old espalier.

Pruning fans

Growing a fruit tree, such as a cherry, in a fan shape can be very attractive but is not suitable for a small garden, as a fan occupies more space than a cordon or espalier. A fan has a series of lateral shoots (ribs) and sub-laterals radiating out in an arc from a short stem, or leg, and is usually grown against a wall or fence.

The aim of pruning a fan is to provide a constant supply of young shoots to replace the old cropping wood. This is usually done after harvesting, when the fruiting shoot is removed and a young shoot from just below the point where the cut was made is tied in its position instead. Tie in the shoot from the end bud of each rib and encourage suitably spaced shoots to grow on the upper side of each rib and one on the underside. Remove any shoots that grow towards or away from the supporting wall or fence.

Fruit

Fruit is a popular crop, with birds and insects as much as with gardeners, so one of the first priorities is to find ways to protect the crop once it is nearly ripe. Netting soft fruit is imperative if you wish to have decent yields, as is correct pruning. These days, modern plant breeding has done much to ensure that good results are obtained with relatively little effort. It is important to remember that some fruits (citrus, apricots and nectarines in particular) are not frost-hardy and will require protection in cold climates.

Currants
Ribes nigrum, R. rubrum

R. n. 'Baldwin'

R. r. 'Versailles' Blanche'

Currants are grown for their juicy red, white or black fruits, which are used in pies and other desserts and for making jams and jellies. Redcurrants are high in pectin and can be added to other fruits when making jam to aid setting. A variety of the redcurrant is the white currant, which has similar cultivation needs.

All red- and white-currants have a similar, upright habit and are quite vigorous; they can easily reach 1.5m (5ft) high and across. In good conditions, blackcurrants will grow even larger: up to 1.5m (5ft) high and 2.1m (7ft) across. However they have a greater variety of habit and vigour, 'Ben Sarek' being the most compact blackcurrant variety you can buy.

Currants prefer an open, sunny position but struggle on exposed, windy sites. Almost any soil will do for red- and whitecurrants, provided it is well-drained but moisture retentive, while blackcurrants require a very fertile soil to do well, although they will produce some fruit even if they are badly neglected. All currants will be ready to crop 12–18 months after planting.

Planting Add plenty of bulky organic matter to the soil before planting. Plant when the bushes are dormant, in autumn and winter. Space bushes 1.5m (5ft) apart.

Cultivation In early spring, mulch the plants with well-rotted compost or manure to a depth of 10cm (4in) to help control weeds and retain moisture. Water the bushes thoroughly in dry periods, especially when the fruit is swelling, as the roots are shallow and can easily suffer from drought.

R. r. 'Jonkheer van Tets'

You will need to net the fruit once the currants start to change colour in order to protect them from birds.

Training and pruning red- and whitecurrants
In late winter or early spring, cut back the main leaders and strongest side shoots of red- and white-currants by one-quarter, and the weaker ones to just one outward-facing bud. This will encourage the formation

Soaking roots
Leave the roots of any bare-rooted bush in water before planting.

Trimming roots
Remove any damaged roots before planting.

of fruiting spurs. You should aim to develop an open-centred bush, which will promote good air flow and help to reduce the chance of pests and disease colonizing the plant.

It is also important to maintain a clear stem, or 'leg', of at least 15–20cm (6–8in) between the lowest branch and ground level, as the fruits hang in long trusses which will tend to trail on the soil if the branches are too low.

Training and pruning blackcurrants

Prune black currants in autumn, immediately after leaf-fall. Remove up to one-quarter of the stems, choosing those that are darkest in colour, to make room for new ones. Black currants produce most of their fruit on shoots made in the previous season, and on regularly pruned bushes no stems should be more than four years old.

Harvesting Never pick currants until they are fully ripe. The uppermost berries on the truss ('strig') will ripen first and the lowest several days later, so wait until all of them are ripe before removing the entire strig from the branch.

Blackcurrants will be ready to harvest in midsummer and red and whitecurrants in mid- to late summer. Cropping can continue for 10–14 days.

Pruning for shape
Aim to create an open, balanced structure so that air can circulate.

Gooseberries
Ribes uva-crispa var. *reclinatum*

R. u-c.* 'Invicta' var *r.

Gooseberries are grown for their green, yellow, creamy white or occasionally red fruits, which can be used in jams, wines and desserts.

Gooseberries grow well in a sheltered position in full sun or partial shade, and need well-drained but moisture-retentive, fertile soil. Mature bushes usually reach about 1.2m (4ft) high. Fruits will be ready to crop 12–18 months after planting.

The plants flower in early spring, so beware of potential frost pockets when planting, and heavy netting or fleece may be needed to protect the flowers and early fruits. Remove netting during the day, however, to allow insects access for pollination.

Planting Before planting add plenty of bulky manure

Gooseberry sawfly
Sawfly larvae will strip the leaves off a gooseberry bush, as here.

to soil that is not particularly fertile. In late autumn or early winter, plant gooseberries 1.2m (4ft) apart, with 1.5m (5ft) between rows.

Cultivation Apply a mulch, 10cm (4in) thick, of well-rotted manure or compost in spring, after plants have been pruned, to help control weeds and prevent the soil drying out. The bushes should then need watering only during very dry periods. In summer, the bushes may need to be covered with netting to protect the fruits from birds.

Training and pruning
Prune gooseberry bushes in late winter or early spring and aim to develop an open-centred bush to promote air flow and protect against pests and disease.

Birds, such as finches, often feed on the buds in winter, and any damaged wood should be removed. Cut back the main leaders by one-half and reduce the strongest side shoots to about 7.5cm (3in). The weaker shoots should be cut back to 2–3cm (1–1½in) to encourage the formation of fruiting spurs.

Harvesting The fruits can be picked while still green for cooking, from early to midsummer, when they are about the size of marbles. They will ripen from midsummer onwards, and will gradually become softer and sweeter, developing their final, red colour.

Frost protection
Cover bushes with fleece or heavy netting in cold weather.

Blueberries
Vaccinum corymbosum, V. australe

***V. c.* 'Bluecrop'**

Grown for their delicious white-bloomed, dark blue fruits, blueberries require cool, moist, acid soil. The bushes will do best in an open, sunny position but will also tolerate partial shade, although they must be protected from cold winds. A mature blueberry bush will grow 1.2–1.5m (4–5ft) high. Bushes can be cropped for the first time two years after planting.

Planting Plant the bushes at any time from late autumn to early spring, into soil that has had 10cm (1in) of peat added. Space plants 1.2–1.5m (4–5ft) apart.

Cultivation Mulch in early summer with a 10cm (4in) layer of well-rotted manure to keep roots moist and control weeds. In dry periods, water with collected rainwater if your tap water is alkaline.

Training and pruning
Blueberries do not require pruning until three years after planting, when the four oldest shoots should be cut back to soil level each winter.

Harvesting Harvesting begins in late summer and lasts several weeks. Pick only the ripest fruits: those which are dark blue, with a white bloom, and slightly soft. Pull them gently from their stalks with a finger and thumb.

Blackberries
Rubus fruticosus

R.f. 'Thornfree'

Most blackberry cultivars produce heavy crops of large, well-flavoured, glossy black fruits. Although the plants are notoriously prickly, there are several thornless cultivars such as 'Oregon Thornless'.

Blackberries need well-drained, fertile soil and prefer a sheltered, sunny position, although they will also tolerate partial shade. They can be cropped for the first time two years after planting.

Planting Plant the canes, 15cm (6in) deep and 3–5m (10–15ft) apart, in well-prepared soil at any time from late autumn to early spring. To make cropping easier, set them in rows spaced 3–5m (10–15ft) apart. After planting, cut back the stems to 25cm (10in) above soil level.

Cultivation Mulch the bushes with a layer of organic matter 10cm (4in) deep and water the plants well during dry periods.

Training and pruning Blackberries are very vigorous, often growing 4m (12ft) in a year, and must have a strong support system to keep them manageable.

Select posts, 10 x 10cm (4 x 4in) square and 3m (10ft) long, and insert these 90cm (36in) into the ground. Fix six horizontal wires, 30cm (12in) apart, to the posts, starting 30cm (12in) above ground level. Then, as they develop, train the canes into a 'fan' arrangement along the wires and tie in position.

Harvesting Cropping can start in mid- or late summer and should last three weeks. When completely black, the ripe berries can be picked by pulling the berry together with its core, or 'plug', from the plant. Pick carefully, as they are easily damaged.

Severing rooted runner
Once it has been rooted, cut the young plant from its parent.

Raspberries
Rubus idaeus

R.i. 'Autumn Bliss'

Raspberries are grown for their good crop of delicious fruit which may vary in colour from a blackish red to golden yellow, depending on the cultivar. Raspberries prefer cool seasons, lots of moisture and a well-drained, fertile soil rich in organic matter. They enjoy a sheltered, sunny position but will also grow in partial shade, especially on dry, exposed sites with light, sandy soil.

There are two types of raspberry: summer-fruiting and autumn-fruiting. Both grow 1.4–2.1m (4½–7ft) high. Harvesting begins from the second year after planting.

Planting Canes can be planted at any time from late autumn to early spring. Add wood ash or another potash fertilizer to the soil before planting. Plant the canes 45cm (18in) apart, in rows 1.8m (6ft) apart. Then cut the newly planted canes back to 23cm (9in) above soil level. Once established, they will sucker profusely; if this is a problem, line the sides of the planting trenches with plastic to contain their spreading habit.

Cultivation Raspberries prefer a cool root run and benefit greatly from mulching with a layer of organic matter 10cm (4in) deep, to help control weeds and retain moisture. Remove the flowers in the first year.

Training and pruning Some cultivars are very vigorous and will produce new canes well over 2m (6½ft) high in a single season. To keep them manageable, use stout posts, 2.4m (8ft) long, and insert them 90cm (36in) into the ground. Fix three wires to the posts 75cm (30in), 1.2m (4ft) and 1.5m (5ft) above ground level. Tie

Planting raspberries
Shorten canes back to 23cm (9in) immediately after planting.

young canes to these wires immediately after the canes that have fruited have been cut down. In autumn, loop over the tops of tall canes and tie them to the top wire. Cut these loops back to 15cm (6in) above the top wire in late winter or early spring, if required.

Prune summer-fruiting raspberries immediately after the crop has been picked, cutting down all canes that have fruited to ground level and removing them, so that only the young canes remain. Prune autumn-fruiting types in late winter, before new growth appears, cutting back the fruited canes to ground level to stimulate the production of new canes.

Harvesting Raspberries are fully ripe when they can be picked cleanly from the fruit stalk, leaving the core, or 'plug', behind. Pick carefully, gripping the fruit gently between finger and thumb.

Training raspberries
Wires stretched between stout posts provide support for canes.

Fruiting raspberries
After the harvest, cut all fruiting canes down to ground level.

Strawberries

Fragaria x *ananassa*

These low-growing, herbaceous plants are grown for their delicious red, occasionally yellow, fruits.

Strawberries, which grow to 45cm (18in) high and 60cm (24in) across, will tolerate most soils that are well-drained. They are relatively short-lived with a cropping life of about three years, so new plants should be planted on a regular basis. The second year is the most productive.

Planting Plant in early autumn at a distance of 45cm (18in) apart and 75cm (30in) between the rows. Plant on a very slight mound with crowns at ground level. The plants must be firmed well and watered.

Cultivation Newly planted strawberries have a shallow root system and must be kept watered until well established. As the fruits develop, they will hang down onto the soil, so a mulch of straw will prevent them from marking and rotting; black plastic can be used as an alternative, but fruits actually touching it may become scorched in hot weather.

Pruning Cut off any runners (modified side shoots) bearing new young plants in summer. Cut down the foliage to approximately

Planting
Young strawberry plants are planted in well-prepared soil.

F. x *a.* 'Calypso'

10cm (4in) above soil level in the autumn, after picking has finished.

Harvesting Harvesting begins in early summer for early-fruiting cultivars, and continues through to autumn for perpetual-fruiting types (see panel). Pick the berries complete with their stalks, when they are red over about three-quarters of their surface and handle them as little as possible, as they are easily bruised. Pick fruits every other day, as they deteriorate fast. Fruits intended for freezing and preserving can be picked slightly earlier than those destined for dessert.

Tidying up
Cut out old leaves and runners once harvesting is over.

Strawberry types

Three kinds of berry
Summer (top), Alpine (right) and Perpetual (bottom).

Strawberries are divided into three distinct groups:
• **Alpine strawberries** produce a light crop of small, delicately flavoured fruits. Reliable cultivars include 'Alpine Yellow'.
• **Perpetual strawberries** flower and fruit in midsummer and again in mid-autumn. Reliable cultivars include 'Gento'.
• **Summer-fruiting strawberries** produce a heavy crop over a three- or four-week period in summer. The season can be extended by selecting cultivars carefully: 'Elvira' fruits early, 'Cambridge Favourite' in mid-season and 'Domanil' late.

Apples
Malus domestica

M. d. 'Discovery'

Apples are one of the most popular fruits, with a wide variety of flavours and uses, as well as a cropping and storing season that runs from late summer to mid-spring. They grow well in most soils, but prefer deep, well-drained soil that does not dry out too quickly in summer.

Most apple cultivars must be cross-pollinated with another cultivar to produce fruit, so it is important to grow cultivars with flowering periods that overlap.

Planting Plant in late autumn or early winter into a well-cultivated soil with plenty of organic matter added. Planting distances vary according to the rootstock used, but an average would be 3 x 4m (9 x 12ft) apart.

Cultivation In early spring apply an organic mulch to a depth of 10cm (4in) to help retain moisture and control weeds. Water the trees in dry summer periods or the fruits may drop prematurely.

Pruning Most tree and bush forms of apple require moderate pruning in winter to stimulate growth for the next season's fruit, so that they will crop well on a regular basis and maintain an open, well-balanced structure The pruning required will vary from year to year, depending on the season and growth of the tree, but strong shoots and leaders should generally be reduced by one-third of the current season's growth, and laterals cut back to four or five buds. The

fruiting habit of the tree must be considered. Spur-bearing trees such as 'Jester' and 'Cox's Orange Pippin' require spur thinning and pruning (see panel, p.187). Tip-bearing cultivars such as 'Discovery' and 'Worcester Pearmain', which produce the majority of their fruit on the tips of the branches, will need 'renewal' pruning, or cutting back in winter to a growth bud to remove bare, unproductive wood.

Harvesting To test whether apples are ripe, lift one in the palm of your hand and twist it slightly. If the apple and stalk come away from the spur easily, then it is ready. Handle apples with care, as they will deteriorate rapidly if bruised. To store, wrap each fruit individually in greaseproof paper and place in a well-ventilated container in a cool place. Early-season apples will be ready to harvest between late summer and early autumn and should be eaten within a few days of picking. Mid-season cultivars should be picked from early to mid-autumn, and late-season apples should be picked from mid- to late autumn, both before they are fully ripe. They will continue to ripen in store, ready for use from midwinter into late spring.

Apple and pear varieties

Not all apple and pear trees are self-fertile and those that are not will need to have a suitable tree nearby with which they can cross-pollinate. Check which pollination group the tree belongs to when you buy it, and perhaps purchase a suitable companion that will cross-pollinate with it. Without pollination, there will be no fruit. Ideally plant two or more from compatible groups that flower at the same period.

Apple varieties
Mid-season apples (compatible pollinators)
'Bramley's Seedling' (cooking), 'Blenheim Orange' (cooking), 'Cox's Orange Pippin' (dessert) 'Worcester Pearmain' (dessert)
Late season apples (compatible pollinators)
'Gala' (dessert), 'Orleans Reinette' (dessert), 'Encore' (cooking)

Pear varieties (Self-fertile or compatible pollinators)
'Conference', 'Beurré Superfin', 'Fondante d'Automne', 'Marie-Louise

Winter pruning
Removing the end quarter of the current season's growth from leader shoots.

Harvesting
When the apple and stalk separate easily from the branch, the fruit is ready for picking.

Pears
Pyrus communis

P. c. **'Conference'**

This very popular fruit can be used fresh in desserts or for cooking and preserving.

Pears are almost as easy to grow as apples, but prefer a warmer climate and flower earlier, so are more susceptible to spring frost damage. They need deep, fertile soil that is moisture-retentive, as they are sensitive to drought. Ideally, at least three different cultivars of pear should be grown in close proximity to allow cross-pollination to occur.

Planting Plant in late autumn or early winter at a spacing of 3 x 3m (10 x 10ft) apart, into a deeply cultivated soil containing plenty of well-rotted organic matter.

Stimulating growth
When a pear tree has ceased to produce new growth, cut back to two- or three-year-old wood. This can be recognised by the annual growth rings on a stem.

Cultivation In early spring, apply an organic mulch 10cm (4in) deep to control weeds and, more importantly, to retain moisture, as dry summer soil can cause the crop to abort.

Pruning Pear trees produce fruiting spurs easily, usually on two- and three-year-old shoots, and will need quite a lot of spur thinning (see p.180) and renewal pruning – cutting back in winter to a growth bud to remove areas of bare, unproductive wood. Most forms of pear require moderate pruning in winter to stimulate the following season's growth and fruit, and to maintain an open structure. The pruning needed will vary from year to year, but strong shoots and leaders should generally be reduced by one-third of the current season's growth and laterals cut back to four or five buds.

Harvesting Timing is critical: pears must be picked before they ripen or they will rot almost immediately in store. To keep pears, place them in a cool, dark position at 0–1°C (32–34°F).

Early-season pears will be ready to harvest between late summer and early autumn, and should be cut from the tree with secateurs.

Mid-season cultivars should be harvested from early to mid-autumn and late-season pears from early winter. They will continue to ripen in store. Always use the smallest fruits first.

Spur systems
With spur-bearing cultivars, apples and pears are produced on shoots that are two years old or more, and the fruits are usually borne in clusters on short, twiggy growths called 'spurs'.

The branches will carry two types of bud: large, swollen buds, which produce flower clusters and then fruit buds (spurs), and other much smaller, pointed growth buds, which develop into shoots for the following year or into laterals (side shoots). These spur systems may become overcrowded over a number of years, and can be thinned out or in some cases removed entirely.

Creating spurs
Lateral shoots should be pruned back to five buds in the winter, to encourage fruiting spurs.

Recognizing bud types
The shoots that are two years or older on this spur system generally contain both pointed growth buds and swollen flower buds.

Plums
Prunus domestica

P. d. 'Giant Prune'

This fruit can be eaten fresh or used for cooking, bottling and jams, but as the trees flower in early spring there is a risk of frost damage.

Plums prefer deep, well-drained soil and a warm, sheltered site. Different cultivars should be grown close together to ensure adequate pollen is available, even for the so-called self-fertile cultivars.

Planting Plant in late autumn or early winter into a deep, well-prepared soil with plenty of well-rotted organic matter. Plants should be spaced 3–4m (9–12ft) apart.

Cultivation In spring, apply an organic mulch, 10cm (4in) deep, to help retain moisture and control weeds. Water the trees in dry periods, or the fruits may drop prematurely. Some thinning of the crop may be necessary in midsummer to avoid major branches breaking under the weight of the fruit. Reduce each cluster to a maximum of five fruits.

Pruning Plum trees should be about 3m (10ft) high, so that most of the fruits can be reached from the ground. If the tree is cropping regularly, do as little pruning as possible. All pruning should be done in late summer to reduce the risk of attack from silver-leaf fungus. Thin out overcrowded branches by removing some completely, and try to keep the rest to about 1.5m (5ft) in length.

Harvesting The ripe fruits will be ready to harvest from midsummer to mid-autumn. Plums for cooking should be picked while still firm; those for dessert when they are slightly soft. Plums do not store well and should be eaten within a few days of picking.

Thinning dense clusters
Remove some fruit, leaving all the stalks on the tree.

Damsons
Prunus insititia

P. i. 'Bradley's King Damson'

These dark purple fruits are noted for their sour taste, which makes them more suitable for cooking and preserving than for eating fresh.

Most cultivars are self-fertile. The trees, which flower in mid-spring, often grow too large for the average garden unless grafted onto a dwarfing rootstock, in which case they can grow to 4m (12ft) high.

Damsons tolerate more rain and will do well with less sunshine than plums. They enjoy a deep, well-drained soil.

Planting Plant in late autumn or early winter into a well-prepared planting hole with plenty of well-rotted manure added. The plants need to be at least 4 x 4m (12 x 12ft) apart.

Cultivation Follow the same guidelines as for plums (see left).

Pruning As with plums, the fruits are carried on the previous season's growth and on spurs carried on older wood. Very little pruning is needed if the tree is cropping regularly. If any pruning is necessary, due to overcrowded or broken branches,

Heavily laden branch
Use a padded, forked stick to support and protect a heavily laden stem.

it should be carried out in summer, to reduce the risk of attack from silver-leaf fungus, to which damsons are prone.

Harvesting Allow the fruits to ripen on the tree. They will be ready to harvest from early to mid-autumn. Damsons for cooking should be picked while still firm; those for dessert when they are slightly soft to the touch.

Greengages
Prunus domestica

P. d. 'Reine Claude de Brahy'

Greengages, which are in fact coloured yellow or green, are ideal for eating fresh or bottling. The trees however tend to produce only about two-thirds of the yield of dessert plums.

Like plums, greengages prefer a deep, well-drained soil and a warm, sheltered site to encourage pollinating insects. They need more sunshine than plums, and most cultivars are self-fertile.

Planting Plant in late autumn into a well-prepared planting hole with plenty of well-rotted manure. Plants should be spaced 3-4m (9-12ft) apart.

Cultivation In spring, apply an organic mulch, 10cm (4in) deep, to help retain moisture and control weeds. Water the trees in dry summer periods, or the fruits may drop prematurely. Some thinning of the crop may be necessary in midsummer, otherwise major branches may break under the weight of the fruit. Reduce each cluster to a maximum of five fruits. Ripening greengages are prone to splitting and rotting in wet weather, and attack from birds and wasps in hot weather, so may need protecting with netting.

Pruning Ideally, greengage trees should be about 3m (10ft) high, so that most of the fruits can be reached from the ground. The fruits are carried on the previous season's growth and on spurs carried on older wood. If the tree is cropping regularly, do as little pruning as possible. All pruning should be carried out in summer, after fruiting, to reduce the risk of attack from silver-leaf fungus. Thin out overcrowded branches by removing some completely, and try to keep all branches to about 1.5m (5ft) in length.

Harvesting Allow the fruits to ripen on the tree. They will be ready to harvest from midsummer to mid-autumn. Greengages for cooking should be picked while still firm; those for dessert when they are slightly soft to the touch.

Cherries
Prunus avium

P. a. 'Morello'

Sweet cherries are delicious eaten fresh. The trees are very vigorous and are usually grafted onto a dwarfing rootstock. Because sweet cherries flower very early – in midspring – they need protection from frost. For this reason, they are often trained against a wall or fence. They require a deep, well-drained, moisture-retentive soil.

Planting Plant in late autumn or early winter into a well-cultivated soil which has had plenty of well-rotted manure added. Space plants 5–7m (15–20ft) apart.

Cultivation In early spring, feed the tree with an organic mulch, 10cm (4in) deep. Water in dry periods and in early summer drape the tree with netting to protect the fruits from birds.

Training and pruning All pruning should be carried out in summer, after fruiting, to promote fruit-bud formation. Each late summer, select two new lateral growths from each branch, tie them into any available space, and remove any other laterals or pinch them back to six leaves.

Harvesting The fruits will be ready to harvest in summer. Pick fruits for freezing when still firm, and those for cooking or dessert when slightly soft.

Shortening laterals
Cut lateral shoots to four or five buds to encourage fruiting spurs.

Tying in new growth
Secure young shoots to the network of supporting wires.

Peaches
Prunus persica

P. p. 'Garden Lady'

Peaches are grown for their downy fruits, eaten fresh or used cooked for desserts and jams. Peach trees will grow in any fertile, moisture-retentive, well-drained soil that is rich in organic matter. They benefit from a sheltered, sunny position, so are often grown against a wall in a fan shape. Flowers in mid-spring are vulnerable to frost. Peaches can be grown as single plants, as almost all cultivars are self-fertile.

Planting Plant in late autumn or early winter at a spacing of 4 x 4m (12 x 12ft) into a deep, well-drained soil. Add plenty of well-rotted manure to the planting hole.

Cultivation Follow the same guidelines as for cherries (p.189). Pollination can be assisted by dabbing each flower with a camel-hair brush. If the crop is heavy, thin out when the fruits are about 2.5cm (1in) across. Aim for one fruit to every 20–25cm (8–10in) of stem.

Training and pruning Peaches produce fruit only on the previous season's growth. Prune in spring to provide a regular supply of new shoots, which will form the ribs/branches of the fan.

Harvesting The fruits will be ready to harvest in mid- to late summer. They are ripe when the flesh yields to gentle pressure if squeezed.

Dwarf peach
Some peaches are ideal for growing in pots, where space is limited.

Peach leaf curl
This fungal disease distorts and causes leaves to fall prematurely.

Nectarines
Prunus persica var. *nectarina*

P. p. var. n. 'Harko'

Nectarines are similar to peaches but are smooth-skinned rather than downy, and are less hardy than their close relatives.

Nectarines, like peaches, will grow in any fertile, moisture-retentive, well-drained soil that is rich in organic matter. They also like shelter and full sun and, as they flower in mid-spring, can be vulnerable to frost.

Nectarines can be grown as single plants, as almost all cultivars are self-fertile.

Planting Plant in late autumn or early winter into a deep, well-drained soil with plenty of well-composted organic matter incorporated into the planting hole. Plant trees 4 x 4m (12 x 12ft) apart.

Cultivation In spring, feed the trees with an organic mulch, 10cm (4in) deep. Pollination can be assisted by dabbing flowers with a camel-hair brush. Water in dry summer periods, or the fruits may drop prematurely. In early summer, drape the tree with netting to protect fruits from birds. If the crop is heavy, thin when the fruits are about 2.5cm (1in) across, aiming for one fruit to every 20–25cm (8–10in) of stem.

Training and pruning Nectarines produce fruit only on the previous season's growth. Prune in spring to encourage new shoots and tie them into any available space. These will replace fruiting branches, which should be removed immediately after cropping.

Harvesting The fruits will be ready to harvest in summmer. Pick when the flesh yields slightly to pressure when squeezed between finger and thumb. Nectarines will store for up to one month if kept in a cool place, but handle them with care as they bruise easily.

Protecting nectarines
Cover the tree with netting to protect the fruit from birds.

Apricots

Prunus armeniaca

P. armeniaca

This succulent, yellow-skinned fruit can be eaten fresh or used for jams and preserves. Apricots are more difficult to grow than other 'stone fruits' such as peaches and nectarines, because they suffer from drought-induced bud drop late in the season. A warm, sheltered site is best, as the early (mid-spring) flowers are susceptible to frost.

Planting Plant from early autumn until late spring when the plant is dormant. Apricots prefer a deep, slightly alkaline, well-drained soil with lots of organic matter. Space plants 4–4.5m (12–14ft) apart.

Cultivation In spring, feed the trees with an organic mulch, 10cm (4in) deep. Pollination can be assisted by gently dabbing each flower with a camel-hair brush. Water in dry summer periods and in early summer drape the whole tree with netting to protect the fruits. If the crop is very heavy, thin when the fruits are about 2.5cm (1in) across, aiming for one fruit to every 20–25cm (8–10in) of stem.

Training and pruning As the fruits are carried on one-year-old growth and on

Spring blossom
A warm wall provides vital shelter for delicate, early spring blossom.

spurs on older wood, all pruning should be carried out in summer to reduce vegetative growth and promote fruit-bud formation. Each early summer, select two new lateral growths from each branch, tie them into any available space, and either remove surplus branches or pinch them back to six leaves.

Harvesting Allow the fruits to ripen on the tree; they will be ready to harvest in late summer. Pick them when they come away from the stalk easily and use immediately, as apricots do not store well.

Figs

Ficus carica

F. c. 'Rouge de Bordeaux'

Figs, which are among the oldest fruits in cultivation, vary in colour from green to reddish-brown. They are used for making desserts and preserves and are also eaten raw.

These evergreen trees like fertile, deep soil that is slightly alkaline, and a warm, dry climate. They can be planted in a brick- or concrete-lined plot to restrict their overall size and to increase their fruiting potential. As a guide, a pit 60 x 60 x 60cm (2 x 2 x 2ft) will confine a fig tree to a mature size of 2.4m (8ft) high and 5m (15ft) wide. Self-fertile fig flowers are produced internally and develop with the embryo fruit.

Planting Fig trees can be planted at any time of year in a deeply dug soil containing plenty of organic matter. Plants should be spaced 4–5m (12–15ft) apart.

Cultivation In early spring, feed the trees with an organic mulch, 10cm (4in) deep, to help retain moisture and control weeds. Water in dry summer periods, or the fruits may drop prematurely. In early summer, drape the whole tree with netting to protect the fruits from birds.

Protect the young fruits from frost by covering the whole tree with fleece.

Pruning In early spring, cut out the old fruited wood as well as any that is frost damaged. Prune back weak, young shoots to a single bud to encourage new shoots.

Harvesting Allow the fruits to ripen on the tree; this can take up to one year before they are ready to harvest, in summer and autumn. The figs are ripe enough to pick when the flesh yields to pressure if squeezed gently between finger and thumb.

Concrete-lined plot
Figs produce more fruit if the root spread is restricted.

Grapes
Vitis Hybrids

V. vinifera 'Schiava Grossa' syn. *V.v.* Black Hamburgh'

Grapes are one of the oldest of domesticated fruits and can be eaten fresh, processed for juice or used in wine-making. Borne in bunches, the fruits are blackish-purple, greenish-white or yellow in colour. Grape vines may reach up to 20m (70ft) when mature and will grow in any fertile, moisture-retentive, well-drained soil that is rich in organic matter. Their flowers, in mid-spring, are susceptible to frost damage. The vines should start to produce fruit in the fifth or sixth year after planting.

Planting Vines may be planted at any time of year.

Cultivation In spring, apply an organic mulch, 10cm (4in) deep. Water the vines in dry summer periods, especially while the fruits are swelling, or they may shrivel and drop. In early summer, drape the plant with netting to protect the fruits. If the bunches are very heavy, thin the crop when the grapes are about the size of peas.

Training and pruning
There are many training methods for grape vines, but the Guyot system is widely used where space is limited. Vines trained by the Guyot method should have all old, fruited wood cut out in winter, leaving only three replacement shoots. Tie two of these shoots down, one on either side of the third, central shoot, and prune the third shoot back to three strong buds. Six weeks before the fruits are to ripen, remove any overcrowded shoots and leaves that are obscuring them.

Harvesting The fruits will be ready in autumn when they are sweet to taste. Cut ripe bunches with a short section of stalk and place in a container lined with tissue paper. If not bruised, grapes will keep for up to two months in a cool, dry store.

Guyot method
A young Muller-Thurgau vine, trained by the Guyot method.

Removing leaves
Remove any overcrowded shoots or leaves that are obscuring the grapes about six weeks before the fruits are expected to ripen.

Kiwi fruit
Actinida deliciosa, syn. *A. chinensis*

A.d. 'Jenny'

This extremely vigorous climbing plant is grown for its hairy-skinned, gooseberry-like fruits, which are about 7.5cm (3in) long and 5cm (2in) across.

Male and female flowers are carried on separate plants, and both must be planted for a crop of fruit to be produced. Generally, one male plant, for example 'Tomuri', should be planted for every 8–9 female plants such as 'Allison'.

Kiwi fruit grow well in a sheltered, sunny position but will also tolerate partial shade. They need a deep, well-drained, fertile soil. The vines flower in early summer and should start to produce fruit in the third or fourth year after planting.

Planting Plant the vines at any time from late autumn until early spring. To make cropping easier, space the plants 4m (12ft) apart, in rows 5m (15ft) apart.

Cultivation In early spring, feed the plants with an organic mulch, 10cm (4in) deep, which will also help to control weeds and retain moisture. Water well during dry periods, to help the fruit to swell and keep the new canes growing vigorously.

Training and pruning
The vines often grow 4m (12ft) in a year, and must have a support system to keep them manageable.

Select posts 10 x 10cm (4 x 4in) square and 3m (10ft) long and insert them 90cm (36in) into the ground. Fix four horizontal wires, 50cm (20in) apart, to the posts, starting 50cm (20in) above ground level. In spring, train the young canes out along the wires and tie them into position as they develop. Cut back the fruit-bearing side shoots to three buds when the plant is dormant. The discarded canes may need to be cut into two or three sections to make removal easier.

Harvesting The fruits will be ready to harvest in late summer or early autumn. They are fully ripe when they begin to feel soft to the touch if squeezed gently between finger and thumb, and can be picked by snipping through the fruit stalk with secateurs. The fruits must be handled carefully as they are easily damaged.

Storing and preserving fruit

The traditional method for storing tree fruit, such as apples and pears, is on slatted benches in a cool, dry loft. Lemons can also be stored in this way. Air must circulate around the fruit to prevent rotting.

Take care when picking and handling fruit for storing, as bruised fruit will quickly cause other fruit to rot if they touch. Soft fruit and some tree fruits can be frozen or preserved, either in syrup or as a conserve. Those with lots of hard pips are better strained and turned into jelly.

Fruits that freeze well

Apples, apricots, blackberries, blueberries, cherries, currants, damsons, plums and greengages, gooseberries, grapes, peaches, nectarines, raspberries.

Citrus fruits
Citrus sinensis, C. limon, C. paradisi

C. sinensis

Oranges (*Citrus sinensis*), lemons (*C. limon*) and grapefruit (*C. paradisi*) belong to the citrus family, grown for their refreshing fruits. These are excellent for eating raw or for making desserts, preserves and drinks, and their peel adds zest to cooking.

All citrus are evergreen, sub-tropical trees, which can withstand frost only for short periods. Most citrus are self-fertile and do not require a pollinator, and many are capable of producing fruits with just a few or even no seeds at all. Citrus do not flower and fruit on a seasonal basis but as a response to warm, humid conditions, and there will often be flowers and fruit present on the tree at the same time. Trees should start to produce fruit four or five years after planting.

C. limon

Citrus trees prefer deep, well-drained, fertile soil, full sun and a warm, dry climate. They can be grown in containers to restrict their overall size, and can be overwintered indoors in cool climates to protect them from frost.

Planting When grown outdoors most citrus will form quite large plants, often needing a 7 x 7m (21 x 21ft) space. They can be planted at any time of year.

Cultivation In late spring, apply an organic mulch, 10cm (4in) deep, to help retain moisture and control weeds. Water the trees in dry summer periods, or the fruits may drop prematurely. In early summer, drape the whole tree with netting to protect the fruits from birds. Protect the young fruits from frost by covering the whole tree with fleece.

Pruning Remove any dead, damaged or diseased branches and prune back long, new growth to encourage bushier plants. Lemon trees can become straggly after a few years and benefit from an occasional hard pruning in early spring, when they should be cut back by two-thirds.

Harvesting Citrus fruit may take up to eight months to ripen. When the flesh yields to gentle pressure, they should be cut from the tree with secateurs.

Watering test
If soil is dry several centimetres into the pot, it needs watering.

Cleaning stems
Remove any shoots below the graft union with the thumb.

Liquid fertilizer
Apply a foliar feed every week, or every two weeks in winter.

The herb garden

Herbs have become increasingly popular for culinary purposes, and even for general medicinal use. They are extremely versatile, producing roots, stems, flowers, seeds and leaves that can have multiple uses, even when they come from the same plant. If you design the herb garden in an attractive, formal way, with the squares or segments divided into different families or species of herbs, it will make using the herbs much simpler. Herb gardens have been popular for centuries, and there is no shortage of information on how to design them, and the best herbs to grow for different purposes. Ideally, however, you should limit your ambitions to a few good, all-round culinary herbs, and some that have medicinal uses. Do not be tempted into practising with home remedies: leave it to the experts, as some herbs are extremely powerful and could endanger your health.

Designing a herb garden

You do not need to come up with an elaborate plan for a herb garden – a small, informal patch close to the kitchen will suffice if you just want to grow a few, well-chosen favourites.

For those looking for a more attractive design, one of the simplest is based on the spokes of a wheel, with each segment being used for a different herb. It pays to put a handsome architectural plant in the hub of the wheel to give the garden structure. A clipped box bush would be good, as would a standard fruit tree, such as a gooseberry, or a standard rose.

The design below will work as well for culinary herbs as for medicinal ones; on the whole, it is best not to mix the two categories.

Much depends on whether your herb garden is ornamental or practical. In either case, if the herb garden is larger than 2m (6ft) in diameter, it will pay to ensure that the paths between the segment are large enough to walk on, so you can tend the garden easily.

If, on the other hand, you have very little space, you can adapt the design to a large-diameter container, simply using fewer herbs in each segment.

The herb garden, left, has six different culinary herbs. A similar design could include medicinal herbs, such as:
a) pot marigold (*Calendula officinalis*)
b) chamomile (*Chaemaemelum nobile*)
c) lavender (*Lavandula angustifolia*)
d) lemon balm (*Melissa officinalis*)
e) mint (*Mentha* spp.)
f) feverfew (*Tanacetum parthenium*)

Parsley
(*Petroselinum crispum*)

Thyme
(*Thymus* spp.)

Sage
(*Salvia* spp.)

Oregano/Marjoram
(*Oreganum* spp.)

Tarragon
(*Artemisia dracunculus*)

Chives
(*Allium schoenoprasum*)

Spoked wheel design
This simple, attractive idea uses six different herbs, one in each segment of the wheel. An ornamental plant is the focal point in the hub.

Medicinal herb display
An attractive collection of medicinal plants in a container: wormwood, tansy, feverfew and hyssop.

Choosing herbs

The herbs you choose to grow are very much a matter of personal taste, quite literally in the case of culinary herbs. In addition to those for the kitchen, and those for herbal remedies, a number attract benevolent insects, such as bees and butterflies, and you could just as easily make a herb garden for encouraging wildlife.

Herbs, like other garden plants, divide into those that have woody stems (shrubs and subshrubs like lavender and rosemary), soft-stemmed perennials that come up year after year, such as lemon balm (*Melissa officinalis*) and thyme (*Thymus* spp.), and annuals that are grown every year from seed such as nasturtiums (*Tropaeolum*) and basil (*Ocimum basilicum*).

In a larger garden, herbs can be grown in their own specific border or mixed with other plants in the perennial border. How you grow them, and even buy them, will depend on which group they belong to. Generally speaking, shrubby herbs can be grown from cuttings while annuals are grown from seed.

Using herbs

Herbs for culinary purposes are used fresh or dried. Although dried herbs can be more pungent, when fresh they give dishes a delicious flavour, notably fresh basil with pasta, rosemary with grilled meat and tarragon with chicken.

For medicinal purposes, herbs can be infused or macerated. Herbal teas are made by infusing leaves in boiling water and letting it stand for a few minutes. Macerated herbs are left in oil for 10 days or so, until it becomes infused with the properties of the herb.

Cultivating herbs

Herbs need a good, free-draining soil and a sunny site. They also need some shelter from cold winds. A good solution for tender herbs is to plant them in a container, and then plunge the container in the ground near the backdoor during the summer, overwintering the herbs under glass. Generally, herbs are pest and disease-free and require little maintenance. Herbs from Mediterranean countries will often withstand drought (generally those with small, much-divided leaves) but those with larger, softer leaves (such as mint) will require regular watering in summer. Plant aromatic herbs in a prime position, such as either side of a path – brushing against the leaves releases their scent.

Herbs in containers
Mint can be contained by growing it in a pot which is plunged into the garden border.

Overwintering herbs
Grow tender plants such as parsley in pots and bring them indoors for winter.

Harvesting and storage

Herbs can be picked daily during the growing season, and many can be dried and stored for use throughout the winter months, providing year-round availability.

If the leaves are harvested correctly, the plant will develop a bushier habit. Pinch out the shoot tips and use these first to encourage the plant to form side shoots. Later in the season, you can then harvest the larger leaves from

Storing seeds
Store herbs in fresh air and put in a plastic bag when thoroughly dry to collect seedheads.

Herbs in containers

If you have very little space, there is nothing to prevent you growing some herbs in a window box, for example. The kitchen windowsill is an excellent spot for cultivating a few culinary herbs, and basil (grown from seed), parsley, chives and thyme will all furnish you with as much as you will need for the kitchen from a relatively small container.

More decorative, larger containers can also be used for more substantial herb displays. Remember that some herbs are quite vigorous so take care when you combine different herbs in the same container. Mint, for example, spreads by runners and will rapidly take over an

these shoots as they develop. When harvesting, the general rule is not to remove more than 20 per cent of the leaves at any one time.

Herbs can be dried successfully, and simply, by being hung upside down in a cool place with a good airflow. Damp and cold may cause the herbs to rot before they dry. Once dried, the herbs can be stored in airtight jars. Culinary herbs can also be frozen, but their aroma and flavour is considerably reduced by this method.

Harvesting fresh herbs
Borage flowers can be harvested and used fresh as a flavouring for summer drinks.

entire container, unless you make provision in the shape of a divider. A roof slate, pushed into the container, is a useful divider.

Culinary herb display
A terracotta pot is home to several culinary herbs, including marjoram, thyme, basil (and purple basil) and sage.

Culinary herbs

By adding herbs to food, not only do you enhance flavour, but you also benefit from the important vitamins and minerals these plants contain. As the types of food we eat has changed, influenced by factors such as health and convenience, and the popularity of exotic foods has grown, demand for more unusual herbs has increased. Many varieties, such as thyme, will keep very well in a dried form. However, to get the maximum benefit and the fullest flavour from herbs, they should be used fresh immediately after harvest. Plant culinary herbs close to the kitchen door to allow you to gather them as you cook.

Chives (*Allium schoenoprasum*)

Horseradish (*Armoracia rusticana*)

Dill (*Anethum gravoelens*)

Chervil (*Anthriscus cerefolium*)

CHIVES
Allium schoenoprasum
Alliaceae
H 30cm (1ft)
The stems of this hardy, perennial bulb have a delicate onion-like flavour and are often used raw in salads or with cheeses. It grows best in a light, well-drained soil, and will keep growing well into the winter in a sheltered position. Plant in clumps 25–30cm (10–12in) apart. Can also be grown in a container.

HORSERADISH
Armoracia rusticana
Brassicaceae
H 60cm (2ft)
This hardy herbaceous perennial has pungent, peppery-flavoured, edible roots. Horseradish will grow almost anywhere, but prefers a rich, moist soil. Once established, it is very difficult to remove. It is served as a condiment, and also complements oily fish, such as mackerel.

DILL
Anethum gravoelens
Apiaceae
H 1.2m (4ft)
The flowerheads and seeds of this hardy annual are used to flavour pickles, while its leaves have an anise-like flavour. Dill likes a rich, well-drained soil and plenty of sun. Plant 30–45cm (12–18in) apart.

CHERVIL
Anthriscus cerefolium
Apiaceae
H 45–60cm (10–12in)
This hardy biennial (usually grown as an annual) thrives in most soil types and conditions. The leaves have an aniseed taste and are sprinkled raw on vegetables, soups and salads. Plant 25–30cm (10–12in) apart.

TARRAGON
Artemisia dracunculus
Asteraceae
H 60cm (2ft)
This hardy, bushy perennial has strongly aromatic leaves. Plant 30–45cm (12–18in)

apart, in a light, free-draining soil. A sunny position is vital for this plant to grow well.

BORAGE
Borago officinalis
Boraginaceae
H 50cm (20in)
This hardy perennial has bright blue flowers and hairy leaves, which have a fresh cucumber scent. Borage flowers and leaves are often used in cool drinks. It likes well-drained soil and sun. Plant 30–45cm (12–18in) apart.

CARAWAY
Carum carvi
Apiaceae
H 50cm (20in)
This hardy biennial plant has fine, fern-like leaves, which are an excellent garnish for soups and salads. The strongly flavoured seeds combine well with casseroles and roasted meats and are also used to flavour cakes and breads. Caraway prefers a fertile soil and plants should be about 30–45cm (12–18in) apart.

CORIANDER
Coriandrum sativum
Apiaceae
H 30cm (1ft)
Cultivated for over 3,000 years, coriander is a staple flavouring in curries and Far Eastern cooking. It is also known to aid the digestion. This hardy annual flourishes in a light soil containing plenty of organic matter, and prefers full sun. Plant 25–30cm (10–12in) apart.

BAY
Laurus nobilis
Lauraceae
H 3m (10ft)

One of the most widely cultivated herbs, the spicy, dried leaves of this slow-growing, hardy, evergreen tree are used to flavour both savoury and sweet dishes. It can spread to 5m (15ft) across, and can also be clipped and trained into neat standards and topiary balls. Bay prefers a fertile, well-drained soil, and a hot, sunny, sheltered position.

MINT
Mentha spp.
Lamiaceae
H 45cm (18in)

The most common species of mint is *Mentha spicata*, or spearmint, which is used to flavour drinks, sauces and salads. An invasive herbaceous hardy perennial, it is best grown in a container to control it. Mints grow well in most soils, and prefer a partially-shaded site.

BASIL
Ocimum basilicum
Lamiaceae
H 35cm (14in)

Originating from India, this tender, annual herb has bright green, delicately flavoured leaves which are delicious when added fresh to soups, fish, meat dishes and salads. Basil prefers a warm, sheltered site and a light, well-drained soil. Plants should be spaced 30cm (1ft) apart, and watered well during dry periods.

MARJORAM
Origanum majorana
Lamiaceae
H 45cm (18in)

This hardy perennial shrub-like plant has a sweet yet spicy flavour, which is excellent with poultry or in egg dishes. This herb thrives in a well-drained, alkaline soil in full sun. Plant about 30cm (12in) apart to allow room for its spreading habit.

PARSLEY
Petroselinum crispum
Apiaceae
H 60cm (2ft)

Used since Roman times, parsley is a hardy biennial herb which prefers a moist, fertile soil. The densely curled or flat (depending on the variety) leaves are rich in iron and vitamins, and are used as garnishes, as well as to flavour casseroles, sauces and mince. Plants are grown 25–30cm (10–12in) apart.

ROSEMARY
Rosmarinus officinalis
Lamiaceae
H 1m (3ft)

The grey-green, needle-like leaves of this shrubby, half-hardy herb have a distinctive flavour and are often used for stuffings. Rosemary likes a free-draining, alkaline soil and a sheltered, sunny site. Plant about 2m (6ft) apart, as it has a spreading habit.

SAGE
Salvia officinalis
Lamiaceae
H 50cm (20in)

The felted, highly aromatic, grey-green leaves of this hardy perennial act as a disinfectant to the digestive system and are often used in stuffings to accompany fatty foods, such as duck. A hardy perennial, sage needs a light, free-draining soil and a sunny position.

THYME
Thymus vulgaris
Lamiaceae
H 15–20cm (6–8in)

The pungent leaves of this half-hardy perennial can be used fresh or dried. It is often used as a seasoning with meats, stocks and stuffings. Thyme should be planted 30cm (12in) apart, and requires a well-drained and sunny position. Clip the plant regularly to prevent it from becoming thin and straggly. Thyme can be grown indoors in winter.

Coriander (*Coriandrum sativum*)

Bay (*Laurus nobilis*)

Spearmint (*Mentha spicata* 'Moroccan')

Basil (*Ocimum basilicum*)

Parsley (*Petroselinum crispum*)

Rosemary (*Rosmarinus officinalis*)

Sage (*Salvia officinalis*)

Lemon verbena
(*Aloysia triphylla*)

Medicinal herbs

Plants have been used for thousands of years to help ease the symptoms of illness, long before chemical drugs became available. Indeed, many of the drugs which are now regarded as common, such as aspirin, had their origins in plants. Even a small garden will hold sufficient plants to make up a basic medicine chest, and by drying and storing them, you will have medicines to hand all year round. The herbs listed are among the most popularly used for common complaints. Warning: consult a herbal medicine practitioner before trying any treatments, as some herbs are toxic and/or have unwanted side effects, particularly in certain illnesses or conditions.

Marshmallow
(*Althaea officinalis*)

Chamomile (*Chamaemelum nobile*)

Pot marigold (*Calendula officinalis*)

LEMON VERBENA
Aloysia triphylla
Verbenaceae
H 1.8m (6ft)

This half-hardy shrub likes full sun and rich soil. It has lance-shaped, lemon-scented foliage and tiny panicles of pale mauve flowers. It can be propagated from semi-ripe cuttings in summer. Its leaves are excellent for infusions for teas as well as for soothing the digestion.

ARNICA
Arnica montana
Asteraceae
H 30–60cm (1–2ft)

Also known as leopard's bane, this daisy-like, hardy perennial likes full sun and rich, acid soil. Small, golden yellow flowers appear from midsummer to early autumn. Sow from seed in autumn. It can be used to make a tincture to relieve bruising and swelling. **Not to be taken internally**.

POT MARIGOLD
Calendula officinalis
Asteraceae
H 30–60cm (1–2ft)

This half-hardy annual, with its bright orange, daisy-like flowers from late spring to autumn, likes most soils but prefers full sun. Propagate from seed sown in late spring. Its flowers have antiseptic properties and are used in creams and tinctures, and in cosmetic preparations.

MARSHMALLOW
Althaea officinalis
Malvaceae
H 90cm–1.2m (3–4ft)

This hardy perennial grows well in damp soil in full sun and thrives in seaside conditions. It has grey-green, downy, 5-lobed leaves and pale pink flowers in late summer. Propagate by cuttings in early summer. The root can be taken as an infusion for insomnia or applied as a poultice to swellings. The leaves soothe irritated eyes.

CHAMOMILE
Chamaemelum nobile
Asteraceae
H 30cm (12in)

A hardy perennial, chamomile will grow in partial shade and likes well-drained soil. It has feathery, apple-scented foliage and tiny, daisy-like flowers. It is used to aid digestion, calm nerves and promote relaxation. An infusion of the leaves can be used to relieve pain. The flowers are used in shampoos to lighten hair colour.

PURPLE CONEFLOWER
Echinacea purpurea
Asteraceae
H 30–60cm (1–2ft)

Used by American Indians to cure snake bites, this purple-flowered, hardy herb grows best on fertile soil in sun or partial shade. It can be propagated from seed sown in early summer. Infusions are used for healing skin complaints and it has valuable antibiotic properties.

WITCH HAZEL
Hamamelis virginiana
Hamamelidaceae
H 3m (10ft)

This small, hardy tree produces tiny, yellow, spidery flowers after the leaves have fallen, in mid-winter. It will do well in sun or partial shade in moist soil. Propagate from softwood cuttings in summer. Its astringent properties are well-known, and are particularly good for eye and skin inflammations.

ST. JOHN'S WORT
Hypericum perforatum
Clusiaceae
H 60cm (2ft)

This hardy perennial does well in partial shade or sun, in well-drained soil. It bears bright yellow flowers in summer. Propagate from seed in spring or autumn. Infusions of the leaves can be used for nervousness, insomnia and depression. Fresh leaves can be crushed and rubbed on bites to reduce pain and swelling. The flowers can be macerated in oil, as a rub for rheumatism.

LAVENDER
Lavandula angustifolia
Lamiaceae
H 60cm (2ft)

This half-hardy sub-shrub has wonderfully aromatic flowers in rich purples and mauves and fine, silvery grey foliage. It grows well in poor soil and full sun. Propagate from semi-ripe cuttings in summer or autumn. The essential oil derived from the flowers has a calming, restful effect, and is much used in aromatherapy. It can also be used as an antiseptic to treat insect bites.

LEMON BALM
Melissa officinalis
Lamiaceae
H 60cm (2ft)

This easy-to-grow, hardy perennial has a golden variety, 'Aurea', which has attractive, buttery yellow-splashed leaves. Does well in partial shade and dry soil. Propagate from cuttings in summer. A valuable bee plant, its leaves are used in teas to calm nerves and ease depression. It has a tonic effect on the digestive system.

PEPPERMINT
M. x *piperita*
Lamiaceae
H 60cm (2ft)

This hardy, spreading perennial has tough, green leaves and small, lilac or white flowers in summer. It likes moist soil and full sun or partial shade. Its leaves are highly aromatic and different species have different aromatic properties – applemint (*M. suaveolens*), and eau-de-cologne mint (*M.* x *piperita* var. *citrata*) among them. The leaves are used to make refreshing teas that help soothe the digestion and promote sleep.

WILD BERGAMOT
Monarda fistulosa
Lamiaceae
H 60–90cm (2–3ft)

This hardy perennial has toothed pairs of leaves and small, mauve-pink flowers in late summer. A lemon-scented species (*M. citriodora*) is also well worth growing. They both thrive in full sun or light shade in dryish, well-drained soil. Propagate from cuttings in summer. Use infusions of the leaves for delicately scented teas, which soothe the digestion.

SALAD BURNET
Sanguisorba minor
Rosaceae
H 45cm (18in)

This hardy perennial has been planted for centuries in herb gardens. It has small, attractive leaves, which are good for ground cover, and insignificant flowers. The leaves are eaten in salads and soups, and are used to treat wounds. Steeped in drinks, they guard against infection.

FEVERFEW
Tanacetum parthenium
Asteraceae
H 60cm (2ft)

This daisy-like, hardy perennial flowers from early to late summer and has toothed, aromatic foliage. Propagate from seeds sown in summer. Its dried leaves make a good moth repellent, and can be used as a sedative in an infusion, and for migraines and arthritis (for which it is now a registered medicine). **Not to be taken in pregnancy.**

HEARTSEASE
Viola tricolor
Violaceae
H 10-30cm (4-12in)

This annual has yellow and blue scented flowers from spring to autumn and dark green, toothed leaves. It likes full sun and a fertile soil. Propagate from seed in spring. Thought to aid healing, its peppery tasting flowers are good in salads.

Purple coneflower (*Echinacea purpurea*)

Lemon balm (*Melissa officinalis*)

Peppermint (*M.* x *piperita*)

Salad burnet (*Sanguisorba minor*)

Feverfew (*Tanacetum parthenium*)

Heartsease (*Viola tricolor*)

Care and Maintenance

For a garden to look its best, and the plants in it to flourish and grow, it must have the right care and attention. This means that to be successful, the gardener has to understand the garden's basic requirements, such as the best possible conditions in which to grow plants, when to supply water or feed, and how to keep them pest and disease-free. This section of the book is an invaluable point of reference for every novice gardener, explaining and illustrating exactly what needs to be done, and when, to keep the entire garden in optimum condition. From choosing the basic tools and equipment, through to learning about and improving the soil, controlling weeds, supporting, pruning and training trees, shrubs and plants, applying fertilizers and increasing your plant stocks, it provides a clear, comprehensive source of expert advice on every aspect of maintaining the garden. A must for all budding gardeners!

The natural environment

The aim of any gardener is to provide the optimum environment in which plants can grow and flourish, not only so that plants are healthy and strong but so that the garden as a whole looks well cared for and is used to its full potential. For successful gardening, it is essential to understand how the natural environment affects plant growth, and how plants respond to their growing conditions. To care for and maintain your garden, you need to organise your environment as efficiently as possible. This means knowing the basic requirements of plants, how climate affects growth, how to deal with soil, how to feed and water plants, and how to shape and control them. It is also useful to be able to increase your stock of plants, cheaply and easily, by growing them yourself from seeds or cuttings.

A border of healthy plants
A perennial border in full swing in summer is one of the great delights of gardening, but behind this seemingly artless mass of flowering plants lies a lot of hard work and hard-won experience.

Healthy plants

Plants need light, air, water and nourishment in order to flourish and thrive. A basic understanding of how plants grow and why each of these factors is important helps you to provide the best growing conditions for your plants. You also need to consider the local climate, as the temperature range, rainfall and wind will have a strong influence on the plants you choose, as well as where you position them and how you care for them afterwards.

How plants grow

Plants manufacture their own food by the process of photosynthesis. Sunlight is the prime energy source. All the green parts of a plant (not just the leaves) contain chlorophyll, which absorbs sunlight and converts it into energy. This energy then converts carbon dioxide from the atmosphere and water and nutrients from the soil into carbohydrates or food for the plant. The process of photosynthesis gives off oxygen as a by-product. To ensure healthy growth, plants need some essential foods (nutrients). The most important of these are nitrogen (N), phosphorus (P) and potassium (K). Plants obtain these foods through their roots, by absorbing mineral salts from the soil. Each of these three nutrients contributes to the growth of the plant in different ways:
Nitrogen is vital for healthy leaf and stem growth.
Phosphorus promotes strong root growth.
Potassium is necessary for flowering and fruiting.
In fertile soils, these nutrients are naturally replenished in the never-ending cycle of plant death and decay. However, to get the best results from your plants, or to cure any nutritional deficiencies, it is often necessary to give extra nutrients in the form of fertilizers (see pp. 214–215).

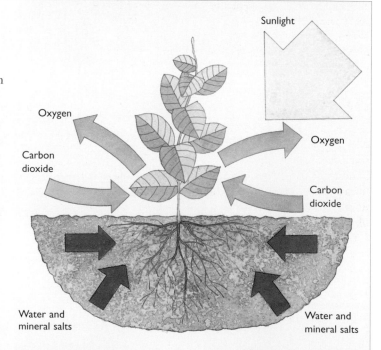

The growth cycle
An understanding of the way in which a plant obtains food makes it clear that light, air and water are essential for healthy growth. The diagram above shows how a plant uses sunlight, air and water to manufacture its food by the process known as photosynthesis. All parts of the plant are involved in this process. The delicate root hairs take up water and nutrients, in the form of mineral salts, from the soil. Green leaves and stems contain chlorophyll which traps sunlight. Energy derived from sunlight is then used to convert the nutrients from the soil and carbon dioxide from the atmosphere into carbohydrate food for the plant. Oxygen, the gas essential to all life, is given off as a by-product. By growing plants, you contribute to the quality of the air we breathe.

Climate

Your gardening possibilities are affected by the climate in which you live, as are your gardening tasks.

Latitude, altitude and distance from the sea all determine local climate. Even in a small garden, it is possible to create some particular 'microclimate' to suit certain plants – a pond for moisture-loving plant types, or a sheltered, sunny spot for sun-lovers.

Temperature, rainfall and wind all play a part in the overall climate and each has a part in determining which plants grow well. In different parts of the world, plants have adapted to take advantage of the natural conditions. Water-retaining succulents and cacti survive in deserts, and plants with huge leaves grow successfully in the shade because they can expose the greatest possible area of leaf to the light and therefore manufacture food efficiently.

Gardening against the natural climate – trying to grow damp-loving plants in dry territory and vice versa – increases your workload enormously and produces disappointing results.

Temperature

The length of the growing season is governed by temperature, which also affects other aspects of plant growth. Air temperature often influences the rate of growth; for example, lawn grass starts to grow when temperatures rise above 6° C (43° F). Summer temperature determines whether or not many plants reach maturity and set seed. The chilling effect of winter, when plants are dormant, often determines the quality of flowers and seed germination in the following season.

Frost

Frost is a great danger to plants when the temperature consistently drops below freezing. Ice crystals form within the plant cells, causing them to split. Rapid thawing can then rupture cells. Symptoms of frost damage include blackened young shoots, shrivelled stems and leaves, and shoots, or even whole plants, that die back.

Frost lift squeezes young plants out of the soil as it freezes and thaws, exposing roots to drying wind and low temperatures. Wind chill (wind and low temperature) causes damage to plants.

Frost pockets

Because it is heavy, cold air runs downhill and frost collects at the lowest point to form a 'frost pocket'. When planting, ensure that you select specimens accordingly or plan to avoid these areas where plants are most vulnerable to damage.

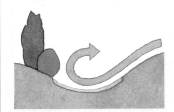

Frost collects in a valley
You can see here how cold air gathers over the frost pocket and extends the area of possible damage as it backs up the slope.

Frost in front of trees
A frost pocket will form in front of obstacles in the path of cold air. Removing them allows the cold air to pass through.

Rainfall

Any country with rainfall distributed evenly throughout the year provides ideal conditions for gardening, because rain and snow are the main sources of water for plants growing outdoors. Either too much or too little rain can be a problem.

Drought Much of the water provided by rainfall is lost through surface run-off and evaporation. Drought is a common problem, especially during summer. Wilting is the first sign of distress as the plant shuts down until more water is available. Plants that are native to dry areas often have specially adapted leaves, with a reduced surface area, to help reduce water loss.

Waterlogging Most plants are able to survive water-logging for short periods of time, but when it is prolonged, the roots are damaged and eventually die.

Rain shadow

In the lee of a house or other building, rain may scarcely penetrate the ground. Susceptible plants may suffer unless you ensure the soil stays moist. Grow plants in open ground, away from buildings and other structures, to get the full benefit from the rain.

Dry areas
The diagram shows that no rain falls on the side of a house facing away from the prevailing wind. Rain shadows also cause problems on the leeward sides of walls and solid fences.

Wind

Wind in the garden disperses seed and pollen, circulates air and discourages diseases. It can also create problems.

Windrock Affects young or recently transplanted plants. They rock to and fro causing root damage, slow growth or even death in dry conditions.

Windscorch May occur on very exposed sites. Plants lean away from the prevailing wind. Cold or dry winds make plant tops misshapen and kill growth buds.

Windthrow Causes the most extreme damage. Branches are torn away. During gales, whole trees may be lifted out of the ground.

Reduced growth The result of excessive water loss in high winds and in high temperatures. A plant's attempts to grow upright in strong winds can reduce its development by as much as 30 per cent.

Wind protection

Windbreaks provide shelter, often crucial for young or recently transplanted plants. Fences, screens and hedges all filter the wind whereas a solid windbreak may create more turbulence. Tie young trees to stakes to protect them.

Hedge windbreak
A hedge provides good shelter from cold winds and allows an early-season display of container-grown tulips and other spring flowers.

Basic equipment

Providing the best care for your plants, and keeping the garden looking good all year round, requires regular maintenance. To do this easily and efficiently, you need a range of gardening tools and equipment. Such tools are often expensive. For the new gardener faced with a vast array of differing shapes and brands, deciding what to buy may present a daunting task. However, with careful planning it can be easier than you think.

First, think about the type of garden you would like. It could be one that takes little maintenance for example, or one with no lawn. Or it could be devoted exclusively to growing vegetables. The style of garden will entirely influence the choice of tools. If you have a lawn, you will need mowing equipment; if you grow vegetables, you will need tools for cultivation.

Invest in the best-quality items you can afford and do not be tempted to economize. If necessary, buy just a few well-made tools for essential tasks, as they will be more comfortable to use, will last longer and do a better job.

Safety is an important consideration in gardening (see p. 207). Your eyes are particularly vulnerable, so it is important to wear goggles if you are using cutting equipment. Always remember to cover up the sharp points of canes and poles, for further protection.

Digging and cultivating tools

These tools are the most frequently used in the garden and it is worth buying the best you can afford.

Forks and spades
A good spade and fork are vital. Use the spade for digging and breaking up the ground and lifting soil. Use the fork for general cultivation, lifting plants and forking manure and compost.

Before you buy a fork or spade, handle it to get an idea of the weight and balance, looking for strength combined with lightness. Check that the joint between the shaft and the head is secure and that all surfaces, especially the handles, are smooth to avoid blisters. Handles are shaped in the form of a T, D, or YD. Try all three to find which design you find more comfortable to use. A smooth surface on the blades or tines makes working with, and cleaning tools much easier.

Spades and forks come in three basic sizes: **digging** (the largest); **medium**; and **border**, (the smallest). Choose the size which feels most comfortable for you.

A Cornish shovel, similar to a spade, has a longer handle and is useful if more leverage is needed.

Hoes
Use these for cultivating the topsoil and weeding around plants. There are two main types:
Push or **'Dutch' hoe** Cuts through surface weeds with a slicing action.
Draw hoe (Also called a swan-neck hoe). Used with a chopping action for weeding. Also for making lines or drills for seeds.

Rakes
Use rakes for breaking up the soil and levelling it before planting. The greater the number of teeth in the rake, the finer the soil surface.

Trowels and hand forks
These, too, are essential. Use a trowel for digging holes and planting. They are also handy for working in containers and raised beds. Use a hand fork for weeding, lifting small plants and for planting. Hand forks are available with round or flat tines. The flat-tined type is better for weeding.

Mechanical digger
For digging large areas a motorized Rotovator can be hired, but do not use them on soils with many perennial weeds as they create ideal conditions for their regrowth by dispersing the stems.

Trowel

Hand fork (round tines)

Hand fork (flat tines)

Spade

Draw hoe

Dutch hoe

Rake

Fork

Cornish shovel

Basic digging and cultivating equipment
These tools will be in use all the time as you care for your garden. Good-quality tools last longer and are more comfortable to work with.

Cutting and pruning tools

Many garden maintenance tasks involve restricting or shaping plant growth. Good training and pruning of plants gives the garden an attractive form, as well as keeping the plants healthy. The kind of cutting and pruning tools you need depends on the planting style of your garden. All cutting tools should be kept clean, sharp and in good condition, ready for use.

Knives
Perhaps the most useful tool is a really good-quality, sharp knife. Most gardeners carry one in their pocket (the kind that closes up safely is imperative). The knife should be well-balanced, strong, light and comfortable to use.
Gardening knife Used for dead-heading plants,
harvesting fruit and vegetables, and taking cuttings, as well as cutting string or canes.
Pruning knife Has a curved blade for controlled pruning.

Secateurs
Heavy-duty cutting – of slender wooden stems and branches – demands a pair of secateurs. These have two blades which meet in a chopping action as the handles are squeezed. Be careful not to pinch your fingers when pressing the secateur handles together. Left- or right-handed models are available, and there are three main types:
Anvil With a single, straight-edged cutting blade that closes down on to an anvil (a bar of softer metal, often
brass). A **ratchet** modification enables the user to cut through a branch in stages which makes pruning less tiring and is ideal for those with a small handspan.
Manaresi Has two blades, both with straight cutting edges. These are often used for pruning vines.
Bypass The best all-purpose secateurs. They have a convex upper blade that cuts against a concave lower one.

When using secateurs, position the stem to be cut close to the base of the blade where it can be held firmly. If the cut is made with the tip, the blades are liable to be strained or forced apart.

Shears
Shears have a similar action to secateurs but longer, flatter blades. There is usually a notch at the base of one
blade for cutting tough stems, but thick stems will need pruners or a saw. Use shears to clip hedges or topiary, cut back herbaceous plants and areas of long grass. They should be strong, light, sharp and comfortable to use.

Loppers and saws
These are used for stouter branches.
General-purpose pruning saw Copes with most pruning needs.
Folding pruning saw The blade closes into the handle (like a pen-knife). Handy for most tasks except sawing through large branches.
Bow saw Good for tougher branches.
Long-handled pruners or loppers Strong secateurs with long handles to give extra leverage when cutting thick stems or branches.

Cutting and pruning tools
Using the right cutting tool for the job is essential if you are to avoid blunting tools and damaging plants by bruising and ragged cuts.

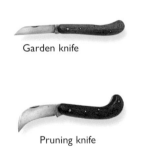
Garden knife

Pruning knife

Anvil secateurs

Ratchet secateurs

Manaresi secateurs

Bypass secateurs

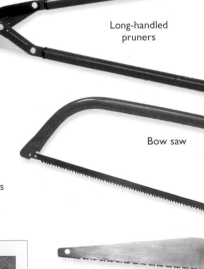
Long-handled pruners

Bow saw

General purpose pruning saw

Folding pruning saw

Shears

Tool care
Tools will not last or function well if they are dirty, rusty or damaged. Clean all tools immediately after use, and wipe metal surfaces with an oily rag.

Mechanized equipment should be regularly oiled. Wipe electrically powered tools dry and clean before they are stored.

It is important to sharpen cutting tools on a regular basis as blunt blades will damage the plants.

Sharpening knives
Hold the knife blade at a 25° angle and push it gently along a moistened oilstone. Repeat this process on both sides of the blade until the knife is sharp.

Lawn care equipment

The kind of lawn you want will determine the lawn tools you need. A formal lawn, complete with stripes of mown grass and neatly cut edges, will require a cylinder mower (see p. 224) and an edging iron and shears. A wild meadow-style lawn will only need to be cut once or twice a year with a sickle or scythe (see p. 225), or an electric strimmer.

The lawn hand tools are illustrated below right. The power tools you need will depend on the size and form of your garden. You would be well advised to discuss your precise requirements with a reputable garden centre.

Lawn tools
There are two vital tools for well-defined lawn edges.
Long-handled edging shears Used to trim any long grass straggling from the lawn edges. Use these every 14 days when the grass is growing vigorously.
Edging iron Use three or four times during the growing season to cut away long grass or rough edges.

Lawn maintenance tools
Such tools will achieve a neat lawn with sharp edges, helping to make a garden appear well tended.

Other useful tools are:
Sickle Has a very sharp curved blade mounted on a wooden or plastic handle. Useful for trimming areas of long grass. It must be kept sharp.
Fan rake A wire rake used to remove moss and to aerate the lawn.

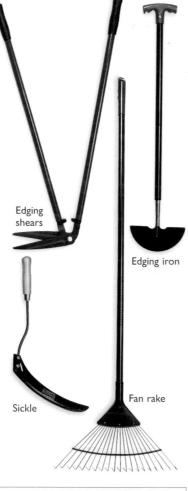
Edging shears
Edging iron
Sickle
Fan rake

Lawnmowers
Choose the lawnmower which best suits your lawn.
Manual lawnmowers Adequate for a small lawn, these are quiet and need little maintenance.
Power lawnmowers Run off petrol or electricity and have one of two cutting actions – cylinder or rotary. For an even, top quality lawn the cylinder type is the best.

Rotary and hover mowers are good for uneven ground but do cut less closely. Rotary mowers have wheels, hover types glide on a cushion of air. For a striped effect, make sure your mower has a fitted roller.

Electric hover mower
This hover mower is good for small areas of lawn. It cuts quickly but not very closely.

Spraying equipment

You may need to spray your plants, either to apply weedkillers or pesticides, or just to mist the leaves with water or give a foliar feed.

Sprayers range from simple, hand-held types, operated by pressing a lever at the top, through to pressurized devices with a pump mechanism. The higher the operating pressure, the greater the risk of harmful chemicals in weedkillers or pesticides drifting onto surrounding plants and harmless insects. Always use on windless days and wear protective clothing, as directed by the manufacturer of the spray and wash sprayers out thoroughly after use.

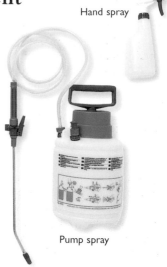
Hand spray
Pump spray

Basic sprayers
Choose from a range of simple hand-held sprayers through to pressurized devices for larger areas.

Carrying equipment

You will often need to move materials within the garden. For instance, you may want to shift soil from one area to another, clear away prunings or move flower pots.

Wheelbarrows
These are essential for moving heavy or loose materials over short distances. Choose a well-balanced model. When the barrow is full, the bulk of the weight should rest over the wheel and not towards the handles. This will make it easier to manoeuvre.

Wheelbarrow

Bags, ground sheets and waste sacks
These are perfect for collecting and carrying light, bulky items such as grass or hedge clippings. They can be folded flat for storage. Woven mesh plastic is the ideal material as it is durable and less likely to rip or tear. Broad, flat handle straps make carrying heavy weights easier.

Trug baskets and buckets
These are ideal for light work such as harvesting flowers and vegetables, or collecting and transporting a few weeds. There are both plastic and traditional wooden types available in a range of sizes.

Carry bag

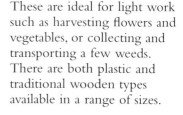
Trug

Watering equipment

Seedlings, newly transplanted plants and those grown in containers all need regular watering for healthy growth. Some kind of watering equipment is necessary, although a simple watering can may be all you need.

Watering cans

A good-quality can is a must. Choose a well-balanced one that starts to pour as soon as it is tilted, with a long spout for extra reach. Watering cans range from 0.5 to 15 litres (16 fl oz to 3 gallons). A rose (nozzle) can be fitted to give an even spray.

Hosepipes and fittings

You will need a hosepipe for watering distant parts of the garden or for heavy watering. Most are made of PVC, but vary in quality and price.
Lances and pistols Fit these to the end of a hose to give a fine jet of water or as extensions for reaching inaccessible plant containers.

Sprinklers

These are useful for an even watering of quite large areas.
Oscillating Gives an even spray over a rectangular area.
Rotary Gives even coverage over a circular area.
Static Sprays water in a circle. This is the best type of sprinkler for lawns.

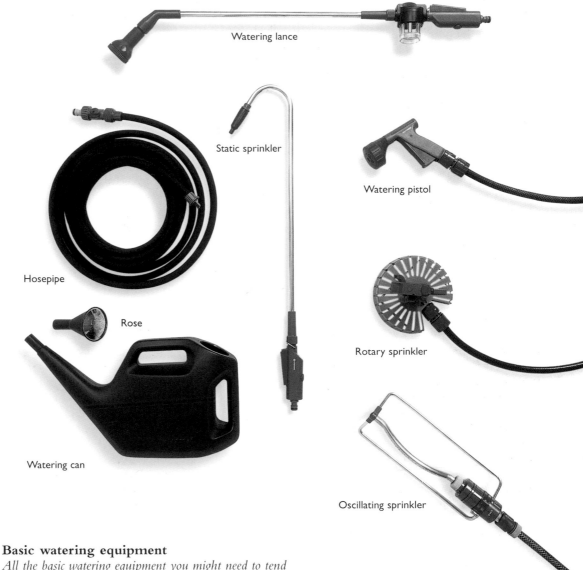

Watering lance

Static sprinkler

Hosepipe

Watering pistol

Rose

Rotary sprinkler

Watering can

Oscillating sprinkler

Basic watering equipment

All the basic watering equipment you might need to tend a garden is shown above. A simple watering can may be sufficient but for larger areas or, to ensure continuous watering, a hose or sprinkler will make life much easier.

Garden safety

Whenever you are using garden machinery or equipment, always play safe by wearing the appropriate protective clothing.

If you are in any doubt about what to wear, look on the machine itself, for safety symbols that show you the minimum you should wear for safe use.

Most accidents occur while mowers, hedge trimmers, spades, forks and secateurs are being used. Do wear strong boots and always have electrical tools fitted with a residual current device (RCD) to cut out the electrical circuit. Do not use electrical tools in damp weather.

Ear protectors

Goggles

Basic safety equipment

Tough gardening gloves are essential for the keen gardener. Protect your eyes with goggles when using power tools or cutting implements. For dusty or dirty jobs, wear a face mask. Cut out the noise of power tools with ear protectors.

Face mask

Gloves

Knowing your soil

The most important resource in any garden is the soil in which the plants grow. Most soil is capable of supporting plant life but by cultivating your soil well, you greatly increase the health and beauty of your plants. Fertile soil is well-drained and aerated, and is rich in organic matter. It is also full of invisible but highly beneficial micro-organisms and bacteria. Digging properly, improving drainage and adding plenty of organic matter and some fertilizer will improve soil texture and structure and the activity of helpful bacteria.

Soil types

Soils are classified according to the proportions of sand, silt or clay. These three materials have quite different properties which determine the character of the soil. **Sandy soils** have little or no clay in them, which makes them very light and free-draining. Nutrients are quickly washed away and the soil can dry out. They are easy to work and quick to warm up in spring.

Silty soils are more fertile and retain water better than sandy soils. They can be difficult to work, though, and often form a surface crust or cap. This can be a problem because rainwater runs off and fertilizers are not taken up very easily.

Clay soils are usually rich in nutrients and retain water well, but they tend to take time to warm up in spring and are slow to drain. They are prone to compaction and can be difficult to work. In hot, dry summers, clays are liable to bake and crack. The ideal is **loam**, a mixture of sand, silt and clay. It has many of the better characteristics of all three, such as high fertility, good water-holding qualities and good drainage.

As well as these main soil types, there is organic soil. Peat, as it is usually called, consists of thick layers of decomposed organic matter (such as leaves, grasses and moss). Peat soils often have poor drainage and lack useful nutrients.

How to improve your soil

Soil type	Problems	Treatment
Sandy	Light and very free draining; loses nutrients quickly	Add humus (p. 212) and fertilizers (p. 214)
Silty	Soil particles are very tightly packed so surface compacts easily; especially sticky to work	Dig over to open up structure (p. 218), then add humus (p. 212) and fertilizers (p. 214)
Clay	Soil is slow to drain, heavy and difficult to work; surface cracks in dry weather	Improve drainage (p. 210); dig thoroughly (p. 218); add lime (p. 215) and humus (p. 212)
Loam	None	Add humus (p. 212) and fertilizers (p. 214)
Peat	Slow to drain and very acid; lacks nutrients unless drained and limed	Improve drainage (p. 210) and add lime (p. 215)

Plants for sandy and clay soils

Once you have ascertained what type of soil you have, you will need to choose plants that suit these conditions. Certain plants, including those listed below, prefer a light, free-draining soil and will do particularly well on sandy soils, although you may have to add well-rotted compost or manure to improve moisture retention. Clay soils can be heavy and difficult to work but there are many plants that will grow well in this type of soil. Despite its problems, it is full of much-needed nutrients and holds water well, making it ideal for the plants listed.

Plants for sandy soil

Trees	**Shrubs**	**Perennials**
Cercis siliquastrum	*Brachyglottis*	*Agapanthus*
Crataegus	*Calluna*	*Alchemilla*
Gleditsia	*Cistus*	*Anthemis*
Laburnum	*Coronilla*	*Centranthus*
	Cytisus	*Echinops*
	Eucalyptus	*Eryngium*
	Fuchsia	*Kniphofia*
	Gaultheria	*Lupinus*
	Genista	*Lychnis*
	Hebe	*Monarda*
	Helianthemum	*Papaver*
	Lonicera	*Scabiosa*
	Potentilla	*Verbascum*

Gleditsia triacanthos

Plants for clay soil

Trees	**Shrubs**	**Perennials**
Fraxinus	*Aronia*	
Laburnum	*Aucuba*	*Bergenia*
Malus	*Buddleja*	*Campanula*
Populus	*Chaenomeles*	*Delphinium*
	Corylus	*Geranium*
	Escallonia	*Gypsophila*
	Euonymus	*Helenium*
	Ligustrum	*Hemerocallis*
	Mahonia	*Ligularia*
	Philadelphus	*Persicaria*
	Pyracantha	*Phlox*
	Ribes	*Ranunculus*
	Spiraea	*Rudbeckia*
	Viburnum	*Solidago*
		Thalictrum

Helenium 'Gartensonne'

The chemical balance

The degree of acidity or alkalinity (the pH) of the soil affects the type of plants that you can grow. Although most plants will grow in soil with a wide range of pH values, certain plants have specific requirements. If your soil is extremely acidic or alkaline, you will have problems and it may be necessary to make some effort to alter the natural balance.

You can easily test your soil to check its natural acid/alkaline balance using a soil-testing kit (see right). The pH level can vary significantly within a given plot, so when testing take samples from different areas within the garden.

Soil pH

Soil acidity and alkalinity are measured on a scale of pH ranging from 0 to 14. A pH below 7 indicates acid soil, and above 7 is alkaline. A pH of 7 is neutral. Between 5.5 and 7.5 suits most plants.

Maintaining soil pH

Cultivated ground tends to become more acidic, which can be corrected by adding lime. Make sure that it is necessary, as applying too much can be harmful. Follow the instructions given for quantities for different soil types. Do not apply lime and manure together because the nutritional value of manure is depleted by chemical reaction.

Growing mediums

If you happen to have alkaline soil, and a particular desire to grow acid-loving plants such as rhododendrons, camellias or heathers, the best way to do this is to grow them in containers using a specially formulated growing medium.

This growing mix would be impractical and much too expensive to use over a large area, but it does allow you to grow a few favourite specimens either in individual containers or in a raised bed. These specially formulated mixes for acid-loving plants are often labelled 'ericaceous' (for heathers) or rhododendron mixes, and are usually based on peat rather than soil.

Bear in mind, however, that if your tapwater contains lime, you may need to use an acid fertilizer from time to time in order to correct the soil balance (see p. 214).

Testing the pH of your soil

Simple pH testing kits are widely available in garden centres. They are very easy to use and enable you to pinpoint exactly where your soil lies in the pH range.

Read the results of your testing against the card provided with the soil-testing kit for an accurate indication of pH. When testing your soil take samples from various areas of the garden because the pH level can vary. If you have a new garden to cultivate it is a good idea to test the soil before you buy any plants.

1 *Using a pipette, put some of the soil solution in the smaller compartment of a soil-testing kit. Shake the solution and let it settle.*

2 *Using the colour chart provided with the testing kit check the colour of the solution to determine the pH level of your soil.*

Sample pH readings

Acid soil
If testing results in a yellow or orange colour it indicates an acid soil.

Neutral soil
If testing results in a pale green colour it reveals that the soil is neutral.

Alkaline soil
If testing results in a dark green/blue colour it shows that the soil is alkaline.

Plants for acid or alkaline soils

Most plants are not fussy about pH values and grow well in a wide range of soils. There are exceptions: rhododendrons and many heathers, for example, only flourish in acid soils. Before buying plants check whether your soil is acid or alkaline and which plants grow best in such soil. Although it is possible, in a minor way to adjust the balance by adding lime or peat, major changes are out of the question and you will always get the healthiest plants by buying those that suit your conditions. It is very difficult to grow lime-loving plants on acid soil and almost impossible to grow lime-hating plants on alkaline soil. However, you can grow both types of plants in containers or raised beds. A selection of the most popular acid-loving and alkali-loving plants is listed below.

Pieris 'Forest Flame'

Plants for acid soil

Acer palmatum
Camellia japonica
Cercidiphyllum japonicum
Cornus kousa
Epimedium grandiflorum
Kalmia latifolia
Liquidambar styraciflua
Pieris japonica
Rhododendron

Brunnera macrophylla

Plants for alkaline soil

Anchusa azurea
Aquilegia vulgaris
Brunnera macrophylla
Kolkwitzia amabalis
Lonicera periclymenum
Morus nigra
Phlomis fruticosa
Syringa microphylla
Verbascum phoeniceum

Drainage

Well-drained soil allows a good supply of air and water to reach the roots of plants. As a result strong, healthy roots are developed that can extract water at a lower depth in the soil, helping plants to survive in dry conditions. In well-drained soil, too, the sun can warm the ground more quickly, making it possible to plant and sow earlier in the year.

On badly drained soil, root growth is restricted and plants develop shallow root systems that are unable to reach water in a drought. In wet weather the ground becomes waterlogged and roots die through lack of air.

Alpine plants

A gravel mulch improves drainage and retains heat well. It is ideal around alpine plants which need a free-draining environment.

Draining the ground

If the drainage problem is not too serious, adding generous quantities of organic matter, such as well-rotted compost, straw or leaf mould improves the texture of the soil and aids drainage. On very heavy, clay soils, digging in large amounts of coarse grit also helps drainage.

If the drainage problem is one of surface water, slope the soil to produce a slight fall, allowing water to run away into drains or ditches. Another option is to grow crops in raised beds or ridges to keep the roots drier. The water can be channelled away in the bottom of the ridge.

If the water table is too close to the surface you may have to install a system of drainpipes, probably with the help of a specialist contractor. Perforated plastic pipes or tile drains are usually arranged in a herringbone pattern, on a layer of gravel, in trenches about 60-75cm (24-30in) deep. Slope the trenches gently towards the lowest point in the garden. On sloping ground lay the pipes parallel to the surface. Place a layer of ash or gravel over the pipes before filling the trench, to intercept the water in the soil and direct it towards the pipes. If there is no natural outlet, such as a ditch or stream, it may be necessary to construct a soakaway (a gravel-filled pit).

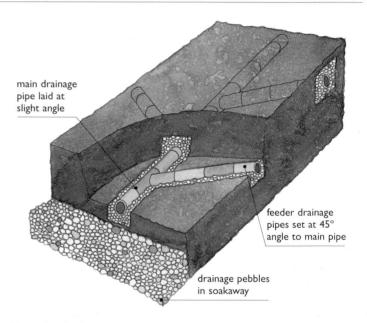

main drainage pipe laid at slight angle

feeder drainage pipes set at 45° angle to main pipe

drainage pebbles in soakaway

Simple drainage system

A herringbone pattern of drainpipes laid in gravel-filled trenches carries away excess water. The branch drains feed into the main drain which carries away the water to an outlet or a soakaway pit.

Testing for drainage

Installing a drainage system is hard work and can be very expensive, so it is well worth testing the soil first to gauge the extent of the problem.

The best and easiest test to carry out is to dig a hole about 60cm (24in) deep. Leave the hole exposed until after a period of heavy rain and then observe how high the water level within the hole rises and, in particular, how long it takes for the rainwater to drain away again. The chart (right) will help you to determine whether any action needs to be taken and recommends the best way to improve the drainage in your garden.

Another simple way of detecting bad drainage is to look closely at the colour of the soil in the hole, particularly in the lower levels. If the soil is a bluish-grey colour with small rusty-brown marks this is a sure sign of very poor drainage.

Drainage	Signs	Action
Good	No water in hole a few days after rain	None
Poor	Some water at bottom of hole a few days after rain	Double dig and add organic material
Excessive	No water in hole 1 hour after rain	Add humus
Impeded	Hole still partly full a few days after rain	Dig in organic material and/or install drains

Mulches

A significant amount of moisture is lost by water evaporating from the soil surface into the atmosphere. This can be a major problem for shallow-rooted plants. Covering the soil with a suitable material – a mulch – drastically reduces moisture loss and will also suppress weeds that compete with your garden plants for water. The open texture of some mulching materials can help to improve surface drainage as well. Always apply the mulch to damp soil, otherwise you reduce the amount of rain reaching the soil. A good time to mulch is after the spring rain when the ground has warmed up.

Inorganic mulches

These mulches (especially plastic sheeting) are extremely effective for conserving moisture.

This continuous 'blanket' over the soil acts as a barrier and also blocks out the light, which prevents weed seeds from germinating. The main disadvantage of such mulches is that they look rather unattractive. To improve the appearance, disguise sheeting by covering it with a shallow layer (2–3cm, or 1in) of composted bark or shingle.

By protecting sheeting from the sun in this way you will also help to extend its working life.

Fibre fleece
A lightweight mulch that raises soil temperatures.

Woven black plastic
Good between vegetable rows Expensive, but re-usable.

Plants in inorganic mulch
Plants benefit from soil-moisture retention and weed supression but gain nothing of nutrional value.

Black plastic
A cheap mulch that is effective at killing weeds and slightly raising the temperature of the soil.

Grit
Useful for plants which need free drainage. Plants self-seed in it if it is not used over plastic sheets.

Pebbles
Useful for absorbing the ambient heat and conserving soil moisture.

Organic mulches

To be totally effective, mulches should be 10cm (4in) thick to form a complete ground cover. Some of these mulches, such as coarsely shredded bark and leaf mould, will help to improve surface drainage.

Over a period of time some organic mulches will gradually improve the fertility of the soil as they decompose and become incorporated into its upper layers. The soil environment around the roots will also improve as this organic layer will encourage the activity of bacteria and worms.

Unfortunately the mulch may get scattered from time to time as birds forage for the worms. The heavier the mulch type, the less likely it is to become scattered by birds or wind.

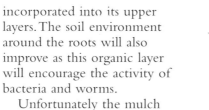
Wood chippings
An effective weed suppressor. With a small electric chipper you can shred your own prunings.

Farmyard manure
Very valuable for enriching the fertility of the soil, it should only be used when it is well-rotted.

Plants in organic mulch
As well as moisture retention and weed suppression, benefits include added nutrients and worm activity.

Cacao fibre
This is fairly slow to break down, as well as expensive, so reserve it for use on your flower borders.

Coarse bark
Larger pieces of bark are longer lasting but expensive. Use them in ornamental borders.

Leaf mould
Good for protecting plants in winter and improving soil drainage. Needs topping up.

Improving your soil

Humus is essential to healthy soil, helping it to sustain plant growth. It consists of well-decayed organic matter, rich in beneficial micro-organisms. By adding humus on a regular basis, you improve drainage of heavy soils and increase the water retention of lighter ones. It promotes air flow through the soil, by improving texture, and as well as feeding plants, it stimulates beneficial bacteria and micro-organisms. These break down the nutrients in the soil to make them more accessible to plants. The end result of regular applications of humus is a more workable and more fertile soil. Humus is a term which is also used to describe partially decomposed, organic matter, such as peat, leaf mould and well-rotted farmyard manure. Producing your own compost from household waste and making leaf mould are both easy ways to provide yourself with ready supplies of humus.

Compost

A compost heap is an inexpensive way of recycling your domestic and garden waste. A properly tended heap accelerates the rotting down of organic matter into valuable, humus-rich compost. Regular applications over the years will make a substantial difference by enriching and improving the structure of all types of soil. Good compost is a rich, dark brown colour and has a light crumbly texture.

For successful compost, do not take large amounts of one specific material, but use each material in small amounts and alternate them in thin layers. Maintain a good supply of air and moisture. Materials decompose more quickly in spring and summer than in autumn or winter.

In summer, compost can be produced in just two to three months, but it could take at least three or four months during winter. You can build your own compost bin or buy one ready-made. If you have space, it is well worth having two bins so that while one heap is decomposing, the already rotted material can be dug in or spread around the garden soil.

Compost heaps

It is best to build a compost heap on level soil, rather than on an impermeable surface such as concrete, so that any rainwater or liquid from the decomposition process drains away freely. Choose a shady, sheltered site to avoid the drying effect of sun and wind.

The bottom layer or 'bed' of the compost heap should consist of a fibrous material such as straw or green hedge clippings, scattered loosely to allow a good flow of air.

Build up the heap in alternating layers of waste materials, ensuring that no single layer of material is too deep and that air can circulate freely. Alternate layers of carbon-rich material, woody fibrous stuff such as wood shavings or bark, about 10cm (4in) deep, with nitrogen-rich layers of green material like annual weeds or cabbage leaves about 20cm (8in) deep. (See opposite for compost materials). No layer should be solidly packed. Varying fast and slow-rotting materials in this way provides the most rapid rate of decomposition.

A compost primer can be used to accelerate the start of the rotting process. There are several proprietary compost primers, but cheap nitrogenous fertilizers, such as sulphate of ammonia, are just as effective. Adding manure or soil to every third layer of material obtains the best results as these natural additives are plentiful in the bacteria that are essential for breaking down waste.

Keep the heap moist if the weather is dry, adding water when necessary. Keep the top covered with a piece of plastic or old carpet to help retain moisture and reduce the heat loss. Turn the heap after two or three weeks, moving the sides to the middle. This will introduce a fresh supply of air to stimulate bacteria and ensure that the material in the heap composts evenly.

Manure or compost accelerator

Finely shredded prunings

Vegetable waste and leaves

Straw and hedge clippings

Layering compost
Alternate nitrogen-rich material, which decays quickly, with layers of carbon-rich waste, which decomposes slowly. Add compost primer to accelerate the rotting process.

Compost bins
A wide range of containers in different shapes and sizes and constructed from various materials can be bought ready-made. It is relatively easy, however, to make your own bin.

The most important factor is to ensure that the bin has a good air flow to promote rapid decomposition of the contents. The main purpose of the bin walls is to hold the composting material in place and keep it tidy. But the bonus of a container is that the compost remains moist at its edges rather than drying out.

For small gardens, a purpose-built compost bin is not necessary; black plastic sacks with holes made in the sides provide a satisfactory environment for composting leaves and garden waste.

Compost covers
Cover compost to conserve essential heat and to stop it from drying out. The plastic bin comes with its own lid while the wooden bins use a layer of carpet and a sheet of clear plastic.

Mulched border
Plants, such as hostas (left), that prefer rich, moist soil will greatly benefit from well-mulched soil, which helps to retain moisture while also adding nutrients.

Healthy harvest
Adding home-made compost to the soil on a regular basis is a cheap way of ensuring a supply of healthy herbs and vegetables from a fertile, productive soil.

Compost materials
Most vegetable material from the garden and kitchen will rot down and be suitable for making compost, provided it is not contaminated with chemicals or diseased.

Suitable materials
✓ Soft pruning and hedge clippings.
✓ Fallen leaves or flowers.
✓ Annual weeds, but not those that are seeding.
✓ Straw and sawdust.
✓ Torn newspapers and egg boxes, soaked in water.
✓ Vegetables and household waste; peelings, tea leaves, coffee grounds, egg shells etc.

Unsuitable materials
✗ Animal remains; encourages scavengers such as mice, rats and foxes.
✗ Cooked and greasy food; also encourages scavengers.
✗ Grass clippings; unless they are added in thin layers. Never use clippings from the first cut after applying selective 'hormone'

weedkillers. These are very persistent chemicals, which may harm plants up to two years after they are used
✗ Woody material; unless it has first been thoroughly shredded.
✗ Badly diseased plants, such as potatoes infected with eelworm or cabbages suffering from clubroot.
✗ Perennial weeds that are flowering or any perennial weed roots.

Shredder
A shredder is very useful for chopping prunings into compostable material.

Leaf mould

This material is an excellent source of humus and a valuable soil conditioner. Decaying leaves contain relatively low levels of nutrients and are essentially a source of bulky, organic matter. Dig decayed leaf mould into the soil, or use it as a mulch. Beech and oak leaves decompose faster than other deciduous leaves and provide a generally acid compost, ideal for mulching acid-loving plants, such as rhododendrons and camellias.

Gathering leaves
Autumn leaves are a valuable source of bulky organic matter. Rake them up and stack them in a wire net cage or in a perforated black plastic bag. Use them to condition the soil a year later.

Plant foods

To grow well, plants need a balanced diet of nutrients. Nitrogen, phosphorous and potassium are the foods plants must have in large amounts to sustain a good growth rate. Nitrogen is needed for healthy growth and leaves, phosphorus is essential for good root development and potassium ensures both healthy flowers and fruits, and disease resistance.

As a gardener, you should supply your plants with these nutrients in various forms depending on the circumstances. Some forms are particularly useful for conditioning the soil, others for supplying a direct source of food to the plant itself. Quantities of nutrients required depend on how intensively the garden is cultivated: closely packed vegetables require a great deal; shrub borders much less. Fertilizers contain plant nutrients in a concentrated form and are used in fairly small quantities. Manures are bulky and need to be added to the soil in large amounts – but they provide only a small quantity of nutrients. However, they do add valuable fibre, which is converted into humus to condition the soil. This also increases the activity of beneficial micro-organisms.

Fertilizers

These may be organic or inorganic in their origin. **Organic fertilizers** consist of dead plant or animal matter that has been processed, such as bonemeal, dried blood and fishmeal. They do not scorch foliage and are natural products. **Inorganic fertilizers**, also known as artificial, chemical or synthetic fertilizers, are derived from mineral deposits or manufactured by an industrial process. These are highly concentrated and faster-acting than organic types, but do not exceed the dosage, or plants may be scorched or damaged. Fertilizers can be applied in dried form or dissolved in water, as in liquid feed.

Soil conditioners

Digging in quantities of bulky, organic matter introduces both nutrients and fibre into a garden soil. Green vegetation and manures with animal content provide some nutrients almost immediately, but very little fibre.

Woody and fibrous material is much better for opening heavy soils and improving the soil structure. It provides materials that improve moisture retention on lighter soils. Fibrous conditioners of this kind are ideal if long-term soil improvement is the ultimate aim. When they decompose they contribute to the formation of humus which absorbs other nutrients applied to the soil, apart from home-made garden compost and the different types of animal manures. Lime, while not a food, is also used to condition the soil. Never apply lime to the soil at the same time as fertilizers and manures.

Composting animal manure
Animal manure is one of the best soil conditioners because it improves soil texture and provides some nutrients while the straw provides bulk. Compost manure for at least six months, preferably for up to a year.

Green manure
Organic matter can be added to the soil by growing a fast-maturing crop as temporary ground cover, on a bed that is empty for a while, usually over the winter. The crop is dug into the top soil six to eight weeks after germinating. This fast-maturing crop is known as a green manure and it is a means of improving both organic matter and nitrogen levels. The release of nitrogen is quite swift and so provides an early boost to plant growth. The greener and younger the manure, the less fibre is produced. Green manure crops should not be allowed time to flower or to set seed.

A green manure returns more to the ground than it has taken out, and eventually forms humus within the soil. Green plants with a rapid growth rate that mature quickly are the most popular green manure crops. Legumes are especially valuable, as they are able to fix atmospheric nitrogen.

Plants that are worth sowing include, for example, borage, comfrey, mustard, red clover and ryegrass.

1 *Mustard* (Sinapis alba) *is a useful green manure. Cut down the crop just before it flowers and leave cuttings on the surface to rot down.*

2 *Incorporate the cut foliage into the top few centimetres of soil with a spade or cultivator. The green leaf will decompose rapidly, thus improving soil fertility.*

Dry fertilizers

These are nutrients in a dry, solid form – granules and pellets. They are mixed together and coated with a wax or resin compound which slowly dissolves and releases fertilizers into the soil. The release can take from six to 18 months, depending on the thickness of the outer coating, soil moisture, temperature and pH. Apply these fertilizers by sprinkling them evenly over the soil and mixing them into the top layer with a fork. If the soil is dry, water the area after application to dissolve the fertilizer and wash it down to the root zone. An even distribution is essential as damage to plants may occur if too much is used. Mark out the area into squares with canes and garden lines, as shown.

Liquid fertilizers

Liquid is usually easier and safer to apply than dry fertilizer, and the plant's response is often more rapid. The concentrated fertilizer can be bought either as liquid or powder which is diluted in water. It is applied either to the soil or to the leaves, depending on the type. Mix the fertilizer thoroughly with the water before application, to reduce the chance of damaging the plants. Do not apply when rain is forecast or it may be washed through the soil away from the plant's roots.

Nutrients applied to leaves as a foliar feed work rapidly and can be directed to specific areas. This is useful for plants with damaged roots, or if the soil is very dry. Apply foliar feed early in the day or when cloudy to avoid sun scorching the sprayed leaves.

Applying lawn fertilizer
Because fertilizers are heavily concentrated it is important to apply exactly the measured amount to a marked out area.

Applying plant fertilizer
Always apply fertilizer evenly, following the instructions given. Avoid touching the foliage as fertilizer can scorch plant leaves.

1 *Dilute liquid fertilizers with water and apply with a watering can or a hosepipe. These fast-acting feeds are useful for correcting nutritional deficiencies.*

2 *Apply liquid fertilizers as a foliar feed, or directly to the soil around the base of a plant. Most foliar feeds are soil-acting so any run-off is absorbed by the roots.*

Feeding container-grown plants

To promote balanced and healthy growth, use proprietary composts that contain measured amounts of fertilizer.

Additional feeds can be given if necessary by applying quick-acting fertilizers as a top dressing, or by using foliar feed or fertilizer spikes.

Fertilizer spikes
These spikes release their nutrients gradually into the compost. Insert them according to manufacturers' instructions.

Applying fertilizers

Type	Purpose and speed of absorption	How and when to apply	How much
Bulky organic matter (manure and compost)	Slow-acting – adds nutrients and fibre to the soil; more quickly absorbed in warm than cold soil	Dig well into the soil every autumn or winter	5kg/sq m (11lb/sq yd)
Concentrated organic fertilizer (bonemeal, dried blood, fishmeal, poultry manure, wood ash etc.)	Same purpose and speed of absorption as bulky organic matter but is more intensive and contains very little fibre	As a base dressing, dig into soil before planting in winter or spring, or apply as a top-dressing around plants at any time	50-200g/sq m (2-8oz/sq yd)
Inorganic fertilizer	Mainly quick-acting; highly concentrated source of nutrients	**Granular and powdered forms:** as a base dressing dig into soil at planting time; as a topdressing apply once a year (generally in spring but check instructions) **Liquid forms:** as a foliar feed apply regularly in growing season	15-30g/sq m ($\frac{1}{2}$-1oz/sq yd)
Hydrated or garden lime	Slow-acting; improves texture of heavy soil; corrects soil acidity	As a topdressing apply after digging, in autumn	450g/sq m (1lb/sq yd)

Watering

Water is essential for all plant growth, although some plants have adapted to drought conditions – cacti and succulents, for example, survive for many months on little water. If you live in a climate with low rainfall it is important to choose plants that will tolerate dry conditions, unless you are able to spend time and thought on watering systems. Roof gardens and other sites exposed to drying winds increase the watering needs of your plants.

A variety of watering systems and devices are available to help you, notably drip-watering systems and water-retaining granules. It is best to water at dawn or dusk when the sun's rays are less powerful and the evaporation rate is much reduced. To encourage deep roots to develop, water thoroughly and regularly rather than little and more often, especially when watering lawns.

Watering plants grown in a raised bed
Plants grown in raised beds or containers need more watering. Choose drought-tolerant plants that grow best in free-draining soils.

Easy-watering systems

In any garden, easy access to water is imperative. An outdoor garden tap is vital, unless the kitchen tap is easily accessible. Also essential is a hosepipe long enough to reach the furthest corners of the garden.

In times of drought, however, water may be rationed and you may well have to recycle washing water from the house. Installing a water butt to collect run-off rainwater is a sensible precaution. Large areas of grass are particularly vulnerable to drought, and although sprinkler systems can be installed to aid watering, you may well find that at the very time your lawn needs water most, you are banned from using watering equipment!

There are some simple systems available which deliver water to the garden, as needed, at the flick of a switch. If you have a small garden in a warm climate, or if you garden on an exposed

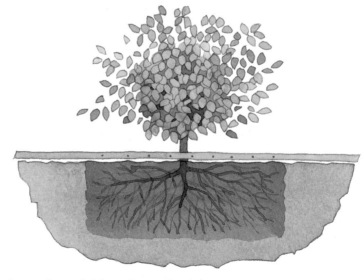

A seephose laid under a shrub
The diagram above shows the benefits of a seephose. You can see how the water is concentrated directly in the root area, with no wastage.

site, such as a roof terrace, consider planning a seephose or drip-feed system, which can be laid permanently in the planting areas.

Drip-feed systems
This consists of a series of fine bore pipes, with drip heads at intervals, that you can position exactly where water is required – at the foot of plants needing frequent watering, for example. A soil-moisture detector can be fitted to the system, ensuring that the automatic system is overridden if the ground is sufficiently damp. Drip-feed systems tend to get blocked

with debris, so it is important to clean the system regularly.

Seephose system
This is useful for watering large areas, such as lawns, or for rows of vegetables. It is an efficient way of using water because it is directed straight at the roots. The hose is punctured with a series of fine holes so that a regular, even supply of water is delivered over the length of the hose. A similar system uses a porous hosepipe. The system can be buried beneath the soil to make it both permanent and unobtrusive.

Water take-up
A regular supply of water must reach a plant's roots. Here a drip feed delivers a steady flow.

How to water containers

Plants in containers lose water very rapidly through evaporation. Terracotta pots especially are notoriously poor at retaining moisture. Hanging baskets, with their small amount of soil and large area exposed to the elements, are very greedy for water and may well need watering once a day in hot weather.

Group containers together to preserve moisture, and have them in shade in hot weather.

Watering the root base
To make sure water penetrates the compost, make a few holes around the edge of the pot with a cane before watering.

Reviving a wilting plant
If a plant is wilting from lack of water, plunge it into a bowl of water so that the pot is covered. Leave it until air bubbles subside.

Watering hanging baskets
To make watering high-level hanging baskets easier, attach a cane to the end of a hose to create a rigid, elongated spout.

Retaining moisture

A major difficulty with growing plants in containers is keeping the plants supplied with water, especially when using loamless composts as these are very difficult to re-wet after drying out. To overcome this, add granules of polymer to the compost. When wetted, these granules swell to form a moisture-retaining gel which can hold vast amounts of water. The water is gradually released into the compost.

1 *When planting, add polymer granules to the compost to help hold in water.*

2 *Water so that granules swell, then add remaining compost before planting up as usual.*

Making the most of water

There are various ways to reduce the need for watering. First and foremost, you need to increase the moisture-retaining properties of the soil, if it is sandy, by adding plenty of organic matter. Secondly, you need to reduce the amount of water lost through evaporation, by screening your plants from the effects of drying winds.

Grouping plants together helps to reduce evaporation, as does using pebbles or stones over the soil surface. Containers, in particular, benefit from having the surface covered with pebbles, and from standing close together on a pebble surface. To keep plants moist, stand the container on a bed of pebbles in a tray of water.

Gravel base
To reduce moisture loss, stand the plants on moist pebbles.

Drought-resistant plants

If you live in a very dry climate with free-draining soil, you need to make sure your plants are as drought-resistant as possible, to give the plants the best chance of success and to save you from spending a great deal of time watering. Generally speaking, apart from those succulent plants which store water in their tissue (either in their leaves or stem), plants that are tolerant of drought can be recognized by their foliage. It is usually silvery-grey, finely divided and sometimes covered in fine hairs or felt, all of which reduce evaporation. The following plants are all happy in dry conditions.

Agapanthus spp.
Agave spp.
Aloe spp.
Artemisia spp.
Buddleja davidii
Buxus sempervirens
Campsis radicans
Clivia miniata
Convolvulus cneorum
Crassula spp.
Cynara cardunculus
Eryngium giganteum

Hedera spp.
Lavandula angustifolia
L. spica
Pelargonium species and
   cultivars
Phormium tenax
Sedum spp.
Sempervivum spp.
Brachyglottis greyi (*Senecio
   greyi*)
Stachys lanata
Verbascum bonariensis

Agave utahensis

Digging

When you dig, you are creating better growing conditions for your plants. Digging opens up the soil and lets in air, which allows organic matter to break down more easily and release nutrients. It also improves drainage and encourages plants to form deeper root systems. As you dig, you have the opportunity to add manure or compost to the soil and to remove perennial weeds, or to bury annual weeds and other plant debris. All will add nutrients to the soil.

As a general rule, autumn is the best time to dig, especially if you are working on a heavy, clay soil. At this time of year the soil should be perfect for cultivation, neither too wet nor too hard. Leave the soil roughly dug over the winter months, so that the frost and rain can break down the larger clods of earth and improve the soil texture. Never dig the ground when it is frozen or waterlogged, as this severely damages the soil structure.

There are three different digging techniques. In **simple digging** a spadeful of soil is lifted and inverted as it is dropped back into its original position. In **single digging** the soil is cultivated to the depth of one spade, using a trench system, and in **double digging** the soil is cultivated to the depth of two spades, again working across a plot that has been divided into trenches.

Simple digging

This is the easiest and quickest method, good for clearing shallow-rooted weeds and creating a fine layer of soil on the surface. It is useful when digging in confined spaces and around mature, established plants.

No trench system is involved. Just lift a spadeful of soil and turn it over before dropping it back into its original position. Then break up the soil with the spade, in a brisk, chopping action.

When the ground has been thoroughly dug, leave it for at least three weeks before any planting or seed sowing is carried out. This will allow the soil plenty of time to settle and should be long enough for any buried weeds to be killed. The surface of the soil will start to disintegrate and separate into smaller clods as it is broken down by the various actions of the weather. This will make it much easier to create a fine tilth, with the aid of a fork and a rake.

Using a fork

If the soil is particularly heavy and difficult to penetrate with a spade, it may be easier to use a fork because the soil does not stick to the prongs in the same way that it does to a blade. Fork tines are ideal for breaking down the soil to a finer tilth, and teasing out unwanted plant roots and debris. However, in normal conditions, a spade is better for slicing through the soil and cutting through weeds.

Forking out weeds
A fork is ideal for removing deep-rooted, perennial weeds.

How to dig
Many people dig incorrectly, with the result that the soil is not properly cultivated and they risk back injury.

It is essential to to adopt the correct posture and to use tools that are the right size and comfortable.

In the winter, make sure you are suitably dressed, as cold muscles are prone to injury. Do not dig too hard or too long on the first occasion, and plan the order of work (see opposite).

1 *Insert the spade, vertically, into the soil, with one foot pressing on the blade. Make sure that the handle of the spade is sloping slightly away from you.*

2 *Pull the handle towards you, slide your left hand down the shaft of the spade and bend your knees, slightly, for correct balance, before starting to lever out the soil.*

3 *Lift the soil onto the spade gradually, straightening your legs so that they take the weight and your back is not strained. Work rhythmically and do not lift too much at one time.*

Order of digging

Approach digging work systematically. Mark out the area to be dug with a taut garden line. Move the soil from the first trench to the end of the plot, ready to fill the final trench. Then fill each trench with soil from the next trench to be dug. If the plot seems too big, divide it in half and work each half in turn. This method avoids any unnecessary handling of the soil, which could compact it and possibly damage its structure.

Sequence of work
Work across and then down the plot, as here, so that all of the ground is thoroughly dug.

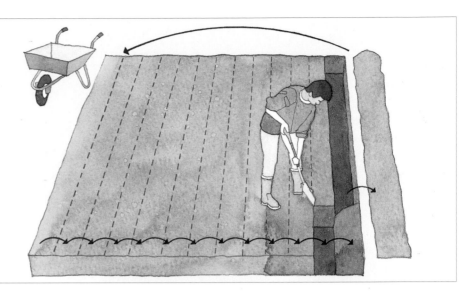

Single digging

This method ensures that an area of ground is thoroughly dug to a consistent depth.

Single digging is usually done with a spade but with heavier soils, a fork can be used. The soil is cultivated to one spade's (or fork's) depth by digging progressive trenches across a plot.

First mark out a trench with a garden line. Dig a trench about 30cm (12in) wide and move the soil from this first trench to the opposite end of the plot. Facing the trench that has already been dug, dig a second trench and use the soil from this trench to fill in the first trench. Twist the spade or fork a little when putting the soil into the first trench so that the upper layers of the soil, and any weeds, fall to the bottom of the first trench.

Repeat the process down the plot. When the final trench is reached, it is filled with soil from the first trench. You can add manure or compost as you dig. Spread the manure around the trench and then fork it well into the soil.

Digging trenches
Mark out the plot with garden lines. Dig trenches about 30cm (12in) wide and to the depth of the spade or fork.

Filling trenches
Fill in each trench with the soil from the previous trench. For the last trench, use soil removed from the first.

Double digging

This is the deepest method of cultivation, and improves drainage by breaking up any hard pan which has formed in the lower levels of the soil. The trenches are twice as wide as for single digging and a spade and a fork are used.

Order of digging

How to double dig
First mark out, with a garden line, the area to be dug, as with single digging.
• Using the spade, dig a trench approximately 60cm (2ft) wide and the depth of the spade. Then remove the soil to the opposite end of the digging area, ready to fill in the final trench.
• Stand in the newly dug trench and break up the bottom soil, using a fork to the depth of its tines (see right). This cultivates the soil to a depth of about 50cm (20in). At this stage, add compost or manure, if required, and fork it into the soil.
• Mark out another trench, parallel to the first one. It is important to get these measurements accurate and have each trench about the same size. They need to be roughly equal so that the same amount of soil is moved from trench to trench and the ground is kept roughly level. To make this easier, turn, so that you are digging across the trench, and divide it into three sections.
• Dig the second trench, filling the first trench with the soil you have just excavated. Fork the bottom of the trench, as before, and continue to the next trench. Proceed in this way, methodically, across the plot. When you reach the final trench, fill it with the soil dug from the first trench.

Double digging
Stand in each trench that has been dug and, using a fork to the full depth of its tines, break up the lower levels of soil to an overall depth of 50cm (20in). This will improve drainage.

Weed control

A weed is any plant growing in a place where it is not wanted. Many cause problems just because they are so tough and versatile that they can adapt to a wide range of growing conditions. For this reason they must always be dealt with before they get out of control. Weeds compete directly with your garden plants for light, nutrients and water. They can also act as hosts to pests and diseases, which can spread as the season progresses. Groundsel, for instance, often harbours the fungal diseases rust and mildew, and sap-sucking greenfly. Chickweed meanwhile, plays host to red spider mite and whitefly.

Gravel mulch
Covering the soil with a mulch such as gravel will block out light and prevent weed seeds from germinating.

Perennial weeds

Digging up perennial weeds is an effective disposal system, provided that every bit of the root system is removed from the soil. If only a few weeds are present, try digging them out with a knife or trowel, but you must remove the top 5cm (2in) of root close to the surface, to prevent the weed re-growing. This method can be used in the lawn to get rid of individual or small patches of weeds, and is a reliable means of eradicating weeds growing close to garden plants. In this situation, often no other weed control method would be effective without risking damage to plants growing nearby.

Digging up perennials
Some perennial weeds, such as dandelions, have very long and tenacious roots. When digging them out, be sure to remove the whole root, or they will reappear.

Clearing weeds
The simplest way to deal with weeds is to remove them physically, either by pulling or digging them out or, if they are small, hoeing them off at soil level.

The biggest problem with this method of control is that most weed seeds require exposure to light before they will germinate. Often, when weeding disturbs the soil, more air is allowed into the surface layers and an ideal seedbed is created. Although the existing weed seedlings are destroyed, the weed growth cycle starts all over again. This problem is often worse when using rotary cultivators because they leave the surface layers of soil light and fluffy, making a perfect seedbed. Perennial weeds are increased, too, because they are chopped into pieces, each capable of growing.

The most effective way to clear weeds, especially established perennials, is to use a combination of cultural and chemical methods. Spray weeds in full growth with a chemical weedkiller and, as they start to die, bury them when the area is dug over. When the new weed seedlings germinate, spray them with a chemical (see right) while they are most vulnerable.

Annual weeds

Clearing annual weeds with a hoe is quick and effective, but the timing is important. The hoeing must be done when the weeds are tiny and before they start producing seed.

Hoeing will sever the stems of young weeds from the root system just below

Hoeing annuals
Hoeing on a regular basis, when weeds are still small and have not set seed, is a very quick and efficient method of weed control.

soil level. This both prevents the stem from forming new roots and stops the roots from producing a new stem. When hoeing, make sure you always walk backwards to avoid treading weeds back into the soil.

There is an old saying, 'One year's seeds make seven years' weeds', which has now been endorsed by scientific research and proved to be remarkably accurate, unfortunately for gardeners.

Annual weeds are capable of producing a staggering total of 60,000 viable seeds per square metre, per year. The vast majority of these seeds are found in the uppermost 5cm (2in) of soil, but they will usually germinate only when exposed to sufficient light levels. This is why mulching, which covers the soil and blocks out light, has become such a widely popular method of weed control. The added benefit of mulching is that there is little chance of contaminating the soil with chemical residue.

Mulching for weed control

Mulching is the practice of covering the soil around plants with a layer of material to block out the light and help trap moisture. In today's gardens, where plastics are commonplace, inorganic black plastic sheeting is often chosen. Though not inviting to look at, it can be hidden beneath a thin layer of more attractive organic mulch.

As a general rule, organic mulches provide the bonus of improving the fertility of the soil, but inorganic mulches are more effective because they form a better weed barrier. To be fully effective as a barrier, organic mulches must be applied as a layer at least 10cm (4in) thick. Both organic and inorganic mulches tend to be less effective against established perennial weeds, unless an entire area can be sealed until the weeds have died out and planting is carried out through the mulch while it is in place. One way of clearing weedy ground in summer is to cover the soil with a mulch of clear or white plastic, sealed around the edges. Weeds are gradually killed by a combination of high temperatures and lack of carbon dioxide.

The plastic can be removed and used elsewhere and the treated area is weed-free, ready to plant and cover with an organic mulch, such as shredded bark or gravel.

Black plastic mulch
Onions are planted through a black plastic mulch. This is a very useful and labour-saving method of suppressing weed growth.

Chemical weed control

Any chemical which is used to kill weeds is a herbicide. Herbicides are preferred by some gardeners as a labour-saving alternative to cultural weed control. They are certainly the most effective method of controlling persistent, perennial weeds, once they have become established. When using any type of chemical weedkiller, do not, ever, exceed the recommended dosage and always handle with care. The weedkillers are grouped into three categories according to the way they work.

Contact These are chemicals which are applied to the leaves and stems of weeds, and they will only injure and kill those specific parts. This type of weedkiller is most effective when it is used to control annual weeds, and especially seedlings.

Residual These are 'soil acting' chemicals which are applied to the soil. They may persist in the soil for some months before they are taken up by the roots of the weeds, and the whole weed will slowly die.

Systemic These chemicals are applied to the leaves and stems of the weeds and are absorbed into the weed by being transported through sap. In time, they injure and kill the whole weed. This type of weedkiller is the most effective one for controlling perennial weeds, especially if the weeds are established.

Applying systemic weed killer
Any chemical sprays should be applied in cool, windless weather, when the leaves are dry. Follow instructions on chemical container carefully and always wear recommended protective clothing.

Plant controls

Certain plants may be able combat weeds by competing with them. They need the following characteristics:
• A low, spreading habit, so that the soil surface is shaded.
• Evergreen or coniferous foliage to keep the soil covered in the spring, when most weed seeds germinate.
• A fast growth rate to cover an area as quickly as possible, and outgrow the weeds.
• The adaptability to cope with a range of growing conditions, with very little care and maintenance.

The soil must be weed-free before planting begins.

Ground cover planting
Periwinkle (Vinca) is an ideal ground-cover plant, as it is evergreen, low-growing and does well in shady parts of the garden.

Reclaiming a neglected garden

The treatment used for reclaiming a garden will depend on a number of factors, such as how long the garden has been left uncultivated, how overgrown the area is and whether there are any existing plants that are worth saving.

Where woody perennials such as brambles are the main problem, the best approach is to cut down all the weed vegetation to ground level, in late winter or early spring, in order to stimulate the development of new growth.

When the new growth is about 45cm (18in) high, spray the weeds with a systemic weedkiller, which will quickly be absorbed, through the soft, new leaves and stems, down into the root system. Within six weeks, even the most tenacious of woody, perennial weeds should be dead or severely damaged.

The soil can now be cultivated to remove the dead and dying weeds and to bring the soil back into good condition. For non-woody perennials the treatment is the same, but the weeds can be buried within two weeks of spraying and they will die in the soil.

Use a follow-up spray to kill germinated seedlings.

Supporting plants

Many plants will need help from you, the gardener, to be seen at their best, and in some instances, to prevent them being damaged by strong winds and heavy rainstorms. Support young trees with slender stems for the first couple of years, until they are strong and well established. Usually a stout, wooden support (see opposite) inserted at planting will do the job. Climbers and wall shrubs, depending on their type and their natural clinging abilities, also need some form of tying in, or supporting, with a wooden trellis or a system of wires nailed to the supporting wall. Tall perennials with thin or lax stems, such as delphiniums, or heavy heads of flowers, such as peonies, require some assistance, too. The best way to deal with them is with a wire or brushwood cage, or a surrounding framework of peasticks.

High summer border
A traditional herbaceous border, designed with taller flowers at the back. Many taller plants need support, so stake them while they are still small and accessible. New growth soon obscures the supports.

Types of support

The equipment available for staking is shown below. What you need will depend on the dimensions of the plant you have chosen to grow but, in principle, make sure that the stake is strong enough for its purpose and that the tie allows room for the plant to grow without cutting into the main stem and damaging it. For perennials, ensure that any support is as unobtrusive as possible, so as not to detract from the flowers. Natural wood and green-coloured stakes blend better into planting than brightly coloured plastic ones. To avoid injury, always make sure you cover the ends of bare canes with plastic tops.

Container plants
Container plants need supports that complement them. Bulbs that tend to flop, like daffodils or hyacinths, can be given cages made of natural materials – canes, brushwood or willow stems. Container-grown climbers can twine over small trellis fans, and ivies can be trained on metal hoops to create a form of instant topiary. Wigwams of canes, tied at the top, are ideal for climbing annuals.

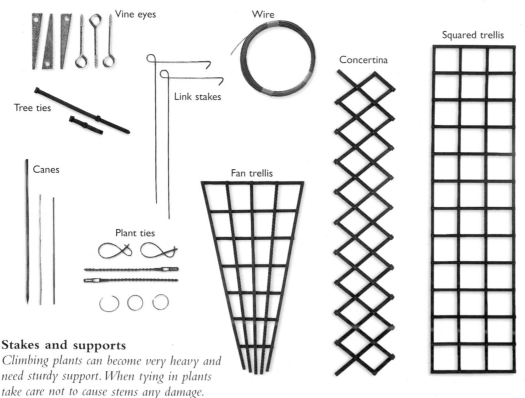

Fan trellis

Stakes and supports
Climbing plants can become very heavy and need sturdy support. When tying in plants take care not to cause stems any damage.

Tree supports

Trees with weak or developing stems may need support until they are well established. A stake, long enough to reach just below the crown, will protect the roots from strong winds. Stake container-grown or rootballed trees at a 45° angle, which clears the rootball, causing no damage. Hammer stakes down so that they penetrate by a third of their overall height.

Young trees
A short stake holds the stem of the tree firmly in the first year.

Older trees
Use a taller stake (to just below the crown) and two ties.

Container-grown trees
Use an angled stake to avoid damaging the rootball.

Supports for climbers

Form dictates the kind of support that will best suit your climbing plants. Those that climb with aerial roots need no help from you, the gardener, as they are self-attaching. Those with twining stems, such as honeysuckle, will need trellis or wires around which their leading shoots can twist, while those that merely scramble will need to be actively tied into an appropriate support.

The support can be unobtrusive or decorative. A wigwam of canes or poles for climbing, flowering annuals like sweet peas, or vegetables like runner beans, can be very eye-catching.

Make sure there is a gap between any wooden support and the surface to which it is attached, to enable air to circulate freely behind the plant, which will help to prevent diseases. Trellis attached to surfaces in need of annual coats of preservative or paint should be hinged at the base. The entire trellis can then be dismounted from the wall once a year, with the plant still *in situ*, and lowered to the ground while the essential maintenance work takes place.

Wires can be strung along, using vine eyes at intervals, leaving a gap of about 5cm (2in) between the wires and the wall. The wire-supporting structure will vary according to the habit of the plant. For fruiting plants that are trained in a fan you will need to have a horizontal wire system to which the branches can be tied at 45cm (18in) intervals.

Tree ties

The best ties are made of thick material that does not cut into the plant's stem, with notches so that it can be let out as the plant's girth increases. A spacer also helps to prevent the tie chafing on the bark. Make sure the tie is secured loosely enough to allow room for growth, and check it every six months to see if it needs releasing.

The tie should be fixed near the top of the stake, ensuring that there is adequate room to prevent chafing.

Supports for perennials and shrubs

Perennial plants vary in how much propping up they need. Tall perennials or shrubs with weak stems will not stay upright without support, and the best systems to use are those that are unobtrusive and loosely support the plant without restricting its growth. To avoid the expense of buying stakes, surround the plant with a low 'fence' of well-branched twigs.

Purpose-made ring stakes are available in various forms. Those that consist of a rigid structure, rather than a clipped one, should be placed in position before the plant is too well-grown, otherwise you risk snapping off any delicate stems.

Trellis support
A natural wood trellis provides support for a Virginia creeper.

Wire support
Horizontal wires attached to a wall support this wisteria.

Link stakes
Metal link stakes can improve the shape of soft-stemmed plants, like this pelargonium.

Twig stakes
Canes and string can be used to train flopping plants with woody stems, like this fuchsia.

Lawns

The lawn is frequently dismissed as merely a flat, green expanse requiring a great deal of work for little reward. However, often the largest single area in the garden, it has an important contribution to make. A healthy, well-maintained lawn makes an attractive area to play or relax in, as well as setting off beds and borders. The most important aspect of lawn care is to grow the appropriate grass for your soil. No amount of care can make a suitable lawn in the wrong situation. When selecting seed, bear in mind the purpose your lawn will serve. An ornamental lawn has fine grass, a child's play area, tougher, hardwearing grasses, and where trees are a focal point in the lawn, the grass needs to be shade-tolerant.

Informal lawn
In large gardens, particularly in orchards, the grass can be much less carefully tended. Tougher meadow grasses are ideal.

Mowing

If you wish to maintain a neat, healthy lawn, regular mowing is very important as it helps the grass to divide and so thicken. Cut little and often, and do not cut more than one-third of a blade in length at any one time. Infrequent mowing allows coarser grass to predominate. Mow most frequently in warm, moist conditions, but keep mowing to a minimum in hot, dry weather. Never allow the grass to grow more than about 4cm (1¹/₂in) long. Cutting too close weakens the grass and produces bare patches, which encourages moss and weeds.

As a rough guide, ornamental lawns should be mown to between 1.5-2cm (¹/₂–³/₄in) to keep the grass growing well. Allow lawns intended for more wear and tear to grow slightly longer, normally to about 2–2.5cm (³/₄–1in) long to enable it to withstand heavy foot traffic.

The choice of mower is largely a matter of personal preference. It does not matter which type of mower you have, provided that the blades are sharp and adjusted to obtain the best cutting action. The striped lawn effect some gardeners prefer is made by the roller on a lawn mower and not by the blades.

In hot, dry weather, raise the height of the cut by about 1.5cm (¹/₂in). This is done to shade the roots and to reduce water evaporation. Remove all grass cuttings, to control pests and disease and discourage worms.

An ornamental lawn
A mown and rollered lawn with fine-leaved grasses does not stand hard wear but looks marvellous.

Mowing over stones
Stones set in a lawn to form a path should be placed below the level of the turf for easy mowing.

Mowing actions
Rotary and hover mowers cut with a scything action, whereas cylinders cut like scissors. The former is useful for informal lawns, the latter for formal, close-cut lawns.

Rotary mower action

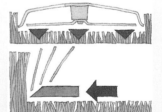

Hover mower action

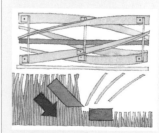

Cylinder mower action

Routine lawn care

If the lawn feels soft and spongy it is probably due to a layer of dead grass clippings – 'thatch' – which has formed on the soil surface. If left, this layer may harbour pests and diseases, as well as weed seeds.

For light layers of thatch, a spring-tine rake is ideal for dragging out the dead material from the soil surface. Remove this waste from the lawn for the raking to be really beneficial. Where thatch has built up to form a thick layer, it is best to scarify the lawn using a spring-tined machine to rip out the dead grass. Set the scarifier up so that the tines penetrate the soil surface and prune the grass roots.

Troublesome lawn weeds are likely to be those with a rosette or spreading habit. Remove them with a sharp knife, or control them with a hormone-type weedkiller applied in spring or autumn.

Moss is encouraged when the grass is growing slowly, usually because of poor drainage and shade. Shading is often caused by leaves lying over the surface in the autumn. This problem is best controlled by raking the lawn vigorously to a depth of 1.5cm (½in) with a fan rake. Always rake from the edges to the centre of the mossy area to help reduce the risk of moss spreading into parts of the lawn which are not affected. Never compost moss, as some may survive and spread again.

Raking up moss
A fan rake is an ideal tool for raking up dead moss and compacted, dead, grass clippings. Rake from the edges to the centre to avoid spreading the moss.

Watering

In an average year, most well-kept lawns only need watering for about two to three months, but occasionally there are dry periods when the soil water reserves are not sufficient. A lawn only needs watering when signs of water stress become visible. The usual signs are grass blades taking on a dull sheen, often with a bluish tint, and footprints that are easy to see as the grass is limp and does not spring back into position. The way in which water is applied is more important than the quantity of water: always ensure the lawn is given a good soaking. Frequent, light applications in dry weather encourages shallow rooting and makes the grass more vulnerable if watering is discontinued. In very dry conditions, it is better to use a slow-running hose to soak the lawn rather than a sprinkler which is not as effective.

Lawn sprinkler
Regular lawn watering is easier with a sprinkler, which needs to be moved to cover larger areas.

Problem solving

Fungal diseases of grasses can cause severe lawn damage. These are worst in autumn when damp conditions tend to favour their development.

A well-maintained lawn can usually withstand most pests and diseases. Surface signs of lawn problems are generally symptoms of grass root problems.

The most common cause of poor growth or disease is grass roots being deprived of oxygen because the soil is compacted and the air pressed out of it. This causes a slow-down in root activity which means the top growth of the lawn becomes weak and unhealthy. Overcome this by aerating the lawn.

Naturalizing a lawn

You may like to try and encourage wild flowers to establish themselves and grow in longer grass, creating more of a meadow than a lawn. Even if you do so, the grass will still need some cutting, roughly speaking about twice each year. A sickle copes better than a mower with longer, woody grass of this sort, and is ideal for cutting grass to 15cm (6in) in autumn.

Using a sickle
Longer grass becomes woody in a naturalized lawn and the easiest way to cut it is to use a sickle.

Lawn repair

Due to the mass of roots beneath grass, it is possible to cut and lift sections of turf and treat them like sections of living carpet. Light damage, such as broken edges to the lawn, can be repaired, quite easily, by cutting out a section of turf that includes the damaged edge and turning it so that the damaged section lies within the lawn. Sow grass seed in the damaged part.

1 *To repair a broken edge, cut out a section of turf including the damaged edge. Slice through the root system of the turf.*

2 *Lift the turf free of the soil. Turn it round and re-lay it so that the damaged edge is in the lawn. Firm the turf into position.*

3 *Fill the hole created by the broken edge with fine soil and sow grass seed. Germination should take 10-14 days.*

Increasing plants

It is both satisfying and economical to create beautiful displays in the garden by growing new plants from seeds and cuttings, or by dividing old, established clumps to form young, healthy plants. Many methods of propagation are very simple, once certain principles are grasped, and they require little equipment. Once you have gained some experience, a simple propagator and a cold frame will allow you to grow wonderful summer bedding displays and a much wider range of plants than is available in the garden centre. An added bonus is that you can easily swap plants with friends and neighbours.

Young chamomile plants
Growing new plants from seed is an easy and inexpensive way to increase plant stocks.

What is propagation?

Propagation is the use of seeds or other parts of living plants to produce more plants. This process can be carried out in two ways – either by seed or vegetatively.

Seed is a sexual method of reproduction where the seed develops following the fertilization of the female part of the plant by male pollen. Vegetative propagation is an asexual method and includes taking cuttings of stem or leaf, dividing rootstock, layering or grafting in order to produce more plants.

Sowing seed is the easiest and most reliable method of producing large numbers of plants quickly. Plants grown from seed are also, generally speaking, healthier and more disease-resistant.

Some plants, however, do not produce viable seed. The seeds may take a long time to reach flowering age, or do not breed true, which means that the seedlings can differ greatly from the parent plant in form, habit and flower colour. This variation allows many new and improved plants to be produced. However, in cases where an exact replica of the parent plant is desired, for instance, in the propagation of especially fine forms of plants or of variegated plants, a vegetative method of propagation is used. This is the only way to be sure that any plant produced is identical in all its features to the parent plant.

Choosing suitable plant material

Always choose cuttings or collect seed from the strongest and heathiest plants available to give the best possible chance of successful propagation. Poor plants provide inferior material, and are rarely transformed into sturdy, new plants.

Seed
Choose the best-formed fruits or seedheads and be aware that timing is critical when collecting seed. If you leave it too late, the seed will already have been dispersed, and if you gather seeds too early, they will not germinate. Gather seed on a dry day and if there is any dampness put them in the sun to dry thoroughly. If you are not sowing them immediately, store them in a cool, dry place out of direct sunlight. If you are buying in seed, select packets which are undamaged and which have the most recent datestamp, as old seed does not germinate so well.

Cuttings
Take cuttings from thriving plants and discard any thin, weak shoots. It is best to choose non-flowering shoots, as these regenerate more readily than older or flowering shoots. If you have to take cuttings of flowering stems, remove any flowers so that all the energy goes into producing roots. Choose shoots from the current year's growth, as this is the most vigorous plant material.

Collecting seeds
Hang thoroughly dry seedheads in a plastic bag to collect seeds.

Taking cuttings
Choose only strong, healthy shoots for making cuttings.

Encouraging root formation
Hormone rooting powder can be used on the cut surface of a cutting to promote root development. There are varying strengths to suit different types of cutting. Follow the manufacturer's instructions.

Rooting powder
Dip only the cut ends of the cuttings in hormone powder before planting.

The propagation environment

Creating the right environment is the key to producing new plants. During propagation, plants are extremely vulnerable. It is therefore essential to provide a protected environment which reduces stress for the young plants and increases their chance of survival. Keeping seeds and seedlings in warm, humid conditions encourages rapid germination as well as healthy growth.

Leafy cuttings, when first taken, have no roots. To prevent them from wilting and encourage the speedy formation of new roots, they need to be in an environment with high humidity. This can be created very simply and cheaply by growing seeds on a warm windowsill, or by raising cuttings in a pot enclosed within a plastic bag. Hold the bag clear of the cuttings with sticks - the leaves will rot if they come into contact with the moisture that collects on the plastic. The addition of bottom heat is necessary for the germination of certain seeds, such as half-hardy annuals, and for the successful rooting of some cuttings. There are various heated units available (see below).

When cuttings and seedlings are ready to leave the protected environment of a propagating unit, they must be very gradually accustomed to the changes in humidity and air temperature – a process that is known as hardening off (see p. 230).

Propagating equipment

There is a range of propagating equipment available to suit any gardener's needs, from basic seed trays to thermostatically controlled mist-propagation units.

A plastic propagator is useful for propagating seeds and cuttings in summer and there are units small enough to fit on a windowsill. Propagating units with their own heat supply speed up rooting and germinating and are necessary for some seeds and cuttings. There are also heating bases that can be bought separately, for placing underneath your seed trays.

If you plan to propagate many plants, it is worth your while investing in a cold frame. The advantages of a frame are that the soil and air temperatures are warmer than open ground and the humidity is higher. Frames are particularly useful as an intermediate stage for 'hardening' plants, so they can be moved gradually from a warm, protected environment to an outdoor site without suffering.

Heated electric propagator
This propagating unit with room for three seed trays has an electric base with an adjustable thermostatic control for flexible temperatures. The rigid lid retains heat.

Degradable containers
You can replant seedlings grown in these containers directly into soil without disturbing the roots.

Plant hygiene
The warm, damp, enclosed space of a propagation environment is an ideal breeding ground for air- and water-borne spores of fungi and bacteria which attack and often kill plants. Always use new or well-scrubbed pots and seed trays. Clean tools regularly and dip them in a solution of methylated spirit between cuttings. Water the propagator with a fungicidal solution once it is planted up.

Bad practice
An encrusted and unwashed pot is a breeding ground for bacteria and fungi.

Cold frame
A cold frame is a great boon in propagation. This model has a sliding glass lid to adjust ventilation when acclimatizing plants, or airing new plants on warm days. Frames are useful for propagating and hardening off plants and for over-wintering alpines that suffer from winter wet.

Seed tray fitted with hoops
Make a simple and inexpensive portable propagating unit by forming wire into hoops over a seed tray. Insert the tray into a clear polythene bag to create a humid atmosphere. The hoops ensure that the leaves do not touch the polythene.

Growing from seed

Growing new plants from seed is the most common, and possibly the easiest, method of propagating a large number of plants quickly. It is ideal for growing plants for bedding displays and containers, and for filling gaps in summer borders. There is great variation between seeds, not only in terms of size and outer covering, but also in the time it takes for them to germinate, and their success rate. The growth rate of seedlings also varies. Plants need specific conditions for their seeds to achieve successful germination. Some of them prefer cool, light conditions, while others need warmth and darkness to trigger growth. Always store seed in a cool, airy place and make sure that you know the individual requirements of a particular seed before you sow it.

Preparing seed

A seed is a complete plant in embryo, but it is in a resting phase. Certain seeds need preliminary treatment to speed up germination.

Soaking seeds
To aid germination soak hard seeds in water to soften the seed coat.

Scraping seeds
Put small, hard seeds in a jar lined with sandpaper and shake the jar.

Chipping seeds
Nick the outer coat of large hard-coated seed with a sharp knife.

Scarification

Seeds with very hard coats take a long time to germinate unless you break down the seed coat so the seed can absorb moisture. This treatment is called scarification. The easiest method is to soak the seeds in warm water for 24 hours. Where the seed coat is very hard, you may have to wear it down in one of two ways:
Scraping Place small seeds in a jar lined with sandpaper and shake the jar.
Chipping Using a sharp knife, make a nick in the outer coat of large seeds.

Do not damage the inner, soft material, the part of the seed that will germinate, or the seed may rot.

Stratification

Use stratification for seeds encased in fleshy fruits, such as hips and berries. It allows the fruit to rot away without the seeds drying out.

Place some broken pieces of flowerpot in a large pot, add 50cm (20in) of sand or seed compost, then a layer of seeds, then another 50cm (20in) of sand or compost. Repeat until the pot is almost full, and finish with a layer of sand. Store in a cool, moist spot outside, and turn the mixture from time to time.

Low temperatures

Some seeds only germinate after exposure to low temperatures of 5° C (41° F) or less, in winter. In the spring, the seeds can be sown in the normal way.

Sowing outdoors

The seeds of hardy perennials and hardy annuals are normally sown out of doors. These seeds can be sown in their final flowering position to avoid transplanting. The best time to sow them is four weeks after the last severe frost in mainland Europe and the USA, or mid-spring in the UK. Check the instructions on the seed packet. Make sure that the soil has warmed up; if it is cold, many seeds will rot.

Prepare the seedbed by digging well in autumn and adding peat or other organic matter at the rate of one cubic metre to every four square metres of soil. On heavy soils, incorporate grit or sand to open it up and improve drainage. A raised bed helps drainage, allowing the soil to warm up more quickly. Now sow the seeds as described in the steps below.

1 *Tread the soil to form a firm surface. Use a rake to remove stones and make a level surface with a fine, crumbly texture.*

2 *Use a taut garden line for guidance on where to sow. Draw the corner of a rake or hoe along the ground to make a drill.*

3 *Sow seeds thinly in the drill, either singly or in groups of two or three. Cover the seeds with a fine layer of soil using the rake.*

4 *Seeds can be watered in after sowing if a very fine spray is used. Alternatively, water the bed the day before you plan to start.*

Sowing under protection

The seeds of more tender plants, such as half-hardy annuals and biennials, need artificial warmth because they will not survive outside in areas where late spring frosts occur. Most of these seeds need temperatures between about 10–21°C (50–70°F) to germinate, but some need high temperatures. To raise the temperature and retain moisture, cover the newly sown seeds with a sheet of glass or with a plastic bag. Your seed packet will give exact instructions as to temperatures required.

Sow seeds in either pots or trays. Plastic containers are the best, being easy to clean and sterilize. Degradable containers are good for large seeds. The seeds are sown directly into a small pot or similar container where they germinate and grow until temperatures are right for planting out. The containers should be planted directly into the soil.

Follow instructions for the depth at which to sow seed. In general, if the seed needs dark to germinate (and not all seeds do) it should only be covered with its own depth of compost. Sow fine and medium-sized seeds evenly in a broadcast fashion over the compost. Space larger seeds at regular intervals. Always label your seeds after sowing.

Germinating seeds
Place seeds in good light in warmth. Cress seedlings germinate very quickly in these conditions.

Sowing fine seeds

1 *Fill the tray with a good seed compost. Firm the soil to within 1.5cm (1/2in) of the top. Scatter fine and medium-sized seeds evenly on the surface.*

2 *If the seed needs dark conditions to germinate, use a fine sieve to cover the seed with the required amount of compost. Do not cover the seed too deeply.*

3 *Stand the tray in a shallow bowl of water until the compost surface moistens. Leave to drain. Cover the tray with a glass sheet and place it somewhere warm.*

Seed viability
The length of time that seeds are viable – or capable of germination – varies. Some are viable for one season only. Most last for a year after harvesting, and many are viable for several years. Some (eg *Paeonia*) can take three years to germinate. If in doubt, check before proceeding further.

Sowing large seeds

1 *For easier handling, sow large seeds in a container. Fill the pot with seed compost and level off the top, removing any surplus.*

2 *To ensure that there are no air pockets in the soil, gently firm and level the compost with a flat-bottomed utensil, like a glass.*

3 *Make sure there is a space between the top of the compost and the pot rim, and then sow the seeds evenly on the surface.*

4 *Cover the seed with a layer of compost if it needs darkness to germinate. Water the pot from below and cover it with glass.*

Care of seedlings

Seedlings must be carefully tended as they are still at a vulnerable stage. Remove glass covers as soon as any shoots are visible and make sure the seedlings are not exposed to any drastic changes in their growing conditions. Protect them from draughts and from very bright sunlight. Make sure that roots never dry out. It is usual practice to sow more seeds than you need so that you can select the healthiest seedlings. To prevent overcrowding, thin out the seedlings. You should remove the weakest surplus plants, which compete for light and nutrients, as soon as they are large enough to handle comfortably, leaving the others to grow on.

Pricking out

Prick out a seedling when it develops its first pair of 'true' leaves (see right) and can be handled with ease. Transfer the seedling to an individual pot, or put three seedlings in a larger pot, so that they have the space and depth of soil to grow into a plant. This must be done very carefully to avoid damaging the seedling, which should never be held by its stem.

1 *Using a plant label, lift each seedling carefully with roots intact, holding the seedling by the leaf and never by the stem.*

2 *Make a hole in moistened soil with a dibber and insert the seedling to the same depth as before. Gently firm in the soil.*

Outdoor thinning
Thin outdoor seedlings when the soil is nice and moist to reduce the amount of root disturbance.

'True' leaves

Recognizing the 'true' leaves on a seedling means that you can tell when to move it. The first leaves to appear are the seed leaves (cotyledons), which swell on germination and force the seedcoat open. These leaves should not be handled. Wait to thin out or repot seedlings until the second pair of leaves emerge and are large enough to hold easily. These 'true' leaves are more complex in shape and look more like the leaves of the adult plant.

The seed leaves will appear first, but wait until the 'true' leaves develop before pricking out seedlings.

Hardening off

Any seedlings that have been grown in a warm, protected environment must grow accustomed to harsher outdoor conditions for a period of about two weeks before it is safe to transplant them outside. The usual method is to move the plants outside when they are well established and place them in an unheated cold frame so that they are still protected by glass or polythene. Gradually increase the amount of ventilation by opening or removing the cover, slightly at first, and then for increasingly long periods, until the plants are acclimatized. Close the frame if there is any threat of a frost at night.

Hardening off
Gradually increase the amount of ventilation in a cold frame in order to acclimatize seedlings.

Potting up

As young plants start to grow and need more space, they should be transferred from a smaller pot to a larger one, to avoid the roots becoming cramped and to provide more nutrients in the new soil.

There is no hard and fast rule about the size of the new pot, but it should be big enough to allow a layer of new compost to be placed around the existing rootball. Do not choose a pot that is a great deal bigger than the original one, as this may cause root problems.

Before transplanting, let the plant become slightly dry so that the rootball slides out of the old pot easily, with minimal root disturbance. Hold the plant by the stem and turn the pot upside down to extract the plant. Fill the new pot with a drainage layer and fresh compost. Tap it on a hard surface to make sure that there are no air pockets and then insert the plant to the same depth as before. Finally, firm it well in.

1 *With the stem of the plant securely between your fingers, and your hand over the soil, ease the plant from its old pot.*

2 *Insert the plant in the new pot, filling spaces with new compost and firming it in gently. Water, and leave it to drain.*

Increasing bulbs

Bulbs can be grown from seed, but it may take as many as six or seven years before the seedlings will flower. For this reason, it is often preferable to use the propagating methods of scaling and scoring. These methods also ensure that the new plants are identical to the parent plant, in contrast to seed-raised plants which are variable in character. One of the major attractions of propagating plants, such as lilies, by scaling is that you can remove up to 80 per cent of a mature bulb's scales for propagation. When planted, the parent bulb, itself, will still produce flowers in the following spring.

Naturalized bulbs

When planted in suitable conditions, like these bluebells in woodland, many bulbs will spread and 'naturalize' successfully.

Scaling a bulb

Use this method to propagate scaly bulbs, such as lilies, which have relatively small, narrow scales that can readily be broken away from the base of the bulb. In the autumn, pull the scales away from the base of a bulb. Place the scales in a polythene bag and add an equal amount of moist peat or sand, and a small amount of fungicidal powder to prevent the scales from rotting. Mix the contents together and expel the air by gently squeezing the bag. Then tie the top, loosely, and label it with the plant name and date. Place the bag in a warm dark room for 12-14 weeks. By the end of this time each scale should have formed at least one embryo bulb, complete with small roots. Plant up each new bulb into a small pot.

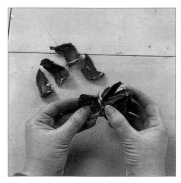

1 In autumn, break off the outer scales from the base of a bulb, discarding any that are damaged. Mix them with peat and fungicide in a polythene bag.

2 Leave the sealed bag in a dark room for 12–14 weeks. After this time, the scales will have developed at least one embryo bulb, complete with small roots.

3 Check each scale and bulblet in the bag and if two or more bulblets have developed from the same scale leaf split them apart with a sharp knife.

4 Fill small pots with a suitable potting compost. Plant the embryo bulbs singly, or in groups so that they are just below the compost level.

Scoring a bulb

This is the most common method of propagation for bulbs, such as hyacinths, whose scale leaves do not readily break away, and which are slow to propagate. In autumn, after the bulbs have been lifted and cleaned, score the base of a bulb to make a series of grooves up to one-third the depth of the bulb. Half fill a pot with loose sand or compost and press the base of the bulb into it. Add more compost until only about the top quarter of the bulb is visible. By the following autumn, young bulblets should have formed. Transplant the bulblets into small pots, or directly into the ground if you prefer.

Scoring a bulb

Using a sharp knife, score the base of a hyacinth bulb by making a series of V-shaped grooves up to one-third the depth of the bulb. Then plant the bulb in compost, with the top visible.

Bulbils

Blackish-purple mini-bulbs often form, just above the leaves, on the stem of certain species of lily, including tiger lilies. Harvest the bulbils three weeks after the flowers have finished.

Sow them as you would sow seed, about 1.5cm ($\frac{1}{2}$in) deep, in a tray or pot, and transplant them after a year. After three years they should flower.

Growing from cuttings

Increasing plants by taking cuttings from their stems is a common way to propagate woody plants. Stem cuttings are divided into three main types, according to the maturity of the plant and the time of year that the cuttings are taken.

Softwood cuttings are taken from shoots of the current season's growth as soon as a shoot's base starts to become firm, from late spring until late autumn.

Semi-ripe cuttings are taken from shoots of the current season's growth just as soon as the base of a shoot has turned woody, in late summer and autumn.

Hardwood cuttings are taken from fully mature shoots of the current season's growth of deciduous shrubs, trees and climbers. They are cut from the parent plant immediately after their leaves have fallen, in late autumn and early winter.

Softwood cutting
A cutting of the current season's growth containing mainly soft, immature tissue.

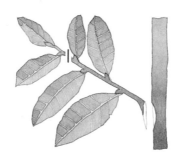

Semi-ripe cutting
A cutting of the current season's growth containing woody tissue at the base.

Hardwood cutting
A cutting of the current season's growth containing woody, fully mature tissue.

Softwood cuttings

There should be minimal delay between removing a softwood cutting from the parent plant and potting it up, because immature stems are very prone to wilting.

Select a vigorous shoot on the parent plant and cut it 7.5–10cm (3–4in) long, with a sharp knife. Protect softwood cuttings, taken outdoors, in a closed plastic bag which should be placed in the shade. Prepare each cutting by trimming the base and stripping away the lower leaves.

Dip just the base in hormone rooting powder and tap the cutting to shake off any excess. Insert at least 5cm (2in) of the stem into a soil-less cuttings compost. Water the pot thoroughly, ideally with sterilized water, preferably containing a fungicide. To prevent wilting, softwood cuttings should be kept in a well-lit, enclosed, damp environment while they initiate roots.

Plants that do not root easily may need bottom heat as well. A heated propagator is best. If you do not have one, simply place a wire hoop or some short canes over the cuttings and cover this with a sealed plastic bag. Every other day, look to see whether the cutting needs water. It should root in 6–8 weeks. Once new growth appears, gradually harden off the cutting.

1 *Cut a strong, young shoot from the parent plant and trim it just below a leaf joint, or node.*

2 *Carefully remove the lower leaves, clearing half the stem for insertion into the compost.*

3 *Fill a small pot with cuttings compost. Dip the cutting in rooting powder, and insert it.*

4 *Water, and cover with a clear plastic bag, forming a mini-greenhouse to retain moisture.*

Semi-ripe cuttings

Semi-ripe cuttings are propagated in a similar way to softwood cuttings, but at a later time of year. The stems of semi-ripe cuttings are therefore harder and more resilient than softwood cuttings. The speed of processing is not quite so critical, because the cuttings will not wilt quite as quickly as softwood cuttings. Semi-ripe cuttings do, however, take longer to initiate roots and therefore various techniques are adopted to improve rooting (see panel, opposite). Unlike softwood cuttings, any soft, sappy growth should be removed from the tip of a semi-ripe cutting before it is inserted into the cuttings compost. Such cuttings should be placed in a propagator or other closed environment while they produce roots. Semi-ripe cuttings, taken in autumn, can be allowed to root slowly over the winter months in a cold frame.

Broadleaved cuttings

A slight variation on the basic method for taking semi-ripe cuttings is used to increase evergreens that have large, broad leaves, often with a thick, leathery texture. Such evergreens can also be propagated over a longer period than semi-ripe cuttings, from mid-autumn to mid-spring. Broadleaved cuttings, 10cm (4in) long, are taken from almost fully mature wood of the current year's growth and are trimmed just below a leaf joint. For flowering plants such as rhododendrons, remove any flower bud in the tip of the cutting. The cutting may, otherwise, develop a flower and not initiate roots. To stimulate a greater number of roots to develop, many broadleaved cuttings benefit from a shallow, angled cut, or wound, made at the base (see panel, right). Because of their leaf size, broadleaved cuttings are often difficult to insert close together within the propagating environment.

In many cases, the leaf surface can be reduced by cutting the leaves in half. However, trimming the leaves in this way puts extra stress on the broadleaved cuttings. Some such cuts may bleed slightly, making the cuttings wet to handle while they are being prepared and inserted. Fortunately the problem is only short-lived, and cut surfaces dry within a few hours. Dip each cutting base in rooting hormone and insert it into a pot of cuttings compost. Water the cuttings, and cover with a plastic bag to reduce water loss.

1 *Trim the leaves by gathering them together and cutting them across, with secateurs, about half way down each of the leaves.*

2 *Dip the base of each cutting into hormone rooting powder and shake off any excess. Insert the cuttings into cuttings compost.*

Improved rooting

To encourage a cutting to produce roots, the base of a stem can be 'wounded'. Make a shallow, angled, downward cut, 2.5cm (1in) from the base of the cutting so that a strip of bark is removed. This stimulates root production both from the base of the cutting and from the edges of the wound itself.

Another way to assist is to take a heel of bark from the parent branch, together with a cutting. This heel exposes the swollen base of the current season's growth, which has a great capacity for stimulating roots. It also gives the cutting a firm base, so it is well protected against rot.

Wounding a stem
Cut a wound near the stem base with a sharp knife. Keep your thumb tucked under the stem and move the knife blade and lower thumb together down the stem, making a shallow cut.

Heel cutting
Hold the shoot between finger and thumb and give it a short, sharp tug, both downwards and outwards, to tear it from the branch. Trim the bark and bruised tissue with a sharp knife.

Hardwood cuttings

Hardwood cuttings can be taken at any time in late autumn and winter, but those taken before the cutting is fully dormant, in late autumn, are likely to be the most successful. Because the soil is moist and relatively warm, they have a chance to produce small roots before the onset of winter and should start into stem growth by mid-spring.

Select a healthy shoot, 23-60cm (9-24in) long, from the current season's growth of the parent plant. Cut it straight across the bottom of the stem with sharp, pruning secateurs. Cut the tip at an angle (but if the buds are arranged opposite each other, as in buddleja, make a straight cut).

In a well-cultivated part of the garden, make a series of holes for the cuttings by pushing the tines of a garden fork up to 15cm (6in) into the soil. Insert one into each hole, so that it presses into the bottom. At least two-thirds of the cutting should be in the ground. Rake the soil around the cuttings and press it firmly around them. If conditions are dry, finish by watering the soil well. Then leave the hardwood cuttings to initiate roots. During the winter, a callus will form at the base of each cutting and it will start to produce roots. Retread around the cuttings after each hard frost. In spring, when the cuttings start to produce leaves, they are at their most vulnerable, so protect them carefully.

Planting cuttings
Press each cutting into the bottom of a hole formed by a fork.

Where to cut a stem

Soft, immature stems are cut 6mm (1/4in) below a leaf joint, or node, where the stem is harder and more resistant to fungal rots. Such a basal cut is called a nodal cut. Woodier, more mature stems are cut midway between the leaf joints. This cut, an internodal cut, is used less often than a nodal one. Use on plants, like vines, that can produce new roots anywhere on the stem, and those whose nodes are spaced far apart.

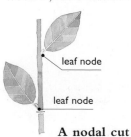

leaf node

leaf node

A nodal cut

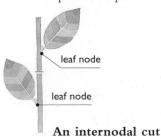

leaf node

leaf node

An internodal cut

Division

You can increase most perennials by splitting a clump of plants, complete with roots and growth buds, into small sections, each of which grows into a new plant, identical to the parent. Either plant the divisions straight into their new site, or into spare ground until they are ready to be planted out permanently. You can rejuvenate many perennials in this way every three to four years as the healthy, new outer sections, when replanted, produce vigorous plants. Division is best carried out when plants are semi-dormant and the soil is workable. Early spring is the main season, but some plants, such as bearded irises, should be left alone until after they have flowered.

How to divide roots

Plants with fleshy roots, such as hostas, need to be cut with a sharp knife into sections, ensuring that each has its own roots and growth buds. Carefully cut away and discard any old and rotten portions of the roots. Replant divisions immediately in well-prepared soil, and water them with a fungicidal solution to prevent them from rotting.

Plants with fibrous roots can be divided by easing the roots apart with your fingers or a knife. If the roots are too tough, you can split them into manageable sections with a garden fork. Replant immediately after division.

Dividing fleshy roots
1 *Wash the soil from the root mass so that healthy roots and new growth buds are clearly visible.*

2 *Use a sharp knife to split the plant into vigorous outer sections with their own roots and growth buds.*

Dividing fibrous roots
Insert two forks back to back in a clump and pull the two forks together to force the tines apart and split the clump into sections.

Runners
Some plants produce runners that develop new plantlets on contact with soil. Anchoring a tiny plantlet into a plunged pot will result in a new rooted plant in about six weeks.

Self-rooting plants
Sink a compost-filled pot under a plantlet and anchor it firmly with a wire hoop.

Root cuttings

Plants that produce shoot buds on their roots can be increased by taking root cuttings in late autumn and winter, while the plant is dormant. Put the cuttings outside in a cold frame. New shoots should emerge by mid-spring.

There are two methods for taking root cuttings. For plants with thick, fleshy roots, take cuttings about 7.5cm (3in) long and 2cm ($\frac{3}{4}$in) thick. Cut the ends with a straight cut at the upper end and an angled cut at the root tip end (so that you work out which way up to plant them). Insert the cuttings into compost vertically with the straight tops level with the compost. Cover with 1.5cm ($\frac{1}{2}$in) of moist, sharp sand, then water with a fungicidal solution.

Thin, fibrous roots should be cut into sections 7.5cm (3in) long, with a straight cut. Place the cuttings horizontally on the compost and then cover with 1.5cm ($\frac{1}{2}$in) of moist, sharp sand, and water with a fungicidal solution.

1 *Lift the plant and remove complete sections of root.*

2 *Cut straight across the end of the root nearest to the plant.*

4 *Insert cuttings so the straight end is level with the compost.*

3 *Cut the thinner end, nearest to the root tip, with a sloping cut.*

5 *Cover with moist, sharp sand to stop the cuttings drying out.*

Layering

This is an ideal method of propagation for the new gardener because no great expertise or risk is involved. The young plant is separated from the parent plant only after it has formed roots and is growing independently. Layering especially suits woody plants and climbers, which are difficult to root from cuttings. The best times for layering are in early spring, before new growth begins, or in early summer as new growth is ripening.

Natural layering
Some shrubs with low branches, like Cotinus coggygria, *will layer themselves. Others can be persuaded by pegging down low branches.*

Simple layering

Select a vigorous, young, flexible shoot from the shrub or climber to be layered. At a point about 30cm (12in) back from the tip of the shoot make an angled cut on the underside, with a sharp knife. The cut should penetrate about a third of the way through the shoot. Twist the shoot to open the cut. Dig a shallow hole in the ground and half fill with good compost. Position the injured section of the shoot into the bottom of the hole, and secure it firmly with a wire peg, making sure the cut is left open. Replace the soil, firm it all down and water well with a fine spray. Do not let the area dry out. It may take a year or more for the shoot to root. Scrape the soil to check if there are roots and when they appear, sever the new plant from the parent plant and leave it for a further growing season before moving it to a new site.

1 *Choose a flexible, young stem that can be bent to touch the ground, and trim the side shoots.*

2 *Bend the stem to the ground and mark its layering position about 30cm (12in) from its tip.*

3 *Make an angled cut, with a knife, about a third of the way into the underside of the stem.*

4 *When the layered stem has rooted, which may take up to a year, sever it from the parent plant.*

Tip layering
Tip layering is the method used to propagate plants that produce long, flexible shoots capable of producing roots at the growing point (tip). Blackberry and other fruit bushes are often propagated in this way.

In early summer, choose one of the young, vigorous shoots and bend it over to touch the soil. Dig a hole, where it touches the ground, about 10cm (4in) deep, and bury the growing point of the shoot in it.

Firm the soil gently and water well. Over a period of six to eight weeks, this tip will first form roots and then produce a new shoot, which will emerge above the soil.

In autumn, sever the new plant from the parent plant by cutting just above a bud with sharp sectateurs. Then dig up the new plant and move it to its permanent site.

New plants from shoot tips
In early summer, dig a hole 10cm (4in) deep, bury the growing tip of a new-season shoot in it and firm in well. By autumn the tip will have rooted and a new plant developed. Sever the plant from its parent by cutting above a bud.

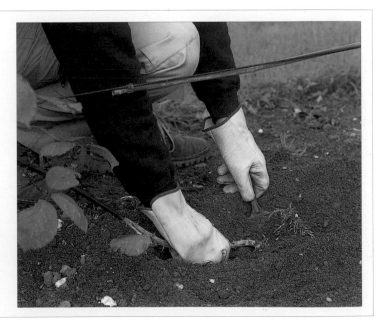

Plant problems

Always purchase strong, healthy, vigorous plants. Plants that do not appear true to type or have obvious signs of pests or disease should be rejected, because a sick plant can easily transfer disease to existing, healthy stock. Never use poor quality plants for the purposes of propagation, since weak cuttings rarely grow into sturdy, flourishing plants.

Choose the right plant for the right place, making sure that the soil pH, texture and type are compatible with the plant. Select an appropriate position to meet the plant's needs. For example, it makes sense to plant salt-tolerant subjects in coastal gardens.

Good preparation and correct planting are essential to promote the quick establishment of newly introduced plants, and to help keep them growing rapidly and strongly, especially during the first year. Plants that struggle to establish themselves are much more likely to succumb to disease. It is vital to check plants regularly, so that problems can be spotted and dealt with early on.

Companion planting
Marigolds are planted close to vegetables in this informal vegetable garden because they attract hover-flies, which feed on aphids.

Pest and disease controls

In a well-cultivated and carefully tended garden, with varied planting, there are unlikely to be many problems. However, when they do arise, gardeners must decide how to deal with pests and diseases.

Organic control
This is based on the use of natural methods to help plants resist, tolerate or recover from pest and disease attacks. In many respects, it is a move back to some of the traditional remedies for gardening problems – methods such as crop rotation. The main aspects of using organic methods of control include:
• **Resistance** Many newly introduced plants have a natural tolerance or resistance to pests and diseases.
• **Safety** Many natural chemicals are derived from plant extracts. They break

down quickly and do not persist in the soil, so they need to be applied regularly.
• **Hygiene** Clearing away plant and weed debris reduces potential breeding sites for pests and diseases. Good crop rotations can prevent the build-up of particular types.

Chemical control
Chemicals offer a quick and simple solution to many pest and disease problems. Many are very effective, but they are better used as a last resort for several reasons:
• **Safety** Many chemicals are toxic and can be harmful to humans, pets and wildlife. Apply with extreme care.
• **Residue** Traces of chemical may remain in the soil and plant tissue for long periods.
• **Tolerance** Many pests and diseases are able to adapt. They develop a resistance to chemicals which are used persistently for long periods.

Simple biological controls
To avoid depending on pesticides, combine methods like the earwig trap, below, with biological controls. An increasing number of pests and diseases can be controlled by a natural predator or parasite. Start early in the season, before pests proliferate. This method works best in an enclosed environment, such as a greenhouse. It is worth bearing the following factors in mind:
• **Safety** There is no need to use protective clothing or dispose of unused chemicals. Most of these natural predators are specific to a limited range of pests and cannot harm pets and wildlife.
• **Residue** These controls do not involve poisonous chemicals, so no poisonous traces remain in the soil or plant tissues.
• **Understanding** For this control to be effective, you

need some knowledge of the life-cycle of the pest or disease.
• **Adaptability** For the predator or parasite to survive and function, a small amount of the pest or disease must be left. This is a new objective – not to totally eliminate the pathogen, but to control it.

Earwig trap
To trap earwigs, fill a pot with straw and invert it on a pole.

How to recognize and control common pests

Aphids
Dense colonies of small pale-green, through pink to greeny-black, insects. Many species transmit viruses from one plant to another, often resulting in plant death.
Symptoms Distorted shoot tips and young leaves, sticky coating on lower leaves, often accompanied by a black, sooty mould.
Plants attacked A wide range of plants.
Prevention Remove and burn badly infected plants.
Control Spray at regular intervals as soon as the first aphids appear in late spring.

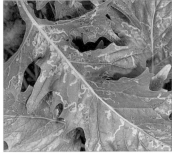

Leaf miners
Very small insect larvae that feed inside the plant leaves.
Symptoms Leaves of plants develop small, pale-green or white lines. These are the feeding tunnels of the insects. They are of nuisance value rather than causing serious damage.
Plants attacked Holly and chrysanthemums are among the many plants attacked.
Prevention Pull off and discard affected leaves as soon as they are spotted.
Control Spray dimethoate or malathion at regular intervals as soon as insects are seen.

Red spider mites
Minute mites that suck the sap of plants.
Symptoms Stunted growth. Yellow, curled and mottled leaves, covered with a fine webbing.
Plants attacked Many, but vines, carnations, cucumbers and chrysanthemums are particularly vulnerable.
Prevention Spray the undersides of leaves frequently with water, and maintain high humidity.
Control Spray with a systemic insecticide at regular intervals, or introduce the parasitic insect *Phytoseiulus*.

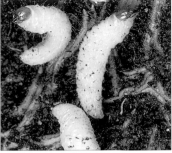

Vine weevil larvae
White, legless grubs with a black/brown head, usually curled into a 'C' shape. Feed on plant roots.
Symptoms Plants wilt or collapse. When examined, most of the roots are missing. Small semi-circular notches bitten out of leaf edges.
Plants attacked A wide range, including begonias, camellias, cyclamen, fuchsias, primulas and rhododendrons.
Prevention Keep soil clear of debris and litter which offer hiding places.
Control Treat soil with parasitic nematodes.

Earwigs
Fast-moving, small, shiny, brown insects, up to 2.5cm (1in) long, with a pincer-like gripper on the tail.
Symptoms Small, circular notches or holes in the leaves and flowers.
Plants attacked Herbaceous perennials, especially dahlias and chrysanthemums, house plants and young vegetables.
Prevention A small amount of damage may be acceptable as earwigs also eat quite a number of aphids.
Control Traps such as straw-filled pots can be used. Spray badly affected plants with HCH or malathion.

Scale insects
Insects resembling small, brown blisters on the stems and leaves of plants. They suck the plant's sap.
Symptoms Stunted growth and yellowing leaves, a sticky coating on lower leaves, often accompanied by a black, sooty mould.
Plants attacked Many trees, herbaceous perennials and greenhouse plants.
Prevention Place a layer of barrier glue around the stems of plants.
Control In mid summer introduce Metaphycus. Apply malathion spray in late spring and early summer.

Slugs and snails
Slugs are slimy with tubular bodies. Snails are very similar, but have a circular shell.
Symptoms Circular holes in plant tissue. Damaged seedlings are usually killed.
Plants attacked A wide range, including hostas, herbaceous perennials, seedlings and food crops.
Prevention Keep soil well-drained and weed-free. Apply gravel around plants as a barrier. Remove plant debris.
Control Apply aluminium sulphate in spring, or scatter slug pellets round the base of plants. Slug traps filled with stale beer are very effective.

Wireworms
Thin, yellow bodies, pointed at each end.
Symptoms Holes in roots and tubers of plants, often causing the above-ground parts to collapse. Attacked seedlings are usually killed.
Plants attacked A wide variety, including herbaceous perennials, bulbs and bedding plants, as well as young vegetable seedlings.
Prevention Avoid planting susceptible plants for up to three years on soil which has recently been grassland.
Control A granular insecticide incorporated into the top 5cm (2in) of soil.

How to recognize and treat common diseases

Botrytis

A fungus infecting flowers, leaves and stems.

Symptoms Discoloured, yellowing leaves, covered with a grey mould. The stem may rot at ground level, causing the plant to fall over.

Plants attacked Any, including roses, house plants, bulbs, lettuce, bedding plants and tomatoes.

Prevention Prune out affected sections, remove and burn badly infected plants, and maintain good air circulation.

Control Spray with thio-phanate-methyl.

Downy mildew

A fungus infecting leaves and stems. Can overwinter in the soil or in plant debris.

Symptoms Discoloured, yellowing leaves, with white patches on the lower surface. Plants often die slowly in the autumn.

Plants attacked Vines, roses and many herbs.

Prevention Avoid over-crowding, use resistant cultivars. Remove and burn badly infected plants, and maintain good air circulation.

Control Spray with the chemical fungicide mancozeb.

Fireblight

A bacterial disease which moves on a film of water, invading plant's soft tissue.

Symptoms Flowers and young shoots become blackened and shrivelled, leaves wilt and turn brown, shoots die back and plants die.

Plants attacked Many members of the rose family; cotoneaster, crab apple, hawthorn, pyracantha, mountain ash and quince.

Prevention Grow as few susceptible plants as possible.

Control Burn plants with the above symptoms, or cut out affected areas.

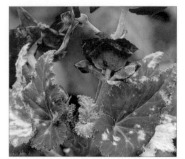

Powdery mildew

A parasitic, fungal disease invading softer tissues inside the leaf.

Symptoms White, floury patches on young leaves, distorted shoots and premature leaf fall.

Plants attacked A wide range of plants, including roses, fruit trees, herbaceous perennials and vegetables.

Prevention In autumn, prune out infected stems.

Control Spray thiophanate-methyl on young leaves at the first signs of fungal infection. The fungus cannot penetrate old leaves.

Coral spot

A common fungus invading the dead wood of plants. May invade live tissue later.

Symptoms Individual branches wilt in summer; grey-brown staining may be found under the bark. In autumn, dead branches are covered in small, salmon-pink, blister-like marks.

Plants attacked A wide range of woody plants, including Japanese maples, magnolias and pyracantha.

Prevention Prune during summer. Do not leave old dead prunings around.

Control Remove and burn infected material quickly.

Silver leaf

A fungus entering woody tissue of members of the cherry family.

Symptoms Leaves adopt a silvery sheen. Branches die back until the whole plant eventually succumbs. As the tree dies, brownish-purple, spore-bearing, fungal brackets appear on branches.

Plants attacked Any relative of the cherry family that has just been pruned.

Prevention Prune during the summer.

Control Prune infected branches from healthy trees, remove and burn badly infected trees.

Damping off

A group of soil-borne fungi which invade and kill the host plants.

Symptoms Seedlings fail to sprout during germination, or keel over, rot and die soon after germination.

Plants attacked Very young seedlings (usually within five days of germinating).

Prevention Good plant care and hygiene. When raising young plants, use sterilized compost and containers. Use seed treated with an appropriate fungicide.

Control Drench infected seedlings and seed trays with a copper-based fungicide.

Mosaic virus

A very simple organism which lives inside the plant, and feeds from it.

Symptoms Yellowing, distorted leaves and poor, weak growth, stunted shoots and striped, misshapen flowers and fruits.

Plants attacked A wide range, including alpines, bedding, house plants, herbaceous perennials, soft fruit and vegetables.

Prevention Buy virus-free plants and control aphids. Do not grow plants in soils infested with eelworms.

Control Remove and burn infected plants immediately.

How to recognize and treat common disorders

Fasciation
Irregular growth which may be caused by bacterial attack or genetic mutation.
Symptoms Twisted or flattened growth, often appearing as many stems joined together and leaves grouped in clusters.
Plants attacked Almost any plant, but it is more noticeable on woody plants.
Prevention None. Some plants are grown for the decorative appearance of the distorted growth.
Control Prune out distorted growths by removing complete stems and shoots.

Frost damage
Temperatures of below 0°C (32°F) causing death or injury to affected plants.
Symptoms Blackening of soft, new growth. Leaves on woody plants, annuals and half-hardy plants blacken and die in a few days. Some vegetables develop split stems as a result.
Plants attacked Almost any plant can suffer frost damage if temperatures fall enough.
Prevention Use fleece, cold frames and cloches to protect young or small plants from sharp frosts.
Control None.

Nitrogen deficiency
Lack of available nitrogen affects plant growth.
Symptoms Pale-green leaves eventually turning yellow and pink, thin spindly stems, stunted growing tips.
Plants attacked Trees, fruit, shrubs, vegetables, herbaceous perennials, greenhouse and indoor plants.
Prevention Regular dressings of well-rotted manure and balanced, compound fertilizers.
Control In emergencies, apply sulphate of ammonia. For a long-term solution, add a high-nitrogen fertilizer.

Sun scorch
Damage caused by heat, due to direct sunlight on the surface of the plant.
Symptoms Dead, dry patches on tree bark. Hard, brittle leaves on greenhouse plants. Hard fruits with flaking skin.
Plants attacked Maples, beech, cherries and poplars; cyclamen and ferns; gooseberries, pears and tomatoes.
Prevention Shade plants, if possible. Protect larger trees by wrapping stems with hessian bandages. Keep greenhouses well ventilated.
Control See prevention.

Drought
Prolonged shortage of water.
Symptoms Plants wilt and collapse, dying within a short time. Leaves dry out and curl, often hanging dead on the plant for long periods.
Plants attacked All plants, but especially those grown in containers and young plants in light, sandy soils.
Prevention Regular dressings of well-rotted manure and organic matter. Mulch to reduce evaporation from the surface of the soil.
Control Water regularly and thoroughly, making sure that the soil is soaked, not just wet on the surface.

Lime-induced chlorosis
Growing plants in soil with too high an alkaline content for their particular needs.
Symptoms Stunted growth. Leaves turn yellow, starting between their veins. Affects older leaves first, and younger ones later.
Plants attacked Any plant, but acid-loving plants show symptoms first.
Prevention Maintain soil pH below 6.5, add peat and well-rotted manure regularly.
Control In the short-term, apply sequestered iron; longer-term, apply flowers of sulphur at 1kg to 10sq m (2lb to 10sq yds) of soil.

Phosphate deficiency
Lack of available phosphates affects plant growth.
Symptoms Reduced plant growth, leaves turn dull green then yellow. May worsen after periods of heavy rainfall.
Plants attacked Any plant, but those growing on clay or organic soils and seedlings are most susceptible.
Prevention Regular dressings of manure and balanced, compound fertilizers.
Control For a quick response, apply super-phosphate immediately. Bonemeal is good for slow, long-term release.

Waterlogging
Roots of plants suffer from a lack of oxygen.
Symptoms Yellowing leaves which often wilt despite having plenty of water. Bark flakes from woody plants. Badly affected specimens die back as their roots are killed.
Plants attacked Any, other than pond and bog plants.
Prevention Regular, deep cultivation and incorporation of organic matter to improve soil structure.
Control Install drainage pipes if the problem becomes severe. Grow plants on raised beds or ridges to overcome localized wet spots.

Pruning

Pruning is an important garden operation, which can significantly improve the look, health and flowering performance of many woody plants. Although it appears to be a complicated process, once you understand the basic principles and methods, you will find it interesting and rewarding to see the benefits it brings.

In its simplest form, pruning is a means of controlling plant growth, productivity and shape, by cutting and training. Sections of the plant are removed to encourage buds to develop lower down. This is essential when growing fruit, to ensure reliable cropping. In the case of ornamentals, rose pruning and hedge trimming are the most frequent operations.

Most trees and shrubs need little routine pruning. The process is performed more as a remedy – when a plant encroaches on a neighbouring plant or obstructs a path. Renovation pruning can improve a plant's appearance, but years of neglect or bad pruning cannot be rectified in one session. Some gardening styles require plants to be cut very precisely. In a parterre, plants are set out in geometric designs; in topiary, they are sculpted into shape.

Pollarded tree
Pollarding is a stylized form of pruning in which a tree is regularly cut back to the top of its trunk, to restrict size.

Pruning principles

The first stage of any pruning operation can be summarized in a rule we will call, 'The four Ds'. This means the removal of any dead, dying, diseased or damaged wood. Afterwards the remaining live, healthy growth can be assessed.

The second stage is to cut out any weak or straggly shoots, to give you a clearer idea of the framework that you have to work with. At this point, you will be able to decide which branches should be pruned back or removed to achieve well-balanced growth.

Remove unnecessary and badly placed growth, such as crossing or congested stems. The aim should always be to try to work with the natural growth habit of the plant. It is important to always retain the inherent grace of the tree, rather than impose an overzealous pruning regime which fights it.

Correct/incorrect pruning
A badly pruned tree (above) fails to reflect natural growth patterns and is prone to disease. A well-pruned tree (right), creates by contrast, a well-balanced healthy shape.

Reasons to prune

The five reasons to prune:
• To maintain plant health
• To obtain a balance between growth and flowering
• To train the plant
• To restrict growth
• To improve the quality of flowers, fruit, foliage or stems.

Plant health

You can eradicate pests and diseases by pruning out dead, damaged and diseased parts, but it is far more effective to prune as a preventative measure to maintain plant health. By thinning out the plant – removing congested growth and overcrowded stems – you allow plenty of light into the centre and encourage a good air flow. This will help to discourage pests and diseases. Prune out crossing stems as these rub against each other, causing damage which makes them more vulnerable to disease.

Balanced growth

Young plants channel their energy into producing vigorous growth rather than flowers. As the plant matures, the emphasis shifts – shoot production declines until little annual growth is added. Pruning encourages mature, woody plants to produce young wood – the source of their leaves and flowers.

Training

Pruning a young plant forms the framework of sturdy, evenly spaced branches which will eventually produce flowers and fruit. You can create a balanced, productive tree of the desired shape and size.

Restricting growth

Trees and shrubs left to develop naturally will grow larger and larger, which can be a problem in a restricted space. Pruning is necessary to keep plants within bounds.

Improving quality

A plant left unpruned will still produce flowers and fruit, but over time these become smaller. You can prune out older shoots and divert energy into the development of larger flowers and fruit.

Some deciduous shrubs, such as dogwood (*Cornus alba*), have brightly coloured bark and the best colour is produced on young stems. The most intense shades are produced by hard pruning.

Health
This shoot has died back due to bad pruning and must be cut back as far as healthy wood.

Training
Fruit tree stems are trained horizontally to encourage flowers and fruits to form.

Restricting growth
The trunk of a grafted tree must be kept clean of suckers as they deprive the top growth of vigour.

Quality
Removing dead flowers is vital to prevent seed formation and encourage further flowers to form.

Positioning pruning cuts

When pruning, it is extremely important not to harm or damage the plant in any way. To avoid this, you need to distinguish the different arrangements of buds on the stem and to make sure that the pruning cuts on a particular plant are positioned correctly.

For those plants where the buds are arranged alternately on the stem, you should make any pruning cut at an angle, 6mm ($\frac{1}{4}$ in) above an outward-facing bud. Any new growth will now grow away from the main stem. The bud itself should be just beneath the high point of the cut.

For those plants where the buds are arranged opposite to each other on the stem, you should make the pruning cut at a right-angle to the stem, just above a pair of buds and as close to the buds as possible, without damaging them.

The reason for cutting close to the buds is because the wound-healing capacity of the stem tissue is greater when close to a growth bud. If the cut is made too far away from it, the stem is more likely to die back to the bud, which not only looks unsightly, but may allow disease to take hold.

Alternate buds
On trees and shrubs where the buds or leaves are arranged alternately, make the pruning cut at an angle, diagonally across the stem, just above a bud or leaf that is outward facing.

Opposite buds
Where the buds and leaves are arranged opposite one another on the stem, make the pruning cut straight across. Cut as close to the buds as possible without causing them any damage.

Pruning trees

Trees give a sense of permanence and maturity to a garden. Once established, they do not need the regular attention that many shrubs require – but pruning can be used to control their shape and size, as well as to influence their vigour.

The method depends on the type and habit of the tree concerned. Flowering trees are pruned specifically to encourage flowers and fruit, others are pruned for their attractive foliage or colourful stems.

Evergreen trees
Many evergreens, like this magnolia, require little or no pruning. In this case, only deadheading of fading flowers is required.

Head formation

The top of a tree is called the head. The form can vary, depending on how the tree grows, has been grafted or is pruned. If the central leader is retained, the main stem of the tree goes right to the top.

To encourage branching, the end third of each lateral branch is removed. Branch-headed trees have the central leader removed so that an open centre develops, with similar-sized branches. To create a clear stem, lower branches are removed.

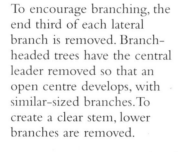

Central leader standard
The central leader is retained to form a feather shape.

Branch headed tree
The central leader is removed in order to develop an open centre.

Feathered tree
The natural form of many young trees, in particular conifers.

Weeping standard
Naturally weeping form grafted onto a clear-stemmed tree.

Training a new leader

If a tree loses its leading shoot by breakage, prune the damaged leader back to a healthy-looking bud. The shoot that develops from the

bud should be trained against a bamboo cane, so that it grows straight. Once the shoot becomes woody it will grow in the desired direction without need of support. If two leaders compete, prune out the weaker.

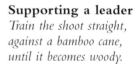

Competing leader
If two leaders are competing, cut out the weaker, more crooked shoots to leave a dominant one.

Supporting a leader
Train the shoot straight, against a bamboo cane, until it becomes woody.

Water shoots

Excessively hard pruning may result in the trunk or branches of a tree producing masses of water (epicormic) shoots, especially around large wounds where branches have been removed. These shoots can then lead to

congested growth, which will deprive the tree of its health and vigour.

They should be removed or thinned out as soon as they develop. You can then train one strong shoot as a replacement for the branch which has been taken away.

Removing water shoots from the base
A hooked pruning knife removes unwanted water shoots growing from the base of the tree.

Removing water shoots from a wound
Water shoots are often produced at the edge of old wounds where branches have been removed.

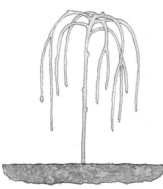

Suckers

Many trees propagated by grafting – artificially joining two separate plants together to form a single plant – may produce unwanted shoots or suckers from below the graft union, or from the roots.

These should be removed by pulling or cutting them from the tree before they become too large.

Grafted tree with sucker
This purple-leafed cherry (left) has a green-leafed sucker growing below the graft union. It must be removed before it becomes too large. Failure to do so will allow the green-leafed rootstock to predominate over the top growth.

Removing the sucker
Trace the sucker as far back as possible to its point of origin (right) and pull or cut it out.

Removing branches

When pruning larger, deciduous trees with well-developed branches, prune after leaf-fall. Care must be taken when removing branches. Do not remove a heavy branch by cutting it from above, flush with the trunk – the results can be disastrous. The branch will tear down into the trunk of the tree, causing a large, gaping wound which is a potential site for fungal infection. To avoid such a catastrophe, adopt safe pruning procedures. Cut the branch down gradually, section by section, to reduce the weight, before you reach the trunk of the tree.

1 *Make a cut, not too deep, on the underside of the branch, 30-45cm (12-18in) along from where it leaves the trunk.*

2 *Make the second cut on top of the branch, further out along the branch, 5-7.5cm (2-3in) away from the first cut.*

3 *When the second cut overlaps the first, the branch will snap along the grain and should fall clear without tearing.*

4 *Make a final cut parallel to the trunk to remove the remaining branch stub. Do not cut into the branch collar.*

Pruning deciduous trees

Deciduous trees are usually pruned when dormant, in late autumn or winter – but do not cut trees such as birch and maple at this time, or the sap will bleed. Prune these later on, in midsummer.

Young trees

Prune young trees to develop a balanced framework with a straight stem and well-spaced branches. Early pruning is important for trees with buds arranged in pairs, such as ash and maple, as, if the central stem is allowed to 'fork' into two, it may split.

During the first three years, prune ornamental trees, such as crab apples, to create a clear, vertical stem. Soon after planting, remove competing shoots and any thin or crossing shoots. In the first spring, prune off all lateral shoots from the bottom third of the tree and reduce all lateral shoots on the tree's middle third by half. In early winter, remove the reduced lateral shoots on the middle third. Repeat over the next two years until you have a clear stem of 1.8m (6ft).

Mature trees

Only prune established ornamental trees to maintain their shape and vigour. Thin any overcrowded, whippy branches in the centre of the head, to allow light and air into the centre of the tree. Any large branches which upset the overall balance and shape of the tree should be reduced in size, to prevent them from dominating the head of the tree. Excessive pruning of vigorous trees, when they are dormant, may result in quantities of long, sappy shoots. It may better to prune in the summer and avoid this eventuality.

Pruning evergreen trees

Conifers and broad-leaved evergreen trees are usually pruned in late spring.

Mature trees

Established, evergreen trees need little regular work. Pruning is usually a matter of removing dead, damaged or diseased branches, by cutting back to a strong, healthy shoot or removing the branch entirely. Cut out badly placed, weak or crossing laterals and remove competing leaders.

Never reduce the height of a conifer by cutting out the top, because this often leaves an ugly, mutilated shape. It is better to dig up the tree.

Young trees

You can establish a strong main stem or central leader by training a strong, vertical shoot upwards. Prune out any leaders that are competing with one another, as well as badly placed laterals or weak and crossing stems.

Pruning shrubs

There are several excellent garden shrubs that need only a light trim in the way of pruning. These include broad-leaved evergreens, such as some cotoneasters, ruscus and sarcococca. However, most shrubs, if left to grow unpruned, gradually deteriorate. Regular pruning enables them to grow and flower well, over a long period, and may even extend their life. Flowering shrubs are usually pruned very soon after the flowers have died away but, inevitably, there are exceptions. *Buddleja davidii* varieties flower in late summer but are not pruned until the following spring, to avoid frost damage to the new growth. The real dilemma comes with shrubs grown for their ornamental fruits, because they cannot be pruned after flowering, or the fruits will be sacrificed as a result. These plants are usually left until the main display of fruit has finished before they can finally be pruned.

Mixed shrub border
The beauty of ornamental flowering shrubs, such as the weigela and viburnum shown here, is enhanced by careful, well-timed pruning.

When to prune

Prune most established ornamental shrubs according to their flowering habit. The majority will produce flowers from a particular shoot only once. This may be a one-year-old shoot, in the case of forsythia, or a two-year-old shoot for kolkwitzia. Shrubs can be divided into four basic pruning groups (see below).

Other significant factors to take into account are the shrub's ability to produce replacement growth and the age of flower-bearing stems. The golden rule is to prune after flowering those shoots which have just flowered.

With all pruning groups, start by removing dead branches and trimming diseased or damaged shoots back to healthy tissue. On variegated shrubs, growth that has reverted to plain green must be pruned out. Then carry out any pruning for shape, or for fruit or flower formation, as usual.

Group 1
Requires very little or no pruning. Includes:

Amelanchier
Buddleja globosa
Camellia
Chimonanthus
Daphne
Elaeagnus pungens
Hamamelis
Magnolia stellata
Osmanthus
Viburnum tomentosum

Group 2
Flowers on the current season's growth; pruned in spring. Includes:

Buddleja davidii
Euonynus europaeus cvs
Forsythia
Fuchsia magellanica
Hibiscus
Hydrangea
Lavatera
Lavandula
Phygelis
Spiraea japonica

Group 3
Flowers on previous season's growth; pruned in summer after flowering. Includes:

Buddleja alternifolia
Chaenomeles
Deutzia
Exochorda
Kolkwitzia
Philadelphus
Rhododendron liteum
Ribes sanguineum
Spiraea arguta
Weigela

Group 4
Has a suckering habit or coloured stems. Includes:

Berberis
Corylus
Fuchsia
Hypericum patulum
Mahonia aquifolium
Rhus
Rosa nitida
Rosa rugosa
Sarcococca
Spiraea x *billiardii*

Daphne bholua 'Gurkha'

Hibiscus syriacus 'Blue Bird'

Weigela 'Florida Variegata'

Berberis x stenophylla

Pruning deciduous shrubs

Before starting to prune any shrub, always look at the habit and growth pattern of the plant. This provides clues to its pruning requirements.

The flowering pattern of mop-head hydrangeas puts them in the category of shrubs that flower on the previous season's wood. Such Group 3 plants should be pruned after flowering – but these hydrangeas are an exception. They flower in late summer and autumn, but the buds are prone to frost damage in the winter. Because of this, rather than pruning soon after flowering, the dead flowers are left on the plant over winter to protect the buds. The shrub is then pruned in late spring.

Young shrubs

Deciduous shrubs are more likely to need formative pruning than evergreens. This is best done in the dormant season, between mid autumn and mid spring, at planting time or soon after.

Cut back crossing branches to one-third of their length, positioning the cut so that the topmost bud faces outwards. This directs growth away from the centre of the plant. Cut out weak and congested shoots, and cut back unbalanced shoots to a suitable outward-facing bud or prune them out altogether.

As a general guide, if an over-vigorous shoot is distorting the framework of the plant, cut it back lightly rather than severely. If there is no balanced framework of branches, cut the plant back hard to promote strong, new shoots. Hard pruning of a vigorous shoot can stimulate even stronger growth – a principle summed up in the adage, 'Prune weak growth hard, but prune strong growth only lightly'. Try to bear this in mind when correcting the appearance of any misshapen shrub.

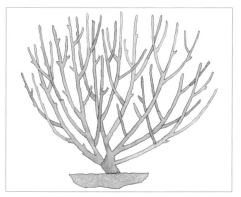

Congested stems
Remove up to one-third of the stems from a congested plant. This encourages a good air flow and discourages pests and diseases.

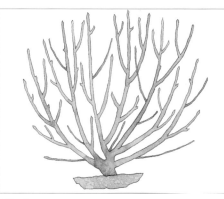

Weak stems
Cut out any thin, weak or spindly stems which are a drain on the plant's resources and are more vulnerable to pests and diseases.

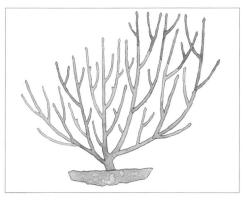

Lopsided stems
Over-vigorous shoots that distort the framework of the plant should be cut back lightly. Pruning too hard stimulates growth.

Pruning shrub and species roses

This is a large and varied group of roses. All of the species and most of the shrub roses, both old and modern, flower on wood that is two years old, or older.

Many flower freely for a number of years without any formal pruning, other than dead-heading old flowers. When they are pruned, remove all weak, damaged, dead and diseased wood. Follow this by a light pruning, leaving as much flower-bearing wood as possible. For the repeat-flowering roses, this is particularly important. The best approach is to remove, completely, two or three of the oldest stems each year, so that over three or four years, all the growth is gradually renewed.

The best time for this method of pruning is immediately after flowering, because this gives the plant the chance to channel its energy into developing new stems. The main exceptions are species, such as *Rosa rugosa*, *Rosa moyesii* and their hybrids, which are valued for their attractive display of hips in autumn and winter. Pruning of these species should be left until late winter.

Standard rose – before
Hard pruning can be used to stimulate vigorous new growth.

Well-pruned standard rose
After pruning, the standard rose has a balanced framework of shoots.

Bush rose – before
Any thin, weak and inward-pointing shoots must be cut out.

Well-pruned bush rose
After pruning, only strong, healthy shoots remain.

Mature deciduous shrubs

The routine maintenance of deciduous shrubs involves the removal of any dead, diseased or damaged wood. This work can be done throughout the year and you should act promptly as soon as you spot any of these problems.

With any shrub which needs to be pruned, it is advisable to remove two or three old stems by cutting them down to ground level. This stimulates new growth, keeps the centre of the plant open and helps air to flow through it, keeping down pests and diseases. Pruning for flowering depends on when the plant's flowering occurs.

Group 1

These plants hardly ever need pruning: most daphne species and hybrids seem to resent pruning and do far better if they are left alone. See below for plants from the other pruning groups.

Group 2

Shrubs in this group flower on the current season's growth and are pruned in spring. Forsythia is simple to prune, as the dead flowers remain on the plant for some time. Remove the old flowering shoots. Cutting them out gives new growth the maximum time to develop and produce next year's flowers. If too many shoots are produced, thin them out in early spring to produce fewer, but larger flowers. If pruning when the flowers have fallen, the stem colour shows which are the older shoots. New growth is dull green, maturing to golden-brown; older stems are a faded, browny-grey and are thicker than younger ones.

Removing stems
Cut out surplus shoots in early spring to produce better flowers.

Pruning after flowering
Prune directly after flowering, when the dead flowers are visible.

Group 3

Summer-flowering plants, such as deutzia, produce flowers on new shoots which formed in the previous growing season. Many of these main shoots will originate from the base of the plant and produce flowers on short, lateral branches. This gives the shrub a tangled, twiggy appearance and it is best to remove about one-third of the stems every year. This pruning is best carried out as the flowers fade, with the oldest, thickest stems being removed close to ground level. A late spring frost occasionally kills the shoot tips of new growth – some tip pruning may be necessary early in the season, to remove the damaged parts.

Thinning out
Remove old flowering stems to encourage next year's flowers.

Reshaping
Cut out the oldest stems at ground level.

Group 4

Shrubs such as kerria, which are grown for their flowers as well as the bright-green colour of their stems, flower on the previous year's wood. Most of the new growth, however, originates from ground level.

Because these shrubs have a suckering habit, it is a good idea to prune out all the old, flowering shoots as close to soil level as possible, as soon as the flowering season has finished. By removing all these old stems, you will stimulate more flowers to grow in future years. It will also encourage the development of new, green stems which show the brightest colour through the winter months, giving you the added bonus of stem colour in the garden.

Cutting out old stems
Cut old stems almost to the base just after flowering, as they will not produce any more flowers.

Removing weak stems
Cut thin, weak stems at soil level as they rarely produce flowers and are prone to pests and disease.

Pruning for colourful stems and leaves

Some shrubs, such as certain dogwoods (*Cornus*), are grown for their colourful stems in winter, and others, such as golden elder, have attractive young foliage. Both are pruned severely to provide plenty of young growth, which has the best colour. Prune dogwoods annually or biennially, depending on their vigour. Cut out all weak shoots and hard prune the previous year's shoots of dogwood in early spring, cutting back stems to a few centimetres above ground. Hard prune golden elder in late winter, to a few centimetres high.

Hard pruning of old stems
In early spring, cut stems to just above ground level.

New stem growth
The red stems of dogwood provide rich colour in winter.

Pruning evergreen shrubs

The pruning method for most evergreen shrubs will depend upon the growth rate and the size of the plant when it reaches its ultimate height. However, regardless of size, there are some rules that apply to all such plants.

Always begin by pruning out any dead, damaged and diseased wood. Cut it back to a point where the shrub has started to regrow, or where healthy tissue can be seen. To judge whether branches are live, lightly scrape away some of the bark with a sharp knife or secateurs. A green layer indicates live tissue, brown indicates dead wood.

General principles

Generally speaking, evergreen shrubs need very little formative pruning. However, excessively vigorous growth will have to be corrected, as it can result in the plant growing into a lop-sided, unbalanced shape.

When evergreen shrubs need pruning, do it lightly in mid spring to reduce the risk of frost damage on the fresh pruning cuts. Cut back any vigorous shoots, by at least a third, to prevent the plants losing their shape, but do not prune too hard, as this results in even more vigorous growth. Remove thin, weak or straggly stems growing in the centre of the plant. Thin out overcrowded shoots, as they can become damaged by rubbing together. When establishing flowering plants, such as rhododendrons, take off flowering shoots before they fully develop in spring.

Repeat this pruning regime for the first two or three years after planting, until the shrub starts to take on the desired shape.

If plants show signs of die-back following a hard winter, especially at the shoot tips, they should be cut back to live growth after the risk of hard frost has passed.

Some smaller shrubs, such as lavender, have a naturally compact habit and only need dead-heading after the flowers have died. Trim back the long flower stalks, with shears or secateurs, close to their base. Trim the shoot tips, too.

Many hybrid mahonias have a tall, upright habit with a large expanse of bare stem below the leaves. In spring, immediately after flowering, cut back the old, flower-bearing stems to form a strong framework of branches about 45cm (18in) above soil level. This encourages a branching habit, with flowers at a more manageable height.

Pruning for shape
Remove any long, straggly shoots as they develop, before they spoil the shape and balance of the plant.

Pruning after flowering
After flowering, cut back the long, bare sections of stem to a cluster of leaves. This encourages new shoots to develop.

Light clipping
Cut dead flower stalks in spring and trim 2.5cm (1in) off the top growth to encourage branching. Do not cut into old wood.

Reversion

Many plant species have varieties with gold- or silver-variegated leaves. These brightly coloured varieties may revert to type and begin to produce shoots with plain, green leaves. Such shoots need to be removed immediately. Cut the reverted shoot back to the first variegated leaf – or, if necessary, remove the shoot completely. Varieties of plants with finely cut leaves may also revert to type and begin to develop coarser leaves. These should be treated in exactly the same way.

Removing green leaves
If a plant with variegated leaves produces a shoot that has reverted to green leaves, you must cut the shoot to the first variegated leaf, or remove the shoot completely.

Renovation

Old, neglected or untidy plants may respond to severe pruning and produce young growth from the base. First, decide whether the shrub is worth trying to renovate. Would it be wiser to dig it up and replant a new one?

To renovate, cut evergreen shrubs down to about 45cm (18in) in mid-spring, just before new growth starts. The following spring, cut back any strong, vigorous shoots which may affect the plant's overall balance. Cut out any weak or crossing shoots. In subsequent years, cut out thin, straggly shoots and shape the plant so that you restrict its growth.

Pruning for renovation
Cut old, untidy shrubs, such as this elaeagnus, down to about 45cm (18in) in mid-spring.

Pruning climbers and wall shrubs

It is important to bear the growth habit of the plant in mind when pruning climbers and wall shrubs, for this should influence your method of pruning and training. Climbers can be divided into groups, based on the way that they hold themselves. The different categories – clinging, scrambling, and twining plants – are illustrated below. Apart from self-clinging plants, such as ivy, climbing plants need some means of support, and these can range from free-standing arches and pergolas to wall mounts like trellis, netting or vine eyes and wire. Climbers can grow vigorously and become very heavy (see p. 224), so support them accordingly. Plant display is always enhanced by proper pruning. Careful training and tying-in, from a young age, are essential.

Vertical gardening
Providing suitable supports, along with careful pruning and training from an early age, ensures the best display from climbing plants.

Types of climber

Climbing plants can be divided up into four basic groups, as follows:
Clinging plants (such as common ivy). These plants attach themselves to surfaces by clinging with **aerial roots** or **sucker pads** and usually need no additional support.
Twining plants. This is a large group, including honeysuckle, clematis and wisteria. Parts of the plant twine themselves around a support – these parts may be **tendrils, leaf-stalks** or **stems**. A support system is usually required for twining plants.
Scrambling plants (such as roses). These have rapidly-growing stems, which grow through other plants, using **hooked thorns**. Scrambling plants must be tied to a support system.
Wall shrubs. These are not true climbing plants, but shrubs that are made to grow against a wall or fence. They usually need careful training to grow them against the vertical surface.

Aerial roots
Climbing hydrangea uses aerial roots to cling on to surfaces. Another plant in this category is Campis *(trumpet vine).*

Sucker pads
Virginia creeper is unusual in that it is the only plant that attaches itself to surfaces and climbs using sucker pads.

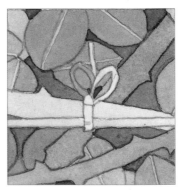

Hooked thorns
Scrambling roses climb using hooked thorns. Another plant in this category is Rubus.

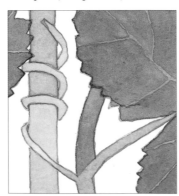

Twining tendrils
Grape vine climbs using tendrils. Other plants in this category include Ampelopsis *and* Passiflora.

Twining leaf stalks
Clematis climbs using twining leaf stalks. Eccremocarpus scaber *and* Tropaeolum speciosum *are also in this group.*

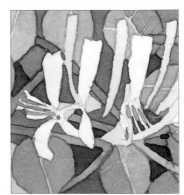

Twining stems
Honeysuckle climbs using its twining stems. Other plants in this category include Akebia quinata *and* Wisteria.

Pruning clingers

These climbing plants attach themselves to a wall or fence by means of sucker pads or aerial roots. They do not require a support system.

Evergreen plants such as ivy help to keep buildings cooler in summer and provide some insulation in the winter. However, when established, climbers with aerial roots can be over-vigorous. They create a problem on the walls and roofs of older houses and can do considerable structural damage. The roots grow into the lime-based mortar, and plant stems thicken, forcing guttering away. It is essential to check the climber's progress and prune the plant back hard, if necessary.

Young plants

Soon after planting, start by cutting the plant's growth back by half. As new extension growth begins, place and tie in the strongest stems, to achieve a well-spaced, balanced framework

Pruning (young campsis)
Cut back the stems to ground level. This will encourage new shoots to develop from the base.

of shoots. Coax them in the right direction, while still soft and pliable, with masonry nails or cable ties. In the second spring, cut back all of the sideshoots to a bud near the main stem. Strong stems will grow from these shoots during the season, forming

Training (a hydrangea)
Tie in shoots as they develop on a one-year-old natural clinger to give the plant a balanced framework.

the plant's framework. Cut back the tip of each stem the following year, to make the shoots branch and cover the wall, extending the main framework. Tie in the stems or help them grip. Cut back any other shoots to within two buds of the nearest stem.

Second-year growth
During the plant's second year, strong shoots develop, with aerial roots to help them grip.

Mature plants

Once plants with a clinging habit have become properly established, there is really very little regular pruning that you need do – apart, that is, from dead-heading to remove any spent flower heads from plants such as climbing hydrangea (*Hydrangea anomala* ssp. *petiolaris*).

The main time for pruning many of these climbers is in mid spring, just after the plants have started to develop new growth and the leaves are small. At this time of year, it is much easier to identify the stems that are dead,

damaged, diseased or weak and which need to be removed. If you leave it too long, they will be obscured by the fully developed leaves and young, new shoots.

Summer pruning will usually include essential maintenance, such as trimming vigorous growth from around doors and windows to prevent them being covered over. Aerial roots and sucker pads should be removed, carefully, from painted surfaces. Shoots that have worked their way under wooden cladding or roof tiles should be cut back with a sharp pair of secateurs.

Renovation

Some climbers and wall shrubs cannot tolerate being cut down severely, and may not survive such harsh treatment. In such cases, it is advisable to carry out the renovation pruning in stages, over a two- or three-year period. Start by removing the oldest stems each year (usually the ones with the darkest coloured bark), so that over a couple of years all of the old growth is replaced by young, vigorous shoots.

The main disadvantage of renovating plants like this over several years is that the new growth that has been

generated may become entangled with the old shoots which have yet to be removed, making it far more difficult to prune. To avoid this, cut down one side only of the plant in the first year.

Train the new shoots into the open spaces created by removing the unwanted growth. The remainder of the old stems are cut away in the second year and replacements trained and tied into the remaining space. It may take a further two years, or possibly even more, before the new growth is mature enough to produce flowers of its own.

Before pruning
Vigorous clingers may need severe pruning to control them.

Pruning clingers
Prune out wayward shoots with a pair of sharp secateurs.

Before hard pruning
This chaenomeles needs its shoots to be cut by half, back to ground level, to increase vigour.

Retraining after pruning
After hard pruning, remaining shoots are trained and tied in to create a fan shape.

Pruning twining climbers

Many twining climbers become very vigorous once established and if they are not regularly pruned, the plant will rapidly choke itself or form an unattractive, tangled ball of shoots. To succeed with this type of plant, make sure that new shoots are produced each spring. To do so, prune to stimulate new shoots and feed the plant in springtime. As the new shoots grow quickly, many of the flowers develop too high up on the plant to be fully appreciated. This problem is worse if the climber is not pruned and new shoots form above those from the previous year. Prune twining climbers regularly, unless they are grown to cover a large surface.

The twining habit leads to self-inflicted damage – stems wrap around each other, and some are crushed and split. Pests and diseases can become established in the wounds. Older stems need to be removed in rotation, and replaced by newer ones.

Young plants

In spring, or soon after planting, prune the new plant severely. Cut the thickest stems down to the lowest pair of strong, healthy growth buds and cut out thin, weak shoots completely. As the new growth begins, adjust its position. If necessary, tie the strongest stems to the support system to achieve a well-spaced, balanced framework of shoots. Until plants mature and start to cling by themselves, they may need to be tied at 30–45cm (12–18in) intervals to prevent wind damage to new shoots. Woody stems that develop while the shoots are maturing cannot be bent into the required position without inflicting damage.

The plant will be established by the second spring. Cut back all the sideshoots to a pair of buds close to the main stem, and tie in any loose shoots to the support system. A number of strong stems will grow from these shoots during the following season, forming the framework of the plant.

First year pruning
Cut back new plants (of honeysuckle here) in spring to the lowest pair of strong and healthy buds.

Second year pruning
Once the plant is well established, cut back all sideshoots to a pair of strong buds close to the main stem.

Tying in
As new shoots grow, train your plants (in this case clematis) by tying the strongest stems into position on their supports with soft twine

Mature plants

For most twining climbers, once a balanced framework of branches has been established, routine pruning consists of cutting back the lateral branches (side shoots) to a pair of buds close to the main stem.

For many plants, this pruning and training can be carried out through the autumn and winter. Tying in growth at this time will also help to prevent any loose stems being damaged by harsh winds.

Any damaged or dead shoots should be removed completely. To encourage flowering, one of the oldest stems is often cut back and a younger replacement tied into position. Neglected, climbing honeysuckles, in particular, may develop tangled stems that bear foliage and flowers at the the tops of shoots only. To correct the problem, prune hard in early to mid-spring, so that new shoots can develop and then be trained in. If children have access to your garden, always prune honeysuckle immediately after flowering too – the berries are attractive but highly poisonous.

Tying in
Spread out the new shoots and tie in position.

Frost damage
Cut out any frost-damaged shoots, back to healthy growth.

Renovation pruning
Shoots are cut back hard to the main stem for a better display.

Pruning wisteria

Wisteria flowers are formed on short spurs, mostly found on branches which are trained horizontally. Prune mature plants twice a year. In summer, tie shoots to be used as part of the framework into a horizontal position. Cut back new, long, lateral shoots, growing at right angles, to 15–20cm (6–8in) from the main stem. In late winter, cut back summer-pruned shoots to form spurs of two to three strong buds. (These will carry the flowers). Cut back to 15–20cm (6–8in), or remove, secondary growths formed after the summer pruning.

Pruning long shoots
Wisteria is extremely vigorous. To prevent sections of the stem being bare, the long shoots will need to be cut back in summer.

1 *In summer, after flowering, cut back new growth to 15cm (6in) to control vigour and promote flower buds.*

2 *In late winter, cut back the summer-pruned shoots to 3–4 buds. Also cut back any secondary shoots formed after the summer pruning to 15cm (6in).*

Pruning clematis

Clematis have the longest flowering period of any group of climbers. During most months of the year, some clematis or other is producing flowers. Prune as for twining climbers, but make sure you know when the clematis flowers, as the key to pruning is the flowering season.

Group 1 Early flowering species. Flowers from January through to late May.
Clematis alpina and cvs
Clematis armandii and cvs
Clematis cirrhosa and cvs
Clematis macropetala and cvs
Clematis montana and cvs

Many of the clematis in this group require little routine pruning. When necessary, the best time to prune is straight after flowering. This allows time for new growth to develop, so that the plant will flower the following spring.

Group 2 Early, large-flowered cultivars. Flowers from early June to early July.
Clematis 'Barbara Jackman'
Clematis 'Carnaby'
Clematis 'Daniel Deronda'
Clematis 'Duchess of Edinburgh'
Clematis 'Elsa Späth'
Clematis 'General Sikorski'
Clematis 'Henryi'
Clematis 'Lasurstern'

Clematis 'Marie Boisselot'
Clematis 'Mrs N. Thompson'
Clematis 'Nelly Moser'
Clematis 'Niobe'
Clematis 'The President'
Clematis 'Vyvyan Pennell'
The flowers are produced on stems up to 60cm (2ft) long, formed during the previous season. Any pruning should be done in early spring. Remove any dead, weak, or damaged growth. Cut back healthy stems to just above a strong pair of leaf buds.

Group 3 Late-flowering species and cultivars. Flowers from early July through to October.
Clematis florida and cvs

Clematis tangutica and cvs
Clematis viticella and cvs
Clematis 'Comtesse de Bouchaud'
Clematis 'Duchess of Albany'
Clematis 'Ernest Markham'
Clematis 'Gipsy Queen'
Clematis 'Hagley Hybrid'
Clematis 'Jackmanii'
Clematis 'Lady Betty Balfour'
Clematis 'Perle d'Azur'
Clematis 'Ville de Lyon',
Plants in this group produce flowers on stems of the current season's growth.

Pruning involves removing the previous season's growth by cutting plants down to a strong pair of buds to within 45cm (18in) of soil level in spring.

C. macropetala **'Jan Lindmark'**

C. **'Nelly Moser'**

C. viticella **'Mme Julia Correvon'**

Pruning scrambling climbers

The scrambling climbers have rapidly growing stems, which clamber through other plants in the wild. They use hooked thorns and a rapid extension of lax, vigorous shoots to attach themselves to, and gain support from, nearby plants and structures.

Scrambling climbers are capable of growing through other plants unaided, but if the intention is to grow them on a vertical structure like a wall or fence, a support system is needed. The plants will need to be tied to the support system and a constant programme of tying and training will need to be maintained to keep the plant growing in the desired direction.

Many scrambling climbers have a tendency to produce most of their flowers on the upper third of the plant, especially when grown up a vertical support. A useful tip is to train the growth at an angle of 45 degrees around the vertical support; this will promote the production of more flowers lower down the plant, providing a more impressive display.

Climbing roses
Rosa *'Madame Caroline Testout, Climbing'* is a vigorous climbing *'sport'* that has graced walls and fences since 1901.

Young plants

Plants such as climbing roses are not true climbers. They must be trained to go in the required direction, and tied to a support. Apart from removing dead, diseased, damaged or weak growth, they should not be pruned in the first year after planting, and, possibly, not in the second year, unless they have made exceptional growth. When the new shoots become long enough to tie in, begin training the plants.

As with most flowering climbers, the shoots should be trained horizontally, by tying them to supports to encourage flowering. Keep the shoots evenly spaced and tied into position. Cut back all sideshoots to within 7.5cm (3in) of a vigorous shoot.

If these scrambling plants are not carefully trained, they will grow into a tangle of unwieldy and unhealthy shoots. This results in poor air circulation and encourages the incidence of fungal diseases, such as black spot, mildew and rust. Dense, bushy growth also makes it very difficult to control diseases and pests.

Tying in stems
Tying and training of young shoots needs to be done on a regular basis, to keep the plant growing in the desired direction.

Neatening up
Trimming away any surplus string after tying is a cosmetic measure to help to give the plants a natural-looking appearance.

Mature plants

Many scrambling plants flower profusely for years without any other treatment than general pruning – the removal of weak or damaged shoots and congested growth in autumn.

Leave the strong, main shoots unpruned, unless they are exceeding their allotted space, in which case, shorten them by cutting them back to a strong, new shoot. Otherwise, simply shorten the sideshoots to within 7.5cm (3in) of a vigorous shoot. Make sure you train all the new season's growth to the supports, while they are still flexible, to establish a well-balanced framework and prevent wind damage.

If the base of a scrambling climber becomes very bare, renewal pruning may be necessary. Cut 25–30 per cent of the oldest shoots to within 15cm (6in) of ground level. This encourages the growth of vigorous, new shoots.

Shortening stems
Flowered stems should be reduced by about two-thirds, to an outward-facing bud.

Removing weak stems
To achieve a healthy, well-shaped plant, remove weak stems by cutting them back to the base.

Pruning wall shrubs

There are a great number of shrubs and a few small trees which can be trained against a wall or fence, and this can greatly increase the range of plants which can be grown in the garden.

For those shrubs that are slightly tender and need a degree of winter protection, a wall or fence can provide the shelter required. In order to manipulate a plant to grow in a flat vertical plane, the shoots and branches must be pruned and trained to cover the support with a framework of evenly distributed stems and branches. This is often difficult as the plant's natural tendency is to grow into the brightest light, which means the shoots will grow away from the support.

To control this natural tendency, pruning and training are combined to direct the growth into the desired directions. In order to achieve the right effect, the plant's natural habit and growth pattern has to be taken into account, and any pruning should be very specific to the plants individual needs.

A sheltered site
Tender shrubs such as this Ceanothus, *a plant originating from California, benefit from being planted against a sunny wall.*

Young plants

Prune young wall shrubs immediately after planting. Cut out any damaged or diseased shoots and remove any thin, spindly stems. Train plants during the first growing season. Position and tie in the strongest stems to the support system to achieve a well-balanced framework of shoots, usually in a fan shape. Do this as the shoots develop, as later they become woody and may be damaged if bent into position. Carry out formative pruning in spring, after the risk of frost is past.

Tying in stems
Tie young, pliable shoots into a fan shape on the wall, before they become too woody to be manipulated easily.

Pruning for shape
Prune any shoots that are growing directly away from the wall, so that you maintain it as a well-shaped wall shrub.

Removing dead stems
Prune out any dead leaves and stems to improve appearance and remove potential sites where pests and diseases can get a hold.

Mature plants

For routine pruning, remove dead or damaged wood to prevent infection spreading, and cut back any weak shoots. Straggly branches, or those growing out at right-angles to the wall, should be removed. Tie in any long shoots which are to be kept as part of the plant's framework. As new growths are tied in, check existing ties to make sure plant stems are not being damaged or restricted by them. As a rule, prune wall shrubs that flower on last year's growth after the plants have flowered, and shrubs that flower on the current season's growth in spring.

New growth of pyracantha appears in summer after flowering and may hide the berries. To avoid this, prune mature plants in mid summer, cutting shoots to within 10cm (4in) of the main stem. These shoots will then form spurs to carry next year's crop of flowers.

Pruning for shape
Saw off any outward-growing branches for neatness.

Pruning after flowering
Cut older spurs to within 10cm (4in) of main stem after flowering.

Pruning hedges

Hedge clipping is, simply, pruning done in certain way to achieve a particular purpose, such as to form a shelter belt. The same general principles apply, but the method depends on the result required.

Formal hedges demand regular clipping or trimming to form a dense mass of compact shoots. Informal hedges take less work to achieve the desired effect. The timing and method is mainly determined by the flowering time but, as a rule, remove old flower-bearing branches as soon after flowering as you can. Plants producing berries should not be pruned until after the fruits have finished.

Tapestry hedges are made up of a mixture of plants, such as beech alternating with yew or holly. Mixing deciduous and evergreen species provides a colourful background, but use plants with similar growth rates.

Flowering hedge
A mature and well-tended Rosa *'Frühlingsmorgen' makes a very exuberant, informal hedge at the height of its flowering season*

Young hedges

The success of a hedge depends on its treatment during the first two or three years. Formative pruning produces even growth over the entire surface, as well as controlling the height.

Immediately after planting, cut back a new hedge to between one- and two-thirds of its original height. Cut back any strong, lateral branches, by about half, to encourage the plants to establish more rapidly and form a dense, bushy habit from ground level. Repeat this process in the second year by severely pruning the sides and top of the hedge. Most of the extension growth forms along the hedge line between the plants, forcing them to grow into one another.

The severity of this initial pruning depends on the type of plant. The aim is to encourage plenty of bottom growth, or the base may remain relatively bare while the upper hedge is dense. If the formative pruning is done well and the new growth trimmed back by half, at least twice each year, a dense, narrow hedge is formed, about 75cm (2½ft) wide at the base, which is ideal for most situations.

Training young hedges

The speed of growth of any hedge depends on the plants used for it, as does its eventual thickness. Some plants are better suited to barrier hedging, others to ornamental screening. It will take four to five years for a deciduous hornbeam hedge to form any kind of protective barrier; an evergreen privet will take three to four, while yew will take up to 10 years but all plants, no matter what their speed of growth, must be pruned back hard in the early years or they will fail to bush out and create the impenetrable screen required.

Broad-leaved evergreen hedges

Pruning broad-leaved evergreens with shears mutilates many larger leaves and spoils the overall effect of the hedge. Leaves cut in half slowly turn yellow and die, and are very prone to attack by pests and diseases.

Use secateurs to prune back new growth. This also helps to reduce the number of damaged stems or branches. Remove any diseased parts quickly.

Removing shoots
Prune back broad-leaved evergreen hedges by removing the tips of growing shoots with secateurs.

Stopping a leader
Cut back the main stem to encourage side shoots to grow.

Trimming laterals
Cut back any laterals by about half to encourage a bushy habit.

Formative pruning
Hard prune when mature to ensure even, vigorous growth.

Mature formal hedges

As the hedge becomes taller, trim the sides to a sloping angle so that the top of the hedge is only about a third as wide as the base, or about 25cm (10in) wide. When the hedge has reached its intended height, a frame or template can be made of the hedge profile, and this can be used as a quick guide, when trimming, to keep the hedge to an even, uniform shape.

Formal hedges should always be shaped to be narrower at the top than at the base. This exposes all parts of the hedge to the light, stops parts of it dying out, (especially at the base) and makes trimming easier. This sloping angle helps the hedge to resist strong winds and to shed snow, rather than have it accumulate on the top, causing damage. This is a particular problem with evergreens, as they can collect large quantities of snow and ice in winter weather.

Clipping sideshoots
Clip sideshoots to remove the growing tip of each shoot and encourage bushy growth.

Trimming to an A-shape
Trimming the hedge to be narrower at the top prevents snow settling and damaging it.

Trimming techniques

Start by trimming the sides of the hedge with shears or hedge trimmers. Work upwards from the base of the hedge so that the clippings fall out of the way as the work progresses. To make sure the top of the hedge is level, use a taut line set at the required height. It is wise to use a brightly coloured line, as this will reduce the chance of accidentally cutting through it. Clip the top of the hedge to the line, clearing clippings as you work.

Cutting line
Use brightly coloured string stretched tautly to make sure that the hedge is cut in a straight line.

Power hedge trimmer

These are ideal for long hedges which are to be trimmed to a formal shape on a regular basis. The electric ones have several advantages over the petrol-powered models. They are lighter, make far less noise and produce no fumes. When using a mechanical trimmer always keep the blade parallel to the surface of the hedge.

Using a trimmer
To protect yourself, wear gloves and goggles. Cut the hedge in a broad sweeping action, working from the bottom upwards.

Renovating hedges

The method used can vary, but in extreme cases the plant is cut to within 10cm (4in) of the base to stimulate the production of new shoots. As the hedge regrows, the process of formative pruning and training will have to be carried out as for a newly-planted hedge.

Phased renovation pruning involves cutting the hedge back in stages so the effect is not so drastic. Cut one side back to the main stems in the first year and then repeat the procedure on the other side of the hedge the following year.

Such drastic action can create problems, such as a sudden lack of privacy, for instance. Or a previously sheltered area might suddenly become exposed, to adverse effect. Consider these risks when planning the operation. Most conifers do not have the ability to produce new growth from old wood and so are not really suited to renovation pruning.

Hard pruning a hedge
This promotes new growth from the base to the top of an old hedge.

Maintaining a healthy hedge

A hedge not only provides shelter for surrounding plants, but also for anything growing or living inside it. At certain times of year, the enclosed environment inside the hedge is warm and humid. These are the ideal conditions for colonization by pests and diseases – and for their spread. This makes pruning even more important.

Any dead or dying wood which is left in the hedge can, potentially, be the very first place where diseases establish themselves – so any infected wood must be removed as soon as it is spotted. For deciduous plants, this may be in the autumn when the leaves have fallen. For evergreen plants, the ideal time is when the hedge is being trimmed and there is less foliage to obscure any plant problems.

When dead wood is being removed, always cut back into live, healthy tissue, as this will reduce the chances of a secondary infection.

Removing diseased wood
Cut out any infected, dead or dying wood as soon as you see it.

Mature informal hedges

Informal flowering or mixed hedges are far less work than formal types, and only need pruning once a year. An informal hedge should be treated as a row of shrubs rather than the single entity of a formal hedge. The timing of pruning depends on the flowering season, as any cutting back is usually done after the flowers have died.

Prune a berrying hedge after the birds have eaten the berries. Remove the old stalks and shoot tips, which held the fruits, to make room for new flowers. Cut back a number of flower-bearing shoots close to ground level.

Mixed hedge before pruning

Mixed shrubs in a hedge will grow at different rates. Prune once a year when hedge starts to look untidy.

Mixed hedge after pruning

Cut back any very vigorous plants, removing long, straggling stems. Lightly clip the remainder.

Flowering hedge

Prune a flowering hedge after flowering. Cut shoots close to the ground to encourage new shoots to grow from the base.

Encouraging growth

Cut flower-bearing shoots to the ground after the flowers have died.

Suitable hedging plants

Plant	Evergreen/ deciduous	Planting distances m/ft	Formal/ Informal/ Either	Best height	When to prune or clip
Berberis thunbergii (Barbery)	Deciduous	90cm (3ft)	Either	0.6–1.2m (2–4ft)	**Formal** once: summer **Informal** once: after flowering
Buxus sempervirens (Box)	Evergreen	1–2m (4ft)	Either	1.2m (4ft)	Twice: late spring and early autumn Once: late summer
Carpinus betulus (Hornbeam)	Deciduous	60cm (2ft)	Formal	1.5–6m (5–20ft)	
Chamaecyparis lawsoniana (Lawson's cypress)	Evergreen	1.2m (4ft)	Formal	1.2–2.4m (4–8ft)	Twice: late spring and early autumn
Cotoneaster lacteus (Cotoneaster)	Evergreen	90cm (3ft)	Informal	1.5–2.2m (5–7ft)	Once: after fruiting
Crataegus monogyna (Hawthorn)	Deciduous	60cm (2ft)	Either	1.5–3m (5–10ft)	**Formal** twice: summer and autumn **Informal** once: in winter
Elaeagnus x *ebbingei*	Evergreen	1.2m (4ft)	Formal	1.5–3m (5–10ft)	Once: mid to late summer
Escallonia spp	Evergreen	90cm (3ft)	Either	1.2–2.4m (4–8ft)	Once: immediately after flowering
Fagus sylvatica (Beech)	Deciduous	60cm (2ft)	Formal	1.5–6m (5–20ft)	Once: late summer
Fuchsia magellanica	Deciduous	60cm (2ft)	Informal	1–1.5m (3–5ft)	Once: spring to remove old stems
Ilex aquifolium (Holly)	Evergreen	90cm (3ft)	Either	2–4m (6½–13ft)	Once: late summer For berries: once, in early spring
Lavandula spp (Lavender)	Evergreen	30cm (1ft)	Either	0.5–1m (1½–3ft)	Twice: spring and after flowering
Ligustrum spp (Privet)	Evergreen	45cm (1½ft)	Formal	1.5–6m (5–20ft)	Three times; not in winter
Prunus laurocerasus (Laurel)	Evergreen	75cm (2½ft)	Formal	1.2–3m (4–10ft)	Once: mid to late summer
Pyracantha (Firethorn)	Evergreen	75cm (2½ft)	Either	2–3m (6½–10ft)	Twice: after flowering and in autumn (avoid berries)
Rosa rugosa	Deciduous	90cm (3ft)	Informal	1–1.5m (3–5ft)	Once: in spring, remove oldest
Taxus baccata (Yew)	Evergreen	60cm (2ft)	Formal	1.2–6m (4–20ft)	Twice: summer and autumn
Viburnum tinus	Evergreen	60cm (2ft)	Informal	1–2.4m (3–8ft)	Once: after flowering

Topiary

Topiary is a form of pruning, training and clipping plants into artificial shapes. The designs can be elaborate or simple, and have a strong architectural element. As well as being suited to hedges and plants in containers, topiary in the garden makes a strong focal point, adding to the structural and vertical interest.

The more intricate the shape, the more frequently the pruning and training has to be done. The secret with topiary is little and often. Trim shoots while they are short, to keep them branching. This is best done by pinching out the growing point between finger and thumb. Most designs are easy to form, if you create a template or framework to help avoid uneven trimming. The plants most suited to topiary are small-leaved, slow-growing evergreens, as they retain their shape and require less frequent clipping. Box (*Buxus sempervirens*) and yew (*Taxus buccata*) are among the most popular shrubs for this purpose. A quick-growing, poor man's topiary centre can be created by training a climber like ivy (*Hedera helix*) over a topiary frame.

Topiary cone
Box is grown into a striking topiary cone (left), adding structure to a perennial border.

Paired topiary
Round box topiary (above) is paired to elegant effect to focus attention on a weathered statue.

Shaping simple topiary

For the beginner, a simple uncomplicated shape is ideal, because topiary requires a fair degree of precision, and techniques which are slightly different than those used for many other forms of pruning. All of the cutting tools used for clipping topiary must be extremely sharp because the shoots are very soft and sappy when pruned and prone to disease if torn.

It is easy to forget that training topiary is a combination of tying shoots into position as well as pruning and trimming.

Training a pyramid
1 *When the shrub is roughly 45cm (18in) tall, create a cone-shaped frame using three canes.*

2 *Pinch out the top growing point so lateral shoots develop, and clip shoots outside the frame.*

Topiary forms

The more elaborate the intended topiary figure, the longer it will take to create, with figures of birds and animals taking years of skill and patience to achieve a recognizable outline and shape.

Basic designs and forms take in cones, globes, obelisks and pyramids, with spirals being introduced into these basic shapes.

To make clipping and shaping more symmetrical, frames or templates (either ready-made or simply constructed from wires or canes) can be used as a guide, with the frame being lowered over the selected plant, and the plant being trimmed to shape as it grows through the frame (see left).

The frame can be left in position to provide structural support throughout the year.

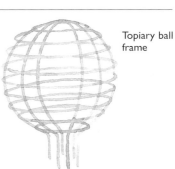

Topiary ball frame

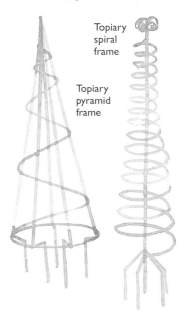

Topiary spiral frame

Topiary pyramid frame

General maintenance

Certain tasks have to be done on a regular basis to keep a garden in good order. Obviously, much depends on the size, scale and nature of your garden. Some tasks are based around the plants – dead-heading fading and dying flowers, removing dead leaves, and cutting down herbaceous perennials in the autumn, for example. But when the weather is inclement, it is also time to turn the attention to the care of any hard surfaces, or man-made features, that the garden contains. Surfaces need to be swept in autumn to remove fallen leaves. Wooden structures and decking may need a coat of preservative once a year, or at least an annual scrub, as does garden furniture. Painted surfaces may need a new lick of paint, and garden tools need to be oiled and their blades sharpened. In a cold climate, bring tender plants under cover as soon as the temperature drops in autumn.

Well-maintained garden
Behind the seemingly effortless profusion of flowers and shrubs lie hours of routine tasks and manual labour diligently carried out.

Clearing a border

In autumn, the dying remains of herbaceous perennials should be cut down and the remains composted or burned. When the times comes for a border to be redesigned, replanted or eliminated altogether, this will inevitably mean that the border has to be cleared completely.

Lift and remove any plants which are to be kept for use in another area of the garden.

If the border is neglected or overgrown, dig out as many perennial weeds as possible, and remove or burn them. Then dig over the border (usually by double digging) to remove any roots and break up compacted soil. Often a chemical weedkiller will be applied 3-4 weeks later to kill off any germinating weed seedlings as they emerge.

Clearing dying plants
Cut down dying perennials and annuals each autumn.

Renovating a border
When the border needs replanting, clear it section by section.

Overwintering shrubs

You can help plants that are too tender to survive cold winters in various ways, depending on the plant's hardiness and the degree of frost. In severe winters, half-hardy or tender plants must be brought under cover, but often they can be over-wintered, in situ, by wrapping roots with hessian, covering them with straw, or wrapping container plants in hessian or bubble-plastic. Larger plants with tender leaves can be netted to protect them from cold and searing winds.

Using bubble wrap
Swathing containers in bubble wrap polythene provides some insulation against the elements

Wrapping shrubs
Insulation is provided for this shrub by a straw base and a wrapping of mesh netting.

Netting a larger plant
Fine mesh netting secured around a framework of canes gives plants some protection from cold winds.

Removing leaves

It pays to remove any dead leaves in autumn as a basic task in garden hygiene – they tend to harbour pests and diseases which may well attack your plants.

You can make good use of the leaves by bagging them in a bin liner, tying the liner up, and then prodding it with a fork to create air holes. In time, this will rot down into good leaf mould for the garden (see p. 213).

Make sure that you remove accumulated leaves that fall or drift onto the centre of herbaceous perennials. If you fail to do this, the result may well be that the crown of the plant dies back, leaving an ugly, dead centre. The leaves also present a risk of disease, and provide a shelter for slugs and snails.

Regularly sweep leaves from paths and steps, as in winter months the leaves become slimy and create a potential hazard.

Maintaining hygiene
It is important to remove fallen leaves from the crowns of plants – this will prevent them from rotting and falling prey to pest and diseases.

Cleaning a pond

If you do not net your pond in autumn, to prevent fallen leaves from fouling the water, or if you fail to scoop most of them out, you will have to remove the debris of rotting leaves from its depths.

Carry out this task in early autumn, and you can use the opportunity to remove any baskets of water plants, and divide those that are outgrowing their pots. If you have stocked the pond with fish, remove them with a net and keep them, in a large container of pondwater, in a shady spot, while you carry out the task. Scoop the debris from the bottom of the pond, using a net, taking great care not to pierce any plastic pond lining you may have installed. Allow the pond water to resettle for at least a day before reinstating the fish.If necessary use a water balancing chemical to improve its quality.

Maintaining a pond
Cleaning a pond is a good opportunity to divide plants that have outgrown their baskets.

Moving heavy containers around

If you live in a cold climate, and have chosen to plant your outdoor containers, permanently, with tender or half-hardy plants,you should overwinter them in a frost-free environment. Moving plants can be difficult and it is very easy to hurt yourself because containers full of soil are often extremely heavy.

There are several time-honoured tricks that should facilitate the move. The first is to use four metal rods. One person inserts them under the pot, while the other person rolls the pot over them. The first rod is then taken out at the back and re-inserted at the front as the pot is pushed along, making a continuous rolling platform. Another simple method is to roll the pot along on the edge of its base. As an alternative, manoeuvre a pot, carefully, onto a heavy-duty hessian sack, with the help of another person, and then drag the pot along the ground, by pulling the sack, to its destination.

Care of decking

First check out what sort of wood the decking is made of. Hardwoods, like teak, need an annual scrub with a stiff brush, and maybe a coat of fungicide to remove any algae growths. Softwoods, like larch, need a yearly coat of preservative. If the decking has been given a coating of wood stain, it may need renewing every couple of years. Finally, go round and tap back in any nails that are protruding from the surface.

Dragging a container
With the help of another person, manoeuvre the container onto a heavyweight cloth. It is much easier to drag the cloth than carry the container.

Rolling a container
To avoid lifting a heavy pot full of soil, roll it carefully on the edge of its base, making sure the plant is held in place, securely, at the same time.

Scrubbing decking
Hardwood decking needs an annual scrubbing and also benefits from a coat of fungicide.

Edible garden calendar

Once you have decided to grow edible plants in your garden, you are committed to certain tasks at certain times of the year. The main tasks in the edible garden are to prepare the soil, plant, water and feed regularly, and harvest. Autumn, spring and summer are the busiest times of year. In autumn, the soil has to be dug over and fertilized, and much harvesting takes place; spring is the time to do most of the sowing and planting and certain plants will need to be protected until the risk of any late frosts has passed. Throughout the summer you will be fully occupied with weeding, watering, feeding and successional planting.

Winter is the quiet time, when you can sit and plan your next year's crops and order seeds and new plants

Spring

Early spring

Plant onion sets and shallots
Apply manures and fertilizers
Prepare the soil for sowing hardier vegetables
Start sowing hardier vegetables outdoors
Sow early crops under protection
Chit seed potatoes
Cover germinating vegetables with fleece or floating mulch
Cover early-cropping strawberries
Check any fruit and vegetables held in store
Continue to harvest overwintered vegetables
Continue pruning top fruit and soft fruit

Mid-spring

Plant out asparagus crowns
Plant onion sets
Plant potatoes
Plant out brassica seedlings
Apply manures and fertilizers
Prepare the soil for sowing hardier vegetables
Start sowing maincrop vegetables outdoors
Sow maincrop vegetables under protection
Cover germinating vegetables with fleece or floating mulch
Cover early-cropping strawberries
Hand pollinate blossom on wall-trained fruit trees
Cover fruit blossom with fleece in frosty weather

Late spring

Plant out greenhouse tomatoes and cucumbers
Plant out maincrop vegetables outdoors
Plant out or sow runner beans
Plant potatoes
Plant out brassica seedlings
Apply manures and fertilizers
Start sowing salad vegetables outdoors
Prepare the soil for sowing vegetables
Sow maincrop vegetables outdoors
Sow sweetcorn, outdoor tomatoes and other tender vegetables under protection
Mulch early-cropping strawberries
Cover fruit blossom with fleece in frosty weather
Protect vegetable plants from birds

Summer

Early summer

Sow sweetcorn outdoors
Plant potatoes
Plant out vegetable seedlings
Sow seeds of brassicas for later crops
Sow runner beans
Sow French beans
Watch for blackfly on broad beans
Watch for root flies on brassicas, carrots and onions
Successional sowings of vegetable and salad crops

Midsummer

Hoe regularly to keep down weeds
Make successional sowings of beetroot, carrots, lettuces and turnips
Check plants for signs of water stress and water regularly
Thin fruits on apples if necessary
Thin out vegetable seedlings
Tidy up strawberries after fruiting
Pinch out the growing points of runner beans when they reach the tops of their supports
Topdress fruit and vegetables with a fast-acting fertilizer to give them a boost
Remove yellowing leaves and sideshoots from tomato plants
Sow seeds of brassicas for later crops
Sow French beans
Watch for blackfly on broad beans
Watch for root flies on brassicas, carrots and onions
Successional sowings of herbs and salad crops

Late summer

Hoe regularly to keep down weeds
Lift onions and shallots when the tops have died down
Check plants for signs of water stress and water regularly
Thin fruits on apples if necessary
Summer-prune trained fruit trees
Protect fruit against birds
Thin out vegetable seedlings
Harvest herbs while the leaves are tender
Feed tomatoes regularly
Tidy up strawberries after fruiting
Pinch out the growing points of runner beans when they reach the tops of their supports
Topdress fruit and vegetables with a fast-acting fertilizer to give them a boost
Remove yellowing leaves and sideshoots from tomato plants
Successional sowings of herbs and salad crops

from the catalogues. It is also time perhaps to oil and sharpen any gardening tools, or apply a coat of wood preservative to the garden shed and fences.

What you choose to grow will determine precisely when you are most busy. The calendar below gives you some good general guidelines, but ideally you should have your own notebook in which you list the tasks you need to prepare for and do. It is also a great help if you note down the names of crops that you find do

especially well in your particular soil. For example, you may have great success with a specific type of potato or runner bean.

Maintaining a successful edible garden demands a methodical, orderly approach, and a commitment to the garden throughout the year. It is not a choice for people who garden only very occasionally or who are likely to be off on protracted holidays when much of their crop is ready to be harvested.

Autumn

Early autumn

Lift onions for storing
Lift and store maincrop potatoes
Prune raspberries
Harvest apples
Clean and store stakes and supports that are no longer needed
Protect outdoor tomatoes with cloches to speed up ripening
Sow green manures

Mid-autumn

Plant cabbages for spring harvest
Earth up celery and leeks
Bend over the leaves of cauliflowers to protect them from frost
Apply greasebands to fruit trees
Prune blackcurrants and take hardwood cuttings of currants
Prune gooseberries and raspberries
Cut down asparagus
Start winter digging

Late autumn

Bend over the leaves of cauliflowers to protect them from frost
Pot up herbs for winter use
Hang up herbs to dry
Plant bareroot fruit bushes and trees
Continue winter digging
Lift and store root crops for winter use
Continue to harvest and store apples and pears
Take hardwood cuttings of currants

Winter

Early winter

Test soil pH before applying lime
Hang up garlic bulbs to dry
Plant bareroot fruit bushes and trees
Continue winter digging
Lift and store root crops for winter use
Continue to harvest and store apples and pears
Check fruit in store
Plant hedges (bareroot)
Lift layered plants
Start forcing rhubarb
Lift leeks and parsnips as required
Take hardwood cuttings of currants
Disinfect canes and supports before storage

Midwinter

Test soil pH before applying lime
Hang up garlic bulbs to dry
Plant container-grown fruit bushes and trees
Continue winter digging
Sow broad beans under cloches
Plant garlic
Lift and store root crops for winter use
Check fruit in store
Plant hedges (bareroot)
Lift layered plants
Start forcing rhubarb
Lift leeks and parsnips as required
Disinfect canes and supports before storage

Late winter

Hang up garlic bulbs to dry
Plant container-grown fruit bushes and trees
Finish winter digging
Sow broad beans under cloches
Prepare trenches for celery and runner beans
Spray stone fruits to combat Peach leaf curl
Lift and store root crops for winter use
Check fruit in store
Plant hedges (bareroot)
Lift layered plants
Start forcing rhubarb
Chit 'seed' potatoes (earlies)
Cover soil with cloches to pre-warm it for early crops
Plant shallots
Lift leeks and parsnips as required

Ornamental garden calendar

Gardening is an all-year-round pastime, with certain tasks that are season-specific. Planting, for example, is normally done when the plants are dormant but the ground is still workable – in early autumn or early spring. It is only too easy to forget tasks until the season is past – if you do not order the seeds you want in time, it will be too late when they arrive to plant them, or if you do not take cuttings at the appropriate time, you will have missed the opportunity until next year.

Garden tasks are numerous, but will depend on the kind of garden you have and the amount of work you are prepared to put into it. You may not, for example, wish to grow plants from seed or take cuttings, in which case the amount of work can be considerably reduced.

Spring

Early spring

Finish planting bareroot trees and shrubs
Continue to plant container-grown trees and shrubs
Plant herbaceous perennials
Sow seeds of hardy annuals
Sow seeds of half-hardy annuals (under protection)
Sow sweet peas
Prick out/pot up seedlings (under protection)
Sow lawn grass seed or lay turf in mild weather
Fertilize and mulch flower beds and borders
Start mowing the lawn (on a high setting)
Prune winter flowering shrubs

Mid-spring

Plant hedges
Continue to plant container-grown trees and shrubs
Plant out sweet peas
Plant herbaceous perennials
Sow seeds of hardy annuals
Sow seeds of half-hardy annuals (under protection)
Prick out/pot up seedlings (under protection)
Take cuttings of pot plants and summer bedding
Sow lawn grass seed or lay turf in mild weather
Fertilize and mulch flower beds and borders
Fertilize the lawn
Mow the lawn regularly
Prune winter flowering shrubs
Prune roses
Stake herbaceous perennials

Late spring

Continue to plant container grown shrubs
Plant up hanging baskets, window boxes and shrubs
Plant herbaceous perennials
Sow seeds of hardy annuals
Sow seeds of half-hardy annuals (under protection)
Prick out/pot up seedlings (under protection)
Take cuttings of pot plants and summer bedding
Fertilize and mulch flower beds and borders
Fertilize the lawn
Mow the lawn regularly
Prune spring flowering shrubs
Stake herbaceous perennials

Summer

Early summer

Deadhead flowers regularly
Continue planting hanging baskets, containers and window boxes
Stake herbaceous plants when they become 15cm (6in) high
Plant out dahlias
Feed pot plants regularly
Take out wood cuttings of shrubs and house plants
Prune late-spring flowering shrubs
Sow seeds of biennials (wallflowers, myosotis etc.)
Fertilize roses as the first flush of flowers ends
Watch for signs of mildew, blackspot and aphids and treat accordingly
Finish hardening off tender bedding plants
Mow the lawn on a high setting in dry weather

Midsummer

Deadhead flowers regularly
Hoe beds and borders regularly to control weeds
Take softwood and semi-ripe cuttings
Transplant biennials (wallflowers, mysotic etc) into nursery beds
Mow the lawn on a high setting in dry weather
Watch for signs of mildew and aphids and treat accordingly
Layer trees and shrubs
Feed pot plants regularly
Use biological control for glasshouse pests
Clip hedges of deciduous plants (beech, hawthorn and hornbeam)
Continue to stake herbaceous plants when they grow

Late summer

Deadhead flowers regularly
Hoe beds and borders regularly to control weeds
Take softwood and semi-ripe cuttings
Take cuttings of fuchsia and geranium
Keep paths and drives weed-free, by hand or using chemicals
Mow the lawn as required
Watch for signs of mildew and aphids and treat accordingly
Layer trees and shrubs
Feed pot plants regularly
Use biological controls for glasshouse pests
Clip evergreen hedges (box, cupressus, holly, laurel and yew)
Check plants for signs of water stress and water regularly
Water lawns if necessary

On these pages we give a guide as to the most likely tasks you will need to undertake, and the season during which they should probably be carried out.

Ideally, you should make up your own garden notebook in a simple diary, listing the things that you need to do, and tasks of particular importance in your garden. It is also well worthwhile keeping a note of what perennials and bulbs you have planted where – without it, you can easily forget and it is only too easy,

once foliage has died down in autumn, to dig up precious plants without even realizing you have done so.

Be as methodical as you can about gardening tasks, but do remember that going out regularly in the garden, armed with a sharp pair of secateurs, will keep your garden in better condition than a once-a-month or once-a-season blitz on it. Pruning, for example, is best done for most flowering plants after flowering rather than in a specific season.

Autumn

Early autumn

Deadhead flowers regularly
Hoe beds and borders regularly to control weeds
Take semi-ripe cuttings
Take cuttings of fuchsia and geranium
Keep paths and drives weed-free, by hand or using chemicals
Plant lilies and spring-flowering bulbs
Mow the lawn as required
Watch for signs of mildew and aphids and treat accordingly
Feed pot plants regularly
Check plants for signs of water stress and water regularly
Water lawns if necessary

Mid-autumn

Lay turf or sow grass seed for new lawns
Hoe beds and borders regularly to control weeds
Take root cuttings
Clear summer bedding
Plant spring bedding
Lift and divide herbaceous plants
Lift gladioli
Take cuttings of fuchsia and geranium
Collect and compost leaves as they fall
Plant lilies and spring-flowering bulbs
Feed the lawn as required, and treat for moss and broad-leaved weeds
Lift and pot tender bedding

Late autumn

Take root cuttings
Lift and divide herbaceous plants
Collect and compost leaves as they fall
Plant lilies and spring flowering bulbs
Cut down the dead tops on herbaceous perennials
Take hardwood cuttings
Continue planting
Plant bareroot trees and shrubs

Winter

Early winter

Test soil pH before applying lime
Make a new compost heap
Take root cuttings
Lift and divide herbaceous plants
Collect and compost leaves as they fall
Cut down the dead tops on herbaceous perennials
Take hardwood cuttings
Order seeds
Check stored bulbs, corms and tubers for mould and rot
Plant bareroot trees and shrubs
Clean and service lawnmower before winter storage

Midwinter

Test soil pH before applying lime
Make a new compost heap
Take root cuttings
Collect and compost leaves as they fall
Cut down the dead tops on herbaceous perennials
Order seeds and bulbs
Check stored bulbs, corms and tubers for mould and rot
Plant container-grown trees and shrubs
Clean and service lawnmower before winter storage
Plant hedges (bareroot)
Lift layered plants
Knock heavy snow off hedges and conifers before it turns to ice
Insulate cold frames against frost

Late winter

Test soil pH before applying lime
Plant climbers
Apply manures and fertilizers
Mulch established fruit trees
Collect and compost garden waste
Order seeds and bulbs
Check stored bulbs, corms and tubers for moulds and rots
Plant container-grown trees and shrubs
Plant hedges (bareroot)
Lift layered plants
Knock heavy snow off hedges and conifers before it turns to ice
Insulate cold frames against frost
Sow sweet peas
Keep off the lawn if it is frozen
Apply mulches to beds and borders

Pests and diseases

Vigorous, healthy plants are far less likely to succumb to pests and diseases than those that are stressed by poor management techniques. This is why it is vital that plants are planted at their appropriate spacing in well-prepared soil in a suitably sheltered, sunny or shady position in the garden, greenhouse or indoors. If a plant appears to be struggling, try to discover the cause and treat the plant as soon as possible.

Some of the most widespread pests that attack fruit and vegetable plants are aphids, birds (soft fruit being very vulnerable), earwigs (which like young vegetables), and slugs and snails (which relish all vegetables). Diseases such as botrytis (grey mould) are common to all fruits, especially soft fruits, and most vegetables. Other common plant disorders that may occur include deficiencies of nutrients such as iron, nitrogen, phosphate and potash, and a lack, or irregular supply, of water (which causes bolting). Some prevalent pests and diseases that affect vegetables and herbs include black spot, downy mildew, leaf scale, powdery mildew and rust.

The more common problems are explained in the charts below and right. You may also refer to the list of fruit and vegetables, as this details which plants are especially vulnerable, and to what type of attack. Prompt action needs to be taken at the first sign of blight in order to protect the remainder of your crops.

Pests

Description	Symptoms	Prevention	Controls
Aphids Pale green, through pink to greeny black coloured winged and wingless insects, which transmit viruses between plants.	Distorted shoot tips and leaves, sticky (honeydew) on lower leaves.	Remove and burn badly infected plants.	Spray with insecticide (pirimiphosmethyl) as soon as first aphids are seen.
Birds Various types and species feed on parts of the plant at certain times of the year.	Holes pecked in fruit by blackbirds, brassicas defoliated by wood pigeons, fruit buds eaten by finches, crocus flowers eaten by sparrows.	Use bird scarers or nets as barriers to deter birds.	Netting or loud noise at infrequent intervals are the most effective controls; bird repellents are very unreliable.
Caterpillars The larvae of butterflies and moths, long tubular bodies, vary greatly in colour and size depending on the species.	Holes eaten in the leaves and young stems, plants may become totally defoliated, reducing vigour and cropping potential. Some caterpillars form a white protective webbing over the feeding site.	Spray fruit trees with winter wash to kill overwintering eggs, small infestations can be picked off.	Spray with insecticide (pirimiphosmethyl), or introduce the bacterium Bacillus thuringiensis to control some caterpillars biologically.
Eelworms Mostly microscopic worm-like pests, which live in the roots, leaves and stems of plants.	Yellowing of the leaves, stunted growth and wilting, small knobbly swellings on the roots. Infected plants do not store well, and often wither and rot.	Resistant cultivars, good drainage, correct crop rotations.	Remove and burn any plants with the above symptoms.
Flies Damage caused by these garden pests is done at the larval (maggot) stage rather than by adult flies.	Brown marks and lesions in roots, flowers, fruits, bulbs and stems. Often leaving a residue of brown waste (frass), crops are inedible, as maggots may still be present.	Sow crops later in midsummer, cover crops with fleece, put insect barriers around plants.	Spray or drench with insecticide (pirimiphosmethyl), or apply (bromophos) granules soon after sowing or planting.
Red spider mites Minute mites which feed on the sap of plants, a serious problem in dry summers when their populations reach epidemic proportions.	Yellow stunted growth, curled and mottled leaves covered with a fine webbing made by the adult insects. Plant vigour greatly reduced, and plants eventually die if not treated.	Resistant cultivars, remove and burn infected plants, maintain good air circulation.	Spray with insecticide (pirimiphosmethyl), at regular intervals, or introduce the parasitic insect Phytoseiulus to control the pest biologically.
Slugs and snails Slugs are slimy, with tubular-shaped bodies, up to 10cm long, creamy white to grey or jet black in colour. Snails are similar, but with shells.	Circular holes in the plant tissue often cause extensive cavities, attacks usually take place during the night.	Keep soil well-drained, weed- and debris-free. Apply mulches of gravel or soot as a barrier.	Apply suitable chemical baits, or use slug traps filled with stale beer.
Wasps Large, scavenging insects which cause damage to ripening fruit.	Holes eaten in fruit: soft skinned fruits, such as plums, are attacked by wasps, but harder skinned fruits, like apples, are visited by wasps after the skin has been injured.	Cover fruiting plants with fine mesh netting or fleece until the fruit is picked.	Use insecticidal traps to catch and kill wasps, if nests can be found, treat with insecticidal dust (pirimiphos-methyl).

Diseases

Description	Symptoms	Prevention	Controls
Botrytis Fungus infecting fruits and flowers, more common in damp, humid conditions.	A covering of grey, felt-like mould, infected plant parts decay rapidly.	Remove and burn badly infected plant parts.	Spray with thiophanate-methyl.
Clubroot Soil-borne fungus which attacks plant roots and may survive for up to 20 years in the soil.	Roots become swollen and distorted, leaves turn yellow and wilt, causing the plant to collapse and die.	Resistant cultivars, good drainage, correct crop rotations.	Dip the roots in a thick paste of thiophanate-methyl and water before planting.
Cankers Swellings or distorted growth on stems, roots, flowers or leaves of plants.	Open wounds, some weeping, uneven scar tissue, irregular stem development or large, corky textured swellings.	Avoid damaging plants, improve drainage.	Fungal: remove infected branches, apply fungicide; bacterial: remove and burn plant.
Downy mildew A fungus which infects flowers, fruits, leaves and stems.	Discoloured, yellow leaves with white patches underneath, plants slowly die.	Resistant cultivars, remove and burn infected plants, good air circulation.	Spray with fungicide such as mancozeb.
Fireblight Bacterial disease, more common in a warm, humid spring, invading soft tissue of plants and eventually killing them.	Flowers and young shoots become blackened and shrivelled, leaves wilt and turn brown, shoots die back and plants eventually die.	Remove and burn any plants with the symptoms listed.	See prevention.
Mosaic virus Organism living in, and feeding on plants.	Yellow, distorted plants, poor growth, striped misshapen flowers and fruits.	Virus-free plants, control eelworms.	Remove and burn any infected plants.
Powdery mildew A fungal disease which invades the leaves, eventually killing the whole plant.	White felt-like patches on the young leaves of plants, distorted shoots and premature leaf fall.	Resistant cultivars, remove and burn infected plants.	Spray thiophanate-methyl on young leaves (the fungus cannot penetrate old leaves).
Rusts A fungal disease invading leaves, tends to be worse in warm, humid conditions.	Orange-brown spots on the leaves and stems, general reduction in growth, yellowing of the leaves and defoliation.	Grow resistant cultivars, improve air circulation.	Remove infected leaves and plants, apply a fungicide such as bupirimate or mancozeb.
Rots Decay caused by fungal or bacterial organism. Infection spreads easily.	Soft watery tissue, often smelling of putrefaction, usually close to a scratch, bruise or other injury.	Avoid damaging plants, improve drainage.	Fungal: remove infected plants, dust with fungicide; bacterial: remove and burn plant.
Silver leaf Fungus entering the woody tissue of members of the plum and cherry family.	Silvery sheen on leaves, dying branches, brownish-purple fungal brackets on branches and stems. Plants die.	Prune in summer when no fungal spores are released.	Prune out infected branches, removed and burn badly infected trees.

Plants affected

Apples: birds, caterpillars, wasps, fireblight, powdery mildew.
Apricots: birds, wasps, fireblight, silver leaf.
Asparagus: rusts, violet root rot.
Asparagus peas: caterpillars, eelworms, flies, birds, downy and powdery mildews, rusts.
Aubergines, chilli peppers: red spider mites, downy and powdery mildews.
Beetroot: flies, downy mildew, rusts.
Blackberries: rusts.
Blackcurrants, celeriac, celery, sweetcorn: flies.
Broad beans: flies, birds, rusts.
Broccoli, kohl rabi: clubroot, caterpillars, flies, downy and powdery mildews.
Brussels sprouts, cabbages, calabrese, Chinese cabbages, cauliflowers: caterpillars, eelworms, flies, clubroot, downy and powdery mildews.
Carrots: caterpillars, eelworms, flies, violet root rot.
Cherries: birds, wasps, canker caterpillars, fireblight, silver leaf.
Courgettes, pumpkins, squashes, marrows: powdery mildew.
Cucumbers: red spider mites, root rots, powdery mildew.
Damsons: wasps, canker, fireblight, silver leaf.
Dwarf beans, runner beans: flies, foot and root rots, rusts.
Endive, lettuces: caterpillars, flies, downy mildew, rusts.
Garlic: eelworms, downy mildew.
Gooseberries: birds, rusts, caterpillars, powdery mildew.

Grapefruits, lemons, oranges, sweet peppers: red spider mites.
Grapes: red spider mites, wasps, downy and powdery mildews.
Greengages: wasps, canker, silver leaf.
Kale: caterpillars, clubroot.
Leeks: caterpillars, eelworms, flies, rusts, white rot.
Lima beans: flies, rusts.
Mangetouts, peas: caterpillars, eelworms, flies, foot and root rots, downy and powdery mildews, rusts.
Melons, strawberries: red spider mites, powdery mildew.
Nectarines: red spider mites, wasps, fireblight, silver leaf.
Okra: caterpillars, powdery mildew.
Onions, shallots: eelworms, flies, downy mildew, root rots.
Parsnips: canker, downy mildew, violet root rot.
Peaches: red spider mites, wasps, fireblight, powdery mildew, silver leaf.
Pears: birds, caterpillars, flies, wasps, brown rot, fireblight.
Plums: birds, caterpillars, wasps, canker, powdery mildew, rusts, silver leaf.
Potatoes: eelworms, violet root rot.
Raspberries: caterpillars, flies, rusts.
Rhubarb: crown rot
Spinach, Swiss chard: downy mildew.
Swedes: clubroot, downy and powdery mildews, violet root rot.
Tomatoes: caterpillars, red spider mites, eelworms, foot and root rots.
Turnips: clubroot, violet root rot.

Plants for particular purposes

The following plants are valuable for particular situations. Some are ideal for planting in hanging baskets or containers, others, such as trees and evergreen shrubs, make especially useful framework plants for the garden.

A range of choices for perennial borders are listed according to colour, and there are also suggestions for plants with interesting foliage colour to add to mixed shrub and perennial plantings.

Key
a = annual and biennial
a/p tender perennials treated as annuals
b = bulb
c = climber
p = perennial
s = shrub
t = tree

Good container plants
Agapanthus (p − blue)
Ageratum (a − blue)
Alonsoa (a − orange)
Argyranthemum (a/p − white, pink, yellow)
Begonia x *tuberhybrida* (a/p - pink, red, orange, white)
Begonia semperflorens (a − mixed colours)
Bidens ferulifolia (a − yellow)
Brachycome iberidifolia (a − blue)
Buxus sempervirens (s − foliage)
Cordyline australis (p − foliage)
Diascia (p − pink, orange)
Felicia amelloides (a − blue)
Fuchsia (s − pink, purple, red)
Helichrysum petiolare (a/p − foliage)
Hosta (p − foliage)
Hyacinthus (b − mixed colours)
Hydrangea (s −blue, pink, white)
Impatiens walleriana (a/p− white, pink, red)
Laurus nobilis (s − foliage)
Lobelia (a − blue, pink, white)
Narcissus (b − yellow, white)
Nemisia (a − mixed colours)
Pelargonium (a/p − orange, pink, red, white)
Petunia (a/p − mixed colours)
Phormium (p - foliage)
Primula (p − mixed colours)
Senecio cinerea (a/p − foliage)
Tagetes (a − yellow, orange)
Tropaeolum (a − red, orange, yellow)
Tulipa (b − mixed colours)

Verbena x *hybrida* (a/p − mixed colours)
Viola x *wittrockiana* (a − mixed colours)

Good hanging basket plants
Ageratum (a − blue)
Alonsoa (a − orange)
Argyranthemum (a/p − white, pink, yellow)
Begonia x *tuberhybrida* (a/p - pink, red, orange, white)
Begonia semperflorens (a − mixed colours)
Bidens ferulifolia (a − yellow)
Brachycome iberidifolia (a − blue)
Diascia (p − pink, orange)
Felicia amelloides (a − blue)
Fuchsia (s − pink, purple, red)
Glechoma hederacea 'Variegata' (a − foliage)
Hedera helix (p − foliage)
Helichrysum petiolare (a/p − foliage)
Impatiens walleriana (a− white, pink, red)
Lobelia erinus (a −blue, pink, white)
Lotus berthelottii (p − orange, foliage)
Narcissus (b − yellow, white)
Pelargonium (a/p − orange, pink, red, white)
Petunia (a/p − mixed colours)
Plectranthus coleoides (a/p − foliage)
Primula (p − mixed colours)
Scaevola (a/p − purple, blue)
Senecio cinerea (a/p − foliage)
Tagetes (a − yellow, orange)
Tropaeolum (a − red, orange, yellow)
Tulipa (b − mixed colours)
Verbena x *hybrida* (a/p − mixed colours)
Viola x *wittrockiana* (a − mixed colours)

Perennial plants for colour
Blue/mauve flowers
Aconitum spp. and cvs
Agapanthus spp. and cvs
Ajuga reptans
Anchusa azurea
Aquilegia flabellata
Aster amellus
Aster x *frikartii*
Baptisia australis
Brunnera macrophylla
Campanula spp. and cvs
Catananche caerulea
Delphinium hybrids
Echinops ritro
Eryngium spp. and cvs
Galega officinalis
Gentiana spp. and cvs
Geranium spp. and cvs
Hosta spp. and cvs
Iris spp. and cvs
Limonium platyphyllum
Linum narbonense
Lithodora diffusa
Meconopsis spp.
Nepeta spp. and cvs
Omphalodes cappadocica
Penstemon heterophyllus
Perovskia atriplicifolia
Platycodon grandoflorus
Polemonium caeruleum
Primula spp. and cvs
Pulmonaria spp. and cvs.
Salvia spp. and cvs.
Scabiosa caucasica
Tradescantia x *andersoniana*
Verbena rigida
Veronica spp. and cvs

Yellow, gold and orange flowers
Achillea spp. and cvs
Aurinia saxatilis
Anthemis tinctoria
Asphodeline lutea
Bupthalmum salicifolium
Centaurea macrocephalum
Cephalaria gigantea
Coreopsis verticillata
Digitalis lutea
Euphorbia spp. and cvs
Geum 'Lady Strathenden'

Helenium spp. and cvs
Helianthus spp. and cvs
Heliopsis spp. and cvs
Hemerocallis spp. and cvs
Hieracium spp. and cvs
Inula spp. and cvs
Iris pseudacorus
Kniphofia 'Little Maid'
Ligularia spp. and cvs
Lysimachia punctata
Lysimachia nummularia 'Aurea'
Oenothera spp. and cvs.
Paeonia mlokosewitschii
Potentilla recta
Primula spp. and cvs
Ranunculus spp. and cvs
Rudbeckia spp. and cvs
Solidago spp. and cvs
Thalictrum flavum spp. *glaucum*
Trollius spp. and cvs
Verbascum spp. and cvs

Red flowers
Achillea 'Cerise Queen'
Alcea rosea
Astilbe 'Fanal'
Astrantia major 'Ruby Wedding'
Centranthus ruber
Cosmos atrosanguineus
Dianthus 'Brympton Red'
Geum 'Mrs Bradshaw'
Hemerocallis 'Stafford'
Lobelia 'Cherry Ripe'
Lupinus 'Inverewe Red'
Lychnis chaceldonica
Monarda didyma 'Cambridge Scarlet'
Paeonia spp. and cvs
Papaver orientale
Penstemon 'Cherry Ripe'
Persicaria amplexicaulis
Potentilla 'Gibson's Scarlet'

Pink flowers
Anemone x *hybrida*
Armeria spp. and cvs
Aster spp. and cvs
Astilbe spp. and cvs
Bergenia cordifolia
Dianthus spp. and cvs
Diascia spp. and cvs
Dicentra spp. and cvs
Erigeron 'Charity'

Erodioum manescauii
Filipendula spp. and cvs
Geranium spp. and cvs
Lamium roseum
Linaria purpurea 'Cannon Went'
Lychnis flos-jovis
Lythrum spp. and cvs
Malva moschata
Monarda didyma 'Croftway Pink'
Papaver orientale 'Cedric Morris'
Penstemon 'Hidcote Pink'
Persicaria spp. and cvs
Phlox paniculata cvs
Phuopsis stylosa
Primula spp. and cvs
Sedum spectabile
Sidalcea spp. and cvs

Purple flowers
Aster spp. and cvs
Centaurea spp. and cvs
Echinacea purpurea
Erigeron 'Dunkelste Aller'
Erysimum 'Bowles Mauve'
Geranium spp. and cvs
Liatris spicata
Linaria purpurea
Lythrum spp. and cvs
Osteospermum jucundum
Penstemon 'Burgundy'
Phlox 'Le Mahdi'
Senecio pulcher
Stachys macrantha
Thalictrum delavayi
Verbena bonariensis

White flowers
Achillea ptarmica 'The Pearl'
Anaphalis margaritacea
Anemone x *hybrida* 'Honorine Jobert'
Anthemis punctata cupaniana
Argyranthemum friutescens
Aruncus dioicus
Astilbe 'Irrlicht'
Campanula latiloba alba
Crambe cordifolia
Dianthus 'Haytor White'
Dictamnus albus
Echinops sphaerocephalus
Geranium sanguineum 'Album'
Gypsophila paniculata 'Bristol Fairy'
Hosta spp. and cvs
Lamium maculatum 'White Nancy'
Leucanthemum 'Everest'
Lysimachia clethroides
Osteospermum 'Whirligig'
Phlox 'Fujiama'

Physostegia virginiana 'Alba'
Polygonatum x *hybridum*
Pulmonaria 'Sissinghurst White'
Romneya coulteri
Smilacina racemosa
Trillum grandiflorum
Yucca spp.

Foliage colour
Silver foliage
Artemisia spp. and cvs (p)
Cerastium tomentosum (p)
Convolvulus cneorum (s)
Cynara cardunculus (p)
Eleagnus 'Quicksilver' (s)
Eryngium giganteum (p)
Hebe pingifolia 'Pagei' (s)
Lavandula angustifolia (s)
Melianthus major (a/p)
Onopordum spp. (a)
Pyrus salicifolia 'Pendula' (t)
Santolina chamaecyparis (p)
Senecio cineraria (a/p)
Stachys byzantina (p)
Tanacetum haradjanii (p)

Purple foliage
Acer palmatum 'Atropurpureum' (t)
Ajuga reptans 'Atropurpurea' (p)
Berberis thunbergii 'Atropurpurea' (s)
Clematis recta 'Purpurea' (p)
Cordyline australis 'Atropurpurea' (p)
Corylus maxima 'Purpurea' (s)
Cotinus coggygria 'Royal Purple' (s)
Dahlia 'Bishop of Llandaff' (p)
Fagus sylvatica 'Riversii' (t)
Foeniculum vulgare 'Purpureum' (p)
Heuchera micrantha 'Purple Purple' (p)
Lobelia cardinalis (p)
Phormium tenax 'Purpureum' (p)
Prunus cerasifera 'Nigra' (t)
Ricinus communis 'Gibsonii' (a)
Rosa glauca (s)
Salvia officinalis 'Purpurascens' (s)
Sedum maximum atropurpureum (p)
Viola riviniana Purpurea Group (p)
Vitis vinifera 'Purpurea' (c)

Golden foliage
Acer japonicum 'Aurea' (t)
Carex stricta 'Bowles Golden' (p)

Filipendula ulmaria 'Aurea' (p)
Fuchsia 'Golden Treasure' (s)
Gleditsia triacanthos 'Sunburst' (t)
Hebe armstrongii (s)
Hedera helix 'Buttercup' (c)
Hosta spp. and cvs (p)
Humulus lupulus 'Aureus' (c)
Ligustrum ovalifolium 'Aureum' (s)
Lonicera nitida 'Baggesen's Gold' (s)
Lysimachia nummularia 'Aurea' (p)
Milium effusum 'Aureum' (p)
Oreganum vulgare 'Aureum' (p)
Philadelphus coronarius 'Aureus' (s)
Physocarpus opulifolius 'Luteus' (s)
Robinia pseudoacacia 'Frisia' (t)
Sambucus racemosa 'Plumosa Aurea' (s)
Tanacetum parthenium 'Aureum' (p)
Taxus baccata 'Aurea' (t)

Blue foliage
Elymus magellanicus (p)
Hosta 'Halcyon' (p)
Hosta sieboldiana 'Elegans' (p)

Variegated foliage
Acer negundo 'Variegatum' (t)
Aktinidia kolomikta (s)
Aquilegia vulgaris 'Woodside' (p)
Aralia elata 'Aureovariegata' (t)
Astrantia major 'Sunningdale Variegated' (p)
Brunnera macrophylla 'Hadspen Cream' (p)
Cornus alba 'Elegantissima' (s)
Cortaderia selloana 'Gold Band' (p)
Elaeagnus pungens 'Maculata' (s)
Eryngium bourgatii (p)
Euonymus fortunei 'Emerald 'n' Gold' (s)
Euphorbia marginata (a)
Fragaria x *ananassa* 'Variegata' (p)
Hakononechloa macra 'Aureola' (p)
Hedera spp. and cvs (c)
Hosta spp. and cvs (p)
Ilex spp. and cvs (t)
Iris pallida 'Variegata' (p)
Lamium maculatum (p)
Lonicera japonica 'Aureo-reticulata' (c)
Miscanthus sinensis 'Zebrinus' (p)
Phlaris arunindinacea 'Picta' (p)
Phormium tenax 'Sundowner' (p)
Pleioblastus auricomus (p)

Pulmonaria saccharata (p)
Rhamnus alaternus 'Argenteovariegata' (t)
Salvia officinalis 'Icterina' (s)
Silybum marianum (a)
Sisyrinchium striatum 'Aunt May' (p)
Symphytum x *uplandicum* 'Variegatum' (p)
Tanecetum vulgare 'Silver Lace' (p)
Vinca major 'Variegata' (s)

Small trees
Acer griseum
Betula pendula 'Youngii'
Cercis siliquastrum
Ilex x *altaclarensis*
Laburnum x *waterei* 'Vosii'
Malus 'Profusion'
Prunus serrula
Pyrus salicifolia 'Pendula'
Sorbus hupehensis

Evergreen shrubs
Abelia spp. and cvs
Azara spp.
Berberis spp. and cvs
Buxus sempervirens
Ceanothus spp. and cvs
Choisya ternata
Convolvulus cneorum
Cotoneaster spp. and cvs
Daphne spp. and cvs
Elaeagnus pungens
Escalonia spp. and cvs
Euonymus fortunei
Garrya elliptica
Hebe spp. and cvs
Ilex spp. and cvs
Laurus nobilis
Mahonia spp. and cvs
Osmanthus spp. and cvs
Photinia spp. and cvs
Pieris spp. and cvs
Prunus lusitanicus
Rhododendron spp. and cvs
Sarcococca spp. and cvs
Skimmia japonica
Viburnum tinus
Vinca spp. and cvs

Index

Glossary

A

Acid soil On a pH scale of 1 to 14, soil with a rating below 7; alkaline soil has a rating above 7, and soil with a value of 7 is neutral. The lime content of soil determines its pH.

Alkaline soil See acid soil.

Annual Plant that completes its cycle of germination from setting seed through to dying in a single growing season.

Aquatic plant Plant that can live in water, either floating or completely submerged.

B

Biennial Plant requiring two growing seasons to flower and seed.

Blanch (-ing) Method of cultivating (e.g. chicory) that protects all or part of plant from light, to promote succulent, white foliage or bulb.

Bolt (-ing) Result of plant producing flowers rather than a good heart; common of lettuces in dry, hot spells.

Bract Leaf at base of flower stalk or flowerhead; may resemble a small, normal leaf or, in some plants, be large and brightly coloured.

Brassica The generic name for the cabbage family.

Bulb Plant storage organ, usually formed underground, containing the following year's growth buds.

Bulb planter Trowel-sized, cylindrical device for removing a plug of soil and enabling bulbs to be planted easily in grass, etc.

Bulbil A very small or secondary bulb that forms eg on lilies.

C

Calyx Usually green, outer part of a flower, formed from the sepals, that encases the petals in bud.

Classification Botanically and for ease of identification, plants are grouped according to family, genus, species and variety or cultivar. For example, with the rose family, *Rosaceae*, **Rosa** = genus, *R. gallica* = species, *R.g.* var. *officinalis* = variety, and *R.g.* 'Versicolor' = hybrid or cultivar.

Climber Plant that uses other plants or objects to grow upwards. Without support, their (usually) lax stems will creep along the ground.

Corm A swollen stem base that acts as a storage organ, similar to a bulb, but of a single piece without layers; it is annual, with the following year's corm developing from a bud close to the original.

Crown The part of a herbaceous plant from where new stems are produced and to where they die back in autumn.

Cultivar A man-made or cultivated variety, produced by hybridization. It will usually have a name chosen by the breeder, e.g. *Clematis* 'Bill Mackenzie'.

Cutting A section of a plant removed for propagation. Cuttings may be root, basal (new growth taken from a herbaceous plant in spring), greenwood (taken from the tip of young growth), softwood (young growth taken at the start of the growing season), semi-ripe (half-ripened stem taken during the growing season), or hardwood (mature stem taken at the end of the growing season).

D

Datum post Peg or similar marked to indicate various layers at different depths (or heights).

Deciduous Plant losing its leaves annually; semi-deciduous plants lose some of their leaves.

Division Splitting of a plant clump into parts containing roots and shoots; normally done when the plant is dormant, for propagation.

Double digging Method of soil preparation whereby the soil is dug to two spade depths (spits).

Double flowers Applied to a flowerhead or bloom having more petals than the original species, e.g. *Bellis perennis* 'Alba Plena', a white double version of the common daisy.

E

Evergreen Plant retaining its leaves at the end of the growing season, though older leaves may be lost through the year.

F

Family See classification.

Floret One of the individual flowers that make up the head of a composite flower, such as a dahlia.

Flowerhead Mass of small flowers that appear as one flower.

Force (-ing) Method of promoting early flowering or fruiting, usually via artificial heat and light.

Friable Used of soil that is in a good, loose, workable condition.

Frond The whole leaf of a fern.

G

Gazebo Ornamental garden structure, usually of wood or iron, used as a raised viewing platform.

Genus see classification

Glaucous Covered in a bluish-grey, bluish-green or bluish-white bloom.

H

Half-hardy Plant that withstands low temperatures but not freezing.

Harden off Allowing greenhouse-raised plants gradually to acclimatize to outside conditions by leaving them out for increasing periods before planting out.

Hardy Plant that tolerates year-round conditions in temperate climates, including normal frost, without protection.

Haulm Name given to stem of, for example, potatoes or peas, after harvesting.

Herbaceous Non-woody plant that dies down to its rootstock in winter.

Humus Largely decomposed organic matter naturally present in or introduced into the top layer of soil; improves soil fertility and water-holding capacity.

Hybrid A plant resulting from crossing two different species, often of the same genus, usually by cultivation, but sometimes occurring in the wild. An F1 hybrid is a plant that is propagated using the seed from two true parent plants, after hand-pollinating. Plants raised from hybrid seed (including F1 hybrids) often do not breed true to type.

I

Inflorescence A group or arrangement of flowers on a stem, such as panicles and racemes.

Intercrop A fast-growing crop grown between rows of a later and slower crop, eg lettuces between onions.

K

Knot garden Ornamental ground pattern of low hedging, infilled with planting or hard materials; intricate interweaving of the linear planting was a favourite device of Tudor and Elizabethan gardens.

L

Layering Method of pinning a stem to the ground and inducing it to form roots, thereby propagating a separate plant.
Limy soil Soil containing a greater proportion of calcium compounds; the lime content of soil determines its pH (see acid soil).
Loam Soil that is fertile and of good structure, that will hold water but is free-draining.

M

Marginal Plant that grows partially submerged in shallow water or moist soil at a pond edge.
Micro-climate Normally refers to small area protected from extreme weather and so experiencing different climatic conditions from its locality. Micro-climates can be created, for example, by walls.
Mulch Layer of organic or inorganic material added to the surface of the soil to retain moisture, help suppress weeds and gradually improve fertility.

N

Naturalize To grow plants in a near-natural condition so that they are capable of maintaining and reproducing themselves.
Node Point at which a leaf grows from the stem.

O

Offset Plant that is reproduced naturally from the base of the parent plant.
Open weather Used to describe periods during winter that are free from frost, snow and rain.

P

Panicle A flower stem (inflorescence) that branches into several small stems or stalks, with the youngest flowers at the top, e.g. lilac.
Parterre An ornamentally arranged level area of flowerbeds.
Perennial A plant that lives for longer than two seasons.
pH See acid soil.
Picotee A dianthus (pink) having light petals edged with a darker colour.
Potager An ornamentally arranged area of chiefly vegetable, fruit and herb beds.
Pollarding The severe cutting back of branches to the main trunk of a tree to restrict its growth.

R

Raceme A long, unbranched flower stem (inflorescence), the flowers opening in sequence from the bottom upwards.
Rhizome An underground, often creeping, stem acting as a storage organ, from which roots and shoots grow.
Root-ball The roots together with the soil adhering to them when a plant is lifted, e.g. for transplanting.

S

Scale leaf A leaf that is reduced in size or modified.
Scarify To scratch the outer surface of a tough-coated seed, enabling moisture to penetrate and so increase the chance of germination.
Screedboard A plank or board used for levelling earth, sand, fine hardcore, wet cement, etc.; it may be notched to sit between two fixed points (e.g. brick path edgings) in order to maintain a constant level.
Sepals Green outer parts of a flower, collectively forming the calyx.
Sharp drainage Condition arising naturally in gravelly soil, and required by many rock or alpine plants where rainfall is high. Achieve by adding a special mix of sand and small stones to the soil.
Shuttering A rectangle of timber planks or boards nailed firmly to pegs to make a fixed template for the laying of cement; also called formwork.

Single flowers Applied to a flower that has the normal number of petals for its species, such as a daisy.
Species See classification.
Spit One spade depth, normally about 25cm (10in).
Spur pruning Cutting shoots back to two or three growth buds to encourage the formation of spurs - fruit or flower buds.
Standard A tree or shrub with a length of bare stem below the first branches; some shrubs e.g. roses and fuschias, can be trained to form standards.
Sucker A shoot arising below ground at the base of a plant; on grafted plants these grow from the rootstock and should be removed.

T

Tamp (-ing) Device for compacting and levelling hardcore, sand etc., with either a long or short handle attached to a rectangular, heavy wood or metal, flat 'plate'.
Tilth Texture of the soil; a fine tilth is like fine crumbs.
Topiary explanation to come explanation to come explanation to come explanation to come explanation to come
'True' leaves Used of seedlings to describe the first leaves that resemble those of the parent plant.
Type Used to refer to an original plant species.

V

Variety A variant of a plant species, arising either naturally or as a result of selection.

Acknowledgements

The photographer, publishers and authors would like to thank the following people and organizations who kindly allowed us to photograph their gardens:
Ansells Garden Centre, Horningsea, Cambs; David Austin Roses Ltd, Wolverhampton, West Midlands; Bressingham Gardens, Diss, Norfolk; Broadlands Garden, Hazelbury Bryan, Dorset; Cambridge Alpines, Cottenham, Cambs; Cambridge Garden Plants, Horningsea, Cambs; Capel Manor, Enfield, Middx; Beth Chatto Gardens, Elmstead Market, Essex; Clare College, Cambridge, Cambs; Docwras Manor, Shepreth, Cambs; John Drake, Fen Ditton, Cambs; Mrs Sally Edwards, Horningsea, Cambs; Peter Elliott, Hauxton, Cambs; Mr and Mrs R. Foulser, Cerne Abbas, Dorset; Holkham Garden Centre, Holkham, Norfolk; Kiftsgate Court Gardens, Chipping Campden, Gloucs; Joy Larkcom, Hepworth, Norfolk; Madingley Hall Gardens, Madingley, Cambs; The Manor, Herningford Grey, Cambs; Paradise Centre, Lamarsh, Suffolk; Royal Horticultural Society's Gardens, Wisley, Surrey; Royal National Rose Society, St. Albans, Herts; Scotsdales Garden Centre, Shelford, Cambs; Trevor Scott, Thorpe-le-Soken, Essex; Scarlett's Plants, West Bergholt, Essex; Mr and Mrs M. Stuart-Smith, Cambridge, Cambs; Anthony Surtees, Crondall, Hampshire; University Botanic Gardens, Cambridge, Cambs; Unwins Seeds Ltd, Histon, Cambs; John Wingate and the Golders Green Allotment Association; Wyken Hall, Stanton, Suffolk; Patricia Zaphros, Fen Ditton, Cambs.

The publishers are also grateful to the following for their help and support in the production of this book: Phoebus Editions Ltd for conceptual work on the *Care and Maintenance* section; Paul Draycott, Roger Sygrave and the staff of Capel Manor; Richard White and Joanna Fowler (for their assistance in photographing of vegetables and fruit) and the staff of RHS Wisley; David Raeburn, John Wingate and the members of the Golders Green Allotment Association; Andrew Lord and the staff of The Garden Picture Library, London SW11.

Suppliers of containers, plants, tools and equipment: Chiltern Seeds, Ulverston, Cumbria; Granville Garden Centre, London NW2; Squires Garden Centre, Twickenham, Middx.

Picture credits:
(Key: R–Right, L–Left, T–Top, M–Middle, C–Centre, B–Bottom)
Introduction
Garden Picture Library: p.2 (all); p.4 (all); p.8 (all); p.9 (TR, BL); p.10 (R); p.12 (all); p.13 (all); p.14 (all); p.15 (all); p.16 (all); p.17 (TL, BL); p.19 (CL). Howard Rice: p.3 (all); p.5 (T, B); p.9 (BR); p.10 (L); p.11 (all); p.17 (TR, C, BR); p.18 (all); George Taylor: p.5 (C). *The Complete Guide to Gardening with Containers* (Collins & Brown, 1995): p.19 (TR, CM, CR, BR).
Designing the Garden, p.20–p.79
All pictures by The Garden Picture Library except: *The Complete Guide to Gardening with Containers* (Collins & Brown, 1995): p.21 (TL inset); p.66 (BL, B C); p.67 (BL, B C). Michelle Garrett: p.66 (BR); p.76 (BL). George Taylor: p.42 (CR, BL, BR); p.43 (CL,CM, CR, BL, BM, BR); p.44 (CL, CM, CR, BL, BR); p.45 (all); p.46 (CL, CM,CM inset, CR, BL); p.47 (CL, CR, BL, BM, BR); p.48 (2nd row L, R, 3rd row L, M, BL, BM); p.49 (CL, CM, CR, BL, BM, BR); p.52 (CL, CM, CR, BL, BM, BR); p.58 (BC, BR, BR inset); p.59 (all); p.61 (BL, BR); p.63 (all); p.65 (TL, TCL, TCR, TR, BL); p.72 (CL, CR, BL, BM, BR).
Plants for the Garden, p.80–p.139
All pictures by Howard Rice except: *The Complete Guide to Gardening with Containers* (Collins & Brown, 1995): p.81 (BR inset); p.129 (TL, TR). The Garden Picture Library: p.82 (BR); p.83 (BR); p.84 (all); p.86 (BL); p.87 (BL); p.92 (TL); p.102 (TR, BR); p.103 (BR); p.106 (BR); p.107 (BL, BR); p.108 (all), p.124 (BR); p.125 (BL); p.128 (TR, BL); p.129 (BR); p.134 (BR); p.135 (TL). Andrew Lawson: p.87 (BR); p.134 (BR); p.135 (BR). *The New Indoor Gardener* (Collins & Brown, 1998): p.112 (3rd row R). George Taylor: p.87 (TL, T, M, TR); p.102 (BL, CL); p.125 (TL, T, M, TR).
Vegetables, Fruit and Herbs, p.140–p.199
All pictures by Howard Rice except: *The Complete Guide to Gardening with Containers* (Collins & Brown, 1995): p.141 (BR inset); p.194 (BR); p.195 (BR). The Garden Picture Library: p.142 (all); p.144 (TR); p.146 (TR); p.151 (TR); p.155 (TR); p.159 (T 2nd L, T 2nd R, TR); p.163 (TC, TR); p.164 (TR); p.165 (TR); p.166 (TC); p.171 (TR); p.173 (TL, TC, TR); p.174 (TL, TR), p.175 (TL); p.176 (TR), p.178 (TR), p.191 (TL); p.192 (TR). *Gardening with Herbs* (Jacqui Hurst for Collins & Brown, 1996): p.196 (TL, third row L, BL); p.197 (2nd row L, 2nd row R, 3rd row L, BL); p.198 (TL, BL); p.199 (TR, 3rd row R); p.214 (TR, BR). Holt Studios International: p.153 (TL). Photos Horticultural: p.162 (TR); p.163 (TM, TR). George Taylor: p.143 (all); p.145 (all); p.146 (BR); p.147 (all); p.148 (all); p.150 (BL, BM, BR); p; 151 (BL); p.152 (BL, B 2nd L, B 2nd R, BR); p.153 (BR); p.154 (BL, BM, BR); p.155 (BL, BR); p.156 (BL, BR); p.157 (CM, BL, BM, BR); p.158 (BL, BM); p.159 (BL); p.160 (CR); p.160 (BL, BR); p.161 (BL, BM, BR); p.162 (BL, B 2nd L, B 2nd R, BR); p.163 (BL, BM, BR); p.164 (BL, BR); p.165 (BL, BR); p.166 (CR, BL, BM, BR); p.167 (CM, BL, BM); p.168 (BL, BM); p.169 (BR); p.170 (BL, BM, BR); p.171 (BL, BM); p.172 (BL, BM, BR); p.173 (BL); p.174 (BL, BM, BR); p.175 (BL, B 2nd L, B 2nd R, BR); p.176 (all); p.177 (TL, TR, B, CL, BL, BR); p.178 (all); p.179 (all); p.180 (all); p.181 (all); p.182 (BL, BM); p.183 (BL, BM, BR); p.184 (BL, BR); p.185 (CL, BL, BM, BR); p.186 (BL, BR); p.187 (CR, BL, BL inset, BR); p.188 (BL, BR); p.189 (BL, BR); p.190 (CL, BL, BR); p.191 (CL, BR); p.192 (BL, BM); p.193 (TL, BL, BM, BR); p.195 (CL, CM, CR, BL).
Care and Maintenance, p.200–p.265:
All photographs by George Taylor except: A-Z Botanical Collections Ltd: p.239 (BR). *The Complete Guide to Gardening with Containers* (Collins & Brown, 1995): p.201 (TL inset); p.215 (BL); p.217 (TL, TM, TR, BM); p.222 (BR); p.226 (BC). The Garden Picture Library: p.202 (TR); p.203 (BR); p.211 (TL, BL); p.213 (TR); p.214 (BL); p.217 (BR); p.220 (TR); p.222 (TR); p.224 (TR, BL); p.225 (2nd row R); p.226 (TR); p.231 (TL); p.236 (TR); p.237 (B 2nd L, B 2nd R); p.238 (BL); p.239 (TL, T 2nd L, TR, BL); p.240 (TR); p.242 (TR); p.244 (TR); p.248 (TR); p.252 (TR); p.253 (TR); p.254 (TR); p.257 (TL, TR); p.258 (TR). *Gardening with Herbs* (Jacqui Hurst for Collins & Brown, 1996): p.214 (TR, BR). Holt Studios International: p.237 (TL, T 2nd L, T 2nd R, TR, BR); p.238 (T 2nd L, T 2nd R, TR, B 2nd L, B 2nd R, BR); p.239 (T 2nd R, B 2nd R). Sam Lloyd: p.215 (BL); p.217 (TM). Peter McHoy: p.237 (BL); p.238 (TL); p.239 (B 2nd L). Howard Rice: p.208 (BL, BR); p.209 (BL, BR); p.244 (BL, B 2nd L, B 2nd R, BR); p.251 (BL, BM, BR).